GENDER AND THE
CIVIL RIGHTS MOVEMENT

Gender and the Civil Rights Movement

Edited by
Peter J. Ling
Sharon Monteith

Rutgers University Press
New Brunswick, New Jersey, and London

Originally published in hardcover by Garland Publishing Inc., 1999
in the Crosscurrents in African American History Series

First published in paperback by Rutgers University Press, 2004

Library of Congress Cataloging-in-Publication Data

Gender and the civil rights movement / edited by Peter J. Ling, Sharon
Monteith.— 1st pbk. ed.
p. cm.
Originally published: Gender in the civil rights movement. New York :
Garland Pub., 1999.
Includes bibliographical references (p.   ) and index.
  ISBN 0-8135-3438-0 (pbk. : alk. paper)
   1. African Americans—Civil rights—History—20th century.   2.
Civil rights movements—United States—History—20th century.   3.
Women civil rights workers—United States—History—20th century.
4. African American women civil rights workers—History—20th
century.   5. Sex role—United States—History—20th century.
6. Sexism—United States—History—20th century.   7. United
States—Race relations—History—20th century.   I. Ling, Peter J.
(Peter John), 1956–   II. Monteith, Sharon.
  E185.61.G284   2004
  323.1196'073'0082—dc22
2003022264

A British Cataloging-in-Publication record for this book is available
from the British Library

Manufactured in the United States of America

CONTENTS

CHALLENGING CONVENTIONS

INTRODUCTION

Gender and the Civil Rights Movement   *1*

Peter J. Ling and Sharon Monteith

CHAPTER 1

Daisy Bates, the National Association for the Advancement of Colored People, and the 1957 Little Rock School Crisis: A Gendered Perspective   *17*

John A. Kirk

CHAPTER 2

Sex Machines and Prisoners of Love: Male Rhythm and Blues, Sexual Politics, and the Black Freedom Struggle   *41*

Brian Ward

CHAPTER 3

"Dress modestly, neatly ... as if you were going to church": Respectability, Class, and Gender in the Montgomery Bus Boycott and the Early Civil Rights Movement   *69*

Marisa Chappell, Jenny Hutchinson and Brian Ward

LEADERSHIP

CHAPTER 4

Gender and Generation: Manhood at the Southern Christian Leadership Conference   *101*

Peter J. Ling

CHAPTER 5

Women in the Student Non-violent Coordinating Committee: Ideology, Organizational Structure, and Leadership   *131*
      Belinda Robnett

CHAPTER 6

The "Gun-Toting" Gloria Richardson: Black Violence in Cambridge, Maryland   *169*
      Jenny Walker

LEGACY

CHAPTER 7

"It's a Doggy-Dogg World": Black Cultural Politics, Gangsta Rap and the "Post-Soul Man"   *187*
      Eithne Quinn

CHAPTER 8

Revisiting the 1960s in Contemporary Fiction: "Where do we go from here?"   *215*
      Sharon Monteith

CHAPTER 9

"The Struggle Continues": Black Women in Congress in the 1990s   *239*
      Britta Waldschmidt-Nelson

CONTRIBUTORS   *261*

INDEX   *263*

Gender and the
Civil Rights Movement

INTRODUCTION

Gender and the Civil Rights Movement

Peter J. Ling and Sharon Monteith

The civil rights movement was primarily concerned with race, but it was also about personal identity. For many of its participants, it was clear that the goal of freedom for African Americans would require all Americans to confront the racism within themselves and what it did to both white and black people.[1] African Americans lead the movement. They rightly regarded it as their liberation struggle and found a new sense of themselves in the empowerment they experienced.[2] Many, though by no means all, African American spokespersons also saw their fight as one over integration. Racial segregation and the systematic discrimination that accompanied it prevented black Americans from enjoying the same life chances as whites. By stigmatizing African Americans, racism attacked their self image so that other key cultural categories of personal identity, such as manhood and womanhood, became problematic.[3] Gender and Jim Crow became entangled in deeply pathological ways that were symbolized in the ritual of lynching, as Ralph Ellison has described:

> usually enacted in a preselected scene (such as a clearing in the woods or in the courthouse square in an atmosphere of high excitement and led by a masked celebrant dressed in a garish costume who manipulated the numinous objects (lynch ropes, the American flag, shotgun, gasoline, and whiskey jugs) associated with the rite as he inspired and instructed the actors in their gory task.

Lynching affirmed white power and, as Ellison shows, broke down all distinctions between the real and the symbolic, since the victim was "forced to undergo death for all his group."[4] It also perpetuated the myth of the innocent white woman on her pedestal whose accusation of sexual assault could put black men and boys in peril at the hands of a lynch mob with the power to punish for a hint of disrespect or even on a whim.[5] As Evelyn Brooks Higginbotham points out, "Lynching rationalized by the white South as its defense of [white] womanhood, served ... to maintain racial etiquette and the socio-economic status quo."[6] This situation was unjust and immoral, and by the middle of the twentieth century it was acknowledged that if this were ended, the United States would live more honorably in conformity with its creed.[7]

Although some African American writers, such as Ralph Ellison and James Baldwin, recognized that racism was very much about the pathology of whiteness, most liberal and radical commentators shared the view that the evil consisted solely of a prejudicial white construction of blackness.[8] African American leaders, such as the Reverend Martin Luther King, who strove to appeal to the white majority, argued that their goal of integration would be liberating to white Americans also, as captured in King's oft-used metaphor of a "single garment of destiny": "We are caught in an inescapable network of mutuality, tied in a single garment of destiny. Whatever affects one directly, affects all indirectly."[9] The small groups of whites who supported the movement actively in the early stage of each phase or local confrontation also commonly felt that racism limited their freedom.[10] But usually they conceptualized the problem in terms of racial barriers of prejudice around a world of universal principles that was invisibly coded "white." It is only in recent years that the scholarship on racism as a historical phenomenon has looked critically at whiteness.[11]

Labor historians such as David Roediger have explored with greater precision the socialist view that racism serves to obscure the objective ties of class interest. His nineteenth-century working-class whites use minstrelsy to construct a racial identity that sets them apart from black slaves yet allows them to express their longing for a pre-industrial world symbolized by the African.[12] Robin Kelley sees the same process at work in more recent popular culture with Native Americans, Africans and Asians serving as "the embodiment of pre-industrial freedom from industrial discipline, hence a model to hate, fear, and emulate simultaneously."[13] But whereas previous writers stressed the creation of the black or colored race as a scape-goat and pariah, more recent writers like Phyllis Palmer have underlined how particularized ethnic identities came to be subsumed in the overriding category of whiteness. Palmer cites Gloria Yamato's call to reclaim ethnicity to illustrate the hegemonic power of whiteness and the need to deconstruct the category if we are to understand racism. Palmer and her students at George Washington University were taken aback by the power of whiteness "as a cultural-ethnic way of building identities and as a crucial thread in the social, economic and political fabric of the United States."[14] In the process of deconstruction, race becomes a dialectical category in which categories of difference need to be seen as continuously contingent upon each other. As a consequence, historical studies of the civil rights movement have now begun to reconstruct a three-dimensional profile of white racists, for example, after decades in which stereotypes have made it easy (and dangerously comforting for white Americans) to regard white southerners of the period as almost cartoon-like exemplars of bigotry and ignorance.[15] The challenge to whiteness, and the institutions that have reproduced it throughout history, is gradually overtaking the preoccupation with individual white supremacists. Whiteness, the last bastion of identity politics, has begun to receive the kind of critical examination that rejects its transparency and breaks open the ways in which the very invisibility of whiteness contributes to its power.[16]

At the outset, the post-war civil rights movement was not overtly or self-consciously concerned with gender inequality. But like other freedom struggles, its critique of existing practices and assumptions provided a position from which to review gender relations. As the movement reached its peak in 1965-66, gender became a stated issue. Included in this collection is an essay by Belinda Robnett looking at gender and leadership roles in the Student Non-violent Coordinating Committee (SNCC). Robnett considers the circumstances surrounding the circulation of a paper on the position of women in SNCC by Mary King, Casey Hayden and others. She argues that after 1966, SNCC, under the leadership of Stokely Carmichael became more macho in style, whereas previously its principles of participatory democracy had made it non-hierarchical and relatively non-prescriptive in terms of gender. After leaving SNCC, such white women activists as Hayden, King and Sara Evans became involved in the women's movement. Women led in this movement and regarded it as their liberation struggle. Many early feminists defined their goal as equal rights, the creation of a society in which men and women shared the same rights and opportunities. Although some women defined the struggle in terms of a patriarchy that was as deeply ingrained in social institutions as racism was, a majority, initially, saw the crucial problem as the widespread acceptance by women of narrow and discriminatory conventions of womanhood. Drawing on the experience of the African American freedom struggle, they stressed the need for women to raise their consciousness and create their own personal and collective identity. From this critical process emerged a dynamic and wide-ranging feminist critique not simply of established social practices and institutions but also of other schools of social criticism, including Marxism, and other social protest movements, including the African American liberation movements insofar as they ignored the issue of patriarchy. As Manning Marable notes, the African American reaction to this critique was decidedly hostile at the outset.[17] The civil rights movement thus informed this women's movement and was itself informed by it.

Although a minority of males openly espoused the feminist cause, the preponderance of female practitioners among analysts of gender has meant that it is only relatively recently that the field of men's studies has attained a status comparable to that more rapidly achieved by women's studies. Like whiteness, maleness was so powerfully positioned as a normative complex that initially issues of inequality were raised without questioning maleness itself. As a result, the demands of women and minorities for equality were often cast as aspirations towards the lifestyle of the white male in terms of employment, sexual conduct, and personal expression. Only thereafter did critics begin to consider the historical peculiarities of this normative model. As an exercise in gender history rather than women's history, this volume also deals extensively with masculinity. It recognizes that the discourse of gender is embedded not only in the conventions governing the social behavior of men and women in both public and private spheres but in the dynamics of differential power in all human relations. Powerfully learned, gender ideals blind us to alternate ways of being. Starkly dichotomized subject positions are often drawn between black men as, for example, when Malcolm X famously differentiated between the "house slave" who, he believed, loved his master more than himself, and the "field slave" who hated that same master with a vengeance. Such hard lines of demarcation between native sons are painful but they have sometimes proved a rallying cry in themselves. Malcolm X warned: "Whites better be glad Martin Luther King is rallying the people because other forces are waiting to take over if he fails."[18] Malcolm's heirs in the Black Panther Party, notably Huey Newton, were also drawn to the propaganda value of seemingly simple dichotomies: white/black; reactionaries and revolutionaries; bourgeois and proletarian; nonviolence/self-defense; and women and men. But such assertion of difference served ultimately, and surely not coincidentally, to divide and destroy them.

Since the 1960s, the scholarship on African American men has been increasing dramatically, through the work of psychiatrists like Alvin Pouissant, sociologists like Robert Staples and Kenneth Clark, historians and philosophers like Manning Marable and Cornel West and cultural critics like Clyde Franklin and Michael Dyson. Film makers like Melvin Van Peebles, Spike Lee and John Singleton have begun to unpick the most pernicious paradigmatic formulations of black men in American society, and film critics, like Donald Bogle and James Snead, have explored the hermeneutics of more traditional cinematic representations. To re-consider the civil rights movement from the standpoint of gender is to assert the dialectical character of both Race and Gender. It is also to insist on their historically constructed character. The term "gender" is used in preference to the term "sexes" to emphasize that the cultural construction of difference is more important to male/female identities than simple physiological differences.[19] These physical differences have given rise to biological explanations of gendered behaviors and the developing science of genetics continues to fuel simplistic sociobiological explanations such as those that argue that endocrinal functions ensure that testerone predisposes males towards aggression, competition, and violence whereas oestrogen inclines women towards passivity, tenderness, and exaggerated emotionalism.[20] The ignominious history of scientific racism, however, tends to make most scholars of race skeptical of such appeals to nature. The gendered body, like the racialized one, has been socially constructed as a cultural, performative text to be read according to changing and contested discourses. It should not be universalized or placed outside of history, or otherwise essentialized.

Despite this emphasis on social construction, the contributors to this volume have not, in the main, embraced post-structuralist attacks on the cult of objectivity that seem to reject the methodological principle that the past should be reconstructed through the critical examination of documents and records. Most of the essays here assay that task and hopefully do so with a certain self-consciousness of their own biases and the complex task of reading texts. They recognize that objectivity is an ideal and that those historians who feel most confident of their objectivity are perhaps those who subject their work to the least rigorous interrogation. Like other narrators, historians do, in a sense, invent a past for their readers, but like other social scientists, they hope that their commitment to what Karl Popper termed "falsificationism" gives their efforts some integrity. Hence, if an earlier scholar's description of the African American activist Mrs Gloria Richardson was historically inaccurate, it is proper and useful both for that description to be corrected here and for us to ask why the earlier description was at variance with the "facts." A key part of that explanation is a too ready acceptance of the explanatory frameworks established by the mass media. Intent on reaching a large audience, such media tend to use familiar narrative patterns and stereotypes. In their difficult task of distilling history, scholars of the civil rights movements have stuck too easily to the established journalistic accounts, and even when they have attempted to publicize neglected heroines like Gloria Richardson, they

have been drawn towards literary devices that mislead.[21] Gender and
race are themselves categories in contest and struggle; they are not fixed
and, consequently, the frameworks through which scholars approach
their subjects also change and develop.

Sociologists have attempted to codify the learned behaviors of
gender via the concept of "sex roles" that encompass the attitudes,
attributes and actions that are seen as appropriate for men and women.
Those who have promulgated rather than questioned such roles have
also added to an earlier prescriptive literature on parenting that has been
a key part of the discourse on gender. Such exhortatory texts have been
among the most conspicuous documents of efforts to enforce the values
of particular groups under the claim of normative status. Hence, to
consider gender in relation to the civil rights movement is also to
highlight the tensions between these normative roles in the United States
that were rooted in white, middle-class, heterosexual, Anglo-Saxon, and
Protestant assumptions and the experience of African Americans and
sundry "others." As Robert Staples has observed, "I see the black male
as being in conflict with the normative definition of masculinity. This is
a status which few, if any, black males have been able to achieve.
Masculinity, as defined in this culture, has always implied a certain
autonomy and mastery of one's environment."[22] In Memphis in 1968 as
black sanitation workers marched to protest the conditions under which
they labored, Ernest Withers took photographs of the men and of the
simple slogan that characterized each of the signs they held up for public
scrutiny, "I Am A Man." The conventional and powerfully repressive
stereotypes of patriarchy to which Staples alludes are unsettled by
Withers's pictures and the interreliance of gender and race is one of the
axioms that underpins this volume. The composure with which the men
march epitomizes the fact that black masculinity was then, and remains,
a contested site of representation. The manipulation of images of black
men by whites to demonize them as sexual predators and rapists or
infantilize them as "boys," subordinates their humanity.

Similarly, Clyde Franklin has observed that to understand black
men you have to realize that "in America adult black males have only
been 'men' for about twenty years." He adds that "even during this time
Black men have not been recognized as 'societally approved' men."[23] A
volume devoted to gender and the civil rights movement necessarily,
therefore, acknowledges the stigma of the term "boy" for African
American adult males in the segregation era, and as a corollary, the
profound association of the attainment of dignity with manhood,
conventionally defined. As Patricia J. Williams has argued, "The
dehumanizing erasure of black men's humanity has created a social

cauldron of much rage, much despair, and even more denial."[24] Traditionally, patriarchy is the rule of the father but in the African American community, as John Edgar Wideman discusses in *Fatheralong: A Meditation on Fathers and Sons, Race and Society* (1994), the role of the father has been assaulted on many fronts. Neoconservative attacks on black families and on black men in particular led to Majors and Jacob Gordon's founding the National Council of African American Men (NCAAM) in 1990. And in October 1995 Louis Farrakhan secured unprecedented attention for his race leadership claims by organizing the Million Man March.

Women historians have noted some of the pernicious effects of black male identifications of manhood in the liberation struggle. As Angela Davis complained of some of her former colleagues in 1975: "some black activists ... confuse their political activity with the assertion of their maleness ... These men view Black women as a threat to their attainment of manhood—especially those Black women who take initiative and work to become leaders in their own right."[25] The black power movement in all its facets perhaps contributed most to a representation of African American men as streetwise but disciplined and politically aware—but it stirred other feelings too as Michele Wallace identified in *Black Macho and the Myth of Superwoman*, describing black power as "a lot of black men strutting around with Afros," who failed to realize that the struggle should involve the full participation of black women.[26] Black men, disenchanted by what they perceived as King's gradualism, found in the Black Panthers' dangerous public image a devastatingly powerful means to rework images of black manhood, and dashiki-wearing black nationalists or unsmiling Panthers holding rifles frozen in history continue to fascinate. The dominant image of black manhood had become interwoven with a political discourse of death and defiance, but it also disregarded the ways in which black power organizations expressed masculine power in ways that marginalized women in the movement.

However, earlier in the movement's course, the sense that black men and women should assert themselves in accordance with these gender stereotypes was one of the motivating forces behind activism for both male and female participants. The role of Mrs Daisy Bates in the Little Rock Schools Crisis is a familiar one to historians of the civil rights movement. Her autobiography *The Long Shadow of Little Rock* (1962) is a standard published source, but reading this text closely and asking questions about how issues of gender identity shaped Mrs Bates's activism, provides a fresh perspective on the movement's early development. As John Kirk shows, Bates's traumatic discovery that her mother had been raped and murdered made her question the conduct of the African American adults around her in terms of their fulfillment of gender stereotypes. It also shaped her future activism so that she wrestled with the dilemmas of despising both the church-going of her female elders and the acute caution of respectable black males. Ultimately, it enabled her to provide unequalled leadership in a black community frequently riven by dissension and hesitation. Thus, the perspective of gender can illuminate neglected aspects of familiar civil rights history.

To give another example, by concentrating on the highly gendered historical phenomenon of respectability and etiquette in Montgomery, Alabama, Marisa Chappell, Jenny Hutchinson, and Brian Ward build upon recent work that has stressed the importance of women within the famous Montgomery Bus Boycott.[27] Their essay stresses that the potency of gender conventions as a glossary for reading social situations made the public conduct of African American demonstrators an important medium of communication. The denial of respectability on public transit was a key grievance behind the boycott. Ralph Ellison described a segregated Southern bus journey as a "haunted gauntletlike passage" for black riders but the time would come when the "bus enscened pantomime" would break apart and change American society. [28] The authors detail precisely how that change came about and show that the public reassertion of respectability was a crucial part of the Montgomery Improvement Association's desegregation battle. James Baldwin has summarized just how important image was in the success of the boycott: "Negroes had refused to be controlled by the town's image of them. And without this image ... the whites were abruptly and totally lost. The very foundations of their private and public worlds were being destroyed."[29]

An attention to gender thus makes more evident facets of movement activity that more general accounts only glimpse. It also strengthens recent lines of interpretation. For a dozen years or more, a cohort of leading scholars has tried to shift the focus of movement studies away from a national narrative of media covered crises, summit meetings, presidential interventions and congressional debates. They have stressed that the movement was most commonly, and in a key sense, most fully experienced, as a local phenomenon.[30] They have insisted that the inclusion of local people and places as milestones along the road to the Civil Rights Act of 1964 or the Voting Rights Act of 1965, or as stopping-off points in the peripatetic life of Martin Luther King from Montgomery to Memphis, has distorted movement history.[31] By looking at local struggles in greater detail, this scholarship has emphasized that the efforts to achieve racial justice had deep roots, that they neither began when the national press arrived nor ended when federal legislation was passed.[32] An important by-product of these studies has been the re-discovery of important activists whose limited exposure on the national stage had marginalized them in standard movement histories. Many of these activists were women.

This volume was partly inspired, of course, by the example of the anthology *Women in the Civil Rights Movement: Trailblazers and Torchbearers, 1941-1965.*[33] Despite this book's important contribution and the concurrent work of Darlene Hine, there are still many women whose activities in the movement are not yet properly acknowledged in its histories.[34] A majority of the essays below deal with women: either individually in the case of Daisy Bates and Gloria Richardson, or collectively in essays on respectability, on leadership in SNCC, or on African American congresswomen of the 1990s. These collective profiles offer an opportunity to posit more general patterns within movement activity. Belinda Robnett's analysis of SNCC provides a particularly rich example, indicating how the dynamics of gender interacted with those of race, class, and region. Using her key concept of "bridge leadership," Robnett also challenges us to re-consider what we mean by leadership and argues forcefully that the movement's rise and fall hinged on the health of its "bridging tier." This tier was primarily composed of women. Some of them, like Miss Ella Baker, Mrs Septima Clark, and Mrs Fannie Lou Hamer have begun to enjoy a fitting status in movement histories. Robnett's essay is frank enough to admit that in the period between the rejection of the Mississippi Freedom Democratic Party delegation in Atlantic City (August 25, 1964) and the expulsion of whites from SNCC (December, 1966), what had once been an organization that had "free space" in which its female members flourished, became a more hierarchical grouping. In doing so, it did not so much have to change as to revert to a patriarchal inclination that the general society had retained.

Much of the ingrained learning of cultural difference occurs early in our development through our primary personal relationships. Thus, it is appropriate that the essays in this volume include biographical sections dealing with the childhoods of Daisy Bates, and Martin Luther King Jr. Remarkably early in our lives, and continuously thereafter, we are immersed in culture, and learn basic rules of social conduct with usually little deliberation. The discourse of gender envelops us most effectively through the most affective cultural texts, those of which we are least self-conscious and to which we are consequently most open. Accordingly, this volume includes two essays on music. Instead of seeing the world of popular music as a reflection of mass struggles raging elsewhere, both Brian Ward and Eithne Quinn see Rhythm and Blues and Gangsta Rap respectively as crucial public arenas in which the battle for civil rights, racial and gender identity, and personal empowerment actually took place. They recognize the truth of Amiri Baraka's recollection: "The lyrics of the blues instructed me. Explained what the world was and even how men and women related to each other, and the problems inherent in that."[35] Ward identifies a change in the instructions and explanations offered for gender relations in R and B during the movement years, before disillusionment led to patriarchal reassertion. Looking at the controversy surrounding the more recent Gangsta Rap phenomenon, Quinn locates not only Gangsta itself but its voluble critics in the context of a "post-Soul" era. In doing so, she comes closer than most of her fellow contributors to a post-structuralist view of interpretation as arbitrary, a practice that imposes order, and silences or excludes other voices.

In a similar vein, Sharon Monteith examines representations of Martin Luther King in recent fiction. Like Ward and Quinn, she sees literary works not as a separate aesthetic product but as part of the public discourse on race and in particular the vexed question of race leadership. The fictional protagonist as movement leader or witness-participator in civil rights struggles serves as a complex model through which to investigate the extent to which civil rights ideology will endure or be finally dismantled in the new millennium. Novelists approach civil rights history as a dialectic between past and present which prefigures the future. By choosing the medium of fiction, writers should acquire a freedom to think beyond the dominant gender discourse and to posit alternatives. Although the genre of historiographical fiction cuts against this tendency to some degree, it may also operate to highlight overlooked possibilities or substantiate alternative scenarios. In the event, novels such as Julius Lester's *And All Our Wounds Forgiven* (1994) and Charles Johnson's *Dreamer* (1998) suggest that even fictive works remain discursively locked.

Monteith and Quinn's essays are grouped in the "Legacy" section of the collection. Both look at contemporary cultural texts as shaped, at least in part, by the weight of the civil rights movement as both a haunting memory and as an episode that somehow failed to pass on an effective program to the current generation. In both respects, its most potent legacy currently seems to be a pervasive feeling of declension. However, the third essay in this section, by German scholar Britta Waldschmidt Nelson, looks specifically at a group of African American politicians—black Congresswomen, primarily those elected in 1992, the so-called "Year of the Woman." Working in a context of a growing pessimism, even among those African Americans whose relative success economically and socially is testimony to what the movement achieved, these women have to press for practical measures to deal with the intensifying problems of those African Americans whose material fortunes have not been improved in the thirty-five years since the passage of the Civil Rights Act of 1964.[36] The statistics are grim and they are gendered. Social scientists speak of the feminization of poverty when they note the growing number of female heads of households below the poverty line and Earl Ofari Hutchinson has referred to the "assassination of the black male."[37] The discrimination that flows from the persistence of racism is ineluctably linked to the inequalities embedded in patriarchy. By fighting against the cutbacks begun in the Reagan era and in collaboration with the Congressional Black Caucus and the Caucus on Women's Issues, these Congresswomen have sustained the struggle for both African American and female liberation.

Among American scholars of the civil rights movement, Belinda Robnett has looked most intently at the dynamics of gender within the movement and thus her essay on the relationship between organizational structure and female movement participation provides a fitting centerpiece for the collection. But this collection also reflects the current preponderance of civil rights studies within the community of scholars devoted to the study of the United States in Britain. The concentration of interest on the recent history of American race relations among younger academics is quite extraordinary. In part, this reflects the work of a generation of senior figures such as Tony Badger, first at Newcastle and then at Cambridge, Mary Ellison at Keele, Richard King at Nottingham and John White at Hull who have consistently promoted historical research on the twentieth-century American South and on the Second Reconstruction. They have also produced work in the field that demonstrated that a European based scholar could meet American standards of research practice.[38] The arrival of labor historian Rick Halpern at University College London and its sponsorship of the annual Commonwealth Fund conference, alongside Brian Ward's inspired organization of the Martin Luther King Memorial conferences at Newcastle, have also boosted the field. Outside of the United States, the only commemorative conference for the fortieth anniversary of the Montgomery Bus Boycott was organized by John White at the University of Hull.[39] For many civil rights scholars in Europe, the exemplar of what can be achieved has been Adam Fairclough, whose study of the Southern Christian Leadership Conference (SCLC) remains the shrewdest assessment of that organization. His more recent epic history of the civil rights movement in Louisiana fulfils many of the aspirations of the current school of civil rights studies with its emphasis on the important and lengthy first act to the "classic" movement, its rendition of local variations and complexities, and its alertness to the interaction of race and class.[40]

Equally impressive is Brian Ward's award-winning study of black popular music during the civil rights era, which provides the foundation for his essay in this collection.[41] Historians are conscious that their writing is shaped as much by their own time as by that of the time they investigate. Thus, just as it is apt that the study of the civil rights movement's legacy should embrace popular culture as well as electoral politics, it is indicative of our times that in an age when a president's sexual conduct can culminate in his impeachment, this collection does not eschew the long-established rumors surrounding the private life of Dr. Martin Luther King. What both instances share is a recognition that private conduct is only fragilely private and can be speedily politicized, and that sexual conduct cannot be simply correlated to public character. Dr. King's private life was invaded by the Federal Bureau of Investigation in an attempt to destroy him and to harm the movement. King was conscious of this danger, yet he and several of his SCLC colleagues had extra-marital relations, nonetheless. In this volume, Peter Ling considers the models of manhood that prevailed at the SCLC and the relationship between nonviolence and sexual license, whilst Sharon Monteith covers similar ground via fictions which imagine King's extra-marital affairs and crises of conscience. Feminist historians, like Robnett, focus on issues of gender equality in SNCC, since women workers raised concerns within the structures of that organization and Ling, exploring Andrew Young's insightful comments in *An Easy Burden* (1996), reveals competing models of black manhood at the SCLC. In a wide ranging essay, Ling examines the contradictions that King's advocacy of nonviolence presents when aligned with assertive masculine roles. He goes on to consider the competition between King's lieutenants James Bevel and Wyatt Tee Walker within the general dynamics of male relations at SCLC and raises important questions about the predilection for martial models within the organization.

In gathering this collection together, the editors are conscious that theirs is only a preliminary exploration of gender in relation to the civil rights movement. John Kirk's essay on Daisy Bates, for example, indicates the need for a more extensive study of the role of women within the NAACP, particularly when one notes that Ella Baker, Septima Clark, Pauli Murray, Constance Motley Bennett, and innumerable local figures like Rosa Parks held office in this pioneering and easily caricatured organization. By the same token, Belinda

Robnett's examination of the impact of organizational structure on female participation in SNCC not only encourages scholars to look closely at the gender implications of the move to black power but invites a testing of her findings in other national movement organizations such as CORE and in the more local and transient movement organizations of the black power era. Among numerous omissions, we are conscious that there is no essay devoted to sexual orientation, even though the work of scholars such as John D'Emilio, John Howard and William Chafe has begun to establish the important roles played by homosexuals in the movement.[42] Nonetheless, we believe that the essays in this collection shed fresh light on both gender and the civil rights movement and hope that they will encourage others to produce comparable volumes illuminating the movement from a class or regional or generational perspective. A great and complex movement committed to freedom deserves a complex and interrogative history and a continuous re-telling.

The editors would like to acknowledge the support of the University of Nottingham and the University of Hertfordshire and most specifically the Department of American and Canadian Studies at Nottingham and the Department of Humanities at Hertfordshire. Robert Cook, Adam Fairclough and Richard King provided valuable comments on individual chapters in the volume. Particular thanks go to Liz Nutt who worked tremendously hard preparing the final manuscript. The work of many librarians and archivists in the United States and in Europe is also appreciated; their work supported the contributors to this collection. Finally, thanks go to Kristi Long, Becca Maclaren and Mia Zamora at Garland Press.

Notes

1. Charles Sherrod, "Mississippi in Atlantic City," in Clayborne Carson, et al., eds., *The Eyes on the Prize Civil Rights Reader* (New York: Viking Penguin, 1991), 189.

2. Richard H. King, *Civil Rights and the Idea of Freedom*, (Athens, GA: University of Georgia Press, 1996), chapters 2 and 3. For the sense of empowerment in SNCC, see the essay by Robnett in this volume.

3. The stigma was well captured by Chief Justice Earl Warren in his ruling against school segregation in 1954. See also, Waldo E. Martin, *Brown v. Board of Education* (Boston: Bedford/St. Martin's Press 1998), 173.

4. Ralph Ellison, "An Extravagance of Laughter" (1985) in *Going to the Territory* (New York: Vintage, 1995), 177; Jacqueline Dowd Hall, "'The Mind That Burns in Each Body': Women, Rape and Racial Violence" in Ann Snitow, et al., eds., *Powers of Desire: The Politics of Sexuality*, (New York: Monthly Review, 1983), 328-49.

5. See Trudier Harris, *Exorcizing Blackness: Historical and Literary Lynching and Burning Rituals* (Bloomington: Indiana University Press, 1984) for a number of examples and Jacqueline Dowd Hall, *Revolt Against Chivalry: Jessie Daniel Ames and the Women's Campaign Against Lynching* (New York: Columbia University Press, 1979).

6. Evelyn Brooks Higginbotham, "The Problem of Race in Women's History" in Elizabeth Weed, ed., *Coming to Terms: Feminism, Theory, Politics* (New York and London: Routledge, 1989), 132.

7. For the idea of an American Creed, see Gunnar Myrdal, *An American Dilemma: The Negro Problem and Modern Democracy*, (New York: Harper, 1944) and Ralph Ellison's even-handed critique, "*An American Dilemma*: A Review" (1944) in *Shadow and Act* (New York: Random House, 1964), 303-317.

8. James Baldwin, *No Name in the Street*, (New York: Dial, 1972), 128-29; Ralph Ellison, *Invisible Man* (New York: Vintage, 1972), for example, 140-141. Raphael Tardon, "Richard Wright Tells Us: The White Problem in the United States," reprinted in Kenneth Kinnamon and Michel Fabre, eds., *Conversations with Richard Wright* (Jackson: University Press of Mississippi, 1993), 99.

9. Martin Luther King, Jr.,"Letter from Birmingham Jail" in Henry Louis Gates Jr. and Nellie Y. McKay, eds., *The Norton Anthology of African American Literature* (New York and London: W.W. Norton, 1997), 1854.

10. In this context, see also David L. Chappell, *Inside Agitators: White Southerners in the Civil Rights Movement* (Baltimore and London: The Johns Hopkins University Press, 1994).

11. David W. Stowe, "Uncolored People: The Rise of Whiteness Studies," *Lingua Franca* 6 (September-October 1996): 68-77; Toni Morrison, *Playing in the Dark: Whiteness in the Literary Imagination* (Cambridge: Harvard University Press, 1992); David Roediger, *The Wages of Whiteness* (New York: Verso, 1991); Alexander Saxton, *The Rise and Fall of the White Republic* (New York: Verso, 1992) and Tomas Alamaguer, *Racial Fault Lines: The Historical Origins of White Supremacy in California* (Berkeley: University of California Press, 1994).

12. Minstrelsy is also examined in Eric Lott, "'The Seeming Counterfeit': Racial Politics and Early Blackface Minstrelsy," *American Quarterly* 43 (1991): 223-254 and the African American reaction to this "whitening" of respectability is covered by Kevin Gaines, "Assimilationist Minstrelsy as Racial Uplift Ideology: James D. Corrothers's Literary Quest for Black Leadership," *American Quarterly* 44 (1993): 341-369.

13. Robin Kelley, "Notes on Deconstructing the Folk," *American Historical Review*, 97 (1992), 1405-1406; quotation, 1406.

14. Phyllis Palmer, "To Deconstruct Race, Deconstruct Whiteness" *American Quarterly* 45 (1993): 281-294. Yamato is quoted on 281. See also, Ruth Frankenberg, *White Women, Race Matters: The Social Construction of Whiteness* (Minneapolis/London: University of Minnesota Press/ Routledge, 1993).

15. One is reminded that veteran civil rights activists were outraged when Freedom Summer volunteers sniggered at films of fat southern white sheriffs during their orientation in 1964. In this context, see Allison Graham, *Reclaiming The South: Civil Rights Films and the New Red Menace* (Memphis: Center for Research on Women Working Papers, 1998). Among recent works that offer a rich portrait of the white southern segregationists, see Charles Eagles, *Outside Agitator: Jon Daniels and the Civil Rights Movement in Alabama* (Chapel Hill: University of North Carolina Press, 1993) and Glenn Eskew, *But for Birmingham: The Local and National Movements in the Civil Rights Struggle Daniels* (Chapel Hill: University of North Carolina Press, 1997).

16. See, for example, *Transition* The White Issue, 7:1 (1998).

17. Manning Marable, *How Capitalism Underdeveloped Black America* (Boston: South End Press, 1984), 95.

18. Malcolm X with the assistance of Alex Haley, *The Autobiography of Malcolm X* (London: Penguin, 1968), 51-52.

19. Gayle Rubin, "The Traffic in Women" in Rayna Rapp Reiter, ed., *Toward an Anthropology of Women* (New York: Monthly Review Press, 1975), 178-80.

20. A classic example would be Steven Goldberg, *The Inevitability of Patriarchy* (New York: William Morrow & Co., 1975).

21. For Richardson, see the essay by Walker below, and for the distortion of histories of the movement by media framing devices, see Charles Payne, *I've Got the Light of Freedom: The Organizing Tradition and the Mississippi Freedom Struggle*, (Berkeley: University of California Press, 1995), 413.

22. Robert Staples, "Black male sexuality" *Changing Men*, 17 (Winter 1986): 34-46; quotation in Kenneth Clatterbaugh, *Contemporary Perspectives on Masculinity* (Boulder, Col.: Westview Press, 1997), 157.

23. Clyde Franklin "'Ain't I a man?': The efficacy of black masculinities for men's studies" in Richard Majors and Jacob Gordon, eds., *The American Black Male: His Present Status and His Future*, (Chicago: Nelson-Hall, 1994), 275.

24. Patricia J. Williams, "Meditations on Masculinity" in Maurice Berger et al. eds., *Constructing Masculinity* (New York and London: Routledge, 1995), 242.

25. Angela Davis, *An Autobiography* (London: Hutchinson, 1975), 161, quoted in Brian Ward, *Just My Soul Responding: Rhythm and Blues, Black Consciousness and Race Relations* (London: UCL Press, 1998), 371.

26. Michele Wallace, *Black Macho and the Myth of Superwoman* (London: John Calder, 1979), 81.

27. David J. Garrow, ed., *The Montgomery Bus Boycott and the Women Who Started It: The Memoir of Jo Ann Gibson Robinson* (Knoxville, Tenn.: The University of Tennessee Press, 1987).

28. Ellison, *Going to the Territory*, 156.

29. James Baldwin, "The High Road to Destiny" in C. Eric Lincoln ed., *Martin Luther King, Jr.: A Profile* (New York: Hill and Wang, 1970), 95.

30. Pioneering local studies would include William Chafe, *Civilities and Civil Rights: Greensboro, Carolina and the Black Struggle for Freedom* (New York: Oxford University Press, 1980) and Robert J. Norrell, *Reaping the Whirlwind: The Civil Rights Movement in Tuskegee* (New York: Alfred A. Knopf, 1985). This trend is confirmed in Armstead Robinson and Patricia Sullivan's collection *New Directions in Civil Rights Studies* (Charlottesville: University Press of Virginia, 1991).

31. An unusual example that follows a civil rights heritage trail is Townsend Davis's *Weary Feet, Rested Souls: A Guided History* of *the Civil Rights Movement* (New York and London: W.W. Norton, 1998). Davis draws specifically on the local and regional to provide what amounts to a "road map" of the movement and a guidebook to the sites of grassroots organizations and activism.

32. Steven F. Lawson and Charles Payne, *Debating the Civil Rights Movement, 1945-1968* (Lanham, MD: Rowman & Littlefield, 1998) which uses the tension between national and local perspectives as its organizing principle.

33. Vicki L. Crawford, et al., *Women in the Civil Rights Movement: Trailblazers and Torchbearers* (Brooklyn: Carlson Publishing, 1990).

34. Darlene Clark Hine, et al, *Black Women in America: An Historical Encyclopedia* 2 vols. (Bloomington: Indiana University Press, 1994).

35. Imamu Amiri Baraka,*The Autobiography of LeRoi Jones/Imamu Amiri Baraka* (New York: Freundlich, 1984), 50.

36. On the pessimism of the black middle class, see Jennifer L. Hochschild, *Facing Up to the American Dream: Race, Class and the Soul of the Nation* (Princeton: Princeton University Press, 1995).

37. Earl Ofari Hutchinson, *The Assassination of the Black Male* (Los Angeles: Middle Passage Press, 1994).

38. Tony Badger, *The New Deal: The Depression Years 1933*-1940 (Basingstoke: Macmillan, 1989); *Richard H. King, A Southern Renaissance: The Cultural Awakening of the American South 1930-1955* (New York: Oxford University Press, 1980); Mary Ellison, *Lyrical Protest: Black Music's Struggle Against Discrimination* (New York: Praeger, 1989); John White, *Black Leadership in America 1895-1968* (London: Longman, 1985).

39. For works based on the Commonwealth Fund and Newcastle conferences, see Melvyn Stokes and Rick Halpern, eds., *Race and Class in the American South Since 1890* (Oxford: Berg, 1994), Brian Ward and Tony Badger eds., *The Making of Martin Luther King and the Civil Rights Movement* (Basingstoke: Macmillan, 1996) and Brian Ward ed., *Media, Culture, and the Modern African American Freedom Struggle* (Gainesville: University Press of Florida, 2001).

40. Adam Fairclough, *To Redeem the Soul of America: The Southern Christian Leadership Conference and Martin Luther King, Jr.* (Athens GA.: University of Georgia Press, 1987); and *Race and Democracy: The Civil Rights Struggle in Louisiana 1915-1972* (Athens, GA.: University of Georgia Press, 1995). For the notion of the twentieth-century freedom struggle as a two-act drama, see Fairclough, "Historians and the Civil Rights Movement," *Journal of American Studies* 24 (1990): 387-98.

41. Brian Ward, *Just My Soul Responding: Rhythm and Blues, Black Consciousness and Race Relations* (Berkeley/London: University of California Press/UCL Press, 1998) was awarded the Organization of American Historians James A. Rawley Prize for the best book on race relations published in 1998.

42. See John D'Emilio, "Homophobia and the Trajectory of Postwar American Radicalism: The Case of Bayard Rustin" and John Howard, "The Library, the Park, and the Pervert: Public Space and Homosexual Encounter in Post-World War II Atlanta" in *Radical History* 62 (Spring 1995), 80-103 and 166-187 respectively; William Chafe, *Never Stop Running: Allard Lowenstein and the Struggle to Save American Liberalism* (New York: Basic Books, 1993).

CHAPTER 1

Daisy Bates, the National Association for the Advancement of Colored People, and the 1957 Little Rock School Crisis: A Gendered Perspective

John A. Kirk

One glaring omission from Vicki Crawford and associates' landmark volume *Women in the Civil Rights Movement* is an in-depth look at Daisy Bates's role in the struggle for civil rights.[1] As a central participant in the 1957 Little Rock school integration crisis and head of the Arkansas State Conference of Branches (ASC) of the National Association for the Advancement of Colored People (NAACP), Bates became one of the earliest women activists in the movement to gain national recognition. Bates won numerous awards and honors from national organizations for her courage in the Little Rock crisis and subsequently worked for the Democratic National Committee and in President Lyndon Johnson's Great Society poverty programs at Washington D.C.[2] Surely this distinguished career deserves more than the meager two pages of analysis provided in Crawford and colleagues' otherwise wide-ranging book.[3]

One reason for the absence of an adequate treatment of Bates's civil rights activism is the approaches to women's history that authors writing in Crawford's book take. Broadly speaking, these fall into two categories. On the one hand, there are essays written from a "contributionist" perspective.[4] This involves writing histories of *what* women, as individuals and as members of institutions and organizations, contributed to traditional patriarchal histories which typically take as their central focus the role played by men and men's organizations. On the other hand, work such as Charles Payne's offers a sociological perspective which seeks to probe deeper into the *how* and *why* of women's participation in the civil rights movement. Payne, for example, seeks to explain the high level of female participation in the movement, analyzing factors such as demographics, religiosity and the function of social and kinship networks in influencing women's activism.[5] Working in a similar vein, Belinda Robnett has offered an even more analytically rigorous framework for looking at the roles played by women in the movement.[6]

Daisy Bates's brand of activism does not seem to fit easily into either of these approaches. From a contributionist perspective there seems little need to "restore" Bates to the historical record since she is already plainly visible in the more traditional patriarchal histories of the civil rights movement.[7] Since Bates is presented as the "leader" of the Little Rock black community during the school crisis, traditionally prescribed as a "masculine" role, this ensures her place in a traditionally masculine gendered history. From a sociological perspective, Bates does not fit into a framework of analysis which has typically examined the role of the "majority" of women in the civil rights movement who operated largely in traditionally defined "feminine" roles, such as organizers, supporters and nurturers through women's social and kinship networks. Bates, therefore, appears to fall between the methodological cracks of studies of women in the civil rights movement.

This essay seeks to provide a gendered perspective on Daisy Bates's activism which attempts to overcome the limitations of existing contributionist and sociological approaches, whilst incorporating their valuable insights. Taking as its base a contributionist perspective by focusing on one particular individual, it also seeks to apply a sociological perspective at a personal rather than group level in order to look at why and how Bates's experiences as a woman were important within the context of the segregated South.

What is immediately striking about the documentation of Bates's life through her personal papers, her memoir *The Long Shadow of Little Rock*, newspaper articles, film footage, and photographs, is the massive imbalance between what we know about her public life and her personal life.[8] Bates's public career is almost exclusively foregrounded whereas much of her personal life remains elusive. Few scholars of the civil rights movement are probably aware, for instance, that Daisy and her husband L.C. Bates had a foster son living with them from 1951 to 1957, who they were forced to return to his former family in order to escape the violence directed at the Bates' home during the school crisis.[9] Neither are the strains in the marriage between Daisy and L.C. Bates, as a result of the school crisis which led to their divorce and remarriage in 1962, apparent in most commentaries.[10] Yet surely these intense personal traumas make up a significant part of the broader picture of Daisy Bates's public life. As Sara Evans has suggested, the distinction between the "personal" and "political" (or "public") sphere is an artificial construct and what happens in one cannot easily be separated from what happens in the other.[11]

Our lack of knowledge about Bates's personal life is partly due to historians having imposed their own (typically masculine) reading of her role in the movement and concluded that what is important about Bates is her role in public life. This has led to historians ignoring or marginalizing how Bates experienced the civil rights movement on a personal level. The situation has been reinforced by the fact that Bates's own accounts of her activism, most notably in her memoir, do not challenge but rather reflect the assumption that her public persona is somehow privileged over her personal life.

The vast majority of chapters in *The Long Shadow of Little Rock* comprise a narrative by Bates about events which happen around her, but only rarely are events in the public realm related to her own private life and feelings. There is one notable exception to this, in chapter two of her book, entitled "Rebirth." Here, we find the only chapter which Bates devotes entirely to a focus on her personal life and on her own private thoughts and feelings, concerning her relationships, experiences, and interactions with other people, black and white, male and female.[12] Largely ignored by scholars, this chapter provides us with a precious insight into Bates's own reflections and representations of the impact of racism on her life.

Gender and Jim Crow

Significantly, "Rebirth" deals with Bates's early experiences from childhood in Huttig, Arkansas, through to the death of her father, followed shortly afterwards by her marriage to L.C. Bates and their move to Little Rock. It appears that Bates feels more comfortable talking about herself within the context of her "pre-activist" life, before she became joint editor of a crusading newspaper and NAACP leader, since there then remains a clear distinction between her private life in Huttig and her public life as a civil rights activist in Little Rock. Bates seems to present her early biography merely as a prelude to her more "important" later work, devoting one chapter to it out of a total of sixteen. Yet the chapter provides important insights into Bates's later activism. Embedded within the narrative of Bates's early personal life are indications of the powerful emotions and experiences, particularly with regard to gender, which fundamentally shaped and influenced Bates's later public career as a civil rights leader. For this reason, a discussion of the influence of gender on Bates's later life must be rooted in a close reading of how Bates chooses to represent her earlier experiences of race and gender consciousness.

Bates's chapter on "Rebirth" deals with her childhood discoveries about the existence of racism in Huttig, Arkansas, during the 1920s and 1930s. At the heart of the chapter is Bates's reaction to the news she learns while just eight years old, that three white men murdered her biological mother when Daisy was just an infant.(10-12) Shortly afterwards, Bates learns the identity of one of her mother's killers, a local drunkard who hangs around Huttig's downtown square, whom Bates refers to throughout simply as "Drunken Pig." Bates proceeds to run a war of attrition with "Drunken Pig," constantly tormenting him by her presence for the evil deed he has done. "Drunken Pig" becomes the embodiment of everything that Bates hates about racism in the South and as such is accorded little status as a person in his own right. Rather, the impact of Bates's biological mother's death is reflected more in her accounts of other relationships that influenced and shaped her early life.

In Bates's mind there seems little doubt that the most influential relationship in her early years was with her adopted father—although she never actually refers to him as such—Bates always simply calls him "Daddy." Bates's father represents the main source of love, tenderness, comfort and affection in her early life, notably the kind of emotions more usually associated with a "mother" figure. When Bates has her first encounter with white hostility at the age of seven, after she is given sub-standard produce at the local white butcher's shop because she inadvertently attempts to get service in front of a white girl, it is her father who stops her tears when he "lifted me in his arms and smiled." (8) When Bates learns of the circumstances of her biological mother's death, it is again her father who is on hand to comfort her. Bates recounts her father saying "'It's time to go home darling' ... He reached out in the darkness and took my hand ... He lifted me tenderly in his arms and carried me home." (12) On another occasion, during a walk in the woods near their home, Bates's father tries to explain why her biological mother's death occurred, within the context of the racist South of the time. "He began in tones so soft I could barely hear the words," Bates recalls, remembering, "I was always happy on these excursions with Daddy." (14) Later, when Bates is coming to terms with the death of "Drunken Pig" and the final part of her childhood trauma is laid to rest, it is her father who is again on hand: "my daddy heard me crying. He came in to comfort me. He sat on a chair next to my bed and took my hand in his." (24)

This tender and loving relationship between father and daughter is drawn together in a moving scene which closes the chapter when Bates lends comfort to her father as he dies of cancer. As Bates tries to deny her father's inevitable death, he raises a hand to stop her. "He knew I knew," Bates recalls, "and to deny it would make meaningless the honesty we'd always held to in our lifelong relationship with each other … How I loved this strong man." On his deathbed, Bates's father passes on to Daisy "a priceless heritage—one that was to sustain me throughout the years to come." Presumably, this heritage rests in an earlier passage where Bates's father delivers his daughter a lesson on hate. "You're filled with hatred," Bates's father warns:

> Hate can destroy you, Daisy. Don't hate white people just because they're white. If you hate, make it count for something. Hate the humiliations we are living under in the South. Hate the discrimination that eats away at the soul of every black man and woman. Hate the insults hurled at us by white scum—and then try to do something about it, or your hate won't spell a thing. (28-29)

The meaning of this "heritage" is left equivocal. Rather than telling Daisy not to hate, which would presage the nonviolence associated with the civil rights movement, Bates's father appears to advise Daisy not to allow her hatred to become self-destructive. This implies an acceptance of hatred as an emotion that may be turned to good use, a view which is markedly at odds with a message of nonviolence.

On his deathbed, Bates's father laments that he found no outlet for his smoldering resentment of humiliations he suffered as a black man in the white South. Before he dies, he recalls one of the most degrading episodes in his life. On the day of Daisy Bates's biological mother's funeral, "three young white hoodlums" accosted him. They mocked him as a "dressed-up ape" and one of them painted a red stripe down his best suit. He recalls that "if I touched one hair on his head I could be lynched." Helpless, Bates's father appealed to a deputy sheriff who belittled him, saying that his assailants were "just having a little fun. Turpentine will take the paint out of your coat." With clenched fists, Bates's father's last words to his daughter are: "I ought to have died the day they put paint on my coat. I should have taken those guys and wrung their necks like chickens. But I wanted to live—for what, I sometimes wonder." (29-30) Certainly, Daisy Bates inherits her father's resentment. Her deep-felt affection for him only serves to increase her anguish that he was never able to stand up against whites as the "real" man he so yearned to be. Bates laments:

How I loved this strong man who all his life had not
been able to use his strength in the way he wanted to. He
was forced to suppress it and hold himself back, bow to
the white yoke or be cut down. And now that his life was
ebbing, he was trying to draw on that reservoir of unused
strength to give me a lasting inheritance. (29)

Hand in hand with the legacy of her father's tenderness, throughout
the text there is an ever-present empathy with the demoralization and
anger which her father feels at never being able to achieve full
"manhood" on an equal basis with whites. After the episode at the
butcher's shop, when he has comforted Daisy and she finally tells him
what has happened to upset her, "his smile faded ... I could feel his
muscles tighten as he carried me into the house." (8-9) Later, when he
tries to explain "the words just wouldn't come. I stood there, looking at
him and wondering why he was acting so strangely. Finally he stood up
and the words began tumbling from him." With Daisy still unable to
fully comprehend, Bates's father

dropped to his knees in front of me, placing his hands
on my shoulders, and began shaking me and shouting.

"Can't you understand what I've been saying?" he
demanded. "There's nothing I can do! If I went down to
the market I would only cause trouble for my family."

Poignantly, Bates asks "Daddy, are you afraid?" In reply, he

sprang to his feet in an anger I had never seen him in
before. "Hell no! I'm not afraid for myself, I'm not afraid
to die. I could go down to that market and tear him limb
from limb with my bare hands, but I'm afraid for you and
your mother." (9)

On another occasion, Bates and her father have been walking in the
woods and he has been explaining her biological mother's death in
terms of the "timeworn lust of the white man for the Negro
woman—which strikes at the heart of every Negro man in the South."
Bates notices that "my daddy looked tired and broken." (15)

In marked contrast to her father, Bates's "adopted Mother"—as she
actually refers to her at one point—is given short shrift. (17) Even in the
snippets of information we are given, there is little of the closeness that
her relationship with her father engenders. It is Bates's mother who

sends her to her first encounter with racism at the butcher's shop because she is "not feeling well" enough to go herself. When Bates returns with her story, her mother tells her to "Go on out to the porch and wait for Daddy," to handle the dilemma. (7-8) In another instance, when Bates picks a wilting single red rose that reminds her of her biological mother, Bates's adopted mother exclaims, "I can't understand that child, crying over a dying flower." But Bates's father makes the connection, telling his wife "Let her be. It just takes time." (14) When Bates is in mourning for her biological mother, her adopted mother's solution is to "send Daisy away for a visit to her grandmother," confessing "I wish I knew what was going on in that mind of hers." When Bates protests, it is again her father who intercedes by saying "All right, darling, if you don't want to go to grandma's you don't have to." (21-22)

In addition, Bates often represents her mother as a repressive force in her life. Curiously, it is her mother who Bates associates with discipline, traditionally the more "masculine" role of the father within the family unit. "I was often clobbered, tanned, switched and made to stand in the corner," she tells us. In part, at least, Bates ascribes this to her mother's religion, since "she believed every word in the Holy Bible—including that passage, 'Spare the rod and spoil the child,' which I later learned wasn't in the Bible at all." (25) Bates's mother also stops her from "playing for keeps" at marbles with the neighborhood boys on religious grounds since "That's gambling and gambling is a sin." (26) Bates curtly notes that her father is allowed to gamble on Saturday nights so long as he seeks forgiveness for it on Sunday mornings. One morning, she impudently asks Daddy in front of her mother, "Daddy, why don't you go to church and ask God to forgive you for a whole month? Then you won't have to go to church every Sunday." Bates tells us, "Mother fanned my tail and sent me off to Sunday school. After that I left it to Mama and God to worry about Daddy's sins." (27) When Bates's mother finds young Daisy has been "playing for keeps" yet again, "[She] didn't allow me to wait for Sunday. She dragged me off that evening for Wednesday night prayer service, so I could ask God to forgive me for my sins." (28)

The association of the church and religion with punishment and oppression are clearly bound up with Bates's feelings about her mother's treatment of her. Bates appears to have little time for religion and the church, identified by scholars as a central focal point of black women's networks and socialization in many southern communities.[13] She views religion as a site of white oppression rather than black liberation. The scene where Bates finally appears to turn her back on the church is particularly poignant. This occurs when Bates is asked by one of the "church ladies" to play the part of "an angel hovering over the straw crib of infant Jesus" in the Christmas nativity play. Bates replies *"No!* I won't ... I don't want no part of that play about a dead white doll ... All the pictures I ever saw of Jesus were white ... If Jesus is like the white people, I don't want any part of him!" Bates's mother, "shocked," tells her daughter "I won't have that kind of talk ... You stop that kind of talk this minute!" Nevertheless, Bates holds firm and "Nothing more was ever said about my appearing in the Christmas play. While my friends and family attended the Christmas pageant, I spent a lonely evening with my dog and colored doll." (20-21)

Bates further mocks the "Church Sisters" in a more light-hearted scene, as they pray at her bedside when she is ill after hearing the truth about her biological mother's death. As they "knelt around my bed and prayed for my soul," Bates's mind fixes on "the fat knees of one praying lady." Bates then proceeds to release the guinea pigs she has been hiding in a box under her bed covers. She describes the ensuing scene of chaos:

> One of them ran across the fat lady's leg. Unable to lift her weight up on the chair beside her, she lumbered around the room, screaming hysterically. The other ladies, managing to keep a few paces ahead of her, joined in the wild demonstration.

The whole scene leaves Bates "helpless with laughter." Predictably, the event ends with Bates having her "behind properly spanked" by her mother. At this spectacle, "The ladies, although convinced that I certainly needed prayer, decided to do their praying for me elsewhere." (13)

Despite her evident disrespect for the churchwomen, Bates does indicate that she is aware of and appreciates their dedication to their faith. When she describes the "two church buildings" with "drab exterior[s]" in Huttig, she does note that it is the "Sisters of the church" who keep them "spotless inside." (7) However, Bates decides, that theirs is not a direction she could follow. Even outside of the church, Bates seems to have little time for the black women in her community. At one point, she declares herself "engaged in open warfare with the neighborhood adults." Although "adult" is not gender specific here, it is clear from Bates's narrative who the enemy is:

> I felt they were a lazy, conniving bunch of porch sitters who were always chasing us kids around town on

errands for them. I resented their rewarding us with stale pound cake and soggy homemade cookies.

One afternoon, after lugging a gallon of milk six blocks for Mrs Coleman, I watched her reach for a piece of cake from her red-and-white cake pan.

"Thank you, Daisy, for fetching the milk. I always seem to be tired these days," she said, handing me my reward.

"Shucks, I get tired too," I said. "And you are always chasing me all over town and then giving me nothing but that old cake. I don't want it—I've been throwing it in the ditch anyhow."

"Well, did you ever!" said the shocked Mrs Coleman. "The nerve! I'll certainly see your mother hears about this!"

It was my last feud with the neighborhood adults. My mother had seen to that. (24-25)

Bates's experiences of racism play an important role in her rejection of the "feminine." Certainly, in terms of religion for example, this is clearly apparent. Yet there are other very subtle "defeminizing" codas to many of Bates's stories about discovering the nature of black oppression. In her first experience at the butcher's shop, she begins, "I put on one of my prettiest dresses and my mother brushed my hair." The episode ends, "That night when I knelt down to pray, instead of my usual prayers, I found myself praying that the butcher would die." (7-9) Again, when Bates has the identity of her mother's killer confirmed in an overheard conversation between three white men in a department store, a similar transition takes place. "I was standing behind them, admiring a big colored doll," Bates tells us, when one of her mother's killers walks in. The men discuss the killer amongst themselves:

You heard about that colored woman they found in the millpond a few years ago? I heard he was involved ... leastwise, he started to drink about then, and he's been getting worse and worse ever since. He's about hit rock bottom. Too bad, 'cause he had a good job at the time.

Bates "stood motionless listening. Now that I was sure of what I suspected I lost all interest in the doll." (19-20)

Most striking of all is the episode in which Bates finds out precisely how her biological mother died. At the outset, she is picking flowers:

> I passionately loved all blooming things. In the woods I hunted out the first of the cowslips and spring beauties, and from the open fields, the last of the Indian paintbrush. I was always bringing home bouquets ... All of the neighbors knew that the flowers in our yard were my garden, not Mother's.

Within one page of text, after Bates's father has explained the death of her biological mother, the soft feminine tones and activities halt and suddenly become more masculine, hardened and embittered, as Bates's mind turns to vengeance:

> Dolls, games ... held little interest for me after that. Young as I was, strange as it may seem, my life now had a secret goal—to find the men who had done this horrible thing to my mother. So happy once, now I was like a little sapling which, after a violent storm, puts out only gnarled and twisted branches. (13-15)

We know little of Bates's biological father, other than he "was as light as a lot of white people" and that he "was so hurt" at the murder of his wife than he left town, never to return. Bates's biological father is notable only as an absence in her life. (12) Although we receive little information about her biological parents, it is Bates's mother to whom she clearly feels closest, no doubt because many people have told Bates that she is "the living image of her." (16) Appropriately, it is Bates's father, who acts as a surrogate mother in gender terms for Bates, and who relates the information about Daisy's biological mother to her, saying "your mother was very pretty—dark brown with long hair." (12) There is also bitterness on Bates's father's part that he was unable to prevent the murder or subsequently secure justice for her killing. As Bates's father briefly narrates the death of Bates's biological mother, he says "your mother was not the kind to submit ... so they took her." (15) As readers, we are left with the curious juxtaposition of Bates's biological mother, who resists humiliation at the hands of whites and is killed for her efforts, and Bates's father who accepts the humiliation of the three white hoodlums on the day of the funeral and survives. There is a great deal of ambiguity over meaning here, especially what this tells us about the relative costs of "protest" and "accommodation" and how these are relevant in terms of the roles played by (and expected of) black men and women in the Jim Crow South.

Bates's early experiences of racism affect not only her relationships within the black community, but also her relationships with whites, male and female. Not all whites are demonic in Bates's narrative. There is, for example, an "elderly and retired mill worker who was now nearly crippled with arthritis" who "knew all the children, both white and Negro" and sat in the town square, often handing out free candy to those who passed. (16) The old man witnesses the daily war of attrition between Bates and "Drunken Pig" and is always silently on hand to help safeguard Bates in these encounters. (17) It is the old man who finally informs Bates that "Drunken Pig" has died and tries to comfort her. (23) Yet Bates cannot fully accept the old man's friendship because he is white. When a friend suggests that they go and get some free candy one day, Bates responds "If I want candy, I have some money to buy it ... I don't want anything from white people." (17) After this episode, her friendship with the old man sours. "The old man had not spoken a word to me since the day I refused his candy," Bates later informs us. (21)

Similarly, Bates's experiences of racism affect her relationships with her female friends. One day, soon after finding out about the death of her mother, Bates is approached by a white girl "with whom I had been friends a long time." The white girl prods Bates in the back and calls, "Look, Daisy, I have two pennies. Let's buy some candy and I'll tell you about my vacation." Bates's anger and frustration is vented on the girl who she slaps across the face: "Don't you ever touch me again," Bates cries "I don't want your penny!"(18) When she arrives home she feels guilt and remorse for what she has done:

> I wanted badly to go back and tell her I was sorry, and that I didn't really hate her. During our friendship we had often met at the store and shared our pennies. We would have so much fun shopping with our pennies. If I bought winding balls, she would buy peppermint sticks and we would divide them. How could I explain to her that ... (18)

At that instant, Bates realizes the significance of her action: "Suddenly I was afraid. Suppose she went home and told her people that I had hit her? Suppose they came for me or my daddy that night?" (19) Within the context of a firmly drawn line of racial etiquette, even a childhood squabble threatens both her life and the lives of her family. Bates decides to keep quiet about the incident. Fortunately, there are no reprisals, but Bates ends up losing one of her best friends and further realizes the significance of minor indiscretions in a racialized world.

Bates's early life presents a confused world of ambiguous, mixed metaphors with regard to gender. By her own admission, Bates wears pretty dresses, picks flowers, and has braids in her hair. She relies upon her male cousin, Early B., to protect her from bullies. She is squeamish about bugs and spiders, whilst declaring herself "a regular tomboy" who enjoyed "competing with the neighborhood boys," climbing trees, gambling with marbles, and keeping guinea pigs in her bed, with only her adopted mother stopping her from keeping hogs in there with her too. (7-21, 25-26) Bates appears to be a product of a childhood which has produced no strong or convincing gender orientation: she neither accepts the "feminine" gender referents offered her, nor rejects them totally for "masculine" referents which also have flaws and weaknesses.

Daisy's marriage to L.C. Bates demonstrates that the ambiguous gender roles inherited from her childhood persisted into her adult life. Daisy met her future husband when she was fifteen and L.C. was twenty-one years her senior.[14] Although L.C. did the wooing with gifts from his travels as an insurance man, and made the first move in the relationship by holding Daisy's hand in the movie theater one night, it was Daisy who made the decision that "I would one day marry him," without revealing her "plans" to L.C. She reaches this decision despite the fact that "Daddy had often declared that a girl should not consider marriage until she could cook and sew. And I could do neither." (33) It was also Daisy who sued for divorce in 1962 on the grounds of "abuse, contempt and studied neglect," and confirmed their remarriage to the press several months later.[15] By all accounts, Daisy Bates was the active and dynamic partner in the marriage.[16] Bates's own memoirs insist that she played an equal role in the founding and running of the *State Press*. (33-34) She also learnt how to run the business side of the newspaper, studying Business Administration and Public Relations at Shorter College. Around the same time, L.C. only just managed to talk Daisy out of taking flying lessons on the grounds that the insurance premiums would be too high. (38-39) It was Daisy who became the public figure in the partnership, first as president of the ASC and later, nationally, as a result of her role in the Little Rock crisis. Although L.C. was the "husband" in the marriage, his role in gender terms was more typically that traditionally assigned to a "wife," as a supporter from the sidelines. Like many other "wives" in history, L.C. Bates has never really received due recognition for the considerable part he played in the civil rights movement in Arkansas.[17]

Gender and Black Activism

Daisy Bates's rejection of the "masculine" as both the site of white male oppression and black male powerlessness, and of the "feminine" as a perceived delimiting sphere which revolved around church groups and seemed apathetic ("a lazy conniving bunch of porch sitters"), rather than overtly political, produced an obvious dilemma. Where, if not in these gendered frameworks of expression, would Bates find an outlet for her anger against whites and against the incapacity of existing black networks to issue that challenge?

One immediate answer was the *State Press* newspaper. Through its pages, Bates was able to have a "say" in community affairs without working through existing networks of black activism. Yet, at the same time, the newspaper had an important impact on those groups, and could stir them to take action. Bates's reporting of the shooting of black army Sergeant Thomas Foster by a white city police officer in downtown Little Rock in 1942, for example, created such an outcry that the normally complacent, male black leaders were forced to investigate the incident through a Negro Citizens' Committee. The newspaper's impact, not only upon the city but throughout the state, was demonstrated by the massive turnout at the First Baptist Church in Little Rock on Sunday March 29, when blacks from all over Arkansas gathered to hear the Committee declare that Foster had been unlawfully killed.[18] Although Foster's white killer escaped punishment in the courts, the *State Press*'s continuing crusade brought some concessions. The first nine black policemen were enrolled into the city's police force soon after.[19]

Bates utilized the *State Press* not only to launch an attack on the wrongdoings of the white community but also to criticize what she viewed as the shortcomings of the black community, in particular lambasting the influential male-dominated leadership. This criticism sharpened, especially during the post-war era when a new black leadership began to emerge in Little Rock. Since Reconstruction, most of the city's influential black public figures had been drawn from the ranks of a small but thriving business community. With the impact of the Depression which crushed many black businesses, and the U.S. Supreme Court's 1944 *Smith* v. *Allwright* ruling, which outlawed racial exclusion in state and local Democratic party primaries and led to an increased concentration on voter registration, a new politically-oriented black leadership began to develop in the city. In the vanguard of this revolt against the older leaders was Charles Bussey who, with a band of black GIs, formed the Veterans' Good Government Association. Bussey also had a hand in forming another new group, the East End Civic

League, led by Jeffrey Hawkins, which concentrated specifically on representing the interests of the run-down, heavily black populated east end of the city. I.S. McClinton, another prominent member of this new band of black leaders, formed the Young Negro Democrats group, which later became the Arkansas Democratic Voters' Association. These new leaders looked to harness the political potential of the black vote in order to use it as leverage with whites to press for improvements in the black community.[20]

Bates remained skeptical about the methods and intentions of these new political leaders. In the pages of the *State Press*, she complained that some who were posing as leaders were only interested in their own self-aggrandizement. They delivered black votes for white politicians rather than advancing the cause of the race as a whole.[21] Even those she deemed sincere were portrayed as misguided in settling for a bargaining of votes to improve conditions within the bounds of segregation, rather than exerting pressure to end racial discrimination altogether.[22] The *State Press* demanded nothing short of a complete end to segregation. "Arkansas needs leadership" ran one typical editorial of 1950: "Arkansas cities need leadership ... the Negro needs leadership which will stand up and be counted ... and above all, Little Rock, Arkansas's capital city, needs leadership badly."[23] In another editorial, male leaders were blamed directly for the inadequacies of the black community's facilities. Their failure, the *State Press* claimed, was "a sounder explanation of our failure to get parks, playgrounds, enough Negro police, employment on the Negro side of the employment office, and other lacks, than any amount of white opposition."[24] Ominously, another 1950 editorial concluded it was "about time for a general showdown on the leadership in Little Rock."[25]

For that "showdown" Bates would need a different vehicle than the *State Press*. Although the newspaper could effectively provide a voice of protest, it could not provide a base from which to mobilize a direct and comprehensive assault on segregation. Even if Bates had wanted to form her own political organization, which from her comments she clearly did not, the gender constraints of that male-dominated world would probably have prevented her from doing so with any degree of success. Neither had Bates discovered any attachment to or affection for the female-dominated networks in the city that revolved around clubs, associations and institutions such as the National Council of Negro Women, the YWCA and the church. Bates was a member of many of these organizations but was a "joiner" rather than a "joiner-inner." She played no prominent part within any of these groups. Indeed, she still showed a private disdain for women's networks. One of Daisy Bates's closest friends in the white community, lawyer Edwin E. Dunaway, vividly remembered the time he approached Bates and asked her to sit on the board of the Little Rock Urban League. The League, established by black schoolteacher Amelia B. Ives in 1939, was an interracial group in which women were heavily represented. The Urban League looked to address the problems that blacks faced in the city, albeit strictly within the bounds of existing Jim Crow. Bates rejected Dunaway's approach, insisting that the executive board of the Little Rock Urban League was "just a bunch of niggers who want to sit next to white folks once every two weeks."[26]

Bates ultimately found that the most effective vehicle for her anger at the conditions blacks faced, was the NAACP. In many ways, it was the perfect organization for Bates since it was not fully incorporated into either the existing male or female networks in the city. The local branch of the NAACP in Little Rock, formed in 1918, confirms Charles Payne's hypothesis that "men led, women organized," yet it remained unclear which role was seen as the most important or who actually held authority within the organization. Most of the city's prominent black male leaders were members of the NAACP board, but none of them played an active role. Rather, it was left to black women to keep the branch afloat, which they did with consummate success. In 1925, for example, Mrs Carrie Sheppherdson won a national NAACP award, the coveted Madam C.J. Walker Gold Medal, for her fund-raising efforts.[27] Still, those women active in the Little Rock NAACP remained exasperated at the lack of effort from the men. As Mrs H.L. Porter, one in a line of female local branch secretaries, summed up in 1933 "the lawyers, Doctors, preachers and businessmen ... are just a bunch of egoistic discussers and not much on actual doings."[28]

Active interest in the NAACP in Arkansas only really took root during the 1940s. Fittingly, it was an initiative led by an organization in which women were in a majority, the Little Rock Classroom Teachers' Association (CTA), which sparked that interest. Throughout the 1930s the CTA had followed the teachers' salary equalization suits championed by NAACP attorney Thurgood Marshall. The success of the *Alston* suit in Virginia in 1940 convinced Little Rock teachers that they too should pursue a similar action. A Salary Adjustment Committee (SAC) was organized and its secretary, Miss Solar M. Caretners, wrote to both Melvin Alston of Norfolk, Virginia, the successful plaintiff in the 1940 suit, and Walter White, president of the NAACP, to ask for advice about "the method of procedure and techniques of bringing about equal salaries for teachers."[29] With preparations in place, Mrs Susie Morris, head of the English Department at Dunbar High School in Little

Rock, was nominated as lead plaintiff for the suit, filed in the U.S. District Court on February 28, 1942.[30] After numerous appeals, the Eighth Circuit Appeals' Court at St. Louis finally decided the suit in favor of Morris on June 19, 1945.[31] The victory marked a significant triumph both for the local and national NAACP. Historian Mark Tushnet describes the Little Rock teachers' salary suit as the "most important of its kind."[32] Certainly, the national NAACP was overjoyed at the outcome, evident in their triumphant press release, which proclaimed "NAACP WINS DOUBLE VICTORY IN ARKANSAS TEACHERS SALARY CASE."[33]

The success of the teachers' salary suit led directly to the formation of the Arkansas State Conference. This stirred a great deal of controversy in the state over the direction of black activism. The national offices of the NAACP divided responsibilities for the ASC between the young, militant activist William Harold Flowers from Pine Bluff, who became chief organizer of branches, and the Reverend Marcus Taylor, an older and more conservative figure from Little Rock, who became ASC president. Animosity between the two as a result of their conflicting styles of leadership soon became apparent. With no real communication between the two rival power bases, two factions, one activist and one more conservative, quickly formed within the organization. Jealous of the support Flowers began to receive, Taylor fired accusations of financial mismanagement at the younger leader, even suggesting that Flowers was keeping half of the funds he collected from the establishment of local branches for himself.[34] An investigation launched by the NAACP to investigate the situation found Taylor's accusations to be untrue.[35] Indeed, Flowers's popularity continued to grow alongside the rapid expansion of NAACP branches and members throughout Arkansas. The battle within the NAACP was finally resolved in 1948 when Flowers was elected as ASC president.[36]

There was no doubt as to which side of the activist versus conservative argument Daisy Bates was on. Both Daisy and L.C. were friends of Flowers. The *State Press* had publicized Flowers's voter registration efforts in the early 1940s as head of the Committee on Negro Organizations, an indigenous organization whose activism pre-dated the NAACP's expansion in the state.[37] Moreover, Flowers wrote a regular column in the *State Press* under the pseudonym of Frances Sampson and considered the Bates' home a welcome stop-over during his visits to Little Rock.[38] In contrast to other male politicians, Bates remembered in later years, Flowers was the only truly "effective" protest leader of the time.[39]

Flowers's election as president of the ASC inspired Daisy Bates to attack the lethargy of male leaders in the Little Rock NAACP. Her difficulties were compounded by the fact that the capital city was the center of black conservatism in the state. Rather than engaging with the existing NAACP in-fighting in the city, Bates attempted to set up her own separate sphere of influence in a rival group, filing application for a "Pulaski County Chapter of the NAACP" in 1948.[40] By forming a countywide chapter, Bates hoped to undercut the authority of older male leaders, such as Reverend Taylor, and provide a new dynamism for the organization. In her application for charter, Bates included fifty membership subscriptions, plus the branch-founding fee, and nominated herself as president. Wise to what Bates was attempting to do, the national headquarters of the NAACP turned down the application. In a curt reply, Gloster B. Current, national director of NAACP branches, pointed out that there was already a branch in Little Rock and that if people were interested in helping the organization they should join up there.[41]

After Bates's unsuccessful attempt to displace Taylor, unrest continued in state NAACP activities. In 1949 when the ASC defaulted on its annual contribution to the NAACP's Southwest Regional Conference fund, the national office demanded Flowers's resignation under threat of dismissal.[42] Flowers resigned but, as a result, talk of mutiny by grassroots members grew. Only the intervention of Roy Wilkins, executive secretary of the NAACP, and Walter White, prevented a wholesale defection. Nevertheless, the deep dissatisfaction of local NAACP activists persisted.[43] Many were extremely reluctant to accept Flower's replacement, Dr. J.A. White, who represented the old guard of black leadership, imposed upon them by national headquarters. Dissension within Arkansas NAACP ranks caused much concern. Mrs Lulu B. White, a member of the Texas NAACP State Conference of Branches, observed "no place in the country is there so much strife and division amongst Negroes as it is in Arkansas."[44]

The internal wrangling was finally resolved in 1952 when Daisy Bates was elected as ASC president. She came to office when Dr. White fell ill and resigned in 1951, resulting in the first popular election of a leader by local NAACP members since Flowers's resignation. Undoubtedly, Bates's connections with Flowers helped her to win office. In contrast to many other organizations in the black community, the issue of Bates being a woman and leader of the ASC never seems to have been broached. This reflected the fact that, at a state level, the NAACP was perceived neither as an exclusively "male" or "female" sphere of influence. Of more concern than Bates's gender was her forthright militancy. Gloster B. Current, who had been present at Bates's election, questioned her ability to work with older, more established leaders in the state, and was wary of her tendency "to go off the deep end at times" in her forceful pursuit of black rights. However, he concluded apologetically, "[although] I am not certain that she was the proper person to be elected I permitted it because there was no one else to be elected who offered any promise of doing anything to further the work of the NAACP in Arkansas."[45]

As ASC president, Daisy Bates began to exercise a more direct influence on the day-to-day affairs of the black community in Little Rock. In particular, the U.S. Supreme Court's 1954 *Brown* v. *Board of Education* school desegregation decision helped to garner support for both Bates and the NAACP. With existing male and female networks unable to handle such a contentious issue as school desegregation, the NAACP filled a void in a black community which saw the *Brown* decision as a signal that "the time for delay, evasion or procrastination was past."[46] As head of the NAACP, Bates spearheaded attempts to press the Little Rock School Board, as well as other school boards in the state, into compliance with the court ruling.[47]

As school desegregation descended into a well-documented crisis in Little Rock during September 1957, Bates's backing from the black community solidified. A 1958 study by sociologists, Tilman C. Cothran and William Phillips, Jr. entitled "Negro Leadership in a Crisis Situation," confirmed Bates's commanding position. Twenty-two out of twenty-six existing black leaders in Little Rock described Bates as "the most influential Negro in the community" whilst twenty-four out of twenty-six named her "the most influential Negro in determining policy on educational desegregation." One interviewee described Bates as "the only outspoken Negro leader," adding "the other Negro leaders have remained silent and have allowed her to become spokesman (sic)." A parent of one of the nine black students undertaking the task of desegregating Central High School agreed that "the NAACP President is the only leader who has stood up for these children. She has been more helpful than anybody." The parent, adding her thoughts on the rest of the black leadership in the city, declared: "We have a shortage of leaders ... There are a lot of would-be leaders, but the problem is that when the trouble starts they won't stand up and be counted."[48]

Although Bates was clearly the sole voice of leadership in the city during the school crisis, her position, working outside of existing male and female networks of influence, remained tenuous. Despite her leading role, Bates was still considered an outsider. One black woman later uncharitably referred to Bates as "sort of an opportunist." Ozell Sutton, who was hired as the first black reporter on the white *Arkansas Democrat* newspaper in 1948 to cover the news in the black community, and who became a major figure in the civil rights struggle in city and state, explained:

> Daisy Bates was a leader for the Negroes in the contending forces concerned with integration, but there was definite disagreement within the Negro community over her tactics and personality. However, there was never any public disagreement because of the unanimity of commitment to desegregation. Because the community power was centered in Daisy Bates, she made arbitrary decisions.[49]

Bates soon discovered that, outside of the immediate problem surrounding Central High school, she was isolated from the rest of the community. Bates became the target of white segregationists after the 1957 school crisis. Missiles were hurled at her home, and she was arrested by the state authorities for refusing to hand over NAACP membership lists. Few in the black community were prepared to take an open stand in her defense. Likewise, the NAACP received little local support for its efforts. In fact, when the organization was attacked by the state authorities through harassing lawsuits, membership figures dropped to an all-time low. When the *State Press* was forced out of business in 1959 through a campaign by segregationists to force advertisers to withdraw their support, Bates's anger at her isolation became clear. In one editorial in April 1959, the *State Press* declared that too many blacks in Little Rock were apathetic, too many satisfied with "the master-slave relationship which the whites called good race relations" and therefore lacked the determination to fight for their constitutional rights.[50]

Bates's final disillusionment came when she played a part in organizing sit-ins with students from Little Rock's Philander Smith College. Following the wave of sit-ins across the South in early 1960, Bates met with black students who staged their first demonstration in downtown Little Rock on March 9 at the F.W. Woolworth lunch counter.[51] City authorities were quick to have students arrested and the courts handed down both harsh fines and long jail sentences.[52] White and black leaders condemned the sit-ins as harmful to race relations. Only the local NAACP and, later, the local branch of the National Council of Negro Women, actively supported the students. The *Southern Mediator Journal*, older black leaders, and especially Dr.

Lafayette Jones, President of Philander Smith College, all strongly dissented. Indeed, Jones had to be persuaded by white college board members not to expel immediately all the students involved.[53] As the students were passed from court to court, deliberately log-jammed in the legal system, local black support for their cause remained virtually non-existent. As a result, further demonstrations ground to a halt. Lack of support proved to be the final straw for Bates. She left Little Rock to concentrate upon national appearances, writing, and then promoting her memoirs. She also supported the "Dollars for Daisy" campaigns run by various black communities across the United States to raise money to revive the *State Press*. From 1960 through 1963 she spent most of her time out of Little Rock.[54]

Although Bates left Little Rock under a cloud of disillusionment, her impact on existing black leaders and black networks in the city was palpable. As those who had been leaders in the community before Bates tried to reassert their authority, factional conflict between different individuals and organizations multiplied. Many in the black community began to express openly their dissatisfaction with the pre-Bates leadership. "Disunity among Negro leaders" wrote an observer from the National Urban League "proved to be of more concern than the school crisis."[55] Young black city lawyer John Walker, who was associate director of the interracial Arkansas Council on Human Relations (ACHR), described black leadership as "virtually nil," whilst adding that "the masses of Negroes are anxious for more progressive leadership from new people."[56] Bates had managed to successfully disrupt existing lines of leadership which older leaders subsequently struggled to restore. However, since the crisis had brought a change in their former constituencies of support, which demanded a more active and dynamic approach to racial issues, older leaders generally failed to live up to the new standards required by the masses. Increasingly, many in the black community felt that there was a need to find a more assertive and capable leadership, which could adapt to a more innovative strategy for the pursuit of black rights.

Initial signs that a new leadership was struggling to establish itself came in the first school board elections after the Central High crisis in November 1959. Dissatisfaction with the newly established pupil assignment system, which limited desegregation at the discretion of the all-white school board, led to a delegation from the black community launching an appeal to abandon the system altogether.[57] When these appeals were ignored, Dr. M.A. Jackson, a young black physician, declared his intention to stand for the school board. Over one thousand black residents signed a petition in support of the action. Although threats from the white community, coupled with disparaging remarks from older black leaders, ultimately prevented Jackson from running, the campaign marked the beginning of a new era of black leadership.[58] Through the offices of the ACHR, working in tandem with the black community, a new forum for leadership emerged. This was rooted in a visit in 1960 by John Wheeler, a black leader from Durham, North Carolina, when he explained how his community had organized a "Council on Community Organizations," with various groups pooling their resources to focus on a common goal of black rights. This paved the way for the formation of a similar group in Little Rock called the Council on Community Affairs (CoCA)

CoCA became the most effective vehicle for local black protest in Little Rock during the 1960s. Formed as a collective body of existing centers and networks of community influence, CoCA proclaimed their intention to "give the Negro community a united voice in all matters concerning their welfare."[59] Significantly, this pooling of community influence began to break down the hitherto clearly defined "male" and "female" roles and spheres of responsibility for black activism. Moreover, the core leadership of the new group, who were all physicians, included a woman, Dr. Evangeline Upshur. She, along with Dr. W.H. Townsend, Dr. M.A. Jackson and Dr. Garman P. Freeman, represented the new breed of leadership in Little Rock and provided tangible links to Daisy Bates. Upshur was Bates's next door neighbor and family practitioner and had been one of her few determined supporters throughout the school crisis.[60] Yet CoCA remained careful to incorporate older leaders into the new structure of community activism, thereby utilizing various avenues of organizational strength and influence, whilst at the same time deploying their energies into new areas of activism.[61] In so doing, CoCA proved an effective voice for the black community. It was CoCA, for example, who, in 1963, linked up with representatives from the Student Non-violent Coordinating Committee and local students to put an end to segregation in Little Rock's downtown area through direct action protests and negotiations with the city's white business leadership. CoCA continued to forge links with white moderate and liberal groups in the city, male and female, and to build important community coalitions which helped to shape the future of race relations in Arkansas's state capital.[62]

Daisy Bates's involvement with the struggle for black rights demonstrates the importance of gender as a potent force in shaping reactions to white oppression in the Jim Crow South. Moreover, it highlights the interconnectedness of the "personal" and the "political." Through an analysis of Bates's activism from a gendered perspective, we can also see that women played multiple roles in the civil rights movement; that, contrary to Charles Payne's hypothesis, they served as both leaders and organizers, including many varieties of involvement within these two categories. Although, as sociological studies have highlighted, the majority of women who participated in the civil rights struggle played their part through women's networks and spheres of influence, clearly not all did. We need to understand the "uncommon" experiences of women alongside these more "typical" experiences if we are to comprehend the multi-faceted roles that women played in the movement. Exploring why some women made an impact in a male-dominated world helps to shed light on why others did not. Contributionist histories do not satisfy the complexities and nuances of women's experiences in the civil rights movement *as* women and not simply as "honorary men." Overlooking the experiences of black women in the civil rights struggle who operated outside of a traditional women's sphere of influence, and failing to recognize that that sphere was itself a product of choices influenced by gender, risks losing sight of the important role played by some of the most influential women in the movement. To be marginalized simply because they were successful against the odds would be an unjust legacy for women, like Bates, to bear.

Notes

1. Vicky Crawford et al, *Women in the Civil Rights Movement* (Brooklyn: Carlson Publishing, 1990).

2. Bates's post-school crisis activism has generally received as little attention as her pre-school crisis years. The best short biographies at present are the finding aids to her papers at the University of Arkansas, Special Collections Division, University of Arkansas Libraries, Fayetteville, and the State Historical Society of Wisconsin, Madison. Hereafter referred to as Bates Papers (Ark) and Bates Papers (Wis).

3. See Anne Stanley, "The Role of Black Women in the Civil Rights Movement" in Crawford, *Women*, 188-190.

4. See, for example, Grace J. McFadden, "Septima Clark and the Struggle for Human Rights" in Crawford, *Women*, 85-97 and Alice G. Knotts, "Methodist Women Integrate Schools and Housing 1952-1959" in Crawford, *Women*, 251-258.

5. Charles Payne, "Men Led, But Women Organized: Movement Participation of Women in the Mississippi Delta" in Crawford, *Women*, 1-11.

6. Belinda Robnett, "African American Women in the Civil Rights Movement, 1954-1965: Gender Leadership and Micro-Mobilization", *American Journal of Sociology* 101 (1996): 1661-1693.

7. Tony Freyer, *The Little Rock Crisis* (Westport, CT: Greenwood, 1984).

8. Daisy Bates, *The Long Shadow of Little Rock* (New York: David McKay Company, 1962). See also, Bates Papers (Ark) and Bates Papers, (Wis).

9. Register of Bates Papers, 1, Bates Papers (Wis).

10. *Arkansas Gazette*, January 1, 1963; September 1, 1963. Hereafter referred to as *AG*.

11. Sara Evans, *Personal Politics* (New York: Knopf, 1979).

12. Bates, *Long Shadow*, 6-31. Subsequent references will be included in parenthesis.

13. Aldon Morris, *The Origins of the Civil Rights Movement: Black Communities Organizing for Change* (New York: Free Press, 1984), 4-12; Charles Payne, "Men Led".

14. C. Calvin Smith, "'From Separate But Equal to Desegregation': The Changing Philosophy of L.C. Bates" *Arkansas Historical Quarterly*, 62 (1983): 254-270. The Register of Bates Papers (Wis) gives Daisy Bates's year of birth as 1922; Smith gives L.C. Bates's year of birth as 1901.

15. *AG*, January 1, 1963; September 1, 1963.

16. For example, see Edwin E. Dunaway, interview with John Kirk, September 26, 1992, University of Newcastle upon Tyne Oral History Collection (collection hereafter cited as UNOHC).

17. Irene Wassall, "L.C. Bates, Editor of the Arkansas State Press", MA thesis, University of Arkansas (1983); Smith, "From Separate".

18. *State Press*, March 27, 1942; April 5, 1942.Herafter referred to as *SP*.

19. *SP*, August 21, 1942.

20. John A. Kirk, "Black Activism in Arkansas, 1940-1970", Ph.D. thesis, University of Newcastle-upon-Tyne (1997), 85-125.

21. *SP*, December 29, 1950.

22. *SP*, November 30, 1951.

23. *SP*, April 14, 1950.

24. *SP*, September 17, 1948.

25. *SP*, December 29, 1950.

26. Dunaway interview.

27. William Pickens to Carrie Sheppherdson, January 5, 1925, Papers of the NAACP (Microfilm Edition, Bethesda: University of America) reel 5, group I, folder "Little Rock, Arkansas Branch," frame 0897. Hereafter NAACP Papers.

28. Mrs H.L. Porter to Roy Wilkins, November 14, 1933, NAACP Papers, frames 0039-0040.

29. Mark Tushnet, *The NAACP's Legal Strategy Against Segregated Education, 1925-1950* (Chapel Hill: University of North Carolina Press, 1987); Miss Solar M. Caretners to Melvin O. Austin, February 22, 1941 and Miss Solar B. Caretners to Walter White, February 22, 1941, group II, series B, container 174, folder "Teachers Salaries, Arkansas, Little Rock, *Morris* v. *School Board* (General) 1941-1943), Papers of the National Association for the Advancement of Colored People, Library of Congress, Manuscript Division (collection hereafter cited as NAACP Papers (LC)).

30. Sue Cowan Morris, interview with John Kirk, January 8, 1993, UNOHC; *AG*, March 1, 1942.

31. *AG*, January 6, 1944.

32. Tushnet, *NAACP's Legal Strategy*, 90.

33. The "double victory" reference was to the overturning of a lower court decision and the favorable ruling of the Appeals' Court, Press release, June 21, 1945, group II, series B, legal files, container 174, folder "Teachers Salaries, Arkansas, Little Rock, *Morris* v. *School Board*" (General 1941-1943), NAACP Papers (LC).

34. Rev. Marcus Taylor to Ella Baker, December 4, 1945, group II, series C, container 9, folder "Little Rock, Arkansas, 1940-1947," NAACP Papers (LC).

35. Gloster B. Current to Thurgood Marshall (memorandum, n.d.), group II, series C, container 11, folder "Arkansas State Conference, April 1945-December 1948,: NAACP Papers (LC).

36. Lucille Black to W.H. Flowers, January 15, 1948, group II, series C, container 10, folder "Pine Bluff, Ark., 1948-1955," and Donald Jones to Gloster B. Current (memorandum, n. d.), group II, series C, container 11, folder "Arkansas State Conference, April 1945-December 1948," NAACP Papers (LC).

37. John A. Kirk, "'He Founded A Movement': W.H. Flowers, the Committee on Negro Organizations and the Origins of Black Activism in Arkansas, 1940-1957" in Brian

Ward and Tony Badger, eds., *The Making of Martin Luther King and the Civil Rights Movement,* (London: Macmillan, 1996), 29-44.

38. Wassall, "L.C. Bates", 36.

39. Daisy Bates, interview with John Kirk, August 14, 1992, UNOHC.

40. Mrs L.C. Bates to Miss Mary Ovington, December 9, 1948, group II, series C, container 10, folder "Little Rock, Ark., 1948–1955," NAACP Papers (LC).

41. Mr Gloster B. Current to Mrs L.C. Bates, January 19, 1949, group II, series C, container 10, folder "Little Rock, Arkansas, 1948–1955," NAACP (LC).

42. Donald Jones to Gloster B. Current, February 24, 1949, group II, series C, container 10, folder "Arkansas State Conference 1949–1950," NAACP Papers (LC).

43. Walter White to Pine Bluff NAACP, February 25, 1949; Roy Wilkins to Arkansas Branches of the NAACP, May 10, 1949, group II, series C, container 10, folder "Pine Bluff, Ark., 1948–1955," NAACP Papers (LC).

44. Lulu B. White to Gloster B. Current, November 1, 1950, group II, series C, container 11, folder "Arkansas State Conference 1949–1950," NAACP Papers (LC).

45. Gloster B. Current to U. Simpson Tate, August 20, 1952, group II, series C, container 11, folder "Arkansas State Conference 1951–1952," NAACP Papers (LC).

46. Bates, *Long Shadow,* 47-48.

47. Bates, *Long Shadow,* 32-69.

48. Tilman C. Cothran and William Phillips, Jr., "Negro Leadership in a Crisis Situation", *Phylon* 22 (1961): 107-118.

49. Irving J. Spitzberg, *Racial Politics in Little Rock, 1954-1964,* (New York: Garland, 1987), 129.

50. *SP,* April 10, 1959.

51. Morris, *Origins,* 192.

52. *AG,* March 18, 1960.

53. *Arkansas Democrat,* March 13, 1960; Dunaway interview.

54. *Southern School News,* January 1960, 6.

55. C.D. Coleman, Director of Community Services, Southern Field Division, to M.T. Puryear, Southern Field Director, October 5, 1959, group II, series D, container 26, folder "Little Rock, Arkansas," National Urban League Papers, Library of Congress, Manuscript Division.

56. John Walker to Paul Rilling, November 17, 1959, Southern Regional Council Papers, Library of Congress, (Microfilm edition) reel 141, series IV, container 234.

57. *Southern School News,* November 1959, 8.

58. *AG,* November 10, 1959.

59. Nat Griswold, "The Second Reconstruction in Little Rock", unpublished manuscript (1968) [provided courtesy of Mr Walter Clancy, Little Rock, Arkansas], Book 1, 129.

60. Bates, *Long Shadow,* 161-170.

61. Griswold, "The Second Reconstruction", Book 2, 11-15.

62. *AG,* September 15, 1963.

CHAPTER 2

Sex Machines and Prisoners of Love: Male Rhythm and Blues, Sexual Politics and the Black Freedom Struggle

Brian Ward

In his essay "Kickin' reality, kickin' ballistics: 'gangsta rap' in postindustrial Los Angeles," historian Robin Kelley described the (mis)treatment of women in some of that music as part of a "very long and ignoble tradition" of venomous sexism in the popular music of African American males. As Kelley recognized, while this tradition has often generated art of great verbal inventiveness, musical potency, and not a little genuine humor, it has also helped to routinize and legitimize debilitating patterns of misogyny and machismo in black male society.[1] Yet neither the intensity, nor the ubiquity, of this sexist strain within black male popular music has been constant over time. Rather, the incidence of macho and misogyny in the most popular black male musical styles of the twentieth century has waxed and waned in conjunction with changing black perceptions of the prospects for meaningful social, political and economic progress in America. In other words, the most important changes in the style and substance of the sexual, sometimes sexist, often sexy imagery in black male Rhythm and Blues have been crucially linked to the state of the black struggle for freedom, respect and equality in America at particular historical moments. This essay explores the shifting sexual politics of male Rhythm and Blues musics within the context of that ongoing struggle.[2]

Myths of Matriarchy and Macho: The Blues Lyrical Tradition

In the male blues tradition, forged in the South just as the false dawns of emancipation and Reconstruction gave way to the long debilitating darkness of Jim Crow and disenfranchisement, portrayals of relationships between the sexes were often deeply pessimistic, vicious, exploitative, and sometimes just plain petrified. In many male blues, women were paradoxically depicted as both the primary source of disorder and grief in the black man's world, and as indispensable to his happiness and self-esteem. Women in the blues were sirens: irresistible yet lethal; they were to be loved, but more importantly, to be tamed and possessed. The historical roots of this perspective were complex. Some writers, like E. Franklin Frazier, and later (with serious repercussions for the black psyche and the struggle for civil rights) Daniel Moynihan, argued that the matriarchal nature of black society and the emasculation of the black male formed one source of the black man's hostility towards the black woman and, for Moynihan at least, a clue to continued black disadvantage in America.[3]

Black matriarchy was traced to slavery when the black man was rendered unable to fulfil his "natural" patriarchal function as breadwinner and protector. As the black male was forced to submit to humiliating physical abuse at the hands of a master or overseer, and compelled to watch impotently while his wife and children were similarly brutalized, so his authority, respect and power within his own family were fatally undermined. This emasculation produced a matriarchal society with the black woman emerging as titular or functional head of the household. This pattern was sustained after emancipation as black women found relatively abundant, if still tightly circumscribed opportunities in the job market, while black males struggled for the economic opportunity, political power, and social status that might restore their patriarchal authority and self-respect.

Subsequent scholarship has both undermined this crude concept of a black matriarchy and refined our understanding of its social origins. The extent to which the black male was emasculated under slavery and afterwards has been re-evaluated by historians like Eugene Genovese and Lawrence Levine, who have stressed cultural modes of resistance to that process.[4] In the 1970s, Herbert Gutman began the process of re-incorporating the black men of history into a more stable, double-headed family structure than previously imagined.[5] Despite powerful disruptive forces working to undermine the black family, North and South, in the main, "two-parent black families had been able to hold together under the buffeting of slavery and war, and most even managed to stand up to the postbellum world as well ..."[6] Indeed, by 1950, 77.7 percent of black families in America still had both parents at home and only 17.2 percent were headed by a female.[7]

The concept of a black matriarchy has also been attacked from other perspectives. Joyce Ladner decried the "confusion of the terms *dominant* and *strong*" in discussions of the black woman whereby she "has almost become a romantic, legendary figure ... almost superhuman, capable of assuming all major responsibilities for sustaining herself and her family through harsh economic and social conditions."[8] Feminist historians like Deborah White and Brenda Stevenson, who rightly stress the centrality of black women to the black social and familial experience, have preferred to think in terms of a community which has often been "matrifocal," rather than matriarchal.[9] Whatever their status within the confines of the family, black women have enjoyed none of the economic, social and status power advantages associated with a real matriarchy. At best, they have historically experienced a relatively elevated situation according to certain economic indices, most notably employment rates and educational opportunities, within a racial group which has been severely disadvantaged relative to American society as a whole.

And yet, as bell hooks has explained, the myth of black matriarchy has remained largely impervious to such empirical refutation and careful analysis, precisely because it has always been such a coherent, flexible and convenient one. The myth of matriarchy and the attendant images of the overpowering, emasculating black woman, have helped to render black America and its apparent failings easily comprehensible to whites. Black matriarchy explained the reality of black disadvantage without raising awkward doubts about the basic soundness of the socio-economic system in which racial and gender inequalities were deeply embedded.[10] The same matrix of racial and sexual stereotypes also offered black males an easy rationale for their own and their community's plight. Frustrated at their exclusion from full social, economic and political participation in American society, convinced that black women enjoyed special privileges and power in that world, and jealous of the white man's patriarchal authority, many black men turned to the myth of matriarchy to explain their distress.

The two poles of the negative female categorizations enshrined in the myth of black matriarchy were personified by the Aunt Jemima and Sapphire stereotypes: one compliant, deferential and domesticated; the other, increasingly dominant during the twentieth century, sexually alluring, vain, fickle, and highly manipulative. These stereotypes, with their capacity for endless refinement, formed part of a discursive regime, the strength of which depended upon its capacity to explain and legitimize a perceived social reality. Sapphire, especially, lay at the heart of the black man's problems. Consequently, she was also the pivot around which much distinctively black male culture traditionally revolved.

The overwhelming psychological imperative of many black male public rituals and forms of popular expression has been the symbolic destruction of the power and dignity of the black woman and the reification of a powerful, compensatory, resolutely macho identity. Many of the jokes, toasts, proverbs, tales and superstitions collected from black America by urban folklorists like Daryl Cumber Dance and Roger Abrahams were, according to Dance, "blatantly anti-female ... most of the jokes are bitter." Indeed, many were terrifying in their conflation of sexual desire, crude sexual objectification and violence towards women. "Frequently the sexual desire for the woman is in itself a longing to violate, to humiliate, to injure and even to kill the woman," Dance noted.[11] Abrahams interpreted the dozens—the ritualistic trading of personal insults in which the mother figure was both the primary vehicle for, and the main object of, the insults—as a means to exorcise matriarchal influence and establish an independent masculine identity.[12]

Those games and tales which did not actually depend for their "humor" on the degradation of women, sought to inflate the black male ego in other ways. Male sexual prowess was valorized and exaggerated to become chiefly a mechanism for asserting an often-brutal authority over the troublesome, unruly and sexually insatiable black woman. This cultural attempt to resuscitate black manhood reached its zenith in the long toasts, or rhymed poems, with their distinctive pantheon of macho heroes. According to Dance, "Bad Niggers" like John Henry, Dolomite and Jody The Grinder were "sexual supermen, but their women are enemies to be conquered, humiliated and controlled, rather than partners to be loved."[13]

This celebration of black macho, and the systematic demeaning of black women, were also central features of the male blues tradition. According to Matthew White, bluesmen "were able to exert power and control" and "exercise the prerogatives and privileges of a man in a patriarchal society through song ... The very act of singing the blues ... is an unconscious exercise in the assertion of male control." Mississippian Charley Patton's 1929 song "Pony Blues" fused this male quest for mastery over the black woman with a strong dose of sexual braggadocio, and a recognition of the woman's own sexual expertise: "Brand new Shetland baby, already trained,/ Just get in the saddle and tighten up your reins." Indeed, while bluesmen readily conceded the black woman's sexual allure they usually did so with a mixture of awe and trepidation, since this sexual power robbed men of agency and empowered women.[14]

Bluesmen routinely blamed the black woman for the breakdown of personal relationships, citing her congenital avarice and promiscuity. Her insatiable quest for greater material riches and better sex may have been viewed as a "natural" trait from the bluesman's perspective, but it was also an unacceptable affront to male pride and authority. Pre-war bluesmen frequently resorted to terror to try to bring their women to heel, as in Robert Johnson's "32-20" ("If she gets unruly ... Take my 32-20, now, and cut her half in two"). Sometimes the violence directed against women in the blues was chilling. "I'm gon' get my pistol, 40 rounds of ball,/ I'm gon' shoot my baby, just to see her fall," sang Furry Lewis on "Furry's Blues."

By contrast, male sexual adventurism and potency were often presented as natural manly traits, to be cultivated as a source of pride not shame. In the blues, a man's social esteem was frequently measured by the number of sexual conquests he could boast, his skills as a lover, or by other macho indices, such as the number of drinks he could down, or the number of fights he had won. This macho posturing was more than simply a matter of lyrical theme, it was projected and validated in the personae of the tough, hard-drinking, womanizing bluesmen and the legends surrounding their lives. In the 1930s, Robert Johnson had set the standard. When Johnson died, poisoned it was said by a lover's jealous husband, his mythic status as the ultimate "Bad Nigger" soared.

Mighty-Mighty Men: The Shouters

The image of the early bluesman as a sexually prolific "Bad Nigger," struggling to control the bewitching, but insubordinate and untrustworthy black woman, was carefully tended by the likes of Peetie Wheatstraw, the self-styled "Devil's Son-in-Law," and endorsed in the work of post-war electric bluesmen like Howlin' Wolf, Muddy Waters, Eddie Boyd, John Lee Hooker and Elmore James. This blues lyrical perspective on sexual politics also passed into the repertoires of the shouters of the late 1940s and early 1950s, and into the ribald side of the vocal group repertoire of the same era, where the Dominoes' insatiable Lovin' Dan, hero of "Sixty Minute Man," was the quintessential macho hero.

The shouters, in particular, were unrelenting in their assertion of black male sexual potency. While a self-deprecating humor occasionally moderated their macho celebrations, the primary thrust of their songs was still to exalt black manhood. The superhuman feats they celebrated were mostly in bed, with sexual domination the favored method of subduing the troublesome black woman and exercising male power. Roy

Brown and his Mighty-Mighty Men, Bullmoose Jackson and his
Bearcats—the names alone revealed much—Wynonie Harris, Joe
Turner, and Amos Milburn constructed powerful macho mythologies
around themselves and their carnal capacities. Brown, for example, was
a "Mighty Mighty Man," a "Midnight Lover Man," and an independent
"Travelin' Man," who offered his women an endless dose of "Good
Rockin' Tonight."

Complementing this celebration of black male sexual prowess was
the objectification of women, usually coupled with a claim of male
propriety, as in Wynonie Harris' "I Like My Baby's Pudding." This
image was chosen from a lengthy menu of ingenious culinary tropes. In
the early 1950s most r&b singers spent at least some of their time eating
cherry pie, baking jelly roll, squeezing lemons, churning milk until the
butter comes, or savoring the delights of dripping honey.

As in the blues, the imperative to cultivate a strong macho image
tended to overwhelm, if never entirely to eradicate, themes that implied
male tenderness or vulnerability. What were perceived as peculiarly
male faults rarely occasioned feelings of introspection, let alone guilt,
but were instead transformed into symbols of manhood and parables of
correct sexual politics. Thus, the failures of marriages and other
relationships, failures which were often rooted in the psychological and
economic ravages of poverty and racism, were explained in terms of the
black man's impressively rampant libido and the black woman's
shameful lust and greed. "You should have seen what a girl of 17 did to
me!" exclaimed the Du-Droppers, who, as real black men, were
naturally powerless to resist such advances and therefore conveniently
absolved of all personal responsibility for seizing the chance to do the
"Bam-Balaam."

While black men were often depicted as sexual supermen in the
male r&b of the early 1950s, black women were often viewed as nothing
but trouble. Their ravenous "unfeminine" sexual appetites placed unfair
demands upon even the indefatigable black man, as in Wynonie Harris's
uproarious "All She Wants to Do Is Rock." The Nebraskan Harris was
perhaps the most gifted of all the shouters. He also fancied himself
something of an expert on female psychology, assuring readers of *Tan*
magazine that what black women really hankered after "deep down in
their hearts was a hellion, a rascal." Modestly billing himself as the
"Hard-drinkin', hard-lovin', hard-shoutin' Mr Blues," Harris was proud
to be of service.[15]

Yet even the mighty Harris sometimes despaired of being able to control the black woman. In "Adam, Come And Get Your Rib," he portrayed himself as the innocent victim of female duplicity, slyly linked black women with original sin, and sought nothing less than to reverse the Biblical account of her creation: "She's been cheatin', she's been lyin'/she's left my poor heart cryin'/So Adam, come and get your bone." As for himself, Harris had already decided that rather than waste his time trying to forge a satisfactory relationship with a flesh and blood black woman, he was better off servicing his not-insubstantial sexual needs with a home-made mechanical "Lovin' Machine" ("put some money in the slot/you hear some buzzin',/kisses while they're hot/five cents a dozen"). The Five Royales had even more obviously dehumanized female sexuality in "Laundromat Blues" ("Her machine is full of suds ... /it will cost you 30 cents a pound"), while the Toppers' "Let Me Bang Your Box" lacked any of the lyrical ingenuity which ironically characterized some of the most demeaning songs.

Many of the shouters' songs, because of, rather than in spite of, their outrageous sexism were genuinely hilarious. A failure to appreciate the politically incorrect humor in this music risks ripping it from its historical context and reducing the true complexities of what was going on to hollow platitudes. The shouters were at one level exaggerating and parodying a jaundiced black male view of relations between the sexes. Black audiences recognized, in a way which often eluded white fans, that this broad mockery revolved around but one possible aspect of black male consciousness and behavior. The shouters depicted an all-too-common, but in no way all pervasive, pattern of black domestic relationships and sexual attitudes rather than their totality.

And yet, at another level, the cumulative effect of drawing almost all their humor from the ridiculing of women, the celebration of a predatory, irresponsible machismo, and the portrayal of preternaturally doomed, exploitative, personal relationships was to help legitimize such attitudes. The blues lyrical tradition to which the shouters and early r&b vocal groups were heirs had by sheer repetition helped to make a peculiarly intense form of sexism, and to nurture a fatalistic resignation to the improbability of stable, mutually respectful, domestic relationships seem commonplace. This did not reflect some aberrant, pathological trait in black male personalities. It was what happened when the particular pressures of racism, economic disadvantage and political impotence at large amplified the patriarchal and sexist patterns of American society.

What was at stake in all these songs, then, and in black male culture more generally, was power. Mastery over the black woman, if only in the cultural arena, could partially compensate for the black man's lack of social, economic and political power; for his inability to control many of the crucial circumstances of his life. Of course, in reality not all black men succumbed to these extreme macho or misogynistic stereotypes, any more than all r&b songs promoted such images and ideas. Nevertheless, their pre-eminence within the broader spectrum of male black secular music before the mid-1950s was striking. Just as striking, however, was the relative decline in the popularity of such songs among black audiences following the emergence of the modern mass civil rights movement in the second half of the 1950s and early 1960s.

An Alternative Vision: The Vocal Groups

The first real signs of important changes in the general tenor of sexual politics in Rhythm and Blues came from the ranks of black male vocal groups. The pioneer vocal groups who emerged alongside the shouters after World War Two had in many respects accepted the blues tradition of macho and misogyny. But what differentiated those groups from almost anything else within the Rhythm and Blues canon was that they also offered some relief from that tradition by featuring sentimental, highly idealistic romantic ballads in their repertoires. The extraordinary popularity of these groups, 15,000 of whom recorded for the first time during the 1950s, may thus have reflected a growing black support for the alternative vision, which they provided.[16]

Sometimes this romantic vision was just the flip of a 78-rpm disk away from machismo and misogyny. The Swallows, for example, are best remembered by historians of r&b for their salacious celebration of the fleshy charms of "Bicycle Tillie," and a ribald variation on a theme by Masters and Johnson, "It Ain't The Meat It's The Motion." Yet, success with their black contemporaries depended at least as much on romantic ballads like "Will You Be Mine" and "Beside You."

Long before the first stirrings of a major white market for r&b in the mid-to-late 1950s, black groups had also regularly recorded white Tin Pan Alley pop such as "A Sunday Kind Of Love" (Harptones), "These Foolish Things" (Dominoes), and "Somewhere Over The Rainbow" (Castelles) to the delight of black audiences. These supplemented a large repertoire of sweet r&b ballads like "Hopefully Yours" (Larks), "I'm A Sentimental Fool" (Marylanders), and the Flamingos' melancholic masterpiece "Golden Teardrops." Lyrically, these songs were much closer to the standard white pop fare of the

1950s than was the norm for either the shouters or the electric bluesmen, whose ascendancy the vocal groups challenged by daring to rhyme "moon" with "June."

In striking contrast to the shouters and bluesmen, and in more subtle contrast to the pioneer vocal groups who had tried to balance romance with ribaldry, and idealism with fatalism, the most popular new male vocal groups of the mid-to-late 1950s tended to eschew the cynicism, macho and misogyny of the blues tradition. Instead, a succession of ever-younger groups evoked a juvenile world of specifically teen trauma and romantic delight. These were the songs—"Gee" (Crows), "Sh-Boom" (Chords), "Earth Angel" (Penguins)—which ushered in the rock and roll era by crossing over into the white pop charts, but they were also hugely successful with black audiences of all ages.

The Spaniels' "Goodnite Sweetheart Goodnite," Moonglows' "Sincerely," and Frankie Lymon and the Teenagers' "Why Do Fools Fall In Love" confirmed and extended the trend towards idealistic, devotional love songs. Moreover, while many of the girls addressed by the bluesmen, shouters, and pioneer vocal groups were sexually experienced—a matter for both censure and celebration by the double standards of the male blues tradition—those solipsized in later songs were more "chaste" than caught. Heroines like "Florence" (Paragons) and "Mary Lee" (Rainbows) were usually respectable and respected objects of male desire. They were waiting, like the Willows, for church bells to ring. Old attitudes and themes did not disappear completely, of course, and even some of the youngest new vocal groups of the late 1950s found themselves back in the bedroom again locked into the old stereotypes. The Cadillacs' "Speedoo" and the Cadets' "Love Bandit" were worthy successors to Lovin' Dan, while the Jayhawks' "Don't Mind Dyin'" and the Orbits' "Knock Her Down" ensured that the blues traditions of sexual jealousy and domestic violence survived. "When your baby goes out and roams around, knock her down, knock her down, knock her down to the ground," the Orbits crooned.

Nevertheless, such sexism and misogyny was simply neither as common nor as intense in the repertoire of black vocal groups after 1954 as previously. Nor, with rare exceptions like "Speedoo," were such records as popular when they did appear. Even when ballads like Little Anthony and the Imperials' "Tears on my Pillow," or Lee Andrews and the Hearts' "Teardrops," did introduce classic blues themes of personal loss, loneliness and pain into the idyllic world of teenage romance, the inescapable youthfulness of the vocals implied a transient, finite, quality to the suffering.

The increasingly lush musical arrangements also served to lighten the tone of such songs, while most of the angst in them stemmed from a failure to fulfil romantic ideals of a stable, mutually respectful, monogamous relationship which was usually depicted as an attainable, if often elusive goal. They were certainly very different in their emotional resonance from the lovelorn laments of the bluesmen or the shouters, who tended to wrap their personal sorrows and romantic disappointments in layers of fatalism, irony and bitter recrimination. The blues had pondered the black experience as it stretched from a horrific past into an uncertain future, and found ways to explain, survive and even celebrate that oppressive reality.

By contrast, the vocal groups of the later 1950s rarely mined the terrifying seams of despair near the heart of the blues lyrical tradition. Indeed, the fatalism and historicism of the blues was almost entirely abandoned. The songs either took place in a perpetual present which, although sometimes problematic, was often wondrous, or else they imagined a future bursting with exciting possibilities. Without condescension, they tackled the faddism, exuberance, idealism and optimism of youth in a way that was largely beyond the repertoire of the blues, except as satire.

Black Pop and the Civil Rights Movement

By the turn of the decade, the new idealistic, romantic ethos that the vocal groups had pioneered, flavored much of the most popular Rhythm and Blues of the era. At the forefront of this trend was a new breed of male black beat balladeers, personified by Sam Cooke. While nothing could entirely hide the gospel roots of his vocals, and notwithstanding his subsequent deification as the father of soul, Cooke's first secular successes were firmly in the teen pop vein, with romantic ballads like "You Send Me" and "Cupid." At the height of this black pop era, roughly from 1956 to 1963, male singers like Cooke, Brook Benton, Sammy Turner, and Clyde MacPhatter enjoyed huge commercial success with both black and white audiences, forming part of what was probably the most integrated popular music market in American history. With 175 white records making the Rhythm and Blues top ten during these years, and black artists regularly comprising a third or a half of the entries in the pop charts, *Billboard* even decided to suspend its separate black record sales listings in November 1963, as a relic of a segregated musical past.

With the mainstream civil rights movement espousing integrationist goals and diligently building biracial support, and with cultural barriers between the races apparently disintegrating—at least in the world of popular music—it is perhaps not surprising that black artists should also move steadily away from the distinctively black, sexual orthodoxies of the blues tradition and nearer to the core ideals of mainstream American sexual politics. Indeed, these singers evoked relatively little of the predatory sexuality associated with either the bluesmen, the shouters, or the lubricious early black rock and rollers like Little Richard ("She's Got It"), Bo Diddly ("I'm A Man") and Chuck Berry ("Sweet Little Sixteen"), all of whom were struggling for black, as well as white, commercial success by the end of the 1950s.

Instead, insecurity, compassion, fidelity, trust and a sense of personal responsibility for the success or failure of relationships were staples of this new black male pop style. Chuck Jackson, for example, admitted: "I Wake Up Crying"; Sammy Turner expected love to last for "Always"; loyal Dee Clark wanted "Nobody But You"; Ben E. King pleaded for a woman to "Stand By Me." In "He Will Break Your Heart," Jerry Butler described—but in a significant departure from the blues orthodoxy, did not glorify or excuse—male infidelity. Similarly, in the magnificent "Man's Temptation" Gene Chandler grappled with his conscience and resolved "to be strong" which, in the new world order, now meant faithful.

Traditional male attitudes did not disappear completely, of course, and neither did the songs of male braggadocio, hostility and suspicion towards the opposite sex. Jackie Wilson's "Doggin' Around," Gene Chandler's "Duke of Earl," and Eugene Church's "Pretty Girls Everywhere" kept the stud tradition alive. Even Motown's Smokey Robinson, whose clever love songs, sweetly sensual voice and image of coy vulnerability encapsulated key values in male black pop, was initially uneasy at exhibiting the kind of sensitivity he so admired in black female jazz singers like Sarah Vaughan: "I loved the way she [Sarah Vaughan] cried with her voice; I was awestruck by her subtlety and sensitivity ... it was a woman who shaped my style. But I wondered: Should a cat like me be singing like a chick?"[17] Nevertheless, the songs of Robinson and many of his black pop and soul contemporaries in the early 1960s expressed and, to some extent legitimized, romantic ideals which had always been present in the black male psyche, but which had previously been eclipsed in most forms of black male popular culture. It was, however, no coincidence that the intense sexism of the blues tradition should generally fall from favor among black audiences at this particular historic moment.

Black macho and black matriarchy were essentially elaborate myths: cultural constructions that served to explain black disadvantage and to compensate for the awful sense of powerlessness which afflicted black males. They symbolically displaced black male frustration at the whole matrix of racial discrimination, social marginality and economic disadvantage into the world of sexual politics where "victories" could be won, "heroic" deeds performed and "evil" destroyed.

Historically, the potency of these myths had reflected the absence of a viable mass movement to remedy black oppression. In the late 1950s and early 1960s, however, many of the resentments that had previously fuelled such sexual demonologies and domestic violence within the black community were channeled towards the racial, economic and political system, which actually accounted for black disadvantage. Vicarious or direct engagement in the freedom struggle gave black men, just as it gave black women, a glimpse of a better future and a sense of empowerment and self-respect that they had previously sought in sexual warfare and other forms of intense internecine competition and conflict. The rise of the civil rights movement and the cautious optimism which initially attended it—even among non-participants, North and South—rendered black matriarchy less compelling as an explanation for the black predicament and an aggressive black machismo less necessary as an outlet for black male frustrations.[18]

Jo Ann Robinson, president of the Montgomery Women's Political Council and a crucial figure in the Montgomery bus boycott of 1955-6, clearly understood the connection between the emergence of the movement and the decline of black domestic—and other forms—of violence:

> Grown men frequently came home on particular evenings angry from humiliating experiences on buses, to pick fights with their wives or children. They needed a target somewhere, a way to relieve internal conflict. These quarrels often ended in cuttings or killings, divorce or separation.

> ... After December 5, 1955, the people were able to release their suppressed emotions through the boycott movement, which allowed them to retaliate directly for the pain, humiliation, and embarrassment they had endured over the years at the hands of drivers and policemen while riding on the buses. There was no need for family fights and weekend brawls.[19]

It is even possible that the conspicuous commitment and courage of women of all ages, from all sections of the black community, who played such a critical role at the grassroots level of the burgeoning freedom struggle, may have encouraged a partial thawing in black male attitudes, conduct and culture. Black men may have begun to see black women more as allies in a common struggle against racism and political and economic powerlessness, and less as the principal source of their distress, or as a surrogate focus for their anger and militancy.

And yet, Stokely Carmichael's celebrated 1964 quip that the appropriate position for women in the Student Non-violent Coordinating Committee (SNCC) was "prone" hardly bespoke a new era of sexual enlightenment among black men; not even in the very heart of what was in other ways the most progressive mass movement in American history. In fairness to Carmichael, this remark has been used altogether too casually by historians to summarize his views, and perhaps even more unfairly those of other black males in SNCC, on the role of women in the movement.[20] Nevertheless, even if Carmichael's position in 1964 was prone to misrepresentation, and scholars and veterans continue to debate whether, in what manner, and to what degree, women in the movement were variously empowered or exploited, liberated or oppressed, June Johnson certainly had no doubts that in the grand scheme of things, "Men ran the Movement ... they made many of the decisions."[21] Moreover, the way in which SNCC's first chairman, Marion Barry, tried to exercise some kind of crude *droit de seigneur* over some of his female colleagues, leaving a paper trail of betrayals and sexual misadventures in the SNCC papers, suggests that some men in the movement were still struggling to shake old stereotypes.

With hard evidence scarce, any conclusions about the relationship between the rise of the civil rights movement, the new romantic ethos in much of the most popular male Rhythm and Blues of the late 1950s and early 1960s, and changes in black sexism and domestic violence are necessarily tentative. It seems unlikely that the romantic idealism, which briefly eclipsed the misogynistic tendencies of the blues tradition, corresponded to a similarly radical re-orientation of male prejudices and practices within the black community. Rather, the sound, sense and image of black pop symbolized a fleeting vision of *possible* changes in those patterns of behavior. It represented alternative modes of male thought, being and action which were not necessarily accurate reflections of what was happening in the "real" world, but which were nonetheless crucially linked to it. Certainly, events in, and changing ways of seeing that "real" world largely determined what earthly dreams it was deemed permissible to dream aloud in black male culture.

In sum, the black male soloists and groups who largely replaced the bluesmen, shouters and early rock and rollers at the forefront of black tastes in the black pop era tended to avoid the "amplified and exaggerated masculinity ... and its relational feminine counterpart" which Paul Gilroy has suggested act as "special symbols of the difference race makes."[22] In the blues tradition, Sapphire and the macho black stud had been mytho-poetic representations of these peculiarly intense, often bitterly antagonistic, sexual identities and had served as critical markers of black racial identity in America. Consequently, by generally refusing to project—or in the case of black consumers, endorse—these conventional sexualized symbols of racial difference, black male pop functioned as a mildly rocking metaphor for the integrationist aspirations and guarded optimism of the early civil rights movement. It was a moment when black Americans dared to have a dream of equality, which embraced the notion of "normalizing" black domestic affairs in accordance with mainstream ideals.

Yet if the racially defined—and defining—Sapphire and stud stereotypes were less conspicuous in the most popular music of the black pop era, there was a price to pay for this apparent progress. In black pop some of the sexual frankness, the genuine humor and eroticism of the blues tradition disappeared along with its more odious misogyny. Furthermore, black pop ultimately traded the aggressive black macho of the blues and r&b for the more insidious, if no less oppressive patterns of sexism and patriarchy practiced by much of mainstream male society. As we shall see, in the soul music of the 1960s and 1970s, male singers often alternated between this mainstream sexism, and a more peculiarly black, almost nationalistic strain of macho and misogyny that revived and extended the old blues orthodoxies.

Black Power and the Return of Lovin' Dan

The passage of the Civil Rights Act of 1964 and the Voting Rights Act of 1965 were momentous achievements for the early civil rights movement. They appeared to place blacks on an equal footing with whites and promised much for a genuinely integrated democratic America. In fact, they were merely markers on the route to an unfinished racial revolution. Statutory equality itself did little to remedy the debilitating effects of centuries of abuse, and left in place myriad systemic manifestations of prejudice and discrimination in education, employment, housing and politics. Greatly expanded black political power after 1965 proved inadequate to prevent the retreat of successive administrations from vigorous federal action on behalf of blacks. Meanwhile, many white liberals joined racial conservatives in a backlash to increasingly desperate black demands that the nation fully recognize its continuing racial dilemmas and commit itself to transforming legal equality into genuine equality of opportunity. These frustrations were further compounded by the growing uncertainly and dissension within the movement regarding how best to confront these obdurate racial, social, political and economic problems. As a consequence, a wide variety of sometimes compatible and overlapping, sometimes wholly antithetical and antagonistic creeds and programs emerged, usually corralled together under the generic term: black power.

As the black community's belief in its own capacity and America's commitment to end racially based discrimination disintegrated, frustrations and energies which had recently been tapped or assuaged by mass insurgency and the optimism it engendered were once more channeled back into an increasingly vicious sexual politics. "We shall have our manhood," pledged self-confessed, political rapist and Black Panther Minister of Information, Eldridge Cleaver, in a statement redolent of the new priorities of the black struggle for some self-proclaimed liberation warriors.[23]

Soledad Prison inmate George Jackson, an honorary Panther Field Marshall and until his death the incarcerated idol of many black radicals, echoed Cleaver's sentiments. In a none-too-coherent outburst, he urged his black brothers to break the emasculating grip of matriarchy, while at the same time condemning black women for being hopelessly parasitic on black men. "All the women I've had," Jackson announced with proprietorial candor, "tried to use me, tried to secure through me a soft spot in this cutthroat system for themselves. All they ever wanted was clothes and money to be taken out to flash these things."[24]

It was not only some of the Panthers who began to erase the distinction between patriarchal assertion and political activity. Other leaders also tried to gender black liberation and make it synonymous with the exercise of various forms of male power and control. In the late 1960s, this sort of agenda had driven Angela Davis out of the cultural nationalist group US, whose leader Maulana Ron Karenga later served time in jail for a sexual assault on a female colleague. Davis later observed that "some black activists ... confuse their political activity with an assertion of their maleness ... These men view Black women as a threat to their attainment of manhood—especially those Black women who take initiative and work to become leaders in their own right."[25]

For some black men, then, during what historian Clayborne Carson has dubbed the "post-revolutionary era," the initially radical struggle for

black freedom and the redemption of American society began to narrow
into a compensatory exercise in interlocking racial and sexual
chauvinism. Once again male Rhythm and Blues reflected these
developments, confirming the basic congruity between the changing
tenor of sexual politics in black popular music and black perceptions of
the potential for securing respect and equitable treatment in America.[26]
But neither the abruptness, nor the extent, of this transition should be
exaggerated, any more than it should be suggested that all black men
suddenly abandoned domestic responsibilities or progressive political
struggle to take refuge in a revived macho and misogyny. The male soul
music that matured during the early-to-mid 1960s had always combined
dreamy romance with raunchy desire, and mixed fidelity, understanding
and respect, with infidelity, sexual objectification, bitter recrimination
and poisonous suspicion. Ian Hoare has generalized that male soul
consistently betrayed "a volatile mixture of self-assertive, free-floating
independence and an almost childlike vulnerability." For him, Wilson
Pickett and Otis Redding represented the archetypes. Pickett was the
super sexual athlete, the predatory "Midnight Mover," the permanently
available "Man And A Half" who reveled in the physical delights of
"Mini-Skirt Minnie." Redding, by contrast, was "Mr Pitiful," tenderly
offering up "My Lover's Prayer," and pledging timeless fidelity on
"That's How Strong My Love Is."[27]

There clearly was something to this distinction, but Pickett could
also deliver tender love pleas like "I'm In Love," while Redding could
belt out storming macho struts like "Love Man." In fact, as Hoare fully
appreciated, there were not really two breeds of soulmen at all. Most
male soul singers of the early-to-mid 1960s had managed to hold macho
irresponsibility and romantic idealism in a dynamic, if often precarious,
creative tension; certainly within their repertoires as a whole, and
sometimes within a single performance. Soulmen like Redding, Pickett,
Solomon Burke, Marvin Gaye and Joe Tex sought to honor both the
psychologically reassuring black macho tradition and more mainstream
patriarchal ideals which required a man to provide not only generous
helpings of great sex, but also fidelity, protection, shelter and economic
security. The preservation of this tension in male soul required at least
some faith that the mainstream ideal was actually attainable. When that
faith began to crumble along with the civil rights coalition in the later
1960s, it often left in its place a harsh, uncompromising battle for sexual
power. The delicate balance which soulmen had fought to preserve in
the mid-1960s proved much more elusive in the very different political
and psychological climate of the black power era.[28]

James Brown provided an influential example of the way in which much male soul lurched back towards a macho and objectifying agenda at this time. Brown's music had always had a raunchy side, with boasts of personal potency mingling with demands for satisfaction and a fine eye for female form on tracks like "Good Good Lovin'." Yet, many of Brown's most successful recordings before 1967, both commercially and artistically, had betrayed a raw sensitivity and an almost desperate romanticism. "I'll Go Crazy," "Bewildered" and "Prisoner Of Love" were impassioned pleas for love and mutual affection. After 1967, however, the macho component in Brown's music was thrust ever more firmly to the fore. Brown massaged his own ego and those of his beleaguered black brothers by becoming a "Sex Machine" who could cast a connoisseur's eye over the contents of "Hot Pants."

Brown's reification of his own sexual potency and the increasingly curt treatment of women in his songs fused seamlessly with the new political engagement of his lyrics as exemplified in "Say It Loud, I'm Black And I'm Proud." On the defiant "I Don't Want Nobody To Give Me Nothing" he explicitly equated black pride and power with a Cleaver-esque assertion of black manhood: "We don't want no sympathy,/ just wanna be a man." Like the despised "nigger" of old, the black woman in Brown's songs had to learn her place, and should she fail in her duties or stray from her man, there was no forgiveness. "Papa Don't Take No Mess" was a blunt declaration of sexual mastery aimed squarely at the potentially treacherous black woman, although the no-nonsense sentiment translated easily into the political arena. "It's A New Day" was simply a list of instructions for the black woman to follow in order to keep her man satisfied. She was told "Never get too confident," and instructed to "Take care of business" since the black man's sexual needs must be serviced. It seemed that Brown's "New Day" would be characterized more by the triumph of black patriarchal authority and sex on demand than by the economic, social or political empowerment of the black community.

Other soulmen also chronicled the revival of black macho and the eclipse of the romantic idealism of the early 1960s. Once more, male paranoia about female infidelity poisoned personal relationships. This was not just the case between men and women, as in the Saints' heart-rending "Mirror Mirror," where a man's unfounded accusations pushed his woman into the arms of another ("The lies you visualized, are now a reality"), but also between male friends. The O'Jay's majestic "Backstabbers" described the black man's fear that the sexually insatiable, shamelessly materialistic black woman was entertaining his so-called friends—sexual opportunists all, of course—behind his back:

"Why do all your friends come to see your lady?/ Man, some of those friends they sure look shady." In the Unifics' "Court Of Love" an unfaithful lover was accused of stripping her man "of all [his] manly pride." Not surprisingly, a jury of the singer's peers found her guilty and the man rejoiced, "I got justice in this courthouse." By the late 1960s, then, justice, a keynote of the black struggle for freedom and equality, was being defined in terms of saving male face and convicting the black woman for the sort of sexual adventurism, which was once again becoming a badge of honor in male Rhythm and Blues.

Alabamian Clarence Carter virtually made a career from tales of unbridled lust and illicit sex like "Slip Away" and "I Can't Leave Your Love Alone." Fittingly, Carter even re-recorded the Dominoes' "Sixty Minute Man." The return of Lovin' Dan was a neat symbol of the way in which the macho-misogynistic strain in black male popular music had revived. Only Carter's broad humor and distinctive chuckle rescued much of his work from its darkest undertones, harking back to some of the more tongue-in-someone's cheek boasts of the shouters. Other soul and funk men were usually far less witty than Carter in their demands for sexual gratification and macho boasts. Songs like General Crook's "Gimme Some" and "Do It For Me" were devoid of any sense of humor or eroticism. Others, like Timmy Willis's "Mr Soul Satisfaction" and the Hesitations' "Soul Superman" suggested that, with an effective freedom struggle fragmenting, this sort of self-congratulatory sexual braggadocio could now be interpreted as correct black male politics. By almost any meaningful standard, songs like Israel Tolbert's "Big Leg Woman (With a Short Short Mini Skirt On)," Johnnie Taylor's "Love Bones," Brothers Johnson's "Land Of Ladies," Intruders' "Me Tarzan, You Jane," 100 Percent Proof Aged In Soul's "One Man's Leftovers (Is Another Man's Feast)" and "Too Many Cooks (Spoil The Soup)" slipped beyond honest sexual admiration to base objectification and voyeurism.

In some respects, what was going on in male Rhythm and Blues during the black power era was simply a reflection of the greater frankness in discussing sexual matters that was a feature of American life in the late 1960s and early 1970s. As David Caute has noted, this was an era when: "Male chauvinism was often decked out as 'sexual liberation', involving a gallop into pornography."[29] Nevertheless, after a period of relative remission, this tendency seemed especially virulent in black male popular music. Certainly, there was plenty in the soul of the period to reinforce Gerda Lerner's dictum that throughout the long history of patriarchy and sexual inequality in western culture, "It is not women who are reified and commodified, it is women's sexuality and reproductive capacity which is so treated." [30]

Male soul was not completely swept up by the macho-sexist wave, which broke across the black power era, any more than all black men succumbed to it. Tenderness, fidelity, vulnerability, respect, reciprocity and romantic idealism still struggled to contain the swell of priapism, misogyny and sexual paranoia. Some artists, among them Tyrone Davis, Joe Simon, the Chi-lites, Delfonics and Stylistics rarely strayed far from themes of love and loss, despair and happiness, yet generally avoided the vindictiveness and cynicism which once more stalked much male Rhythm and Blues. Others, like Al Green, Marvin Gaye and Barry White unashamedly put sex to the fore, but usually strove for a more reciprocal, less exploitative, erotic vision.

While faithless and demanding lovers and wives tended to bear the brunt of male resentment in black power era soul, mothers were generally spared. The former were viewed by black men as both potential rivals for, and impediments to, their exercise of social, economic and sexual power; the latter were often accorded special status as the repository of black wisdom, culture and stability. And, of course, mothers could also be defined purely in terms of the primary role assigned to women in a patriarchal society, as the bearers and nurturers of children. Certainly, some of male soul's more compassionate and thoughtful treatments of black women involved mother figures. The Intruders' cloying "I'll Always Love My Mama" was typical in its depiction of the black mother as the rock of both family and communal life, while Funkadelic's first hit, "Music For My Mother," was dedicated to those who held the black world together. The pointed context for such sentiments was that by 1970, more than 34 percent of all black households were headed by a woman; virtually double the figure in 1950.[31]

While the dread of ego-shattering female infidelity, or indeed any expression of female sexual freedom or power, permeated much male soul and funk, prostitutes, like mothers, were largely exempt from criticism. Again, there was a clear logic to this, since the prostitute exemplified conventional sex roles, enabling men to define, evaluate, and exploit women purely according to their sexual, if not reproductive function. The prostitute was the quintessential embodiment of sex as a commodity, to be coveted, bought and owned by men. Yet, if there was little guilt about the sexist dimensions of prostitution, with successful pimps elevated to the status of ghetto heroes in blaxploitation films and songs, there was often a genuine sympathy and understanding of the economic imperatives that compelled black women to sell sex. Syl Johnson's "Don't Give It Away," for example, acknowledged that "romance without finance won't get you nowhere ... make 'em all pay."

The most remarkable of all soul's depictions of prostitution actually involved a mother figure. O.C. Smith's 1968 country-soul "Son Of Hickory Holler's Tramp" described how a mother, abandoned by her drunken, womanizing husband, had pledged to raise her fourteen children alone. It was told from the perspective of a son who only realized years later that she had kept her promise by "sacrific[ing] her pride" and turning to prostitution. Rather than condemnation, the son is full of understanding and gratitude: "Let them gossip all they want,/ she loved us and she raised us,/ the proof is standing here a full-grown man." It is revealing to compare these mother songs with soul's songs about fathers. While some, like the Chi-lites' "Let Me Be The Man My Daddy Was" and Joe Tex's "Papa's Dream," depicted dutiful fathers who took care of their families as best they could, others like the Temptations' epic "Papa Was A Rolling Stone" revealed the ravages wrought upon the black community by the interplay of racism, poverty and macho irresponsibility. The finest musical creation of the Motown label's psychedelic phase, the brooding "Papa Was A Rolling Stone" told the cautionary tale of a family whose father "Spent all his time chasing women and drinking ... And when he died, all he left us was alone."

"Papa Was A Rolling Stone" was a good example of the way in which, even in the heart of the black power era, male soul did sometimes manage honest critiques, rather than blind celebrations, of black macho. Johnnie Taylor's "Who's Making Love?," for example, pointed out the perils of playing the errant black stud: a lifestyle which undermined the family unit, and thereby black solidarity, and also risked driving the good black woman into the arms of another. Clarence Reid's "Real Woman" was an even more telling indictment of black macho and the failure to forge mutually respectful relationships. The record begins with Reid extolling the virtues of his "real woman" in classic sexist clichés: "She stays home alone when I'm gone/ She stays there with the kids and keeps her dislikes hid." As the song progresses, Reid acknowledges the mistake of taking her so for granted. Yet he is unable to resist the lure of "slippin' around" and in a marvelous dénouement gets his just desserts: "One night I came home and all her clothes were gone ... Made me realize my real woman/ had gone to find herself a real man."

What makes Reid's sensitivity and insight on this track especially intriguing was that shortly afterwards he reinvented himself as a carnal character called Blowfly and released a string of highly successful X-rated comedy funk albums. There were some genuinely funny ribald riffs on the black stud stereotype on these records, but their humor revolved almost exclusively around graphic tales of sexual hunts, conquests and the routine humiliation and degradation of women. It is as if Reid had simply given up on the struggle to maintain the balance between honest descriptions of powerful sexual needs, lusts and longings, and other aspects of black life and relationships. Instead, he creates a crudely sexist alter ego and gives the macho, voyeuristic, exploitative element of his soul full vent. It certainly did not appear to matter much to Reid that Blowfly sacrificed a broader, more nuanced vision of black life and sexual politics for a reductionist set of racialized stereotypes. What mattered was that this stuff sold. It was a set of priorities which Blowfly and similar acts like Rudy Ray Moore and Red Foxx passed on to the gangsta rappers of the 1980s and 1990s, along with their nascent rap style, street subject matter and easy misogyny.

Epilogue: Rap, Respect and Misogyny in the Post-Revolutionary Era

Since the mid-1970s, the black struggle for freedom, equality, power and respect in America has continued at any number of local and national, political and cultural, economic and educational levels. However, as countless historical, sociological, political and economic accounts grimly testify, that struggle has at best yielded fitful progress and uneven rewards for the black masses, while racial suspicion, hostility, and misunderstanding continue to rend the fabric of American society. Certainly, despite the expansion of a black professional and middle class, and a dogged battle to maintain and extend black political power, literally millions of African Americans are still engaged in a struggle against poverty, un- or under-employment, inferior housing, inadequate medical provision, meager educational opportunities, and sometimes chronic levels of crime in and around their often still functionally segregated communities. In this struggle for survival, contemporary black popular musics, especially rap music and the broader hip-hop culture in which it is embedded, have continued to serve as a bulwark against the psychological ravages of racism, the frequent poverty, and, on occasion, understandable despair of the black masses, particularly among youths trapped within America's inner-city ghettos. Whether as musical creators or as creatively participating listeners and dancers, blacks have continued to find in their musics a means to express themselves, earn respect and in some cases secure material success, within a society where many obstacles to black progress, recognition, security and self-esteem persist.

By boasting of their own superhuman capabilities in the urban battlegrounds or the ghetto bedroom, while "dissing" their rivals' inadequacies in the same arenas, rappers at the microphone or turntable have staked their claims for recognition and respect. Indeed, male rappers have displayed the boastful self-aggrandizement of the shouters writ *badder* and even more sexist as befits an era of deep despondency, disillusionment and cynicism among many young blacks. Songs like 2 Live Crew's "Pop The Pussy," NWA's "She Swallowed It" and "One Less Bitch," Slick Rick's "Treat Her Like A Prostitute," and Kool G. Rap's vile "Talk Like Sex" have helped to publicize a peculiarly intense black variant on the sexism which still pervades much of American society. Like gangsta's songs of glorified violence, raps of rape and sexual exploitation have risked making bland and commonplace acts that should always be horrific and unacceptable. In the process, these songs have also helped to perpetuate racial stereotypes about black animalistic hyper-sexuality, while further undermining the sort of mutually respectful, stable domestic relationships which a combination of racism and poverty have already made harder to achieve in black communities. Just as critically, this sort of sexism has helped to ensure that youthful black energies are often diverted from genuinely progressive political organizing and social activism into macho ego gratification and sexual one-upmanship.

It is certainly sobering to think that whereas Black Panther Afeni Shakur was once jailed for her attempts to secure power and opportunity for her people, her son, the rapper Tupac Shakur, was imprisoned in 1995 after coercing sex for himself and his road crew from a young woman they had imprisoned in a hotel room. For Tupac and many other young black men, such brutal sexual assertiveness—alongside the martial gangsta posturing which provided the context for his later murder in Las Vegas—had become vital indices of personal respect and esteem. It was no coincidence that one of Shakur's main concerns in his post-prison interviews was to deny rumors that he had been raped in jail. Thus, he affirmed his unimpeachable manhood and aligned himself with the vicious homophobia that has plagued much gangsta rap.[32] This may have had something to do with a rejection of disco's gender ambiguities in the late 1970s and early 1980s, as reflected by the success of gay black artists like Sylvester and a whole host of disco divas (Gloria Gaynor, Donna Summer, Linda Clifford). Yet, they also betrayed the deep male insecurities, and the lack of real social, economic and political power, which lurk behind the compensatory balls, bluster and belligerence of the most aggressively macho gangsta rap. No wonder that the black critic Greg Tate has written frustratedly that in the 1990s "the impotence of Black nationalist politics comes from its being phallocentric to the core ... "[33]

Certainly, the attempts of 2 Live Crew's Luther Campbell to excuse his own misogyny and sexual predation in the name of both broad humor and a desire to document all aspects of black sexual proclivities, revealed that he was more committed to making a buck than bucking the racial and economic system within which blacks, female and male alike, remain oppressed. "Some women deserve respect," Campbell generously conceded, but there were others, "The whore, the ho, the big stinker pussy," who deserved only contempt and vilification. While Campbell protested his social conscience, arguing that rappers like him "do more for our communities than the basketball players or football players. We don't ever leave our communities," it is hard to imagine exactly what he thought a song like "Up A Girl's Ass" actually contributed to black progress and empowerment. Ultimately, any claims of social responsibility have been seriously undermined by the willingness of Campbell and others to allow sexism and the systematic degradation of women to so inform their music.[34]

The tenor of the sexual politics in much of the music emanating from the most disaffected sections of contemporary black America conforms to the broader historical pattern described in this article. The intensity and ubiquity of sexism and misogyny in black male popular music have always tended to increase whenever black optimism about the possibility of achieving freedom and equality has ebbed. At a time when many young black males are utterly disillusioned about the prospects of ever competing on anything resembling equal terms for their share of the American Dream, and when the traditional male role of bread-winner and protector in a stable double-headed household often seems permanently beyond their reach, such youths feel impelled to find other avenues to personal empowerment and self-respect.

Thus, the machismo, misogyny and sexual violence that form a significant part of gangsta rap's repertoire, represent essentially cultural vehicles for arriving at a measure of personal respect, power, status and control, rather than the terminus of inner city, black male ambitions. This is not to excuse such songs, merely to suggest that in a world of greater legitimate black opportunity, or where there existed a viable and progressive mass movement for black liberation, such personal empowerment might be pursued by other, more constructive means.

Contrary to the impression given by its many hostile critics, not all rap, not even all gangsta rap, is this sexist. As befits a music of great power and innovation, rap has embraced a wide range of subject matter, perspectives and ideologies. For example, despite its regular descent into sexual irresponsibility and macho adventurism, since the mid-1980s black music has lead the way in songs explicitly urging safe sex practices and personal accountability (De La Soul's "Buddy," Coolio's "Too Hot," Spearhead's "Positive"). This sense of sexual responsibility became even more pronounced after the death from Aids of former NWA rapper and entrepreneur Eazy-E. Moreover, it is clear that rap's sexism has generated more than its fair share of black, as well as white, criticism and protest. Many committed rap fans have objected strongly to what a correspondent to the hip-hop magazine *Vibe* decried as gangsta's "nihilistic 40s-and-blunts nonsense." A 1992 survey, for example, found that 97 percent of Philadelphia's black teens listened to and enjoyed rap music, but also reported among the same youths "a significant desire to see their culture portrayed in a more positive and multi-faceted fashion."[35]

For many blacks, hostile critics and alarmed fans alike, the real problem with gangsta rap is that, for all the claims that these songs accurately capture the grim realities and sexual politics of contemporary black life, gangsta rap does not actually depict a reality which many blacks recognize from their own day-to-day experiences. Nor does it enshrine the moral values and elusive dreams with which most blacks identify. That too many young blacks have slipped into the Thug lifestyle is incontrovertible, and gangsta may indeed reflect aspects of that urban experience, if often with more cartoonish exaggeration than documentary realism. Yet gangsta rap has had relatively little to say about the millions of blacks—poor, rich, young, old, male, female, employed, unemployed, small town, urban and suburban—who continue to try to forge constructive, meaningful, responsible lives, protecting themselves, their families, and their communities as best they can from poverty, racism, and precisely the sort of anti-social behavior which gangsta rappers celebrate, or at least portray as routine.

This credibility gap helps to explain why the most successful black acts of the 1980s and 1990s have not been rappers at all, but crossover artists like Michael Jackson, Whitney Houston, Mariah Carey, Prince and Janet Jackson. These artists have all enjoyed major white followings, but in that respect they are no different from many rappers. In 1992 it was estimated that whites bought 74 percent of all the rap music sold in America.[36] Moreover, the continued black popularity of these crossover acts, like that of other essentially non-rap—although often rap influenced—black stars such as Regina Belle, Boys II Men, DeBarge, R. Kelley and Tony Toni Tone, suggests that for all its undeniable creativity, rap, gangsta or otherwise, has failed to address all the needs or agendas of a black audience which is far from homogenous.

Indeed, although African Americans are united by color, heritage, and a shared appreciation of the myriad ways in which racism can impinge on black lives regardless of socio-economic status, the encrustation of a black underclass at one extreme, and the steady expansion of a black middle and professional class at the other, means that black Americans now have more widely divergent, day-to-day experiences than ever before. The sexual politics of contemporary black popular music thus reflects a similarly wide range of lifestyles, ideals, aspirations and expectations. Consequently, without for a moment denying the diversity of black experiences in the past, it is probably more perilous than ever before to generalize about the tenor of sexual politics in black society, and therefore in black popular music, as a whole. Nevertheless, with its potent depictions of a range of lived and imagined black lives and relationships, black music continues to present rare—if seldom unproblematic—insights into the workings of contemporary black culture and consciousness.

Notes

1. Robin Kelley, "Kickin' reality, kickin' ballistics: 'gangsta rap' and post-industrial Los Angeles" in *Race Rebels: Culture, Politics and the Black Working Class* (New York: Free Press, 1996), 214.

2. For the purposes of this essay, the generic term Rhythm and Blues (capitalized) has been used to encompass all forms of post-World War Two black popular music outside the jazz and gospel traditions: namely, r&b, black rock and roll, black pop, soul, funk, disco and rap. It is important to recognize that the male artists with whom this essay is concerned did not work in a vacuum. Black women singers also had their perspectives on black sexual politics and frequently engaged with their male counterparts in a dialogue which was by turns witty, scathing, and vengeful, dutiful, rapt and boastful. It is also important to note the influence of the music and broadcasting industries in manipulating the sexual content of black popular music at various times, particularly when they have been eagerly pursuing white markets for black musics. Nevertheless, black consumers were never passive in their consumption and, regardless of the machinations of the industry, the broad changes in black attitudes towards sexism and misogyny, romance and idealism in Rhythm and Blues which are described here were, in part at least, a consequence of discernible black consumer preferences. For more on the sexual politics of female Rhythm and Blues, the role of the Rhythm and Blues industry, and a much fuller discussion of the themes of this essay, see Brian Ward, *Just My Soul Responding: Rhythm and Blues, Black Consciousness and Race Relations* (London/Berkeley: UCL Press/University of California Press, 1998).

3. E. Franklin Frazier, *The Negro Family in the United States* (Chicago: University of Chicago Press, 1996) and Daniel P. Moynihan, *The Negro Family: The Case for National Action* (Washington, DC: Government Printing Office, 1965).

4. Eugene Genovese, *Roll Jordan Roll: The World the Slaves Made* (New York: Vintage 1976), and Lawrence Levine, *Black Culture and Black Consciousness: Afro-*

American Folk Thought From Slavery to Freedom (New York: Oxford University Press, 1986).

5. Herbert Gutman, *The Black Family in Slavery and Freedom* (New York: Pantheon, 1976).

6. Edward Ayers, *The Promise of the New South: Life After Reconstruction* (New York: Oxford University Press, 1992), 69.

7. Harry Ploski and John Williams, eds., *The Black Almanac: A Reference Work on the Afro-American* (New York: John Wiley, 1984), 476.

8. Ladner, *Tomorrow's Tomorrow: The Black Woman* (Garden City, NJ: Anchor Books, 1972), 30-35.

9. Deborah White, *Ar'n't I A Woman* (New York: Norton, 1985) and Brenda Stevenson, *Life in Black and White: Family and Community in the Slave South* (New York: Oxford University Press, 1996).

10. bell hooks, *Ain't I A Woman* (Boston: South End Press, 1981), 71-86.

11. Daryl Cumber Dance, *Shuckin' and Jivin'* (Bloomington: Indiana University Press, 1978), 110-111.

12. Roger Abrahams, *Deep Down in the Jungle* (Chicago: Aldine, 1970), 46-58.

13. Dance, *Shuckin'*, 224, 225-226.

14. Matthew White, "'The Blues Ain't Nothin' But A Woman Want To Be A Man'": Male Control in Early Twentieth Century Blues Music," *Canadian Review of American Studies*, 24 (1994): 19-40. For a fuller discussion of sexual objectification, domestic violence and machismo in the blues, see also Paul Oliver, *Blues Fell in the Morning: Meaning in the Blues* (Cambridge: Cambridge University Press, 1990), 95-116; and Levine, *Black Culture*, 276-279.

15. Wynonie Harris, quoted in *Tan* (October 1954), 76; see also 28-31, 76-77.

16. Bill Millar, *The Drifters: The Rise and Fall of the Black Vocal Group* (New York: Macmillan, 1971), 9. Of course, beyond Rhythm and Blues, there were many black male artists working nearer to the jazz or straight pop fields, who, like Nat King Cole, Billy Eckstine, Cecil Gant and the Ink Spots, offered a more idealized, romantic vision of relations between the sexes. For more on vocal groups, Stuart L. Goosman, "The Social and Cultural Organization of Black Vocal Harmony in Washington, DC and Baltimore, Maryland, 1945-1960," Ph.D. dissertation, University of Washington, (1992); Phil Groia, *They All Sang on the Corner* (New York: Phillie Dee, 1983); and Ward, *Just My Soul*.

17. Smokey Robinson with David Ritz, *Smokey: Inside My Life* (London: Headline, 1989), 49, 101-102.

18. Unfortunately, there are few reliable statistics regarding the levels of black domestic violence during the peak years of civil rights activity, let alone comparisons with earlier periods. Nevertheless, anecdotal evidence suggests that black domestic violence and internecine black violence more generally, declined when and where movement activities flourished. Bernice Johnson Reagon, for example, recalled that in Albany there was a black business and entertainment district dubbed Harlem "where things could get rough and people could get cut, shot, or even killed, except during the Civil Rights Movement, when the violence level almost disappeared." Bernice Johnson Reagon, et al., eds., *We Who Believe in Freedom* (New York: Anchor, 1993), 155-6.

19. Jo Ann Gibson Robinson, *The Montgomery Bus Boycott and the Women Who Started It* (Knoxville: University of Tennessee Press, 1987), 36-37.

20. Julian Bond, "The Politics of Civil Rights History," in A.L. Robinson and P. Sullivan, eds., *New Directions in Civil Rights Studies* (Charlottesville: University Press of Virginia, 1991), 10; Clayborne Carson, *In Struggle: SNCC and the Black Awakening of the 1960s* (Cambridge: Harvard University Press, 1981), 148; Sara Evans, *Personal Politics: The Roots of Women's Liberation in the Civil Rights Movement* (New York: Knopf, 1979), 87; and Mary King, *Freedom Song* (New York: William Morrow, 1987), 452.

21. June Johnson, interview with Brian Ward, 22 January, 1996, University of Newcastle upon Tyne Oral History Collection.

22. Paul Gilroy, *The Black Atlantic: Modernity and Double Consciousness* (Cambridge: Harvard University Press, 1993), 85.

23. Eldridge Cleaver, *Soul on Ice* (New York: Dell, 1968), 61.

24. George Jackson, *Soledad Brother* (New York: Coward McCann, 1971), 62-4, 118, 220. Under the influence of Angela Davis and others, George Jackson would later recant some of these misogynistic rants.

25. Angela Davis, *Angela Davis: An Autobiography* (London: Hutchinson, 1975), 161.

26. Clayborne Carson, "Black Political Thought in the Post-Revolutionary Era," in Brian Ward and Tony Badger, eds., *The Making of Martin Luther King and the Civil Rights Movement* (London/ New York (Macmillan/ New York University Press, 1996): 115-127.

27. Ian Hoare, "Mighty, Mighty Spade and Whitey: Black Lyrics and Soul's Interaction with White Culture" in his edited collection, *The Soul Book* (London: Eyre Methuen, 1975), 137.

28. For the sexual politics of soul in the late 1960s and 1970s, see Nick Kimberley, "Paranoid Sex in 60s Soul," *Collusion 2* (February-April 1982), 9-11; James Stewart, "Relationships between Black Males and Females in Rhythm and Blues Music of the 1960s and 1970s," in Irene Jackson ed., *More Than Dancing: Essays on Afro-American Music and Musicians* (Westport, CT.: Greenwood, 1985): 169-186; Ward, *Just My Soul*.

29. David Caute, *1968* (London: Hamish Hamilton, 1988), 235.

30. Gerda Lerner, *The Creation of Patriarchy* (London: Eyre Methuen, 1986), 213.

31. Andrew Hacker, *Two Nations: Black and White, Separate, Hostile and Unequal* (New York: Ballantine Books 1995), 74.

32. For Shakur's comments, see *Vibe* 4 (February 1996), 51.

33. Greg Tate, *Flyboy in the Buttermilk* (New York: Fireside 1992), 283. See also, Tricia Rose, *Black Noise: Rap Music and Black Culture in Contemporary America* (Hanover, CT.: Wesleyan University Press, 1995).

34. Luther Campbell and Jim Miller, *Nasty as They Wanna Be: The Uncensored Story of Luther Campbell of the Two Live Crew* (New York: Barricade, 1992), 190; Campbell, quoted in *Rolling Stone* (30 November 1995), 37.

35. Paul Scott, *Vibe* 4 (June/July 1996), 31; *Washington Post*, 15 July 1992, F-7.

36. Figures on black artists and audiences taken from, *Ebony*, (June 1996), 116-120; *Los Angeles Times*, (19 June1992); and (15 September 1992).

CHAPTER 3

"Dress modestly, neatly ... as if you were going to church"[1]: Respectability, Class and Gender in the Montgomery Bus Boycott and the Early Civil Rights Movement

Marisa Chappell, Jenny Hutchinson and Brian Ward

In late February 1960, *Time*, one of the leading journals of middle-American opinion, reported on the wave of student sit-ins which had broken out across the South to challenge segregation at lunch counters and in other public accommodations. The magazine insisted that the student demonstrators were simply demanding the sort of basic civil rights which should be accorded to all decent Americans. In pictures and words, *Time* contrasted the admirable goals and dignified demeanor of the protesters with those of the white youths, "the duck-tailed sideburned swaggerers, the rednecked hatemongers, the Ku Klux Klan," who abused and repeatedly assaulted those who waited for hamburgers and justice.[2]

There are few more striking images from the southern freedom struggle than those which, as in the *Time* article, or in reports from any number of civil rights flashpoints in the late 1950s and early 1960s, juxtaposed perfectly coiffured, immaculately dressed, quietly dignified, and stoically nonviolent black demonstrators with violent, foul-mouthed, unkempt and hysterical white mobs. Such reports in the press and on television vividly rendered the movement as not only a battle between black rights and white wrongs, but also as a clash between accepted notions of decency and respectability, and those of vulgarity and barbarism. Even southerners generally sympathetic to the aims of the resisters recognized the potency of such imagery and felt the rug of moral righteousness being tugged from beneath their feet. James Jackson Kilpatrick, editor of the *Richmond News Leader*, contrasted the well-scrubbed black students with their shameful white adversaries: "a ragtail rabble, slack-jawed, black jacketed, grinning fit to kill, and some of them ... waving the proud and honored flag of the Southern states in the last war fought by gentlemen. Eheu!"[3]

The symbolic contrast between mob and movement was especially heightened and complicated whenever southern women were involved—which they were in the ranks of both civil rights protesters, and of the white mobs who opposed them in the streets. In both cases, such conspicuous public activism presented a serious challenge to prevailing ideas about the proper role of respectable women in American civic and political affairs. Ironically, however, by diligently observing and publicly exhibiting many of the accepted ideals of respectable female behavior—even in the midst of their bold insurgency—black women frequently managed to appear rather more "lady-like" than many of their white segregationist opponents. For example, at Little Rock in 1957, the much-publicized photograph of Sammy Dean Parker's contorted face as she hurled obscenities at Elizabeth Eckford, one of the nine black students attempting to desegregate Central High School, not only embodied the racial spite and hatred of the white South, but was a particular affront to acknowledged standards of female behavior. Such intemperate, unlady-like behavior and cowardly outbursts from the safety of snarling mobs contrasted dramatically with the obvious bravery and impeccable conduct of young black women like Eckford, and thereby helped to discredit white claims of moral superiority and greater civility.[4]

This contrast was no accident. Just as movement leaders like Martin Luther King carefully appealed to mainstream American civic ideals in their rhetoric, so the whole style, tenor and symbolism of black protest was carefully orchestrated to appeal to mainstream white sensibilities about proper behavior in pursuit of legitimate goals.[5] This strategy was hardly unique to the civil rights movement or even to African Americans. It has been common practice among oppressed peoples to employ the key ideological and moral touchstones of the dominant culture in order to find leverage within a hostile system. Such groups rarely accept all of those core values unequivocally or consistently, since they often enshrine and serve to perpetuate existing patterns of oppression. Nevertheless, marginalized and outcast social groups frequently internalize and redeploy aspects of the dominant ideology in order both to survive and protest their situation.[6]

African Americans had long exhibited such tendencies as part of a much broader repertoire of survival strategies. Blacks hoped to insulate themselves from the very worst manifestations of racial oppression by showing fealty to mainstream, putatively white, ideals of respectable, civilized behavior, even as they remained at all times acutely aware of their marginalized position outside that mainstream. This was the tension at the heart of W.E.B. Du Bois's turn-of-the-century articulation of black "double-consciousness," but it had its roots deep in slavery.[7] For example, Eugene Genovese has described how female slaves were very deliberately schooled by their parents in matters of Victorian moral rectitude and encouraged to "carry themselves as women with sensibilities as delicate as those of the finest white ladies." Thereby they could potentially circumvent stereotypes of black female promiscuity and humanize themselves in white eyes, perhaps even securing a minimal measure of personal safety in the midst of a system where rape by white men and their "unwomanly" position in the labor force constantly threatened to render them not only less than ladies, but sometimes less than human.[8]

This tradition persisted after slavery, as African Americans utilized respectability as part of a whole range of tactics—from confrontation, through accommodation, to separatism—to resist the full brutality of southern racism. Barbara Welke has suggested that wealthier black women could sometimes even use their conspicuous respectability, as revealed by their dress, to evade a form of segregation on southern streetcars which was initially informed by class and gender, as well as racial, protocols.[9] More systematic was Booker T. Washington's accommodationism, in which he sought—among other social and economic goals—to protect blacks from the worst manifestations of racism by insisting that they shared with all decent white folks a staunch belief in the value of religion, thrift, hard-work, education, civic duty, temperance, matrimony and family. At a time of rapidly deteriorating race relations in the South, this tactic was not without its successes, especially for the small black business and professional elite. In 1900, Washington assured a meeting of his National Negro Business Association that blacks who succeeded in business, but who also "possessed intelligence and high character," could expect to be "treated with the highest respect by the members of the white race."[10]

Of course, there were numerous occasions when audacious black entrepreneurial success led to white censure or worse against "uppity niggers." Yet, Washington's argument that those successful blacks who exhibited proper, respectable behavior might evade the worst victimization and reprisals was not entirely unfounded. Certainly, Gregory Mixon's work on Atlanta in the early twentieth century has revealed that African American elites in that city ultimately prospered after the carnage of the 1906 race riot by carefully aligning themselves with their white counterparts in denouncing various forms of unruly lower-class behavior. In a city where whites were stirred to murderous frenzy by rumors of black rapists attacking white women, elite blacks like Dr. Garland Penn were especially keen to pledge the support of the "educated Christian members of his race ... in protecting white women from crimes ... against them by the criminal negro classes." If this tactic did not always save black professionals from attack at the height of the riot, in its aftermath it did encourage a measure of white tolerance and even protection for that black elite—not least because white leaders hoped that right-thinking blacks would act to internally police the black community; imposing order and stability on the black masses at a time when Atlanta was embarking on a major and unsettling burst of economic and demographic change.[11]

As historian Kevin Gaines has suggested, this emphasis on black civic and moral virtue and careful alignment with middle-class American ideals, became a keynote of black leadership in the twentieth century. Indeed, in a world where whites routinely judged all blacks according to the lowest common black denominator, the black better classes often sought to distance themselves from the more disreputable behavior of some from the black lower orders. Yet, they also sought to regulate that behavior, using churches, missions, fraternal societies, schools, colleges, and newspapers to promote respectability as a means of collective protection and advance for all blacks.[12] Moreover, as Glenda Gilmore has noted, simply affecting the social and moral mores of the middle class could provide a bulwark of sorts, even for those who did not really have the material accoutrements of that class. Consequently, shared ideas of respectability, and a common belief in its political and social efficacy, could provide a solder between diverse sections of the black community.[13]

The paradox in all of this was that blacks were using ideas of middle-class respectability, which had from their inception been coded in racially exclusive ways, in order to break down that very pattern of racial exclusivity. Blacks increasingly reified and adopted standards and styles of respectable behavior which whites had traditionally proclaimed impossible for uncivilized blacks to appreciate, let alone practice. Since that alleged inability had always provided an important justification for the banishment of blacks to the margins of society and beyond, the conspicuous embrace of respectability both undermined that justification, and helped to create a potent case for black inclusion in the American plurality.[14]

In the 1950s and early 1960s, the southern civil rights movement extended and refined this dimension of black resistance, skillfully tapping pervasive ideas of respectability to gain moral and political leverage within the system. Respectability provided the movement with an important antidote to the claims of intransigent southern whites that segregation was absolutely essential to defend American civilization from contamination by uncivilized blacks with their congenital ignorance, sloth, promiscuity and irresponsibility. It helped to affirm in many skeptical white minds the essential worthiness of blacks to enjoy the citizenship rights they were demanding. Thus, a careful adherence to responsible tactics like nonviolence, coupled with the promotion of eminently respectable public leaders espousing perfectly American ideals in pursuit of quintessentially American democratic goals, helped to create the powerful sense of moral rectitude which was one of the early movement's most effective weapons.

And yet, respectability in the movement was more than a simple tactical expedient, donned at a particular moment to woo white sympathy or acquiescence, only to be cast aside when the new day of black freedom dawned. By mid-century, mainstream middle-class American ideals of respectability, especially as they pertained to matters of gender roles, family responsibilities, child-rearing, sexuality, employment, frugality, and education, were genuinely—if still not uniformly or unequivocally—endorsed by most African Americans. Even though racism, poverty and myriad forms of discrimination often made it difficult for blacks to realize these ideals, they nonetheless retained a powerful psychological force within a mass black consciousness which was far from homogenous, and which was always constructed from a myriad of intersecting, nominally black and nominally mainstream, influences. Indeed, ultimately, the civil rights struggle was inextricably linked to, if never synonymous with, a quest to "normalize" black domestic and gender relationships in accordance with conventional middle class patterns—even though those patterns were riddled with class, racial and gender iniquities of their own. In other words, the movement was, in part at least, a struggle for access to the educational, economic and political opportunities which might make middle-class status and ideals of conventional respectability and domestic stability more attainable for the mass of blacks. Consequently, in the course of that struggle, respectability became simultaneously a tool of protest and an index of black progress.

This essay considers the ways in which black and white notions of respectability, traversed and partially created by gender and class considerations, shaped the form and trajectory of the early civil rights movement in the South. The first section briefly considers how ideas of respectability were constructed and promoted in mass black consciousness through various forms of black public discourse, most notably the black press. The second section moves from the general to the particular to consider how the black tactical and psychological preoccupation with forging a respectable movement can help historians to understand the origins, style and substance of the Montgomery Bus Boycott of 1955-56. In particular, it examines the emergence of Rosa Parks and Martin Luther King as key figures in that protest in terms of their respectability, and the ways in which the movement traded on such credentials in order to present itself favorably to the wider and whiter world.

The Black Press and the Coordinates of Post-War Respectability

When E. Franklin Frazier wrote his stinging critique of the black bourgeoisie in 1957, he depicted it as a rather pitiful, self-absorbed class without culture or values of its own. Unwilling to embrace the grassroots vernacular culture of the black masses, yet unable because of racism to fully engage in the notionally more sophisticated world of the white middle classes it so envied, Frazier's black bourgeoisie aped the manners and mores of that middle-class mainstream in a sort of fantastic parallel black universe. Furthermore, he argued that the black press were crucial in helping "to create and maintain the world of make-believe in which Negroes can realize their desire for recognition and status in a white world that regards them with contempt and amusement."[15] Black newspapers and magazines were, in Frazier's view, the vehicles for a "small intelligentsia among Negroes," dedicated to shoring up an established black hierarchy, with themselves securely in place at the top by virtue of their apparent proximity to white codes of behavior and standards of excellence. The black press, he claimed, passionately celebrated black achievements in the arts, sports, business and politics, in part to boost black confidence that they could succeed against the odds, but also as sort of compensatory gesture in the absence of a more systematic struggle against widespread racial discrimination. In much the same vein, the press also reified an exaggerated black conformity to the precepts of mainstream respectability. In Frazier's opinion, this too was basically a surrogate for not being able to compete successfully in other areas of American political, social and economic life.[16]

There are a number of striking things about this analysis. One is that, although Frazier was writing in the immediate aftermath of the Montgomery Bus Boycott and the founding of the Southern Christian Leadership Conference (SCLC), he betrayed little sense that a mass black insurgency was germinating which would flower into a genuinely mass movement just a few years later. Even more pertinent here, is Frazier's complete disregard for the positive potential of the notions of respectability advanced in the black press, both as a means to unite disparate groups within black America around certain shared values and ideas, and as a means to present black demands for equality within an ideological framework which white America might recognize and respect. As we shall see, the protesters in Montgomery self-consciously employed respectability in precisely these ways. Moreover, in so doing, the boycott leaders sought to carefully align the protest with ideas about proper, decent behavior—in particular, notions of correct gender roles and family life—which the black press had done much to articulate and promote. While the middle-class social and sexual values enshrined in the black press seemed to Frazier nothing more than a sorry imitation of white codes and mores, for the black protesters in Montgomery they actually provided a crucial weapon in their struggle.

As regards the depiction of proper gender roles within this code of respectability, the black press essentially endorsed patriarchal authority, and consigned women to traditional and subordinate domestic roles. Pioneering black female journalists like Freda De Knight prospered in the "women's pages" of mass-circulation magazines like *Ebony* by steadily reinforcing prevailing middle-class ideals of respectable womanhood. De Knight and others stressed the need for black women to work hard to run their homes and care for their children efficiently, while providing physical satisfaction and psychological reassurance for black men whose self-esteem was frequently undermined by the ravages of racism, and its attendant blights of economic, social and political impotence. The *Chicago Defender*'s syndicated "Glamour Clinic" column by Gerry Masciana, director of a school of modeling and charm, similarly stressed the importance of women looking good at breakfast time, in order to send husbands off to work "with an indelible memory of fresh, rose-like, dew-kissed loveliness" that would both strengthen their marriage and improve his day at work. Otherwise, "through her sloppy appearance and unsanitary attention, she can drive him to the liquor bars, the arms of another woman ... or to court for a divorce."[17] Even the *Arkansas State Press*, run by Little Rock NAACP activists L.C. and Daisy Bates, was at pains to remind its female readers that "with the coming of summer we must all work even more faithfully to keep lovely to look at," so as to keep black men happy at home.[18]

"Marriage is a full-time occupation that has to be worked at to be successful," *Tan* magazine advised its largely lower-class black female readership, again insisting that black women were expected to take prime responsibility for a successful relationship or marriage. "Usually it's a wife's own stupidity that deals her the short end of what might have been a lasting, happy marriage," the magazine explained.[19] Indeed,

in the case of infidelity by a male partner, black women were instructed
to "make an honest examination of yourself ... Do you nag and
complain?"[20] If black women were thus charged with keeping their men
happy at home, sexually interested and therefore faithful, they were also
expected to warm to this role with good grace and gratitude. As Franklin
Fosdick explained in the *Negro Digest*, "A wife who is unselfish, who
does not feel herself a martyr, gains more than she loses by striving to
make her home and herself attractive to her husband."[21]

As many commentators have noted, because of the black experience
in both slavery and freedom, there has historically been a pronounced
tendency towards matrifocality in black culture.[22] This often left black
women with a measure of authority, influence and responsibility within
their communities which was far in excess of that experienced by most
of their white female counterparts, and certainly some way removed
from conventional ideals of proper gender roles. Consequently, the
black press devoted considerable effort towards encouraging black
women to downplay the affront to patriarchal norms which their
peculiarly prominent social and economic profiles within the black
community appeared to represent. Black women were certainly
counseled that, in no circumstances, were they to make their men appear
inadequate, or to ridicule them, if they proved unable to fulfil their
proper patriarchal functions as provider and protector for their
womenfolk and families. *Tan* ran many cautionary tales along these
lines, warning women—especially those who worked at a time when
their menfolk were suffering the indignity of under-or
unemployment—that they should not seek to dominate or nag their
partners as this would only make them feel even more inadequate and
further erode their pride and self-confidence. In "Chained To Him
Forever," a contrite wife told of how she had responded inappropriately
when money problems rocked her marriage, leading her husband to
drink, and eventually to abandon his job: "I got frantic when my
husband left a situation he couldn't endure any longer, and stormed at
him, and finally I simply took over by going out and getting a job when
he pleaded with me not to. He knew by that act that I had lost faith in
him and he needed my faith above anything else." Thus, what appeared
at one level a sensible survival strategy, was actually portrayed as a
transgression against the natural order of things, with the man the
principal breadwinner.[23]

Of course, black women had always worked, in greater numbers
proportionately than white women, and the black press was eager
enough to report on inspirational black women who were successful in
the arts, sports, business, or any of the professions. Yet, when it did so,

it was careful to stress the importance of maintaining the integrity of conventional gender roles and domestic responsibilities alongside a successful career. Thus, singer Hazel Scott, who married black Harlem congressman Adam Clayton Powell, Jr., was only too happy to subordinate her own career to her more pressing duties as mother and homemaker. "As important to me as my music was—and still is—I decided I would never permit it to interfere with my marriage," she explained and "Hazel Scott would have to play second fiddle to Mrs Adam Powell Jr." This, Scott insisted, was her decision, not her husband's: "Woman has been given a special job—to produce children and to be the hub of the family. If she has another talent, that's just what it should be—*another*—talent."[24] Similarly, while the black press often applauded the efforts of politically active women, as when the *Arkansas State Press* celebrated the work of Mrs Gwendolyn Floyd, "the dynamic and alert president of the local National Council of Negro Women," such women were still expected to honor conventional priorities pertaining to family life.[25] *Tan*, for instance, noted approvingly that while Count Basie's wife was "very active in social and civic affairs," she "always finds time to look after her home."[26]

Black women who had successful careers, or who were conspicuously active in political and civic life, potentially at least, presented a serious challenge to traditionally gendered structures of power, prestige and responsibility in post-war America—even if, as Joanne Meyerowitz and Susan Lynn have rightly pointed out, there was a good deal more female activity and creativity going on during this period than one might imagine from the reification of the "feminine mystique."[27] In order to reconcile their public assertiveness and political activism with dominant notions of proper female behavior, it became important for female black participants in the early civil rights movement to somehow minimize the radicalism of such apparent violations of the patriarchal order. As we shall see, nowhere was this balance between feminine respectability and "un-feminine" militancy achieved more successfully than in the construction of Rosa Parks as both the symbol of and catalyst for black insurgency in Montgomery and beyond.

In the black press, descriptions of male roles and responsibilities conformed to the same mainstream patriarchal ideals which framed the depictions of proper female behavior. Black men were supposed to be sober ("Wasn't it silly to drink all of that liquor and throw away all of that money only to end up with a hang over," chided the *Chicago Defender*), dependable fathers and husbands, who worked hard to provide food and shelter for their families, and served as responsible members of their communities.[28] *Tan* demonstrated its fidelity to those mainstream gender assumptions by carrying a column on "Child Care" by the white pediatrician Dr. Edward Beasley, an instructor at Northwestern University. The column emphasized the importance of inculcating "proper" gender roles and responsibilities in young children. Beasley idealized a father and husband who would enshrine the correct male characteristics by being "assertive and demonstrate initiative," as well as being a reliable and sensitive sex partner. Above all, however, the man must be the visible and unimpeachable head of the household, or else, Beasley warned, children would be confused and psychologically scarred by this violation of the natural order of things.[29]

Amidst all these idealized images of masculine virtue and respectability, the errant black stud, irresponsibly satiating his own sexual urges, was not an uncommon figure in the post-war black popular press. Yet he was seldom celebrated, and was often roundly condemned for contravening the acceptable standards of respectable male behavior. This attitude was vividly revealed in an *Ebony* profile of the Rhythm and Blues vocal group, Billy Ward and the Dominoes—who, in 1951, had achieved great celebrity and not a little notoriety with their paean to "Lovin' Dan," the sexually insatiable "Sixty-Minute Man." *Ebony* was at pains to distinguish the behavior of the group from that of their macho hero, whose main mission in life was to service the sexual needs of women whose partners were failing to measure up in the bedroom. "Off-stage all five young men are mannerly, sophisticated, and reserved," the magazine reported.[30] Thus, the magazine sought to undermine traditional stereotypes of black men as somehow primal sybaritic forces, untempered by culture, decency and civilization. Similarly, an article on ex-heavyweight champ Joe Louis—the quintessential example of raw black male physical power—was keen to emphasize his humanity and intellect. Not only was Louis a great fighter, he was portrayed as a true gentleman and sportsman; sensitive, incorruptible, and generous of spirit.[31]

The underlying message in all these depictions of black male behavior, was that black men needed to distance themselves from the racial stereotypes which haunted the white imagination with dark images of black hyper-sexuality, brute force, and overly corporeal and sensual drives. Instead, they were to cultivate and stress their capacity for intellectual activity, social refinement, artistic sensibility, hard work, and respectable, responsible behavior towards family, country and community. Indeed, as William Berry has suggested, *Ebony*'s ideal male readers and its stock heroes were patriotic gentlemen scholars; the "sophisticated, cosmopolitan, urbane, diverse, affluent, intellectual person who contributes to the NAACP."[32] Certainly, the black press was at pains to stress black educational initiatives and achievements, believing that these would help facilitate black acceptance in the mainstream by both increasing black access to middle-class job opportunities, and by undermining white stereotypes of black ignorance. The *Chicago Defender*, for example, urged blacks to make donations to the United Negro College Fund specifically in these integrationist terms, insisting that "college is where a real American kid belongs." Educated blacks, the paper argued, would "move up to first-class citizenship and take the whole race with them."[33] The heroine of one *Tan* story similarly articulated the link between educational achievement, job opportunities and respectability, when she told her brother, "Don't you see our only chance is to study hard and get a job and be decent someday."[34]

Predictably, the black press devoted a lot of copy to the achievements of blacks who had already used their intellect and education to secure prestigious jobs as doctors, lawyers, teachers, engineers and military officers, and to entrepreneurs who had succeeded in businesses of their own. Yet, the annealing value of the press's steady emphasis on middle-class values and conduct, as opposed to simply on the conspicuous material trappings which announced middle-class status, was that the black poor and lower class could also subscribe, or at least aspire, to that brand of respectability. Consequently, the respectable black poor were the regular subject of praise and exemplification too. In 1954, for example, eminent black journalist Ethel Payne reported on her meeting with Mrs Sarah Belling, a woman who made a very modest living as a book binder in Washington DC—and whose son Spottswood had been the plaintiff in one of the school desegregation cases consolidated as *Brown vs Topeka Board of Education*. Payne applauded the widowed Mrs Belling's desire to get a decent education for her son, and lavished praise on other manifestations of her essential respectability as a regular church-goer and proud custodian of "a modest row home, unpretentious, immaculately kept."[35]

While eager to see their children educated, many black parents—much like their white counterparts in the 1950s—were wracked by fears that instead of being immersed in their school books, their offspring might be succumbing to the lure of juvenile delinquency and sexual impropriety.[36] These twin concerns about youthful deviation from middle-class social expectations merged dramatically in popular adult opposition to the raunchier side of black Rhythm and Blues. Indeed, while black concerns about the morality of some of that music and its rock and roll derivatives lacked the clear racist overtones of much adult white hostility to the style, the middle-class coordinates of this unease were common to both races. Ironically, the apogee of this black and white criticism came around 1956, by which time black Rhythm and Blues had already curtailed many of its more bawdy themes and risqué lyrical elements. Yet, if this process of gentrification was accelerated by the recording and broadcasting industries' response to the emergence of a mass white market for the music, its black roots went rather deeper. As blacks became more heavily concentrated in urban communities, and became increasingly exposed via personal observation and a deeply penetrative mass media to urbane middle-class standards of respectable behavior, their principal popular music increasingly reflected their acceptance of those mainstream values.[37]

Certainly, long before Rhythm and Blues music had begun to cross over to reach a youthful white market, middle-class blacks in Cleveland had protested against songs which they felt perpetuated old stereotypes of blacks as dissolute, over-sexed hedonists, with uncurbable appetites for violence, drink and sex.[38] Similarly, the Houston Juvenile Delinquency and Crime Commission—headed, not by a southern white guardian of racial and moral purity, but by the eminently respectable black sociology professor, Dr. H.A. Bullock, of Texas Southern University—was just one of many such bodies which spent the mid-1950s compiling lists of objectionable rock and roll records which appeared to infringe the National Association of Radio and TV Broadcasters' ruling that broadcasters should "observe the proprieties and customs of civilized society ... honor the sanctity of marriage and the home."[39] Even Martin Luther King joined the chorus of respectable black voices raised against the more bawdy side of early rock and roll. In his *Ebony* "Advice For Living" column he warned black teenagers that the music "often plunges men's minds into degrading and immoral depths."[40]

Much of the problem with Rhythm and Blues was its relative sexual explicitness at a time when blacks were especially keen to disavow stereotypes of congenital promiscuity, and to demonstrate their allegiance to middle-class ideals of pre-marital chastity. Given this agenda, it is no surprise that by the late 1950s and early 1960s the most popular black music of the period with black consumers was a big beat black pop style personified by the likes of Sam Cooke, the Platters, Brook Benton, and the Shirelles. This black pop largely eschewed the more ribald adult themes and sexual frankness of early Rhythm and Blues, and instead favored lyrics which idealized monogamous, mutually respectful relationships, solemnized by wedding vows. Thus, black pop became yet another vehicle by which conventional social expectations and proper sexual conduct were transmitted to the black community, particularly to its young.[41]

The black press shared this concern to impress upon black youth the need to observe mainstream sexual codes of behavior. The *Carolina Times* was not the only black newspaper to carry a "Youth Page," devoted to giving young blacks a thorough grounding in middle-class sexual codes. The page featured a cautionary "Date Data" column, tellingly signed by "The Chaperone."[42] The content of *Tan's* regular "Teen Talk" section revealed that sexual double-standards had been imbibed along with other mainstream values, since it directed almost all of its advice on proper sexual conduct towards young black women, warning that "Boredom, loneliness, too much idle time and even the strong desire to be popular, account for a number of good girls going astray."[43] The magazine averred that pre-marital virginity was the "moral ideal" in American society, and had numerous lurid tales to tell of young women whose premature sexual experimentation had lead to deep unhappiness and social ruin.[44] "Our love, that only a moment ago had been so sweet and clean, was spoiled now and somehow sordid," rued one fallen black girl after surrendering to her boyfriend's ardor.[45]

While such immorality was often condemned outright, the black press often saved its worst criticism in these cases, not for the unfortunate youths, but for their lax parents. These girls—and to a lesser extent, their male companions—were shown as in dire need of correct moral example, and close adult supervision at a time when *Tan* claimed that, "juvenile delinquency is rampant." Moreover, the love, succor and example of a conventional nuclear family—ideally, but not necessarily, a church-going family—was repeatedly presented as the best vehicle for such moral education. A well-adjusted, stable patriarchal family imbued with all-American middle-class values and beliefs represented the best hope of producing a "poised, charming youngster who will soon become a courteous and respected citizen." And such black young citizens, of course, like such black families, were believed to stand the best chance of impressing upon mainstream America the fitness of blacks for basic civil rights and political equality.

The ideals of respectable behavior and accepted gender roles codified in the black press, were replicated—and therefore further reinforced—in many other areas of black public life and leisure in the 1950s and early 1960s. In addition to black popular music, the mass media of television, radio and movies, whether notionally black or white-oriented, reified conventional moral codes and values, and were vitally important in helping to define respectable behavior and legitimate ambition among post-war black Americans. Bernice Johnson Reagon of the SNCC Freedom Singers, and subsequently leader of Sweet Honey In The Rock, vividly recalled "conversations we had at college about what our ideals were. We were all going to have this really nice house ... and the guys were talking, 'my wife is not going to work'. And that had nothing to do with anything which comes out of the black community, that really comes straight off TV."[46] As Reagon recognized, for many black women, and, indeed for black men, there was still a substantial gulf between media depictions of domestic bliss and the black experience. Nonetheless, such images and ideals clearly had a considerable impact on black consciousnesses which were always constructed from a multitude of messily overlapping racial, class, gender and status considerations.[47]

The black pulpit, dominated by men even as the congregations were often dominated by women, expressed much the same concern with probity, sexual restraint, education, industry, thrift, and civic responsibility as the black press. Black fraternal lodges encouraged members to pursue similar ideals. The Arkansas state branch of the Benevolent Protective Order of Elks of the World even sought to ban bad language among its members as part of a 1955 "Good Conduct" campaign. More generally, the Elks insisted that if members behaved like respectable first-class citizens, they could expect to be treated as such.[48] Black schools and colleges were another means of disseminating such values. In 1950, Ouachita County Training School in Arkansas organized a "good citizenship and good grooming club," the objectives of which were to "promote sound citizenship by observing good health habits, safety rules and to have pride and respect for home, school, community and finally nation."[49] Even black astrologers confirmed the importance of cultivating such habits. In the wake of *Brown* and the optimism it initially inspired, *Tan*'s "Your Stars and Numbers" predicted a time of profound change and opportunity in all areas of black life. "Those who lead orderly lives and conduct their affairs in a well organized and non obligated manner, will be in a position to act upon such inducements and advantages as will prevail," the magazine assured the respectable. "But those who have been careless, negligent, or have complicated their lives with extravagance, emotional, domestic or social irregularities may feel a squeeze or encounter some sort of a crisis with an aftermath of regrets or disillusionment."[50] Respectability, then, really did seem to be the key to a better future for black Americans as the latest phase in an age-old freedom struggle dawned. In Montgomery, the black community would make good use of that key in unlocking the system of segregation on the city's buses.

Rosa Parks, Martin Luther King and Respectable Protest in Montgomery

At the first mass meeting of the Montgomery bus boycott on the night of December 5, 1955, Rosa Parks received a standing ovation from the 7,000 people gathered in and around Montgomery's Holt Street Baptist Church. "She was their heroine," remembered Martin Luther King, Jr., "They saw in her courageous person the symbol of their hopes and aspirations." Reverend Ralph Abernathy later explained that Parks had been presented that night "because we wanted her to become symbolic of our protest movement."[51] Parks herself was no movement manqué, of course. She was a very self-conscious, experienced and trained political activist; a fully cognizant agent of the events which surrounded her arrest and the protest it sparked. Yet, in the construction of Parks's public image as a symbol of African American pride and aspirations, leaders of the protest and the black press consistently downplayed her activist credentials in favor of an emphasis on her middle-class respectability and femininity, thereby revealing just how deeply those notions had penetrated mass black consciousness. This was somewhat ironic, given that Parks had actually seriously challenged those gendered ideals and assumptions, as well as the racial status quo, when she refused to vacate her seat for a white passenger after being instructed to do so by a Montgomery bus driver. Nevertheless, shared middle-class ideals and aspirations ultimately served as a cohesive force in Montgomery, helping to unite diverse groups of Montgomery blacks around common goals and tactics.

While boycott leaders sometimes suggested that the protest was spontaneous, initiated and maintained by the city's black masses, interest in a bus boycott long pre-dated Parks's act of defiance. E.D. Nixon, an official of the Brotherhood of Sleeping Car Porters and former president of the local chapter of the NAACP, had been looking for the proper persons or incident around which to build a protest for at least a year before December 1955. According to Jo Ann Robinson, the Women's Political Council had been waiting since 1949 to stage a boycott. Its representatives had met with and petitioned Mayor Gayle on several occasions in 1953 regarding the bus situation, offering thinly veiled warnings of mass black action if its initial demands for a more polite form of segregated bus service were not addressed. Yet, prior to Rosa Parks's arrest, Montgomery's black activists lacked the appropriate symbolic figures around when to build a mass movement that might transcend the city's class and gender divisions.[52]

Parks's most basic qualification for this symbolic role was her gender. Southern racism, as observers and historians have frequently noted, is inextricably linked with sexual anxieties. The specter of any interracial sexual relations provoked anger and fear among many whites, and segregationist organizations like the Klan and the White Citizens' Councils played on this fear to galvanize support for Massive Resistance. Integration, they argued, would lead irrevocably to intermarriage, "amalgamation," and the fall of American civilization. Segregationists tied sexual and racial anxieties to Cold War political rhetoric, portraying interracial sex as a Communist weapon to destroy the country. Black male sexuality was particularly feared and demonized. "How would you like your daughter to marry a Negro?" became, according to one *Crisis* columnist, "the question designed to end all argument."[53] Citizens' Council literature reported countless alleged sexual offences by black men in integrated areas, while Montgomery police commissioner and Citizens' Council member Clyde Sellers felt the whole quest for desegregation stemmed from the desire of black men to find "white women to marry them."[54]

Arguments against integrating public transportation also focused specifically on white fears of black male sexuality. Montgomery City Lines attorney Jack Crenshaw rejected a "first-come, first-served" seating plan, which fell within city segregation laws. Because of the angles of the bus seats, he argued, white nurses getting on a bus just leaving a Negro section of town would be "rubbing knees with Negro men." State Representative Nick S. Hare suggested that if a woman was the first occupant of a two-person seat, she should retain her right to the entire seat. This would eliminate the fear of a black man sitting next to a white woman and thus preserve "the dignity, safety and security of women." A Citizens' Council newspaper played on these anxieties in an article entitled "Ten Cents Per Lady." It claimed that the Supreme Court, by outlawing segregation on South Carolina's intrastate buses, had "evaluated Southern [white] womanhood at 10 cents per lady" because "that is the price any colored man can pay for the *right* to sit next to a white lady on a bus." Because of this sexual paranoia, and because, as Rosa Parks recognized, "a woman would get more sympathy than a man," the catalyst for any bus boycott in Montgomery was always likely to be a woman.[55]

Not just any woman would do, however. The woman, Parks wrote later, "would have to be above reproach, have a good reputation, and have done nothing wrong but refuse to give up her seat." The protest symbol, then, had to meet certain behavioral and class-specific qualifications in order to gain sympathy from the country's middle-class population, both black and white, and to refute pro-segregationist claims that African Americans were unworthy of full citizenship. These class and behavioral requirements were revealed in the fate of two rejected candidates for the role.[56]

When 15-year-old Claudette Colvin was arrested in March 1955, police reports claimed that she was dragged "kicking and clawing" off the bus.[57] Consequently, Colvin could be charged, not only with disobeying the city's segregation ordinance, but with disorderly conduct and assault and battery. Some sources also reported that Colvin, an unmarried teenager, was pregnant. Rosa Parks appreciated that these behavioral transgressions would have given the press a "field day," jeopardizing any possible case which might be brought against the segregation laws, and above all denying black community activists the sense of moral superiority upon which their wider appeal for black justice was dependent. Thus, while the arrest "seemed to arouse the Negro community" and "there was talk of boycotting the buses in protest," E.D. Nixon had rejected Colvin as an inappropriate figure around whom to try to organize a mass movement in Montgomery.[58]

While more than a dozen witnesses insisted that Colvin had not been disorderly, and the arresting officer even admitted under oath that she had not hit, struck, or scratched him, white press accounts continually stressed Colvin's violence.[59] One white witness claimed that Colvin had "sorely provoked" and "struck" the officers and contrasted this behavior with that of the police officers, who—fulfilling equally powerful stereotypes of southern male gallantry—were described as "gentlemanly almost to the point of turning the other cheek."[60] Female violence and out-of-wedlock pregnancy clearly contradicted pervasive middle-class standards of respectability and both appeared frequently in segregationist literature as if they constituted the normal behavior of black women. Just as they fell back on venerable stereotypes of all black men as potential rapine beasts, so opponents of integration revived arguments that black women were, in Paula Giddings's phrase, "morally obtuse" and "openly licentious."[61] Citizens' Council newspapers repeatedly cited high rates of venereal disease and illegitimate births among black women, arguing that "as a race" Negroes "make a mockery of the white man's holy institution of matrimony."[62]

In October 1955, Mary Louise Smith, an 18-year-old black girl, was also arrested for violating the bus segregation laws. But when E.D. Nixon went to her house he reputedly "found her daddy in front of his shack, barefoot, drunk." Nixon duly rejected Smith, not simply for her actual lower-class background, but because of her links, in Nixon's view, with all manner of dissolute lower-class black stereotypes—a drunken father, an unkempt house.[63] To function effectively, the symbolic figurehead for any bus boycott in Montgomery needed not only to be far removed from any white stereotypes of black incivility or moral lassitude, but also to be able appeal to, and rally, a number of different constituencies within black Montgomery. Unlike the previous candidates, Rosa Parks was admirably suited to play such a centrifugal role. Her socio-economic position as a seamstress allowed Montgomery's working-class blacks to identify with her easily enough as one of the respectable poor, so frequently venerated in the black press. Virginia Durr, a Southern white liberal for whom Parks worked occasionally, and whose husband Clifford acted as an advisor to boycott attorneys, wrote about the "straitened circumstances" under which the Parks family lived. Rosa Parks "made only twenty-three dollars a week," while her husband, a barber, "was sometimes sick and unemployed." Living in a housing project with her husband and mother, Parks took in extra sewing to supplement her income from her department store job. Working-class blacks also respected Parks's activist credentials. In 1945 she had joined the local NAACP branch—only the third woman in Montgomery to do so—and subsequently served as branch secretary under E.D. Nixon. She founded, and for a while headed, the local NAACP youth chapter, and in the summer of 1955 had attended interracial workshops at Tennessee's Highlander Folk School, a bastion of racial liberalism and civil rights education.[64]

Parks occupied a place within the ranks of the black working-class women who, participants and observers frequently noted, were at the heart of the protest. Notwithstanding the important organizational and leadership roles of Jo Ann Robinson and other members of the Women's Political Council, and of individual women like Johnnie Carr, many rightly saw black domestics as the "backbone of the movement": its foot soldiers.[65] Yet, Montgomery's working-class black women not only had the collective economic power to bring the city and bus company to their knees by means of a boycott, they also wielded considerable power and influence within the social and material economy of many southern white households. In a very real sense, these black women were integral to the middle-class aspirations and pretensions of many white families. Despite the post-war cult of domesticity, many white wives worked outside the home in order to maintain middle-class lifestyles which were defined principally by the preservation of nuclear families and certain patterns of leisure and conspicuous consumption. Cheap black domestic help often made both of these things possible. According to Virginia Durr, when

Montgomery's Mayor Gayle implored white women to stop transporting their maids to and from work in an attempt to undermine the boycott, a "roar of indignation" arose from white women, who were "just furious ... They said, okay, if Tacky Gayle wants to come out here and do my washing and ironing and cleaning and cooking and look after my children, he can do it, but unless he does, I'm going to get Mary or Sally or Suzy."[66]

The national black press used this situation to discredit the claims of white women to some kind of racially superior brand of respectability. White dependency on black house workers was denounced as indicative of a mass white middle-class flight from much vaunted standards of domestic and familial responsibility into a world of self-centered ego-gratification. The *Chicago Defender*, for instance, argued that many white women wanted "release ... from the drudgery of housework and minding babies," used their free time for "garden clubs and other social functions," and had a "general distaste for mops and ironing boards." According to Wilma Dykestra and James Stokely, writing in the *Nation*, the black domestics in Montgomery "knew instinctively that these people might tolerate injustice but never inconvenience."[67]

Montgomery's small but significant professional middle-class black population, could also warm to Rosa Parks. It, too, could admire her political engagement and willingness to take a public stand against the indignities of Jim Crow. But just as crucially, as a consequence of her value-orientation and reputation as a good Christian family woman and upstanding citizen, it could accept her as a sort of honorary member of the middle class, despite the fact that she lacked most of the economic, educational and status indicators by which membership of that class was usually measured. Her age—she was 42 when the boycott began—fused with her gender and impeccable behavior to create an image of a strong, mature, dignified and resourceful women, deserving of respect from all sectors of the black community. In sum, Rosa Parks was a perfect symbol of resistance for the black preachers and professionals in Montgomery, as well as for the black domestics and laborers whose spurning of the buses was at the heart of the protest. That symbolic power flowed from her apparent conformity to pervasive middle-class ideals of chastity, Godliness, family responsibility, and proper womanly conduct and demeanor as codified in America's black and white media.[68]

From the outset, these sterling, thoroughly conventional, qualities were stressed by movement leaders, and by the black press, allowing blacks of all classes throughout the nation to rally around Parks as a symbol of a righteous struggle, properly pursued. At the initial Holt Street Baptist Church meeting, King had praised Parks's civic virtue and respectability for the benefit of an approving black audience who needed little persuasion, but also for a wider public who clearly did. King pointedly described Parks as "one of the finest citizens in Montgomery (Amen)—not one of the finest Negro citizens (That's right), but one of the finest citizens in Montgomery." King continued, "since it had to happen, I'm happy that it happened to a person like Mrs Parks, for nobody can doubt the boundless outreach of her integrity ... nobody can doubt the height of her character ... nobody can doubt the depth of her Christian commitment and devotion to the teachings of Jesus."[69] Emphasizing Parks's respectability in this way helped to throw the injustice of her treatment, and of the Jim Crow system more generally, into stark relief.

Given her respectability, Parks's gender provided additional moral leverage for the boycotters. At the Holt Street meeting, Reverend Edgar French had directly challenged southern white male chivalric pretensions by noting the distinctly ungentlemanly attitude towards Parks. "Mrs Parks was a lady," French insisted, "and any gentleman would allow a lady to have a seat."[70] Such attacks on the avowed chivalry and good manners of southern segregationists were common in a freedom struggle where claims of superior respectability were fiercely contested. In 1949, Al Smith of the *Chicago Defender* had gleefully reported on an encounter between Odis von Blasingame, a black news advertising salesman in Washington, and his new neighbors in a previously all-white block he had just desegregated. When a group of hostile whites came to his house, "Odis, who has a keen sense of humor, refused to talk with them unless they would come inside, let him take their hats and coats and sit down like ladies and gentlemen in his living room. Naturally they wanted to stand on the porch and talk."[71] In the aftermath of *Brown, Ebony* had run a photo editorial asking "Where is Southern Chivalry?," which argued that, for all its protestations of grace, good manners and even dignity in defeat, the region had responded to the Supreme Court's desegregation decision like a "petulant kid." In contrast to this emotionalism and intemperance, blacks "were anxious to sit down at the Conference table and work the problem out intelligently."[72]

In order to reinforce Parks's image of unassailable respectability, movement leaders and the black press consistently downplayed—in fact, rarely mentioned—her involvement with the NAACP or Highlander, whose links with radicals and communists made it an especially sensitive issue in the midst of the Cold War.[73] Indeed, at Holt Street,

Martin Luther King appeared concerned to distance Parks from her own history of political engagement by stressing that she was not "a disturbing factor in the community."[74] Several other leaders, including Edgar French, pointed out that before the boycott, Parks "devoted her extra hours to the affairs of St. Paul AME Church," and described her as "mild-mannered and soft-spoken." Jo Ann Robinson called her a "lady ... [who] was too sweet to even say damn in anger."[75] The black press similarly neglected the more radical implications of mass black female working-class insurgency in favor of an emphasis on middle-class propriety and domesticity. One black newspaper described Parks as "retiring and perfectly poised," and noted that she "doesn't appear to fit the role in which she is now cast."[76] Other published reports referred to her variously as "unassuming," "genteel," "attractive," "soft-spoken," "quiet," and "refined."[77]

In a similar effort to make Parks the militant female activist conform more closely to ideals of female domesticity, while she herself described her position at the Montgomery Fair as "assistant tailor," Martin Luther King and others feminized her job description by calling her a "seamstress." Reverend French further sought to reconcile her work with prevailing middle-class values by insisting that Parks was "a typical American housewife who shared in the support of her household by working as a seamstress in a downtown department store." One boycott supporter described the childless Parks as "attractive and quiet, a churchgoer who looks like the symbol of Mother's Day," while an interviewer for the *Philadelphia Afro-American* even quizzed the mother of the modern black freedom struggle about her favorite dishes to cook.[78]

By emphasizing those aspects of Parks's life which conformed most closely to proper womanly behavior as defined by post-war society, and by deliberately representing other aspects of her life—such as her employment outside the home—in ways which could also be reconciled with those norms, boycott leaders, the black press, and the sympathetic sections of the white press which followed their lead, partially defused, or at least redefined, the full radicalism of Parks's defiance. After all, her bold act of resistance was actually a challenge to the gender expectations of American politics and society in the 1950s, as well as to the racial codes of the South. Yet, it was interpreted primarily as an act of racial, not gender, defiance. While this construction played well for white audiences, it may also help to explain the effectiveness of Rosa Parks as a symbol in black America, particularly among black men, for whom the attainment of the sort of patriarchal power, deference and respect prescribed as normal by middle-class ideologies was always one index of racial progress. Often grappling with the myths of matriarchy which blighted both black and white perceptions of black domestic politics, and afflicted by the very real sense of political, social, economic impotence which mass activism would partially assuage, black men may well have recoiled from supporting a female activist who entirely rejected the domestic values and behavior conventionally assigned to her sex. Rosa Parks was not a militant of that stripe at all. But, in a sense, it was far more significant for the future of both feminism and the black struggle that she should emerge, a powerful and portentous black women activist, from the ranks of those who appeared in most other respects to embody conventional gender roles.

Like Rosa Parks, Martin Luther King, Jr., president of the Montgomery Improvement Association (MIA) and premier spokesman for the bus boycott, was immediately embraced as both a proponent of black activism, and a potent symbol of black aspirations. King was portrayed in the black press as a "symbol of the South's new order," who embodied "the spirit of the New Negro, seeking equal justice under the law in the democratic tradition and Christian spirit."[79] An *Ebony* article reflected on the combination of militancy and respectability which characterized this "New Negro." Confronting intransigent southern whites was "a Negro willing to go hungry if it means his children would attend decent schools, willing to lose his job rather than withdraw his membership from the NAACP, who would rather mortgage his farm than deny himself the right to vote"; someone who would "even be willing to die, if it meant that other Negroes might live in a race-free America." Opposite the text was a full-page photograph of an African American man, dressed in a suit and tie, with smart hat and briefcase, boarding a plane. He does not look homeless, jobless, or hungry. King, hero of the piece, represented the strength and commitment required to fight oppression tirelessly, but through his dress, speech, demeanor, education, and above all his family, he also represented the post-war middle-class respectability necessary to gain support for that fight from a wide range of African Americans and much of the nation at large.[80]

King's election as president of the MIA, just like his appointment to Montgomery's Dexter Avenue Baptist Church a year earlier, reflected the middle-class aspirations of the city's black professionals. According to Taylor Branch, King's predecessor at Dexter, Vernon Johns, had no pretensions to "middle-class respectability." Looking like the "farmer that he was," with "a square head and jaw, flaring nostrils, a barrel chest, and huge hands that he joked were like Virginia hams," Johns promoted self-sufficiency as a means to race advancement. Dexter's congregants, who harbored very different ideas, recoiled at his schemes, which included selling fish from the church basement and watermelons from a truck parked on the Alabama State University campus.[81] The reserved, well-educated King represented for Dexter patrons, 95 per cent of whom numbered among the city's black professional class, the more respectable middle-class image they wanted to portray.[82]

E.D. Nixon had been Montgomery's most influential black activist for many years, and in many ways he, rather than the newcomer King—who in his brief time in Montgomery had shown a marked lack of interest in political activity, and had earlier declined an invitation to become president of the NAACP—was the obvious choice to head the MIA. Yet Nixon lacked the charisma, quite possibly the diplomatic skills, and certainly the conventional forms of respectability necessary to unite Montgomery's factionalized black community into a coherent mass movement. "Mr Nixon was a hardworking man, a fine leader and everything," recalled MIA stalwart Mrs Johnnie Carr, "but he [didn't] have that thing that could weld people together in a movement like ours."[83] His bluff manner and obvious impatience with the protocols of middle-class behavior in his fight for racial justice, was anathema to the college-educated black clerics, professionals and elites who formed the core of the MIA's leadership. It also meant that Nixon, who at one point was referred to even in the black press as "a hulking, rough-hewn Pullman porter," was more vulnerable than other black leaders to white propaganda and criticism. Grover Hall, the editor-in-chief of the *Montgomery Advertiser*, at one point attempted to discredit the boycott, merely by pointing out the under-educated and intemperate Nixon's pivotal role in "uncorking" it. The admittedly "courageous" Nixon was described by Hall as a "fuming white-hater" and "a veteran of the street-fighting, pre-revolutionary days before Dr. King had earned his degree of doctor in systematic theology."[84]

By contrast with Nixon, as David Garrow has noted, King "was extremely well educated and an articulate speaker. Those qualities appealed strongly to the wealthier, professional segment of the black community, people who otherwise might be ambivalent about the conditions on public buses that they rarely patronized."[85] Those same qualities were repeatedly emphasized in the black press coverage of King and the boycott. In an *Ebony* profile, Lerone Bennett described King as "A third generation Baptist preacher, well read in philosophy and psychology ... a short, stocky intellectual who quotes Hegel, Kant and Louis Jordan with equal ease." The reference to the popular black jump 'n' jazz jester Louis Jordan alongside the intellectual heavyweights Hegel and Kant was highly significant. Part of King's genius as a civil rights leader was his extraordinary capacity to fuse religion, deep-learning, respectability and good strategic sense, with a folk-pulpit sensibility to create a rhetoric which transcended class and educational divisions in the black community, and inspired all those who "reached out to touch the threads of his faultlessly tailored suit"—the raiments of his respectability.[86]

Even the most celebrated tactic to emerge during the boycott—nonviolent direct action—revealed black efforts to conform to ideals of middle-class respectability. Following the bombing of King's and Nixon's homes, and again during the mass arrests under the state's anti-boycott law, MIA leaders demonstrated a restraint and dignity in the face of extreme provocation which surprised white America and helped to sway opinion to their cause. The nonviolence and orderliness of the protest, which a *Washington Post* account called "impeccably lawful, orderly, [and] dignified," belied pro-segregationist arguments that African Americans were purely instinctual beings, lacking the capacity for level-headed thought or restraint, and proved "especially gal[ling]" to white Montgomery. Restraint, order, and propriety were hallmarks of post-war middle-class respectability, and they proved powerful weapons for gaining public support.[87]

The proceedings of *The State of Alabama vs Martin Luther King, Jr.* also illustrated the extent to which middle-class respectability, including proper gender roles, acted as both a goal and a tactic for the MIA. "Some 20" black witnesses "marched to the stand," one article reported: "school teachers, washer-women, ministers, school children, store clerks, employed and unemployed, widows, persons polished of speech, the inarticulate, the placid, the resentful, the angry and the tolerant."[88] As a group, the evidence they presented, not only through their words, but also by their carriage and appearance, revealed the "New Negro" capable and deserving of respect based on dominant middle-class standards of patriotism, propriety, and proper gender roles. Judge Eugene Carter, who presided over the trial, betrayed prevailing white views of southern blacks when he "repeatedly warned the crowded courtroom" to remain quiet. "This is no vaudeville," he admonished, "If you came in to be entertained, you're in the wrong place."[89] As one press account noted, the judge was "learned, polished, a Harvard graduate, and far more polished than a bus driver." And yet, the judge was admonished for retaining a paternalistic attitude no longer appropriate for Montgomery's "new Negroes," and giving the "impression that he regards the colored people in his court room as wayward children."[90]

Protesting this patronizing attitude in the courtroom and on the buses, defense witnesses complained of not only being called "apes" and "niggers" but also "boy" and "girl." When asked by lawyers how bus drivers addressed black riders, Mrs Odessa Williams replied, "I never heard a bus driver call no Negro Mr or Mrs; I never heard that ... I heard 'Girl,' 'Boy,' or 'Nigger.'" Louise Osborne described bus drivers yelling at black passengers for being too loud, screaming, "'Baby' or 'Honey' or 'Son,' ... if you don't all shut up I will put you all off." In a particularly poignant episode, one male witness described how a bus driver called him "nigger" in front of a busload of white schoolchildren. The trial revealed that the complaints of Montgomery's black bus patrons went far beyond any particular seating arrangement, with the southern custom of treating all blacks like "wayward children" emerging as perhaps the most grievously felt indignity.[91]

The paternalistic admonitions of Judge Carter contrasted sharply with the images of black defense witnesses and spectators presented in the African American press. Despite the implications of Judge Carter's warning, journalist Charles Loeb insisted that "Negro spectators, witnesses and defendants were well-behaved and amazingly unperturbed." The same writer later noted that among the black witnesses and spectators, "hair was well-groomed, apparel selected with an eye to crease and cleanliness, and backs were straight and heads up."[92] Throughout the boycott, supportive press accounts repeatedly commented favorably on the sartorial appearance of the participants: King's dress was "nattily collegiate," Thelma Glass was "smartly attired," Rosa Parks "wears smartly tailored suits." When the *Chicago Defender* reported the comments of a defiant Montgomery black woman that, "there is just no way in the world that they can make us ride the buses," it was careful to note that she was "well-dressed."[93] Through their poise and appearance, the defense witnesses—wealthy or poor, formally educated or not—evinced middle-class respectability and thereby articulated their claim to full membership in America's public life.

Press articles repeatedly contrasted the "New Negro" with the disreputable past that he or she was leaving behind. According to the *Cleveland Call & Post,* the only "light note" of the trial was when three black witnesses testified on behalf of the prosecution. The state had hoped that the testimony of Willie Carter, Ernest Smith, and Mrs Beatrice Jackson would "establish that Negroes who persisted in riding the buses after December 5 were subjected to threats and intimidation." While the article mocked Carter's testimony (he claimed to have been threatened and assaulted for riding a bus but could not identify the perpetrator), it also mocked Smith—"clad in overalls"—and Jackson—"a huge, unkempt woman"—for their appearance.[94] Jeanetta Reese also appeared in black press accounts as the epitome of the old disreputable order. An original plaintiff in Parks's federal case, Reese had recanted, prompting white officials to charge black attorney Fred Gray with misrepresenting a client. According to James Booker in the *Amsterdam News*, Reese arrived at King's trial "in typical fashion" just "like the old order to which she is desperately trying to cling." Reese had "got the aid of a sheriff whom she once worked for to let her in the back door," and "came dressed in a neatly-pressed blue domestic's uniform, with a white apron." It was duly noted that "Every other Negro in the courtroom, except for one state witness in overalls, was wearing his Sunday best." Reese—whose profane insistence that she was "damned mad" about the boycott, contrasted vividly with Rosa Parks's chaste mouth—and the other prosecution witnesses provided perfect foils to the black press's depiction of the "well-groomed" defense witnesses, the new respectable negroes, who were making their dignified appeals for justice.[95]

Defense witnesses reserved their most scathing attacks on segregation for its effects on black family life. The male-headed nuclear family was revered as the pinnacle of Cold War middle-class respectability, and many pro-segregationist arguments cited the instability of black families, particularly high rates of illegitimacy and female-headed households, as evidence that blacks had inferior morals. Montgomery's blacks responded by affirming their commitment to middle-class ideals of respectable family life, while denouncing segregation as antithetical to the attainment of those ideals. Testimony from MIA witnesses repeatedly noted the ways in which bus segregation had challenged the sanctity of the family and made it difficult for black women to discharge their proper maternal and domestic responsibilities. Sadie Brooks described "women with babies in their arms" having to stand over empty seats, and violence to pregnant women figured prominently in the testimony. Joseph Allen described an incident in November 1955: "I was trying to help a pregnant woman off the bus with her heavy packages, when the driver impatiently drove off before she could get both feet on the ground. She stumbled and fell." Richard Jordan described the situation faced by his pregnant wife: "The driver would yell out at negroes to get back in the bus, and swear out in public, 'damn, dumb Negro,'" and would "race and swear and slam on the brakes, and had everybody upset on the bus." Most national press accounts noted the power of defense witness testimony, which told of men and women, young and old, pregnant and elderly, facing indignity and potential violence every time they rode a segregated bus.[96]

During the boycott, every effort was made to ensure that the King family took on iconographic significance as the epitome of middle-class family life. Press coverage during the boycott focused on King's attempts to maintain his patriarchal role at the head of a loving, supportive family in the midst of craven white harassment, real and threatened violence, and a crushing work schedule. Similarly, it was vital that the musically talented and politically engaged Coretta was also seen to fulfill her assigned female role as mother and homemaker. Pausing before an important meeting, the press carefully reported how King "greeted his lovely wife Coretta affectionately" and "asked about his seven-weeks old daughter, Denise Yolanda." After King's trial, a picture of the "attractive Mrs Coretta King as she kissed her husband affectionately on the cheek" became a staple photo in African American newspapers. The Kings were revealed as models not just of activism, but of refinement and cultivation. Even when describing King's visit to discuss the racial situation with Georgia's segregationist senator Eugene Talmadge, *Ebony* was sure to note that he traveled with Coretta, and that en route they listened to "Saturday afternoon opera on the car radio"—none of that dubious rock and roll for the respectable King family.[97]

Family stability and good citizenship, hallmarks of postwar middle-class respectability, converged in King's defense of black protest against Jim Crow in Montgomery. At his trial, he argued that economic, political, and social oppression had conspired to deprive southern blacks of an opportunity to meet middle-class standards of consumption, behavior, and home life. According to King, "our most fundamental social unit—the family" was "tortured, corrupted, and weakened by economic insufficiency." "When a Negro man is inadequately paid," King wrote later in his account of the boycott, "his wife must work to provide the simple necessities for the children." In a statement reminiscent of those made by numerous psychologists and columnists in hundreds of post-war periodicals, King argued that "when a mother has to work she does violence to motherhood by depriving her children of her loving guidance and protection."[98]

The veneration of the King family continued after the boycott, as entertainer-activist Harry Belafonte maintained secret payments to the family for domestics and nannies to make sure that the King family home was a model of neatness and decorum whenever the press called. When *Ebony* visited for one of many picture spreads, it revealed Coretta, a "stunningly attractive young woman," in domestic bliss, dressing her children and preparing a meal. Other captions described her serving "punch and cookies" while "entertaining young matrons of

Dexter Avenue Baptist Church" and consulting with an "early-morning caller" discussing a "family problem." Mrs King, the article assured readers, had advised her troubled visitor "to return to her husband," thereby restoring the patriarchal nuclear family to its proper glory.[99]

When an all-white jury predictably convicted King of conspiracy to boycott, the disappointing legal outcome of the trial paled into insignificance next to the opportunity it had given Montgomery's blacks—those who formally testified and those who took advantage of the unprecedented influx of press attention—to show the nation that they fully embraced the ideals of middle-class respectability. As a consequence, it was more often the protesters, rather than the southern segregationists, who appeared to the nation as the true followers of "The American Way"; as the guardians of American domestic ideals and even proper gender roles. An editorial in the *Arkansas State Press* neatly summarized the magnitude of this achievement, noting after the victorious conclusion of the protest in December 1956, that the boycotters had won both "from a moral and financial standpoint," and gained "a new dignity throughout the world."[100] They had also conclusively proved the value of respectability as both a tactic and a rallying point for civil rights activities in the South, where it would play a conspicuous role.

Notes

1. This advice was given to black students Vivian Malone and James Hood in June 1963, when they were being briefed prior to their attempt to register for classes at the previously segregated University of Alabama at Tuscaloosa.

2. *Time*, February 22, 1960, cited in Richard Lentz, *Symbols, The News Magazines and Martin Luther King* (Baton Rouge: Louisiana State Press, 1991), 45.

3. *Richmond News Leader*, editorial, February 22, 1960, cited in Clayborne Carson et al., eds., *The Papers of Martin Luther King, Jr.: Volume 3: Birth of a New Age* (Berkeley: University of California Press, 1994), 14.

4. The stories of Sammy Dean Parker and Elizabeth Eckford, and the symbolic resonances of this famous photograph are described by Pete Daniel, "Bibles and Bayonets: The Little Rock Central High School Crisis," paper presented at University of Newcastle upon Tyne, December 1, 1997.

5. For more on the ways in which King appealed to American civic ideals in his rhetoric, see Keith Miller and Emily Lewis, "Touchstones, Authorities, and Maria Anderson: The Making of 'I Have A Dream'," in Brian Ward and Tony Badger, eds., *The Making of Martin Luther King and the Civil Rights Movement* (London: Macmillan, 1996), 147-161.

6. An excellent example of this pattern can be seen in Jonathan Glassman's account of slavery in North Africa. See Jonathan Glassman, "The Bondsman's New Clothes: The Contradictory Consciousness of Slave Resistance," *Journal of African History* 32 (1991): 277-288.

7. W.E.B. Du Bois, *The Souls of Black Folk* (Chicago: A.C. McClurg, 1909), 3-5.

8. Eugene Genovese, *Roll, Jordan, Roll: The World the Slaves Made* (New York: Vintage, 1976), 471.

9. Barbara Welke, "When All Women Were White, And All the Blacks Were Men: Gender, Race and the Road to Plessy, 1855 – 1914," *Law and History Review* 13 (1995): 261-316.

10. Booker T. Washington, quoted in E. Franklin Frazier, *Black Bourgeoisie* (Glencoe, IL: Free Press, 1957), 192.

11. Gregory Mixon, "'Good Negro – Bad Negro': The Dynamics of Race and Class in Atlanta during the Era of the 1906 Riot," *Georgia Historical Quarterly* LXXI (3), 1997: 593-621.

12. Kevin Gaines, *Uplifting the Race: Black Leadership, Politics, and Culture in the Twentieth Century* (Chapel Hill: University of North Carolina Press, 1996).

13. Glenda Elizabeth Gilmore, *Gender and Jim Crow: Women and the Politics of White Supremacy in North Carolina, 1896 – 1920* (Chapel Hill: University of North Carolina Press, 1996).

14. This argument builds on Nancy MacLean's insight that "American ideas of middle-class standing and citizenship rights were coded in racially exclusive ways. So, too, was American middle-class consciousness molded and galvanized, from its very origins, by notions of appropriate gender roles and moral respectability." Nancy MacLean, *Behind The Mask of Chivalry: The Making of the Second Ku Klux Klan* (New York: Oxford University Press, 1994), 187.

15. Frazier, *Black Bourgeoisie*, 27-8.

16. Frazier, *Black Bourgeoisie*, 146-161, 326. The white *Ebony* editor, Ben Burns, broadly shared Frazier's assessment, insisting that in the 1950s, "*Ebony* was never even close to the forefront of the movement and paid only lip service to the achievements of the militants who were challenging the racial status quo." Instead, the magazine served up an endless diet of black achievements and exemplars of respectable behavior. See Ben Burns, *Nitty Gritty: A White Editor in Black Journalism* (Jackson: University of Mississippi Press, 1996), 109.

17. *Chicago Defender*, May 7, 1949, 26.

18. "Things That Interest Women," *Arkansas State Press,* June 2, 1950, 3.

19. "Should You Fear The Other Woman?" *Tan*, May, 1958, 9.

20. "What To Do When Your Mate Cheats," *Tan*, May, 1960, 12.

21. Franklin Fosdick, "How To Stay Happily Married," *Negro Digest*, October, 1950, 8.

22. bell hooks, *Ain't I A Woman? Black Women and Feminism* (Boston: South End Press, 1981), 71-86; Joyce Ladner, *Tomorrow's Tomorrow: The Black Woman* (Garden City, NY: Anchor, 1972), 30-35; Brenda Stevenson, *Life in Black and White: Family and Community in the Slave South* (New York: Oxford University Press, 1996), 206, 286-319.

23. "Chained To Him Forever," *Tan*, August, 1959, 72.

24. Hazel Scott, quoted in "I Have Love and My Career," *Tan*, April, 1954, 22, 23, 67.

25. "Little Rock Women Organize to Support Loy for Mayor," *Arkansas State Press*, July 20, 1951, 1.

26. "Modern Home - Harmony in Musician's Home," *Tan*, July, 1954, 38.

27. Joanne Meyerowitz, "Beyond the Feminine Mystique: A Reassessment of Postwar Mass Culture, 1946 – 1960," in Meyerowitz, ed., *Not June Cleaver: Women and Gender in Postwar America 1945 – 1960* (Philadelphia: Philadelphia University Press, 1994); Susan Lynn, *Progressive Women in Conservative Lives: Racial Justice, Peace, and Feminism, 1945 to the 1960s* (New Brunswick: Rutgers University Press, 1992).

28. *Chicago Defender*, January 1, 1949, 12.

29. Dr. Edward Beasley, "Child Care," *Tan*, November, 1953, 44-5.

30. "The Dominoes: Bully Ward And His Frenetic All Bachelor Quintet Shatter Top Box Office Records From Coast To Coast," *Ebony*, February, 1954, 23-4.

31. "How I Discovered Joe Louis," *Ebony*, October, 1954, 64.

32. William Earl Berry, "Popular Press as Symbolic Interactionism: A Socio-Cultural Analysis of *Ebony*, 1945 – 1975," Ph.D. dissertation, University of Illinois, 1978, 43.

33. "Your Help Is Needed," *Chicago Defender*, May 7, 1949, 6.

34. "I Tried To Hide My Past," *Tan*, May, 1961, 25.

35. "Ethel Meets Boy Made Immortal By U.S Supreme Court Decision," *Chicago Defender*, May 29, 1954, 12.

36. See, for example, Era Bell Thompson, "Girl Gangs Of Harlem," *Negro Digest*, March, 1951, 40.

37. The complex links between the gentrification of Rhythm and Blues music, changes in mass black consciousness after the Second World War, and the emergence of a mass white audience for—and of a diverse opposition to—rock and roll music, are discussed in Brian Ward, *Just My Soul Responding: Rhythm and Blues, Black Consciousness and Race Relations* (Berkeley/London: University of California Press/UCL Press, 1998), 40-42, 71-122, 146-159.

38. John Jackson, *Big Beat Heat: Alan Freed and the Early Years of Rock and Roll* (New York: Schirmer, 1991), 78.

39. For the "Broadcasters' Creed," see *Broadcasting Yearbook*, January 19, 1953, 31-3. For the Houston Commission, see Arnold Shaw, *Honkers and Shouters* (New York: Macmillan, 1978), xxiv-xxv; Lynn Martin and Kerry Seagrave, *Anti-rock; The Opposition to Rock 'n' Roll* (Hambden, CT: Archon, 1988), 23-24.

40. Martin Luther King, "Advice For Living," *Ebony*, April, 1958, 104.

41. Ward, *Just My Soul*, 150-151.

42. *Carolina Times*, (Afro Magazine Section), November 16, 1957, 10.

43. Jane Walters, "Teen Talk," *Tan*, May, 1954, 14.

44. "The Most Dangerous Time Of Your Marriage," *Tan*, November, 1959, 10.

45. "Too Easy with Men," *Tan*, July, 1954, 55.

46. Bernice Johnson Reagon interview with Brian Ward, January 24, 1996, University of Newcastle Oral History Collection (hereafter, UNOHC).

47. The relationship between enduring black female ideals of conventional domesticity and the female black experience in the 1950s and early 1960s is discussed in Ward, *Just My Soul*, 1998, 153-9.

48. *Arkansas State Press*, March 18, 1955, 8.

49. *Arkansas State Press,* February 24, 1950, 3.

50. "Your Stars And Numbers," *Tan*, October, 1954, 12.

51. Martin Luther King, Jr., *Stride Toward Freedom: The Montgomery Story* (New York: Harper, 1958), 63; Ralph D. Abernathy, "The Natural History of a Social Movement: The Montgomery Improvement Association" in David Garrow, ed., *The Walking City: The Montgomery Bus Boycott, 1955-1956* (Brooklyn, NY: Carlson Publishing, 1989), 124.

52. Taylor Branch, *Parting the Waters: America in the King Years, 1954 – 1963* (New York: Simon and Schuster, 1988), 120-123; Thomas J. Gilliam "The Montgomery Bus Boycott of 1955-56" in Garrow, ed., *Walking City*, 124; Jo Ann Robinson, *The Montgomery Bus Boycott and the Women Who Started It* (Knoxville: University of Tennessee Press, 1987), 17; John White, "'Nixon was the One': Edgar Daniel Nixon, The MIA and the Montgomery Bus Boycott" in Ward and Badger, *The Making of Martin Luther King*, 49.

53. Dorothy Schiff, "Looking and Listening," *Crisis*, 63 (3), March, 1956, 155.

54. Howard Shuttle, "Scandal of the Century! Facts of 'Nations Model Schools' Shocks America," *The Citizens' Council*, November 3, 1956, 3. Clyde Sellers, quoted in S. Heron, "Southern Negro or Northern Liberal?," *Christian Century*, June 20, 1956, 744. For links between anti-communist rhetoric and segregationist fears of miscegenation, see John Barlow Martin, *The Deep South Says "Never"* (Westport, CT.: Negro Universities Press, 1957), 57; James Graham Cook, *The Segregationists* (New York: Appleton-Century

Crofts, 1962), 62 and Neil R. McMillen, *The Citizens' Councils Organized Resistance to the Second Reconstruction 1954 – 1964* (Chicago: University of Illinois Press, 1971), 71.

55. Jack Crenshaw, in Gilliam, "The Montgomery Bus Boycott," 283-4. See also Rosa Parks, *Rosa Parks: My Story*, (New York: Dial Books, 1992), 110-111.

56. Parks, *My Story*, 1992, 110-111.

57. Parks, *My Story*, 1992, 110-111.

58. King, *Stride*, 41; Parks, *My Story*, 112; Robinson, *Montgomery*, 17, 37-39, 41-43; White, "Nixon was the One," 49.

59. Preston Valien, "The Montgomery Bus Protest as a Social Movement" in Garrow, ed., *Walking City*, 86; Lamont H. Yeakey, "The Montgomery Alabama Bus Boycott, 1955-56," Ph.D. dissertation, Columbia University, 1979, 240-243.

60. Anonymous witness, quoted in "A Difficult Assignment Well Handled," *Montgomery Advertiser*, March 6, 1955, 4A.

61. Paula Giddings, *When and Where I Enter: The Impact of Black Women on Race and Sex in America* (New York: Bantam, 1984), 31.

62. "The Truth Is Painful," *The Citizens' Councils*, 1(5), February, 1956, 2; see, also, "Disease, Prison Record Reflect Lapse in Morals," *The Citizens' Councils* 1(6), March, 1956, 1.

63. E.D. Nixon, quoted in Steven M. Millner, "The Montgomery Bus Boycott: A Case Study in the Emergence and Career of a Social Movement" in Garrow, ed., *Walking City*, 546.

64. Virginia Durr, *Outside the Magic Circle: The Autobiography of Virginia Foster Durr* (Tuscaloosa: University of Alabama Press, 1985), 278; Parks, *My Story*, 94-105.

65. See, "Boycotters Say 'Buses Can Rot'," *Chicago Defender*, May 26, 1956, 18. See also, Wilma Dykeman and James Stokely, "Montgomery Morning," *Nation*, 1957, 12.

66. Durr, *Outside the Magic Circle*, 1985, 282; "Free Rides End Asked By Mayor In Bus Boycott," *Alabama Journal*, January 25, 1956, 1. See also, Ted Poston, "Boycott Capital Can Not Do Without Servants," *Philadelphia Afro-American*, (Magazine), August 11, 1956, 5.

67. "Boycotters Say 'Buses Can Rot'," *Chicago Defender*, May 26, 1956, 18.

68. Parks's ability to symbolically straddle the divide between classes in black Montgomery is also discussed in Millner, *Voice*, 441.

69. Martin Luther King, Jr, "MIA Meeting At Holt Street Baptist Church," December 5, 1955, in Carson et al, eds., *Birth of a New Age*, 72.

70. Edgar N. French, "Beginnings of a New Age" in Glenford E. Mitchell and William H. Peace III, eds., *The Angry Black South: Southern Negroes Tell Their Own Story* (New York: Corinth Books, 1962), 75.

71. Al Smith, "Adventures in Race Relations," *Chicago Defender*, May 14, 1949, 7.

72. "Where Is Southern Chivalry?" *Ebony*, December, 1954, 118.

73. Joanne Meyerowitz's study of media presentations of women in the postwar period, singles out the African American press for its particularly strong celebration of women's political and economic activism. However, as has been shown, African American newspapers and magazines during this period reveal a preoccupation with "respectable," middle-class standards of appearance, behavior, and gender roles. The depiction of Parks conformed to this pattern whereby even politically or professionally active women were often described in terms of their feminine charms and domestic proclivities. See, Meyerowitz, "Beyond the Feminine".

74. King, "MIA Meeting," in Carson, *Birth*, 72.

75. French, "Beginnings," 34 and 5. Jo Ann Robinson, quoted in Millner, "Bus Boycott," 541.

76. Al Sweeny, "A White Man Took My Seat ..." *Philadelphia Afro-American*, March 3, 1956, 7.

77. Inez J. Baskin, "The Montgomery Bus Strike," *Crisis*, 63(3) March, 1956, 7; Evelyn Cunningham, "'More Determined Than Ever': Fight For Freedom Goes On,"

Pittsburgh Courier, March 3, 1956, 3; Ethel Payne, "Link Ala. Bus Boycott to Gandhi's Technique," *Chicago Defender,* February 18, 1956, 1.
   78. See French, "Beginnings," 33; L.D. Reddick, "The Bus Boycott in Montgomery" in Garrow, *Walking City,* 70; Sweeney, "A White Man," 7.
   79. James Booker, "Who Is Martin Luther King?" *Amsterdam News,* March 31, 1956, 2; "Montgomery Bus Boycott Leader Cited By Fisk Alumni," *Philadelphia Afro-American,* July 9, 1956, 10.
   80. "A Brand New Negro," *Ebony,* July, 1956, 70-1.
   81. Branch, *Parting the Waters,* 8, 17-18.
   82. See Lerone Bennett, "The King Plan For Freedom," *Ebony,* July, 1956, 68.
   83. Mrs Johnnie Carr, quoted in Millner, "Bus Boycott," 530.
   84. Grover C. Hall, quoted in "Alabama's Bus Boycott: What It's All About," *U.S. News and World Report,* August, 1956, 84.
   85. Garrow, *Walking City,* 20
   86. Bennett, "King's Plan," 65. See Keith Miller, *Voice of Deliverance: The Language of Martin Luther King and Its Sources* (New York: Free Press, 1992).
   87. *Washington Post* editorial, cited in "U.S. Editors Are Saying," *Montgomery Advertiser,* February 27, 1956; "The Montgomery Boycott," *Nation,* February 11, 1956, 102.
   88. Charles Loeb, "Alabama Bus Boycotters Get Chance To Tell Nation, World of Wrongs," *Philadelphia Afro-American,* March 31, 1956, 11.
   89. Judge Carter, quoted in Tom Johnson and Frank McArdle, "Records of Association Reveal Thousands Spent To Support Bus Boycott," *Montgomery Advertiser,* March 20, 1956, 1.
   90. Charles Loeb, "Legal Dual In Bus Trial Affecting Alabama Mores," *Philadelphia Afro-American,* March 24, 1956, 8.
   91. See *The State of Alabama vs M.L. King Jr., et al,* Vio. Sec. 54, title 14, 1040 Code of Alabama, Circuit Court of Montgomery, Alabama (Alabama Department of History and Archives, Montgomery), 440, 476, 482.
   92. Charles Loeb, "Courtroom Highlights In Montgomery Trial," *Cleveland Call & Post,* March 24, 1956, 3A; Charles Loeb, "Convict Rev. King, Bus Boycott Continues," *Cleveland Call & Post,* March 24, 1956, 2A.
   93. Alfred Maund, "We Will All Stand Together," *The Nation,* March 3, 1956, inside cover; Loeb, "Alabama Bus Boycotters"; and "Arrests Fail To Halt Ala. Bus Boycott," *Chicago Defender,* February 22, 1956, 1.
   94. Charles Loeb, "Rev. King Is Target Of Montgomery Trial," *Cleveland Call & Post,* March 24, 1956, A1-2.
   95. James Booker, "Most Pathetic Woman In Alabama: 'So Damn Mad'," *Amsterdam News,* March 31, 1956, 1.
   96. *Alabama vs King,* 197-8, 363, 366.
   97. "The South And The Negro," *Ebony,* April, 1957, 77.
   98. King, *Stride,* 203, 223
   99. "The Woman Behind The Man," *Ebony,* (January 1959), 37. Harry Belafonte, interview with Brian Ward, March 12, 1996, UNOHC.
   100. S.S. Taylor, "Editorial," *Arkansas State Press,* December 30, 1956, 4.

CHAPTER 4

Gender and Generation: Manhood at the Southern Christian Leadership Conference

Peter J. Ling

The Three Sins of SCLC

Students of the Southern Christian Leadership Conference (SCLC) have viewed three aspects of the organization from a gendered perspective. First, they have noted the clash between the male ministers and Miss Ella Baker that culminated in her departure and subsequent mentorship of the Student Non-violent Coordinating Committee (SNCC) in 1960.[1] Secondly, they have related how J. Edgar Hoover's Federal Bureau of Investigation (FBI) used its knowledge of Dr. Martin Luther King, Jr.'s extra-marital relations to try to discredit him as a public figure.[2] Thirdly, biographers have stressed the volatile, competitive character of relations within Dr. King's inner circle of male associates, referring frequently to the clash of egos and bawdy "macho" style of its deliberations.[3] Taken together, these issues have branded SCLC as a highly male chauvinist organization. By comparison, the older civil rights bodies—the National Association for the Advancement of Colored People (NAACP) and the National Urban League—have not faced the charge of sexism to anything like the same extent. Even SCLC's rivals in terms of direct action campaigns, the Congress of Racial Equality (CORE) and SNCC, have faced less criticism, a key exception being their joint efforts to recruit female volunteers for the Mississippi Freedom Summer campaign of 1964 which had clear sexist elements.[4] Feminist attention has focused more on SNCC than CORE because women working within the former drafted a now famous memorandum on the role of women in the movement.[5] However, the male chauvinism detected in SNCC men is commonly seen as typical of its time while the organization itself, because of its principles of participatory democracy, is remembered as progressive in its attitude to women, at least until 1966.[6]

In this essay, I want to reprise these three issues. I will also consider other aspects of gender relations at SCLC that are revealed by a close consideration of the work of the Reverend Andrew Young. Of Dr. King's senior associates—Ralph Abernathy, James Bevel, Jesse Jackson, Bernard Lee, Wyatt Tee Walker, Hosea Williams—Young has offered the most thoughtful reflections on his time at SCLC.[7] A critical examination of his autobiographical account therefore provides fresh insights into the complexities of gender relations at SCLC.

The Rejection of Miss Baker

> I was old enough to be the mother of the leadership.
> The combination of the basic attitude of men, and
> especially ministers, as to what the role of women in their
> church setups is—that of taking orders, not providing
> leadership—and the ego that is involved—the ego
> problems involved in having to feel that here is someone
> who had the capacity for leadership and, certainly, had
> more information about a lot of things than they
> possessed at that time—this would never had (sic) lent
> itself to my being a leader in the movement there.
>
> Ella Baker[8]

The SCLC grew out of a succession of meetings in early 1957 designed to sustain and expand the momentum of nonviolent protest against segregation in the South. Derived from the bus boycotts in Montgomery and elsewhere, it was originally titled the Southern Leadership Conference on Transportation and Non-Violent Integration. A key advisor to Dr. King by this time was Bayard Rustin, despite the fact that aspects of his background could be exploited by enemies of the movement. Forty-five years old in 1956 and a striking figure, Rustin had joined the Young Communist League in 1938 while at college in New York. The pacifist convictions of his Quaker upbringing led him to serve a prison term for draft resistance during World War Two. Completing a list of "dangerous characteristics" for the America of the McCarthyite era, Rustin had been convicted of gross indecency with two other men in a parked car in 1953.[9] Thus, King's leading advisor on nonviolence could have been portrayed to mainstream America as black, "Red," "unpatriotic," and "queer."[10]

Rustin introduced King to a New York associate, Miss Ella Baker. An established African American activist, she had been director of branches for the NAACP during its rapid wartime expansion. At the

NAACP, Baker had pressed branches to be more active locally rather than relying on the NAACP to advance the cause of racial equality exclusively by litigation and lobbying. Elected president of the NAACP's New York branch, she re-located its office to "where it would be more visible to the Harlem community."[11] The fifty-three year old Miss Baker agreed with Rustin that the Montgomery campaign suggested that a new phase of community activism had begun. To support such activism against retaliatory violence and intimidation, Baker and Stanley Levison established the organization In Friendship in 1956.[12] A successful white New York businessman, Levison had had direct ties to the Communist Party. Rather than abstract Marxist analysis, however, he offered King what he described as the skills acquired "in the commercial jungle where more violence in varied forms occurs daily than is found on many a battlefront." He wanted to turn these male-coded traits against the culture that celebrated them.[13]

The more secular New York trio represented a different generation of activism from that of King and his southern activist preacher colleagues. The Great Depression framed the older group's ideas of politics and justice. They shared a left-wing politics linked to the rise of industrial unionism in the US, and a critique of the business civilization that had celebrated how strong, ingenious, entrepreneurial men battled for supremacy in the capitalist marketplace. During the Depression too many strong and ingenious men had been brought down by unemployment and financial collapse. King's generation had its views shaped more sharply by World War Two. Their militancy drew on the democratic creed that America espoused in its struggle with the Axis powers, and on the renewed determination of African Americans to assert their rights within the republic for which they fought. Often too young to have fought themselves, King and his contemporaries felt nonetheless what is now clearly a gendered potency of the soldier-citizen ideal to which black veterans appealed.

No one would dispute the claim that Miss Baker was poorly treated at SCLC. Her expertise and energy kept the fledgling organization going between 1957 and 1960. However, when Baker left SCLC, it was not the first time that she had left a civil rights organization in disgust. On Valentine's Day 1941, the NAACP announced her appointment as an assistant to the deputy director of branches, Mrs Daisy Lampkin. Baker was to tour the nation assisting with branch membership drives. Barely a month into her new post, she reported to Roy Wilkins on the drive in Birmingham, Alabama, one of the NAACP's southern flagships. The drive's leader, Reverend Goodgame of Sixth Street Baptist church was "all preacher," according to Baker, "but unlike most of them, he knows that it takes work to produce and he will work." At the end of her stay, Baker was confident that she had deepened interest in the branch's work. "The ministers were put on the spot," she reported with satisfaction, "and had to commit themselves to more definite support." Similarly, in a later report from Jacksonville, Florida, Baker grumbled that she had been trying to get ministers to devote at least part of one Sunday service a month to civic matters.[14] By this standard, Martin Luther King, Jr.—one of whose first actions at Dexter Avenue Baptist church in 1955 was to establish a political action committee—was far better than the average black minister, a fact confirmed by his later troubles with the National Baptist Convention.[15] However, Ella Baker was never entirely satisfied with the contribution of the clergy to local activism.

In April 1943, without bothering to consult Baker herself, the NAACP executive announced that she would succeed William Pickens as director of branches. Despite misgivings, Baker took the job and was soon pressing the committee on branches to seek vigorously "to transform local branches into centers of sustained and dynamic community leadership." Addressing the national convention in 1943, she recommended the tactic of developing neighborhood units that had boosted membership in Birmingham, presumably with the help of ministers who would actually work. These grassroots units, she explained, had meant that "you have more people participating in branch work and you are able to contact more persons who perhaps will never get to the general branch meeting but will attend little neighborhood meetings." She reminded delegates that the branches' work was "in the final analysis the lifeblood of the Association," and urged them to ensure that their own branch was geared to local needs. "Any branch which says it has nothing around which it can build a program," she complained, "is simply too lazy to concern itself with things on its own doorstep." To implement her strategy, Baker organized Regional Leadership Training Conferences "to instruct local workers in methods of attacking local problems and promoting an efficient program in their community." When Baker resigned in May 1946 with angry recriminations towards the NAACP executive for its high-handedness and undemocratic tendencies, Roy Wilkins in a lukewarm tribute singled out these conferences "as a distinct contribution to the NAACP's effectiveness."[16]

Following the NAACP's argument that an increasing black vote would secure and extend legal victories, the right to vote became a stated priority of the early SCLC. King's speech to the Prayer Pilgrimage in 1957 stressed the potential power of black ballots and

SCLC announced an ambitious Crusade for Citizenship in 1958.[17] Baker was enthusiastic about the latter campaign because it required the kind of mass participation that could draw the people into direct engagement with the system that oppressed them. In October 1959, she vented her frustration at SCLC's failure to nurture mass participation. She stressed that it needed to "provide for a sense of achievement and recognition for many people, particularly local leadership."[18] To Baker's dismay, the SCLC sought recognition primarily of the leadership of Dr. King and of the ministers who led the various SCLC affiliates. Alongside King at SCLC before 1960 were other Baptist preachers, such as his Montgomery colleague, Reverend Ralph Abernathy, Reverend Fred Shuttlesworth of Birmingham, and Reverend C.K. Steele of Tallahassee. All four shared an egotism that at least matched their considerable courage and populist sympathies. They saw their leadership as divinely inspired and they were accustomed to working in an ecclesiastical environment that was clearly hierarchical.[19] Baker's view, that you should begin with the people and empower them to act, was at odds with a tradition that emphasized a prophetic charismatic ministry.

Like Baker herself, Andrew Young sees the tensions she aroused at SCLC as the result of a generational conflict as well as a gender conflict, both exacerbated by the black Baptist background of King and his senior associates. He writes:

> Ella Baker was a determined woman and she reminded them of the strong Momma's (sic) they were all trying to break free of. The Baptist church had no tradition of women in independent leadership roles, and the result was dissatisfaction all around.[20]

This reiterates what Young told interviewer Nick Kotz in 1973 when he asserted that the clash stemmed from the fact that:

> Martin's mother, quiet as she was, was really a strong domineering force in that family. She was never publicly saying anything, but she ran Daddy King and she ran the church and she ran Martin, and so Martin's problems with Ella Baker, for instance, in the early days of the movement were directly related to his need to be free of that strong matriarchal influence.[21]

Momma King probably did exert significant private influence in family matters. But, it is notable that just as Ella Baker in her Civil Rights Documentation Project interview and Coretta Scott King in her 1969 autobiography alluded to the then popular hypothesis of the emasculation of African American men in American society, so Reverend Young four years later alluded to the allegedly matriarchal tendencies of the black family.[22]

His multi-faceted explanation is plausible. Daddy King was a disciplinarian prepared to use physical coercion. King's mother, Mrs Alberta King, and grandmother, Momma Williams, were female figures who provided the young Martin with an affection that gave positive reinforcement to the Christian conventions of behavior that they wished to instill. In my opinion, however, Young may also have projected his own relationship with his mother onto King's. His parents' relationship, Young writes, reminded him of:

> an old Moms Mabley joke in which she affirms that her husband is the head of the household and makes all the big decisions, like who'll be president, while she makes all the small decisions, like where they live and what they eat. My father was head of our household, and my mother ran his life.

Similarly, when Young explains his refusal to follow his father's career of dentistry, he anticipates a vocal struggle with his mother. "Mother minced no words," he declares, "she was always emotional and assertive in her opinions. Nonetheless, I knew it was time to break away from her control and take charge of my own life." He later emphasizes the contrast between his parents: "I had always been able to reason with my father. Mother *told* me what to do, Daddy made suggestions." [original emphasis][23]

In describing her departure from SCLC, Ella Baker saw the basic problem as her gender, compounded by her lay status among an overwhelmingly ministerial group. As corroboration, Mrs Septima Clark, another veteran activist who came to work at SCLC in 1961, also found it to be a man's domain. Although she was on the Executive, and responsible for a major SCLC project, the Citizenship Education Program, she found that she had little influence. Interviewed for an oral history project at the King Center, she complained that "those men didn't have any faith in women, none whatsoever. They just thought that women were sex symbols and had no contribution to make."[24] Baker and Clark have attracted scholarly attention because, unusually for women in the movement, they had prominent titled positions. Their rare executive status highlights gender inequality because it did not translate into genuine authority within SCLC. Both women had previously enjoyed formal leadership positions within women's organizations, notably the Young Women Christian Association (YWCA), and within the NAACP. They had also exercised what Belinda Robnett would term "bridge leadership" in earlier phases of the Freedom Struggle at the local level.[25] Despite their inexperience, the status of the young ministers of SCLC gave them prominent positions in all-male organizations and in local NAACP chapters, but simultaneously deflected them from bridge leadership, except insofar as they linked their local activities to larger state and national campaigns.

Given this divergence, the implied, but largely unaddressed, question arising from Miss Baker's sacking is: how did it affect the development of the civil rights movement? It is implied that if Dr. King had deferred to the more experienced and astute Miss Baker in the period 1957 to 1960, the SCLC would have become more like the SNCC of the early 1960s. The element of continuity would have been the channelling of popular energies aroused by local direct action campaigns into sustained voter registration and political campaigns. After the Montgomery bus boycott of 1955-56 ended, Baker felt that King and Abernathy failed to sustain the momentum of protest by using the lessons of their experience to help organize other areas of the South.[26] By comparison, after the dramatic sit-in movement in the Spring of 1960, Baker called together the student leaders to ensure that the momentum of protest was sustained. The key to this development was bridge leadership that persuaded individuals, even in high-risk areas like rural Mississippi, to move to activism. This kind of face-to-face recruitment was to become characteristic of SNCC fieldwork.[27]

To suggest SCLC's untaken path highlights the way in which the civil rights movement of the late 1950s was struggling to find its next vulnerable target, given the vigor of southern resistance to school desegregation and the agony of overcoming the discriminatory practices of the region's voting registrars. The sit-in movement of 1960 identified these targets. Like buses, retail stores were service institutions partly dependent on African American consumers. Sit-ins also exemplified the means by which the movement became firmly associated in the public eye with nonviolent direct action. Yet for Baker and her generation of local activists like Amzie Moore in Mississippi or Esau Jenkins in South Carolina, direct action campaigns were high-risk measures of last resort. They were also superficial in their aims alongside the goal of reenfranchisement in rural areas where African Americans were still numerous, or even the majority population. It is true that, with Baker's guidance and the support of many largely uncelebrated, and often female, grassroots figures in Delta towns like Greenwood or Clarksdale,

SNCC came to focus on the vote rather than the lunch counter.[28] It was a shift that provoked internal dissension and which, by 1964, had cost a great deal in terms of suffering with less to show in terms of tangible, political or social change.

Ultimately, with its Freedom Summer campaign and recruitment of white volunteers to attract media cameras, SNCC aped SCLC in its keenness to capture the nation's attention. Andrew Young condemns the young men of SNCC for their seduction into the martial histrionics of confrontation in the same way as he castigates his militant SCLC colleagues. He alleges that during Freedom Summer the former "had a way of riding around in cars playing macho on two-way radios, while the actual door-to-door canvassing was done by women."[29] The existing scholarly record rightly celebrates SNCC's brave and vital contribution to the process of micro-mobilization in the Deep South and stresses their commitment to nurturing and empowering local people. But the important balance between these movement activities and the more externally oriented protest campaigns of SCLC in achieving legal and political change needs to be re-asserted. Sadly, when the implementation of the Voting Rights Act for the 1966 mid-term elections increased the importance of grassroots organization and mass participation that Ella Baker had always favored, SNCC was ill-equipped to assist. Its local offspring, such as the Mississippi Freedom Democratic Party, found it difficult to become self-sustaining.[30] This suggests that while SCLC overlooked the importance of the kind of bridge leadership that Miss Baker venerated, she in turn underestimated the value of the kind of formal leadership—a combination of prophetic ministry, media politics and summitry—that Dr. King exerted between 1963 and 1965. King's chauvinism aggravated his inability to see the value of Miss Baker's counsel, but his mode of masculinity also prompted him towards a program of dramatic protest that pushed civil rights to the top of America's legislative agenda.

Nonviolence and the Return of the Repressed

My husband was always sensitive to the way the public would respond, not out of personal pride, but for fear that any of his actions might reflect negatively upon the Movement.

One of the difficulties American black men must face is that the whole social system beats down upon them harder than on women ... With this background, it has been difficult, until very recently, for black men to take their natural place as the head of the household and the protector of their families ...

Martin had none of these inhibitions nor any of the psychological insecurities that seem to beset so many men in white America. He always made me feel like a real woman because he was a real man in every respect.

Coretta Scott King[31]

I'm away from home twenty-five to twenty-seven days a month. Fucking's a form of anxiety reduction.

Martin Luther King Jr.[32]

The practice of nonviolence by the SCLC was primarily shaped by the two interactive elements of public relations and economic coercion. Keen to cultivate national support, Dr. King was acutely aware of his own image. In some respects, this simply accentuated the division between the public and the private man that was an integral part of any preacher's life. However, the playing out of conventional masculine roles by an African American male was clearly problematic.[33] It became still more complicated when a commitment to nonviolence was grafted onto the challenge of public manhood for black males. King and his male colleagues experienced tensions in their personal lives as a result of the pressures of their public crusades. These tensions produced considerable friction, even to the point of physical confrontation among male staff in meetings, and a voluble and fairly bawdy approach to sex.[34] However, promiscuity was only one product of a regime that placed acute strain on SCLC members. King and his colleagues had to find ways of making nonviolence "manly" and of dealing with the feelings of anger and frustration that it left.

On April 27, 1957, the *Pittsburgh Courier* issued a thinly veiled warning that a "prominent minister in the Deep South, a man who has been making the headlines recently in his fight for civil rights, had better watch his step." The widely read black newspaper had learned that white segregationists had hired detectives to catch "the preacher in a hotel room with a woman other than his wife, during one of his visits to a Northern city."[35] Although not referred to by name, this was an early indication that those seeking to discredit the movement would monitor King's personal conduct. Later, the FBI sought information about King's private life via covert surveillance. In early 1965, Mrs Coretta King opened a package containing a letter threatening her husband with public humiliation unless he withdrew from public life, preferably committing suicide. The parcel contained a tape recording of King telling dirty jokes, making bawdy remarks, and allegedly having sex. According to FBI informants interviewed by Taylor Branch, the tapes caught Reverend King *in flagrante* loudly declaiming: "I'm fucking for God!"[36] The tape had been prepared on the order of assistant FBI director, William C. Sullivan.[37]

The iconic status of Dr. King, both at the time of the movement and subsequently, has ensured attention for these salacious aspects of his life. King recognized that such revelations were potentially very damaging to his public role, but he complained to friends that such intimate matters were properly "between me and my God." Prophets, like presidents, have private lives. His wife, Coretta, has largely dismissed the tape as "a lot of mumbo jumbo." But historian David Garrow also quotes her as saying that she would never have questioned her husband about his fidelity since "anything so trivial ... just didn't have a place in the very high-level relationship we enjoyed."[38] Accepting that her response was a defensive rationalization, it still suggests that she had a conventional, middle-class view of sexuality, rooted in a binary opposition of mind and body. She thus accorded carnal desires a lower status than intellectual concerns, and believed that success often required the denial of physical desires. A product of the Platonic and Pauline elements in Christianity, this outlook also meshed well with Gandhian nonviolence in its subordination of emotional responses.

This attitude to sexuality was by no means unchallenged by the time Coretta Scott married Martin Luther King, Jr. in 1953 and it would be questioned vigorously in subsequent decades. Whatever its deficiencies, it had reinforced middle-class women's claims to social power as guardians of moral, cultural and civic probity. Within the African American community, whose respectability was denied by the malignant logic of racism, the need to advance such claims was strong. Both the Scott family of Perry County, Alabama and the King family of Atlanta, Georgia had powerful incentives in the segregation era to sustain their self-respect by struggling to secure economic independence and by demonstrating moral respectability. Within the black church tradition, the repression of carnality had enforced segregation of the sexes in some churches. A reading of the body as the source of passion and sin, found even more commonly in white Protestant churches in the South, was evident in the African Methodist Episcopal tendency to look down on the emotional "carryings-on" of the Baptists. Coretta Scott's lady-like demeanor, her trained singing voice and educated manner, reflected her family's status aspirations and the ideals she absorbed at the American Missionary Association's Lincoln High School in Marion, Alabama.[39]

Similar influences informed the social world of the Reverend Martin Luther King, Sr., and his wife, Alberta Williams King, in Atlanta. Mrs King managed the domestic sphere with the assistance of her mother-in-law, "Mama Williams," but "Daddy" King set the disciplinary standards. Martin Luther King Jr. remembered that his father had "whupped" him until he was fifteen, by which time, King had entered Morehouse College. A teenage friend, Larry Williams recalled vividly the day Daddy King caught he and Martin dancing with girls at the YWCA. Shouting furiously at this public gathering, Reverend King insisted that the two teenagers leave. This reflected a puritanical prohibition of public dancing by certain black churches.[40]

During his childhood, King internalized the role models of a gentle, pious mother figure and a vigorous, aggressive father figure. He remembered how his father demanded respect from a white Atlantan policeman who had pulled him over and snapped: "Boy, show me your license." Daddy King had pointed to Martin and retorted: "Do you see this child here? That's a *boy* there. I'm a *man*. I'm Reverend King." Underlining the significance of the episode to his son, King Sr. had declared "When I stand up I want everyone to know that a *man* is standing."[41] The widespread practice of denying adult status to African Americans was felt keenly by those whose professional status and education deepened their expectation of civil treatment and increased the likelihood of their involvement in the white dominated public sphere. Poorer African Americans faced such poverty and high unemployment that it was more difficult for them to conform to mainstream gender stereotypes of law-abiding fathers providing for and protecting their families and of mothers devoting their lives exclusively to home-making. King's black bourgeois upbringing made his father's insistence that he was not a "boy" memorable, but the slogan of the striking Memphis sanitation workers in 1968—"I Am A Man"—illustrates the saliency of questioned manhood as an issue also for the black working classes.

But what was it, to be a man? If it was a job, war mobilization had provided more jobs for black men in urban centers, with important military bases developing near southern cities like Montgomery. The Cold War sustained both the bases and the rhetoric of an American democratic creed, thus providing both a material and an ideological support for African American civil rights demands. It made the incidents of white racial violence in the post-war period against returning veterans and other black males internationally embarrassing. It also made de-colonization (particularly Gandhi's struggle in the Indian subcontinent which was presented to Americans largely without the distorting effects of anti-Communism) a compelling example of the changing world order. If the sun could set on the British Empire, then the so-called southern way of life could equally be overturned.

Black men could look around the world and see their counterparts fighting successfully for freedom, and many of them had first-hand military experience. War veteran, Medgar Evers named his first child after Kenyan leader Jomo Kenyatta in 1953 and "thought long and hard about the idea of Negroes engaging in guerilla warfare in the Delta."[42] Tim Tyson cites several further examples in his recent article on Robert Williams of Monroe, North Carolina and concurs with John Dittmer's judgement that Williams's military background, NAACP membership, and willingness to use force if necessary to defend home, family, and community made him "typical of the generation of southern blacks who launched the civil rights movement in the 1950s."[43] In this context, one understands why—despite the interest in Gandhi which Indian independence and partition aroused—support for nonviolence was largely limited to middle-class intellectuals of a religious temperament. The Mahatma's ascetic life-style made him an unusual role model for African American males. More commonly, black men delighted in the athleticism, financial success and physical power of Joe Louis and Jackie Robinson. It was too easy to confuse nonviolence, sometimes misleadingly referred to as passive resistance, with a pacifism that seemed to require an "unmanly" repudiation of the right to self-defense.

Against a backdrop of widely publicized white violence in the late 1950s, notably the Emmett Till lynching in 1955 and the mob attacks at Little Rock Central High School in 1957, both of which raised the question of defending one's children, African Americans remained wedded to the ideal of self-defense. As Tyson makes clear, the so-called "kissing case" in Monroe, in which two African American boys aged eight and ten were beaten by local police and sent to reform school for kissing an eight-year-old white girl, was what first drew Robert Williams into the public spotlight.[44] A Korean war veteran, Williams had publicized the incident to put pressure on state authorities to release the boys. He had also organized a para-military group to counter increasing Klan activity in Monroe. Williams believed that armed defense was the only way to assert black rights in a white majority society in which legal authorities failed to provide adequate protection. The rapid acquittals of two white men charged with sexual attacks on African American women in Monroe in 1959, confirmed this failure to provide equal protection under the law. An angry Williams told reporters "if it's necessary to stop lynching with lynching, then we must resort to that method." Publicized by segregationists as the NAACP's advocacy of vigilantism, Williams's words prompted national executive secretary Roy Wilkins to remove him as president of the Monroe branch. Denounced by a succession of speakers including Martin Luther King Jr. and Jackie Robinson at the NAACP annual convention, Williams retorted: "We as men should stand up as men and protect our women and children," adding defiantly, "I am a man and I will walk upright as a man should. I WILL NOT CRAWL."[45]

Shortly thereafter, Williams debated the merits of nonviolence with Dr. King in the pages of *Liberation* magazine. Nonviolence was inappropriate given the immorality of the white South, Williams claimed. It was "no repellant for a sadist." In his own community, nonviolent ministers had pleaded with the city council to curb the Klan to no effect. Only his military preparations had prompted an ordinance against Klan motorcades. As an NAACP official, Williams had persistently tried legal avenues of redress but all his "appeals to constituted law were in vain." Appropriating the gendered rhetoric of southern white supremacists, Williams presented nonviolence as "turn-the-other-cheekism," an approach that would stop African American men from protecting their women from "the southern white beast."[46] In his reply, Dr. King insisted that not even Gandhi had believed that nonviolence required the repudiation of self-defense. He accepted Williams's contention that the use of force in self-defense had historically been celebrated not condemned, but he warned against the initiation of violence. Yet Williams was not only endorsing *self*-defense but a more masculinist defense of dependents; of women and children. King realized that pure nonviolence would attract only a small following, partly because it flew in the face of this convention. But, equally, he believed that the armed struggle would never attract sufficient numbers to be sustainable. Pragmatically, the varied repertoire of nonviolent direct action was much more likely to induce the masses to participate in some form of systematic non-cooperation.[47]

King never doubted the challenge that the gendered appeal of self-defense represented to his nonviolent approach. No doubt remembering his father's words, he grinned with delight when Ella Baker's successor, Wyatt Tee Walker told how "this big Negro guy" had stood up to a white bus driver, with the words: "I want you to know two things. One, I ain't no boy. And two, I ain't one of those Martin Luther King nonviolent Negroes."[48] From the armed black farmers of Mississippi to the street-hardened youths of the northern ghettos, King's public advocacy of nonviolence generated serious contradictions with the largely conventional gender norms that he espoused. As late as 1967 when Dr. King was openly opposing the war in Vietnam, this vulnerability in gender terms was evident in his insistence that: "There is a masculinity and strength in nonviolence."[49]

At the time of his debate with Williams in late 1959, nonviolence was associated primarily with bus boycotts. But the principle of non-cooperation embodied in a boycott, was not the only element within nonviolence. Equally important was the positive principle of direct personal engagement with injustice. Nonviolence required its practitioners to put their "bodies" on the line. This was dramatized effectively in the sit-ins and Freedom Rides where protesters deliberately targeted specific practices within the segregation system. The air of normality and civility which expedited transactions at southern lunch counters and on Jim Crow transportation depended on the absence of protest. The placing of well-groomed, respectable, outwardly civil African American youths at such counters exposed racist lies about black conduct, and triggered the use of overt force in a way that delegitimized segregation. In this confrontation, the gendered body was a key part of the script.

One set of images of the masculine body stresses aggression. There is a rich iconography in America of the armed male as not simply a defender of family, nation, and race but as an agent of self-expression. The Western, as a major narrative genre in both movies and television in the 1950s, presented stories that hinged on just such a figure. However, while African Americans like Williams foreshadowed the later black power era in their celebration of "Negroes with Guns," they, like most positive depictors of masculinity, placed a strong emphasis on the capacity of the masculine body to endure. Thus, while King's nonviolent philosophy was denounced as unmanly, if it left women and children unprotected, it was also seen as courageous, disciplined and defiant when men endured pain sacrificially on their behalf. When King calmed the angry crowd that gathered outside his bombed Montgomery home in 1956, he was applauded for his appeal to Christian principles and admired for his self-control and his bravery also. He had mastered the anger and fear that this threat to himself and his family would have stirred in most men. He was in control of his emotions. He certainly spoke defiance to those who used violence against him, asserting his superiority by indicating that there was nothing—not even lethal violence—that would stop the movement of which he was a part.[50]

This emphasis on the will to accept pain remained a conspicuous and problematic aspect of SCLC's work. King celebrated the bravery of the students who sat in at lunch counters but, as historian Adam Fairclough points out, "he showed little eagerness to lead a sit-in himself."[51] He was very reluctant to engage in the Atlanta sit-ins and refused to join the Freedom Rides. By 1963, to the disdain of his SNCC and CORE critics, King's personal nonviolent witness, commonly ,was to lead a march and accept imprisonment with maximum publicity. Demonstrations that were likely to meet street violence were usually led by others and involved mainly local people. There was an irony to this in that Dr. King, beginning with his knifing in 1958, showed extraordinary courage and composure on those occasions when he was physically attacked, but found confinement hard to endure.[52] Nonetheless, it appeared to some that SCLC devolved the pain onto local "foot-soldiers," while its general stayed safely aloof. This made King's celebration of redemptive suffering hard for his critics to stomach. At the climax of the SCLC's Birmingham campaign of 1963, for example, King told local activists:

> We must say to our white southern brothers all over the South who try to keep us down: We will match your capacity to inflict suffering with our capacity to endure suffering. We will meet your physical force with our soul force ... Do to us what you will. Threaten our children and we will still love you ... Say that we're too low, that we're too degraded, yet we will still love you. Bomb our homes and go by our churches early in the morning and bomb them if you please, and we will still love you. We will wear you down with our capacity to suffer. In winning the victory, we will not only win our freedom. We will so appeal to your heart and your conscience that we will win you in the process.[53]

This belief in the redemptive power of unearned suffering was a key element in the Christian tradition. But to Malcolm X, such suffering appeared degrading and pathological. This was particularly so because of King's use of the term, "love" in accordance with Christ's admonition—"Love Your Enemies." According to the Honorable Elijah Muhammed, whites were irredeemable devils. On this basis, Malcolm X saw King's claim that black suffering might "win" whites as not only too costly, but fundamentally wrong. However, as King explained to anyone who misunderstood his talk of "love," the confusion was largely one of language. It could be avoided by maintaining the Greek distinction between *eros*, *philia*, and *agape*.

Eros had come to mean romantic love and powerful sexual attraction, while *philia* referred to the reciprocal affection between friends. According to Coretta King, her husband declared that "No one could be such a fool as to expect a person to feel that kind of love for his oppressor."[54] The third kind of love—*agape*—was what King asked his followers to display. It corresponded to Gandhi's concept *Satyagraha* and constituted an imperative that obliged an individual to act in such a manner as to create and preserve the beloved community. The objects of *agape* were worthy of redemption not because of their individual qualities but because of their inalienable humanity. Thus, King was speaking of an intense, but actually cool and rational, relationship when he used love in this profoundly unsentimental sense. *Agape* was ascetic not simply in terms of the disciplined way in which its practitioners deployed their own bodies as subordinate instruments but also in its disinterest in the visible body and personality of the oppressor.

If nonviolence drew selectively on the suffering warrior cult within American culture, its practice in the civil rights movement was tied to the emotive rituals of African American Christianity. As a preacher, King drew on the "Sustainer" tradition within the black Baptist faith. The drama and musicality of his charismatic performance provided an emotional immersion that gave meaning and huge significance to everyday lives. As a young man, he had been embarrassed by the emotional liturgy in his father's church, echoing those critics who saw such pietism as an opiate. Within his own ministry, however, he saw such practices as vital to the development and sustenance of insurgency. While the philosophy of nonviolence stressed the efficacy of mind over matter, soul force over physical force, its practice required the mobilization of actual people, a matter of a visceral commitment as well as intellectual conviction. In short, such personalism in practice revealed the inseparable nature of body and mind.

As a nonviolent protest organization, SCLC would find itself continuously dealing with what is termed the return of the repressed. The rituals of its protests could not serve as channels for the sublimation of all aggression. The rudimentary biochemistry of confrontation—the flight-or-fight response—made each march and demonstration an adrenaline sauna. Concurrently, these dramatic experiences were incorporated into the mental cartography or narratives of identity of individual participants. The tropes and symbols of gender were basic to how such events were anticipated, experienced, and remembered. While putting one's body on the line was an act of self assertion that gave many participants a more positive sense of self, maintaining nonviolent discipline when others were attacked around you was deeply unsettling.

In both SCLC and SNCC, the leadership was shaken by the suffering of others. King was deeply distressed by the murder of the four girls in the Sixteenth Street Baptist Church bombing in Birmingham and Robert Moses was haunted by the unpunished murder of Herbert Lee, a Mississippi farmer whom he had asked to register to vote.[55]

The classic secular model for male acceptance of peer suffering was a martial one and it is striking how SCLC leaders were attracted to military terminology to describe their nonviolent campaigns. Wyatt Tee Walker, James Bevel and Hosea Williams competed for influence at SCLC partly by their escalation of nonviolent direct action. While scholars have argued that the competition among different civil rights groups for publicity and funding in the early 1960s benefited the movement by prompting experimentation and fresh initiatives, they have overlooked that this process was also at work within organizations.[56] Examining this rivalry at SCLC highlights the way in which gendered self images contributed to these developments. As executive director, Wyatt Tee Walker made good Ralph Abernathy's claim to be the man who could put Martin Luther King's ideas into practice. "Our personalities sort of merged," is how Reverend Walker describes his time as King's alter ego. He tried to limit access to the SCLC president and to insist that everyone address Martin as "Dr. King" as a mark of respect for someone who looked so young. He referred to King simply as "the leader" and to himself variously as "Dr. King's chief-of-staff," "attorney-general" (a big claim during the Kennedy years) and as his "nuts-and-bolts man."[57]

At SCLC's Nashville convention in September 1961, Walker downplayed James Lawson's suggestion to the press that SCLC was going to recruit a "nonviolent army" of 10,000 people, all willing to oppose segregation with their bodies and to endure lengthy jail terms.[58] This was not because Walker doubted the coercive power of mass protest or was unattracted to military metaphors. On the contrary, Walker was somewhat infatuated with the masculine mystique of military organization. His clashes with colleagues at SCLC were a product of his vain desire for a strict, authoritarian, hierarchical structure within which he barked orders and his colleagues obeyed. He was also drawn to the hyper-rationalism of military-style planning with code names, targets, tactical contingency plans and a fascination for maneuvers. This was especially evident in his preparations for the Birmingham campaign or "Project X," as Walker called it.[59]

Walker saw the earlier campaign in Albany as a mistake, born of sentiment and good intent. He was determined that SCLC's next effort would be meticulously planned, even ruthless. "We've got to have a crisis to bargain with," he argued, "to take a moderate approach, hoping to get help from whites doesn't work. They nail you to the cross."[60] To produce this crisis, an escalating campaign of protest had to be prepared to compel the Birmingham business community to respond. "Project X" would begin with "B Day" (Birmingham day) when demonstrators would attempt to integrate the Alabama metropolis's downtown lunch counters. Interviewed many years later, and making the pattern of the campaign appear more planned than it was, Walker still spoke with obvious relish about his own role. He had visited each lunch counter, counted the number of seats and the points of access and egress, measured the length of time it would take for demonstrators to reach their goal, and lined up secondary targets should the police prevent them from reaching their destination. To move the city's police and firemen away from downtown, he dispatched "eight or ten guys to different quarters of the town to turn in false alarms."[61] When James Forman of SNCC witnessed Walker's delight at the first use of attack dogs, he was appalled. It "seemed so very cold, cruel and calculating to be happy about police brutality coming down on innocent people, bystanders, no matter what purpose it served."[62] Walker's martial approach was also apparent when he supported James Bevel's proposal to use teenage demonstrators to maintain the mass character of the protests as the number of adult volunteers petered out. "We needed more troops," he explained later, "We had run out of troops. We had scraped the bottom of the barrel of adults who could go."[63]

But although willing to support Bevel's tactics, Walker still expected Bevel to follow his orders. The result was an explosive dispute during the Birmingham campaign. "You cannot order me to give my life," Bevel declared dramatically to Walker, "This is a movement, not a military operation." When King refused to sack Bevel for insubordination, Walker believed that his own authority had been critically undermined.[64] Bevel's background explains his reaction to Walker's martinet approach. He had been dishonorably discharged from the navy for insubordination because he refused to accept a galley assignment at a time when African American servicemen were routinely allotted kitchen duties.[65] But while refusing to defer to organizational superiors, Bevel relished his own ability to sweep along young volunteers by the power of his argument and his presence. He had recruited the many high school students who had filled the jails for SCLC during the Birmingham campaign. He began to talk to these excited followers about the next dramatic phase of the struggle: a children's march (8,000 strong) from Birmingham to Washington, and aroused considerable enthusiasm among them, despite his colleagues' misgivings about the practicality of such a scheme. When the actual March on Washington of 1963 acquired a more ceremonial character, he was disappointed. "You all turned my march into a picnic," he complained.[66] Much later, after Dr. King's assassination and the faltering of SCLC under Ralph Abernathy, Bevel was dismissed. He embarrassed the organization by transforming his scheduled sermon to the women of Spelman College from an hour-long chapel service to a weekend retreat in his Atlanta hotel room. He illustrated his themes by writing on the hotel room walls before his spellbound young protégés. Thus, although Bevel rejected Walker's strict military discipline, he too enjoyed the thrill of command.[67]

Bevel's chief rival in militancy was Hosea Williams. Williams was a World War Two veteran. Wounded in action, he had returned home to Georgia on crutches, but when he tried to drink from the water-fountain at Americus bus station, a policeman and several local whites set upon him. Like Bevel, Williams's military experience deepened his anger at racial discrimination. The GI bill enabled him to take a degree in Chemistry, and he secured a well-paying job with the US Department of Agriculture in Savannah. There, he began his career as an NAACP activist, organizing the Chatham County Voters' Crusade. His voter registration work brought him into contact with SCLC and, watching the Birmingham campaign, he decided to launch a direct action campaign to desegregate Savannah. The ensuing demonstrations had more enthusiasm than discipline with Williams himself held in jail for sixty-six days, a longer consecutive period of imprisonment than for any other movement leader. In Andrew Young's negative assessment, however, Savannah resembled the Albany campaign far more than it did Birmingham.[68]

Whatever Williams's deficiencies, Dr. King invited him to join SCLC in 1964. King was under no illusions that Williams was "confrontational" but regarded this aggressiveness as preferable to becoming "too comfortable with injustice." Hosea, King explained, is "going to go out there and start something, and though we don't know what it might lead to, we need people like that."[69] Williams himself saw SCLC as a vehicle for his ego. "Ain't no money out there, ain't no nothing," he observed, "you've got to have ego to stay in that movement."[70] The statement was revealing, suggesting how Williams, like Wyatt Walker, shared the common view that the merits of a man should be evident in the money he earned. Walker, who had haggled over salary before joining SCLC, left in 1964 for a more remunerative position in New York. Williams, too, was well known for his financial demands.[71] While King was drawn to the ascetic ideals of Gandhi, other staff members expected a middle-class "family" wage. Young reports that the United Church of Christ agreed to pay Williams the same relatively high salary that he had received in his previous job, making him the highest paid person at SCLC.[72]

For men like Williams, movement activities provided excitement, fame, and power. From the hostile perspective of Andrew Young, the newly hired Williams used the St Augustine campaign in 1964 as a personal proving ground to place himself on a par with the SCLC veterans of the Birmingham campaign. The four hundred year old Florida city was a center for Klan activity and local black leaders like Air Force veteran Robert Hayling had narrowly escaped lynching. Such documented violence made Williams's decision to schedule night marches to the old Slave Market particularly hazardous. Justifying the move on the grounds that it enabled black adults to participate outside of the working day, Williams acknowledged that it increased the likelihood of attack by white segregationists.[73] He believed "it was necessary for the movement to stay on the front pages" and violence secured media attention. The spotlight also allowed the leader of such demonstrations to be, so-to-speak, king-for-a-day. "Everybody wanted to be like Martin," one staffer explained.[74]

Andrew Young: A Different Kind of Man

In his autobiography, Andrew Young sees himself as consistently representing a different approach to the authoritarian, egocentric and reckless attitudes of his SCLC Baptist colleagues. He believes that his Congregationalist background made him more appreciative of issues of gender equality than his Baptist counterparts. Joining SCLC as part of the Citizenship School Program (CS), Young's immediate staff was female: Mrs Septima Clark and Mrs Dorothy Cotton. Having noted that the SCLC board did not take the CS seriously in the beginning, Young aligns himself with Mrs Clark as someone excluded from the "high-level strategy sessions." In doing so, he declares that the schools were "laying the foundation for a Southwide movement" and describes himself as "content to spend my energy on training rather than engage" in internal squabbles.[75]

From the outset, however, Young saw the CS differently from Mrs Clark who appreciated the slow face-to-face work of developing the movement at the local level in the manner of a bridge leader. Young actually saw the CS from the more centralized position of formal leadership, regarding them as serving SCLC's larger strategies by providing a network of contacts across the region. "A trained local leadership would be on hand to coordinate a wide variety of SCLC programs in the future," he noted in June, 1961. In the winter of 1961-62, when SCLC was drawn into Albany, Young was keen to visit the area and recruit for the CS program. He felt that he had a greater rapport with the SNCC activists and the local youths they attracted than did "the more authoritarian SCLC staff." Thanks to his youth ministry work for the National Council of Churches (NCC), he "had a lot of experience dealing with prickly young adult males who were still trying to assert their manhood." His NCC background also gave Young contacts in "the white liberal church community in the South and across the country." He soon began responding to mail on Dr. King's behalf, explaining SCLC's work to this white liberal constituency. Both tasks accentuated his role as a formal leader bridging the movement to external constituencies.[76]

Young accepts that his role at SCLC began to change at the end of 1962. The SCLC meeting at the Dorchester Center near Savannah, which normally housed the CS teacher training courses, gave Young a chance to establish himself in the fraternal inner circle that ran SCLC. He recalls fondly how during the recreational periods each afternoon, the "thirty-somethings" played softball or basketball, and how the cook catered attentively to King's taste for "soul" food. This bonding session established Young in SCLC's inner circle. The meeting planned the Birmingham campaign and according to Young, it was clear that the CS, which in Albany had developed from the protest campaign, could be valuable in Birmingham as a pre-campaign mechanism for training and mobilizing demonstrators.[77]

Once it was agreed that the CS program would work with the Birmingham based Alabama Christian Movement for Human Rights, Young became effectively the SCLC's "advance man." He was in regular communication with black community leaders, and using his NCC contacts, he also volunteered to "initiate contact with white business leaders in Birmingham." Such diplomacy was an uncoveted job at SCLC and Young's attraction to it prompted others to tease him as an "Uncle Tom." With the possible exception of Dr. King, Young was the most "image-conscious" of the SCLC staff. When he met with white business leaders, he dressed formally and maintained a strict courtesy in his exchanges so as to overcome the demonization of the movement by the segregationists.[78]

As the campaign progressed, Young became more involved in negotiations, press work, and the supervision of demonstrations than in the CS program itself. But despite the drama of the campaign, he insists that, unlike some of his colleagues, he never became addicted to confrontation.[79] He characterizes local leader Fred Shuttlesworth's dissatisfaction with the Birmingham settlement negotiated by SCLC as a product of this addiction: "After so many years of suffering, the taste of victory felt too good to quit."[80]

Young was clearly attracted to the idea that a higher faculty of reason should restrain emotional responses. He and James Bevel prided themselves on their coolness under pressure. Summarizing the lessons of the Birmingham campaign, he stresses that nonviolence is a rational process whose success is threatened by emotionalism.[81] To underline his point, Young recounts how, immediately after the Birmingham campaign, he accompanied Dorothy Cotton and James Bevel on a desperate night drive to Winona, Mississippi. They went to check on the safety of a group of jailed CS teacher trainees that included Mrs Fannie Lou Hamer and the CS state field director Annell Ponder. Since hers was the only car available, Cotton insisted on coming. Bevel and Young had tried to discourage her because her emotionalism might trigger a confrontation with a clearly vicious, local sheriff. Mrs Cotton took the wheel and the trio set off at high speed with Cotton still lambasting her companions for their chauvinism. In her anxiety and fury, she drove recklessly until the car narrowly escaped a head-on collision with a huge truck. Shaken by the near miss, Cotton then allowed Young to drive. Young continues to portray Cotton as emotionally unstable, ascribing her behavior to the guilt she felt over the women's plight which she had indirectly caused by inviting them to train at Dorchester. "It was as if she wanted to be in jail right along with the other women," he declares. In contrast, he writes: "I did not make my decisions out of guilt, though, and I wasn't about to go to jail just because she felt guilty. My goal was to get everyone out of Winona in one piece."[82]

After relating the mission's successful outcome, he records that "We used to joke that Dorothy had initiated the women's rights movement on that mission to Winona." He then pays tribute to the courage of all the women in the movement and admits that male activists "probably too often tried to 'protect' them," before noting the "special vulnerability of African American women under segregation." Despite these extenuating remarks, Young attempts here to strengthen his argument that emotionalism is a liability by appealing to negative gender stereotypes.

The celebration of "coolness" as a key attribute of leadership sets Young's model of masculinity against the manhood personified by Hosea Williams. Sent to assist the Savannah campaign, Young stresses how it has suffered from Williams's lack of forethought. Its youthful protesters have no personal provisions and no guidance as to how to conduct themselves in custody. Packed into an overcrowded police van, they start to panic until Young teaches them to "use mind over matter."[83] Simlarly, in April 1964, Williams, without prior consultation, announces to a St. Augustine mass meeting that Young will lead that night's march. Accordingly, Young twice approaches the local segregationist leader, "Hoss" Manucy, to negotiate safe passage. While TV cameras roll, he is kicked and beaten by a white mob.[84] After the experience, Young supported Williams's call to make the city SCLC's main focus in 1964. With hindsight, he believes that the resulting images of racial brutality facilitated passage of the 1964 Civil Rights Act. Underlining the gender tensions within nonviolence, Young remains "haunted by the sight of young women with blood streaming down their faces from head wounds, and the sheer terror of those racist mobs." He disliked SCLC's shock tactics. "You would reason your way out of segregation," King reportedly told him, "but it takes more than just reason to get this country straight."[85]

Ultimately, St. Augustine enhanced Young's status among his male colleagues. However, his growing importance within general SCLC operations between 1962 and 1964 occurred at the expense of his CS work. In December 1963 Mrs Clark wrote a memo to Dr. King complaining that Young had neglected his duties. She had been left to run the CS program virtually alone while Young and Cotton were swept up in first the Birmingham and then the Savannah campaigns. Many states, she reported, "are losing their citizenship schools because there is no one to do the follow-up work" assisting new teachers. It "seems as if Citizenship Education is all mine, except when it comes times to pick up the checks," she complained. Implying that SCLC was not using the foundation grants for the CS appropriately, she warned, "We can't fool the foundations." The officers of the Southern Regional Council who were overseeing the Voter Education Project had already complained about SCLC's inadequate reporting and had temporarily withheld funds. Clark viewed Young and Cotton's neglect of their CS duties in generational rather than gender terms. "Direct action is so glamorous and packed with emotion," she wrote, "that most young people prefer demonstrations over genuine education."[86]

Young's mistrust of emotionalism probably made Clark's last accusation sting. On December 12, 1963, he gave his thoughts on how the CS staff could "fulfill our obligations to both the Field Foundation and to the Negro people." From the outset he stressed that he felt a greater "responsibility to the Negro people" and that his "first concern is their Freedom." The terms of the Field Foundation grant required SCLC to "teach 300 persons to run classes and operate 300 schools per annum," and in 1963 they had exceeded this target. But Young also declared that "we all know that Negroes will not be significantly better off socially and civically if we do this alone." The CS program must not repeat the mistake of the American Missionary Association during Reconstruction and "assume that education was in itself an answer to the Negroes (sic) problems. Education must be related directly to social change and social action." Explaining his role in Birmingham, he stressed that he had tried "not to get involved in demonstrations very much" because this was not CS work, but he added that "we must train the youth of the nation to appreciate nonviolent means of social change and to consult with them as they apply these means in their community." This justified his involvement in the previous year's major campaigns. He indicated that other staff "closer to the field" should "do more of the field work in citizenship schools." Rebutting Clark's charge of neglect, Young averred "that I can do more through training our field staff of 23 full time persons than I ever could by running around the South trying to do it all myself."

Young largely ignored the question of the emotional appeal of direct action campaigns to a younger generation. His argument was that the education provided by the CS must be integrally linked to nonviolent direct action. In contrast, Clark—an activist nurtured in the NAACP era—tended to view direct action as a distraction from the more substantive process of local leadership development and education. Ironically, Young responded to her call for greater attention to grassroots movement building by urging the devolving tasks to others "closer to the field." From a gendered perspective, this reflected Young's commitment to what Belinda Robnett has termed formal bridge leadership and Clark's devotion to informal grassroots bridge leadership. The latter was the role played most extensively by women in the civil rights movement and was characterized by sustained face-to-face contact which drew people into activities until they were immersed in a movement culture that altered consciousness and impelled action.

Wyatt Tee Walker's departure from SCLC added to Young's organizational responsibilities and the St. Augustine campaign confirmed his disengagement from the CS program. As the latter campaign wound to a close at the end of June 1964, Young as the new executive director issued fresh job descriptions and assignments. Forwarding these details to Clark on July 9, he apologized for missing the recent Dorchester training session. Once again, Clark complained about the neglect of the CS program. Despite her previous criticisms,

Young's authorization of payments to the volunteer teachers continued to be slow, and clearly secondary to other business. This had caused hardship and disappointment for local workers, which was hard to justify, given other discretionary expenditures. Young now proposed adding Randolph Blackwell and Hosea Williams to the CS budget and raising the salaries of male staff such as C.T. Vivian, Jim Bevel and Harry Boyte who had families to support.[87] In her reply, Clark wondered what qualifications Blackwell had for CS work and whether Williams—whom she knew well—would "develop leadership so as to have classes observed while he is on the firing line." During the St. Augustine campaign a term of schools in south-east Georgia had been cancelled because the supervisor could not secure formal approval of expenditures. While sharing Young's concern for "the men with families," Clark felt compelled to remind him that "women have great responsibilities also." She herself had three grandchildren reliant upon her for financial support, and like Dorothy Cotton, she had to cover the upkeep of two homes, one in Atlanta where SCLC was based and another in her hometown of Charleston, South Carolina.[88]

Writing on July 20, Young conceded his administrative shortcomings but placed them in the context of what he termed "perhaps the most confused and complicated year of my life." He was defensive on the pay question, insisting that he had "tried to give every consideration to women and salaries." Female staff had received raises with each new grant, while he had remained on the same salary that he had earned at the NCC. He concluded that the established practice was to pay staff according to their previous salary, a policy that ignored how much this favored men like Williams over women like Clark. More confidently, he declared that "ever since Albany," he had been prepared to be fired over the impact of his protest involvement on his other responsibilities. He reasserted that protest had to take precedence over education. "The schools and colleges have been educating Negroes for 100 years," he wrote, "and all you have is educated slaves. There must be some assault on the slave system—segregation—and Direct Action is the best way to do that." Reversing the logic that had seen the CS as laying a foundation for direct action, he concluded that: "Our training program has prospered because Action has freed the Negro to want to vote and learn."[89]

This is a fascinating statement to come from Andrew Young, the SCLC's in-house conservative, the moderate who sought to restrain the fire-brands like James Bevel or Hosea Williams. First and foremost, it reflected the immediate impact of his baptism of fire in St. Augustine. His autobiographical account of this experience is another exercise in psychological projection. According to Young, it is Williams who is intent on boosting himself within SCLC's inner circle by orchestrating a heroic confrontation. Williams recklessly maneuvers Young into leading a march. Beaten but unbowed, however, Young emerges with an enhanced status, and, judging by the above comment, a new militancy. But within his later autobiographical narrative, he remains critically independent, a man above the fray.

The martial predilections of the men of SCLC and their experiences from 1962 to 1964 shaped an SCLC strategy that became rooted in the idea of "creative tension." As Dr. King explained in his *Letter from Birmingham Jail*,[90] direct action served to create such a crisis that established groups, who had previously refused to surrender any of their privileges, were compelled to address the concerns of the oppressed, and make concessions. By 1964, creative tension was a widely accepted idea within the movement. While some older activists agreed with Bayard Rustin that the movement had reached the profitable end of its protest phase by late 1965, most SCLC, SNCC and CORE staff regarded direct action as an essential continuing element. At the same time, both within SCLC and among the other direct action groups, there were deep disputes about the tactics, targets and timing of protest.

In these disputes, Andrew Young tended to return to the "cool" pose he had adopted prior to 1963. In his response to Mrs Clark's criticisms in late 1963, he had commented that staff needed to recognize that because of a common background of segregation, "we are part of the problem we are trying to cure." He attributed "the emotional problems, lethargy, misguided enthusiasm and impetuosity" within the movement to "our being Southern Negroes," and warned that it "takes time to overcome these ills."[91] These ills aggravated both gender and generational conflicts. Together, they gave rise to emotional clashes and reckless outbursts that wasted both human and material resources and political and personal opportunities. But the competing models of cool and hot-headed manhood at SCLC should be seen as simultaneously a source of strength and weakness. They overcame fear and courted attention in a way that compelled federal action. They may have under-valued the less conspicuous, movement sustaining work of frequently female bridge leaders but such manhood compelled action and the will to act was the very essence of the Freedom struggle.

Notes

1. Belinda Robnett, *How Long? How Long? Women in the Civil Rights Movement* (New York: Oxford University Press, 1997); David J. Garrow, *Bearing the Cross: Martin*

Luther King Jr and the Southern Christian Leadership Conference (London: Jonathan Cape Ltd., 1988).

2. David Garrow, *The FBI and Martin Luther King, Jr.: From "Solo" to Memphis* (New York: Norton, 1981); Taylor Branch, *Like A Pillar of Fire: America in the King Years, 1962-1965* (New York: Simon & Schuster, 1998).

3. Stephen B. Oates, *Let the Trumpet Sound: The Life of Martin Luther King Jr.*(New York: Penguin USA, Mentor Books, 1985); Adam Fairclough, *To Redeem the Soul of America: The Southern Christian Leadership Conference and Martin Luther King, Jr.,* (Athens, GA.: University of Georgia Press, 1987), 169.

4. Doug McAdam, *Freedom Summer* (New York: Oxford University Press, 1988).

5. Sara Evans, *Personal Politics: The Roots of Women's Liberation in the Civil Rights Movement and the New Left* (New York: Alfred A. Knopf, 1994); Mary King, *Freedom Song: A Personal Story of the 1960s Civil Rights Movement* (New York: William Morrow, 1987); Mary Rothschild, *A Case in Black and White: Northern Volunteers and the Southern Freedom Summers, 1964-1965* (Westport, Conn.: Greenwood Press, 1982).

6. Robnett, *How Long? How Long?*, 37- 41.

7. Andrew Young, *An Easy Burden: The Civil Rights Movement and the Transformation of America* (New York: Harper Collins, 1996).

8. Robnett, *How Long? How Long?*, 94.

9. Jervis Anderson, *Bayard Rustin: Troubles I've Seen: A Biography* (Berkeley: University of California Press, 1998), 153-54.

10. Garrow, *Bearing the Cross,* 67-69.

11. Carol Mueller, "Ella Baker and the Origins of 'Participatory Democracy," in Vicki Crawford et al., eds., *Women in the Civil Rights Movement: Trailblazers and Torchbearers, 1941-1965* (Bloomington: Indiana University Press, 1993), 58.

12. Fairclough, *To Redeem the Soul*, 31-32.

13. Oates, *Let the Trumpet Sound*, 242.

14. August Meier and John Bracey, eds., *Papers of the National Association for the Advancement of Colored People,* microfilm series, [hereafter NAACP papers] Part 17, (National Staff Files 1940-1955) reel 1: 23-24; 41; 54; 190. Baker would probably judge that Reverend John W. Goodgame reverted to type when he opposed later civil rights protests, v. Glenn Eskew, *But for Birmingham: The Local and National Movements in the Civil Rights Struggle* (Chapel Hill: University of North Carolina Press, 1997), 70,137-38, 351: note 48.

15. Branch, *Like A Pillar of Fire*, 25.

16. NAACP Papers, Part 17 reel 1: 193, 204, 569, 574; Part 1 (*Meetings of the Board of Directors, Records of the Annual Conferences, Major Speeches and Special Reports*) reel 11: 202-203; Part 16 B reel 5: 522.

17. Fairclough, *To Redeem the Soul*, 39-40, 47-49

18. Mueller, "Ella Baker," 67.

19. For Shuttlesworth, v. Eskew, *But for Birmingham*, 122-24, 196-197.

20. Young, *An Easy Burden,* 137.

21. Garrow, *Bearing the Cross*, 655, note 12.

22. Coretta Scott King, *My Life with Martin Luther King, Jr.,* (London: Hodder and Stoughton, 1970), 104-5.

23. Young, *An Easy Burden,* 16, 60-61.

24. Robnett, *How Long? How Long?*, 94.

25. Robnett, *How Long? How Long?*, 19-23.

26. Robnett, *How Long? How Long?*, 74.

27. Clayborne Carson, *In Struggle: SNCC and the Black Awakening of the 1960s* (Cambridge, Mass: Harvard University Press, 1981); Howard Zinn, *SNCC: The New Abolitionists* (Boston, Mass.: Beacon Press, 1964).

28. Charles Payne, *I've Got the Light of Freedom: The Organizing Tradition and the Mississippi Freedom Struggle* (Berkeley: University of California Press, 1995); John

Dittmer, *Local People: The Struggle for Civil Rights in Mississippi* (Urbana: University of Illinois, 1994).
29. Young, *An Easy Burden*, 400.
30. Dittmer, *Local People*, 324-28,362, 408-23.
31. Scott King, *My Life With Martin*, 30, 104-5.
32. Garrow, *Bearing the Cross*, 375.
33. See, for example, William Grier and Price Cobbs, *Black Rage* (New York: Basic Books, 1968), 59.
34. Garrow, *Bearing the Cross*, 586.
35. Garrow, *Bearing the Cross*, 96.
36. Branch, *Like A Pillar of Fire*, 207.
37. Garrow, *Bearing the Cross*, 125-26, 133-34.
38. Garrow, *Bearing the Cross*, 374.
39. Scott King, *My Life With Martin*, 39-42, 45, 49-51.
40. Garrow, *Bearing the Cross*, 32-34.
41. Oates, *Let the Trumpet Sound*, 10.
42. Payne, *I've Got the Light of Freedom*, 49-50.
43. Tim Tyson, "Robert Williams, 'Black Power', and the Roots of the African American Freedom Struggle," *Journal of American History,* 85:2, (September 1998), 545-46; John Dittmer, "Robert Williams," in *The Encyclopedia of Southern Culture*, ed., Charles Reagon Wilson and William Ferris (Chapel Hill: University of North Carolina Press, 1989), 231.
44. Tyson, "Robert Williams, 'Black Power'", 551-55.
45. Tyson, "Robert Williams, 'Black Power'", 556-58.
46. Clayborne Carson, et al, eds., *The Eyes on the Prize Civil Rights Reader: Documents, Speeches, and Firsthand Accounts from the Black Freedom Struggle, 1954-1990* (New York: Penguin, 1991), 110-12.
47. Carson, *Eyes on the Prize Civil Rights Reader*, 112-114.
48. Oates, *Let the Trumpet Sound*, 273.
49. Garrow, *Bearing the Cross*, 566.
50. Scott King, *My Life With Martin*, 143.
51. Fairclough, *To Redeem the Soul*, 58.
52. Scott King, *My Life With Martin*, 183; Young, *An Easy Burden*, 174-75.
53. Oates, *Let the Trumpet Sound*, 228-29.
54. Scott King, *My Life With Martin*, 72.
55. Branch, *Like A Pillar of Fire*, 250 note.
56. Nancy J. Weiss, "Creative Tensions in the Leadership of the Civil Rights Movement," in Charles Eagles, ed., *The Civil Rights Movement* (Jackson, Miss: University of Mississippi Press, 1993), 39-64.
57. Oates, *Let the Trumpet Sound,* 138, 151.
58. Garrow, *Bearing the Cross*, 168.
59. For how "Project X" became "Project C" during the course of the Birmingham campaign rather than in advance, v. Eskew, *But for Birmingham*, 210-12.
60. David L. Lewis, *Martin Luther King: A Critical Biography* (London: Allen Lane,1970), 173-74.
61. Garrow, *Bearing the Cross*, 248.
62. James Forman, *The Making of Black Revolutionaries* (New York: Macmillan, 1972), 312.
63. Garrow, *Bearing the Cross*, 247.
64. Young, *An Easy Burden*, 221.
65. Young, *An Easy Burden*, 190.
66. Young, *An Easy Burden*, 269-70.
67. Young, *An Easy Burden*, 503-4.
68. Young, *An Easy Burden*, 259-63.

69. Young, *An Easy Burden*, 281.

70. Garrow, *Bearing the Cross*, 464.

71. Fairclough, *To Redeem the Soul*, 269.

72. Garrow, *Bearing the Cross*, 136; Oates, *Let the Trumpet Sound*, 292; Young, *An Easy Burden*, 281.

73. Young, *An Easy Burden*, 291; Oates, *Let the Trumpet Sound*, 285-93.

74. Garrow, *Bearing the Cross*, 464; Young, *An Easy Burden*, 355, 358.

75. Young, *An Easy Burden*, 144.

76. Young, *An Easy Burden*, 173, 171.

77. Young, *An Easy Burden*, 189-90.

78. Young, *An Easy Burden*, 203, 228.

79. Young, *An Easy Burden*, 228-29.

80. Young, *An Easy Burden*, 247.

81. Young, *An Easy Burden*, 252.

82. Young, *An Easy Burden*, 253-56.

83. Young, *An Easy Burden*, 260-63.

84. Young, *An Easy Burden*, 291-93.

85. Young, *An Easy Burden*, 294.

86. Garrow, *Bearing the Cross*, 309.

87. Andrew Young to Septima Clark, July 9, 1964 in Southern Christian Leadership Conference Papers, Martin Luther King Center for Non-violent Change, Atlanta, Georgia, [hereafter SCLC], Box 154: file 4.

88. Septima Clark to Andrew Young, July 12, 1964, in SCLC, Box 154:4.

89. Andrew Young to Septima Clark, July 20, 1964, SCLC, Box 154:4.

90. Martin Luther King, Jr., *Why We Can't Wait* (New York: Harper and Row, 1963), 76-96.

91. Andrew Young to Septima Clark, July 20, 1964, SCLC, Box 154:4.

CHAPTER 5

Women in the Student Non-violent Coordinating Committee: Ideology, Organizational Structure, and Leadership

Belinda Robnett

This essay argues that ideology shapes organizational structures of social movement organizations that, in turn, are critical determinants of women's leadership positions in movements. Such factors determine the extent to which women are able to exercise their leadership capabilities. Specifically, organizations built on an ideology of a participatory democracy that discourages the centralization of leadership, seek consensus and are anti-hierarchical, empower women even in the absence of an explicit feminist doctrine or in the presence of gender bias. The Student Non-violent Coordinating Committee (SNCC) was this type of organization. Conversely, organizations such as the Southern Christian Leadership Conference (SCLC), with an ideological commitment to a centralized nucleus of leadership, and that are hierarchical, impede women's leadership.

Joyce Rothschild-Whitt distinguishes between collectivists' organizations and bureaucracies, arguing that the relationships in the latter are instrumental, segmented and role-based while those in the former are holistic, community oriented and affective.[1] As Myra Ferree points out, "These different forms of relationship may also be grounded in the organizational structure of the movement itself."[2] Several scholars have noted the importance of organizational structure in other social movements in determining organizational goals.[3] Moreover, feminist scholars have analyzed the importance of organizational structure to patterns of women's participation in women's movement organizations, but only a few, such as Suzanne Staggenborg, have examined them in the context of gender-integrated organizations.[4] Those who do, often argue that women gain power and leadership in organizations that incorporate a feminist awareness into their leadership structures.[5] Yet, in the case of the civil rights movement, which predated the 1970s feminist movement, women were leaders. In other words, something other than a clear ideological commitment to feminism facilitated their participation as respected leaders. Moreover, the extent to which an organization impedes a woman's ability to lead directly affects her decision to remain with or leave a movement organization. This suggests that the ideology that governs an organization extends beyond the rhetoric of activism as a mobilizing tool. It includes structural and organizational forms that facilitate or impede the inclusion and empowerment of otherwise excluded groups.

SNCC's Ideology and Organizational Structure in its Early Years

In creating SNCC, Miss Ella Baker, a seasoned activist and former national director of NAACP chapters, contributed her clear ideology regarding leadership, goals and tactics. She did not believe that leaders should define a movement and often stated that "strong movements don't need strong leaders." Instead, her focus was upon the development of community leadership and grass roots mobilization.[6] Baker's views became central to the operation of SNCC.

With Ella Baker's guidance, it was decided that rotating the chairmanship would ease some of the tensions between groups and would prevent a single "strongman" from usurping power. Unlike the centralization of power within other movement organizations, SNCC was a decentralized organization. There were rotating chairs and an executive committee. Men dominated the official positions within SNCC, much like those in other movement organizations, but women in SNCC were more visible and held more power than their counterparts in other organizations. These differences are attributable to Miss Baker whose emphasis on group-centered leadership required that decisions be made through group consensus. Such a consensus automatically included women's input. As Carol Mueller in her description of Baker's ideology states:

> The emphasis on participation had many implications, but three have been primary: 1) an appeal for grass roots involvement of people throughout society in the decisions that control their lives; 2) the minimization of hierarchy and the associated emphasis on expertise and professionalism as a basis for leadership; and 3) a call for direct action as an answer to fear, alienation, and intellectual detachment.[7]

This emphasis on group participation and the decentralization of power in the decision-making process created an organizational structure in which everyone was expected to participate, including women. This tended to mitigate, though it did not eliminate, traditional beliefs that encouraged deference to males or ministers as leaders. Even if one held traditional beliefs, one was expected to participate.

Yet, there is still a disparity that needs clarification. Though the women in SNCC held considerable power, here too most were not part of the formal leadership. Although SNCC's decentralized structure prevented the development of oligarchy, it did not ensure that power was any less gender determined than in the centralized organizations. Though their philosophy was one of group-centered leadership, visibility was still heavily dictated by traditional beliefs about the legitimacy of male authority. Even with its decentralized structure and relatively decentralized power relations, male leaders dominated SNCC. As Fay Bellamy states: "there was a hierarchy, [but] ... there was more than one, let me say that ... there was a Forman kind of hierarchy ... a Stokely kind of hierarchy. [A] Bob Moses kind of hierarchy ..."[8] Other interviewees confirm Bellamy's perception of three distinct groups. But while these power groups each formed around a male leader, taken as a whole, SNCC women had greater access to organizational power than in organizations where power was centralized around one key figure. The town-meeting style, "consensus required" nature of decision-making, and the relatively decentralized nature of leadership created what Sara Evans and Harry Boyte term "free spaces" where women could lead.[9] Even though most men held the formal titles, women found ways to circumvent any barriers to power and leadership.

Titled Positions, Women Leaders and Power

Titled positions in SNCC did not convey the same meaning as in organizations with centralized power. Power was more diffuse, and one's title did not always convey one's power. For women, titled positions were more restrictive than for men. They were gendered even though the structure was decentralized. One respondent recalls, "If you had a title, you were in the office."[10] Since women could type, and men generally could not, women assigned to the office would end up doing the typing. Many of my respondents stated that women did not want to be relegated to the office but preferred to work in the field. Hence, for women, titled positions often translated into less power while the titled positions for men often signified greater decision-making power. On the other hand, when a woman participated without a title, her workload could more easily stretch beyond her job description. In other words, women could have the power without the title or the title without the power. Within SNCC, the combination of an emphasis on grass roots leadership and the decentralization of decision-making created an atmosphere where women could lead as long as the position was untitled, or given a unique title (though a few women did hold titled leadership positions). Yet, titles in SNCC were relatively unimportant because the absence of a title or a relatively unimportant title did not mean one necessarily lacked power.

Women participants understood that women's leadership was no less important to the movement than men's. Miss Ella Baker, who was considerably older than the students in SNCC, provided a role model for both the young men and women. One woman respondent, who wished to remain anonymous, recalls how, despite having no leadership title, Diane Nash Bevel and Miss Baker were key players in shaping SNCC's "basic philosophy, strategy and tactics" and were widely consulted before decisions were taken.[11] Titles failed to reflect women's authority in the movement. In Nash Bevel's case, her titled position of "office manager" completely disregarded her repeated leadership during moments of crisis when she often acted as a formal leader. Miss Baker was an "outside consultant" though clearly her influence dominated and created SNCC's structure and philosophy. Like Miss Baker, powerful leader Ruby Doris Smith Robinson's position as personnel manager and bursar was uniquely buried, placed in the "Others" category. Aware that such titles might restrict their leadership opportunities, women either chose to avoid them or to ignore the restrictions imposed by their titles. They wasted no energy challenging these inequalities, aware of the vastly greater goal of liberation that all movement members pursued.

Women preferred to work in the field, though here too, they did not often hold titles. Still, such positions allowed for more autonomy than office work. They worked at canvassing in local communities and on a day-to-day basis were able to make decisions within the local community. Canvassing included finding out what was on people's minds—what kinds of things they would like to see done; getting individuals to register to vote; and, recruiting individuals for local demonstrations. Few women became project directors, though more were appointed to the position with the beginning of the 1964 Freedom Summer that brought scores of new volunteers to the South. Between 1964 and 1965, of the fifty staff in Mississippi, there were twelve women. In Mississippi, Southwest Georgia and Alabama, there were twenty-nine project directors, seven of whom were women working in Mississippi. These included Muriel Tillinghast in Greenville, Mary Lane in Greenwood, Willie Ester McGee in Itta Bena (who worked alongside district director Stokely Carmichael), Mary Sue Gellatly in Shaw, Lois Rogers in Cleveland, Cynthia Washington in Bolivar County and Gwen Robinson in Laurel. Women project directors did not generally supervise more than one field worker, while most men supervised three workers or more.[12]

Some of the women became project director because no man was willing or able to take the post. Muriel Tillinghast, for example, received her position after her friend, Charlie Cobb, decided to move on. Tillinghast had had movement leadership experience prior to joining SNCC as a member of the Nonviolent Action Group in Washington, D.C. Later, she became project director in Jackson, Mississippi in an equally spontaneous way, when Jessie Morrison announced his departure. As she explains, Morrison had declared:

> if anybody wanted to take over the reins feel free but at 12:00 in such and such day he was leaving ... I guess I got there about a quarter to twelve ... and it turns out that I was the only one who showed up and he handed me the keys and left ... that way I got to inherit the cohort operation in Jackson and by that time most of the major civil rights organizations had pulled out. The killings ... ha[d] really frightened a lot of people.[13]

In 1963, under similarly intimidating circumstances, another powerful leader, Prathia Hall, though not on the official roster of project directors, became head of the Selma project at Jim Forman's request. Hall explains:

> It was an extremely dangerous time. I remember the first mass meeting and how the church had been ringed by the sheriff on horseback and carrying these huge carbines and rifles and Al Lingo and the Alabama State troopers surrounding the church ... in the week ... which followed ... all of the men who had been involved in the project were in jail and at that moment I became the project director ... Need determined how people were utilized.[14]

Such pressures prevailed throughout the South and it was impossible to plan and organize every decision and activity. Women moved in and out of positions frequently and served the movement in ways that were critical to its continued momentum and sustenance. The fact that women's participation options, as titled staff members, were limited neither suggests that women were not leaders nor that they were not looked to for leadership. Likewise the women interviewed did not perceive their activities as limited. Women felt themselves to be an important and integral part of SNCC.

Women's Empowerment and the Transformation of Gender Positions

Before 1965, women felt empowered and liberated by their participation in SNCC. Most of the women interviewed, in telling me their stories, included the courageous acts of men and women, and did not perceive their actions as having been limited by male domination. For most, the civil rights movement has remained in their memories as a special and unique period in history, one which evokes memories of cooperation, love, fear, accomplishment and empowerment. All of them considered their participation liberating, because for the first time in their lives they could participate openly in organizations targeting the extreme oppression of their people in America. Any level of participation in such an endeavor was a form of empowerment. The fact that men held the offices or overt power was not perceived as the critical issue. Rather, men and women equally were admired for their courage and skills. Bernice Johnson Reagon, an active participant in the Student Non-violent Coordinating Committee, provides an insightful summary of many women's feelings about their participation in SNCC:

> my whole world was expanded in terms of what I could do as a person. And I'm describing an unleashing of my potential as an empowered human being. I never experienced being held back. I only experienced being challenged and searching within myself to see if I had the courage to do what came up in my mind. And I think if you talked to a lot of people who participated in the movement, who were in SNCC, you find women describing themselves being pushed in ways they had never experienced before.

Reagon acknowledges that she and her colleagues had conventional expectations of men and women for their time but:

> none of those ideas, whether they were carried by me or some man, had any limiting effect on what I would do as a powered person in the world. I was challenged to go further than I'd ever gone before. And to that extent, it was an incredible experience.[15]

Reagon and her male and female colleagues were challenged to transcend not only personal boundaries, but political and social ones as well. Nothing was sacred, neither their identities nor society's boundaries. As she eloquently explains:

> Men who grew up in the Student Non-violent Coordinating Committee were pushed as hard as we were in their own way to go beyond any models we had for behavior. All of us were day by day doing things that our parents thought would get us killed. So we'd been socialized to go as far as you can go, but don't go do X, Y, Z, if you're Black. And SNCC was saying, 'We're breaking this thing up. We're breaking it down. We're challenging this structure.'

> So SNCC needed people who were willing to go further than they'd ever been trained to go. So we were all boundary breakers. And what I've experienced that doing, for me, was freeing me as a person in the world so that I never thought that anybody could tell me where I could go or not go. I thought that somebody else could kill me, but short of that, there wasn't any way they could stop me.[16]

While some movement theorists view social movements as ordinary organizations, Reagon's comments suggest that the movement provided a particular cultural context that transformed the identities of both male and female participants beyond the confines of societal norms.

It is clear that a strict adherence to gender norms was precluded by the context of the movement, even within the hierarchy of the church.[17] Historically, women's leadership in black churches was limited to activities centered on family, community and education. In these areas, women were expected to lead, to forge ahead as brave soldiers. Since the nineteenth century, women's church auxiliaries have existed, concerning themselves with the well-being or uplift of the community. During the 1900s, numerous women's clubs were formed whose extensive community activities addressed: "the plight of working women, limited economic opportunities, inferior housing, severe health problems, the political strait jacket of Jim Crowism, care for the aged, and programs for the very young."[18] In spite of the enormous importance of such activities, black women were largely viewed as the "backbone" of the church and of the community, and were often scorned if they stepped beyond the confines of their acceptable positions. E.

Franklin Frazier noted that after emancipation, the church helped to reinforce the patriarchal position of the male in the black family.[19] Similarly, Jacquelyn Grant discusses the male-dominated church hierarchy and its continuing failure to apply a liberation theology to gender questions as well as racial ones.[20]

Social prestige is often derived from one's position in the church hierarchy. Males typically dominate the higher positions of leadership while women work to organize the activities, run the Sunday schools, and raise money for the church.[21] Historically, women have been largely barred from the upper echelons of the mainstream churches, and their attempts to step beyond these limits have met with strong disapproval.[22] For these reasons, many black women seeking formal leadership positions have been attracted to black spiritual churches rather than the more institutionalized black churches.[23] Again, Bernice Johnson Reagon provides an example of how the movement challenged this pattern:

> You have to understand that I grew up in a church and the women sat on one side in the Amen Corner and the men sat on the other side in the Amen Corner. The pulpit was in the center and the only time the women went up was on Women's Day. Now the civil rights movement was one time I saw women going up into the pulpit because they were leaders of the civil rights movement ... like Fannie Lou Hamer who was not a minister. She was always in the pulpit. I always during the mass meetings saw women in the pulpit with the ministers ... And it had to do with your willingness to put your life on the line and your courage and your character. But we were all products of a culture that had roles for various people. My mother always belonged to a women's group. That is not a sexist phenomenon within the black community. That is the way the organizations operated, to a large extent.[24]

SNCC's ideology cultivated a movement culture in which societal norms were questioned. Within the context of that culture, women and men often viewed women as capable leaders. Fay Bellamy, who late in SNCC's history became a member of its Executive Committee, recalls, "they didn't assume that you were not capable. They would assume that if you showed them that, but they would assume first that you are capable and, therefore, you can do certain things."[25] Another interviewee indicated that what was most important was not what men thought of them, but what they thought of themselves. She explained that since SNCC was a voluntary organization, no one told others what projects they could work on or that they had to participate in certain activities. Everyone in SNCC, by virtue of being a part of SNCC, was putting his or her life on the line. This act alone was a source of empowerment.[26]

Other SNCC women expressed this sentiment as well. Though there were restrictions on the titled positions women could hold, they were still able to lead in particular areas and to contribute in significant ways.[27] Women, who were responsible and hard working, who were not afraid of confrontation or of expressing their own viewpoint in debate, were considered leaders, Bellamy recalls. She also remembers that some of the men were afraid for the safety of women with highly visible roles in the field projects and others didn't want to work for women or "just thought it was not a woman's place to play that kind of role."[28]

Yet, such misgivings about women's capabilities were not enough to stop women's leadership. As Bernice Johnson Reagon recalls:

> ... if you wanted to go into the field and somebody didn't want you to go into the field because you were a woman, that was their opinion. But it never stopped you from doing it. So when I talk about men's and women's relationships in the Student Non-violent Coordinating Committee, I am not describing an organization where men were progressive when it came to women, and they were for women being equal, I'm not saying that. I am saying that we were in a movement and the structure of that organization was such that you were the only person who could limit what you did. And you had to find the courage to challenge anything that didn't feel right to you, and you could do it in the organization.[29]

Status was gained through acts of courage, and gender divisions, while quite real, were irrelevant to the day-to-day struggle to survive as a people. The atmosphere of ever-present danger precluded strict adherence to commonplace gendered expectations. Movement participants were constantly confronted with aggressive white southerners willing to stop their efforts by any means necessary. Dorie Ladner, a SNCC field secretary, recalls that there were too few SNCC workers to permit a policy of restricting women:

> I would say that a lot of times the guys might have wanted to protect us, but all of us were in it together.

There was no hiding from anything. You must also understand that there in Mississippi, those of us who were working with Bob Moses, there were probably about five or six of us ... There were only three girls and maybe four or five guys in the whole state. So we were running up and down the highways on these lonely, dark roads by ourselves. So when you talk about a particular role, we were all fighting a battle, like a war. It was war, not like war—it was war.[30]

Race, in these dangerous circumstances and times superseded other identities such as their gender and class. "It was war," and the battle-lines were drawn along those of color.

Therefore, in determining the nature of gender relations in SNCC, what is of great significance is the way these relationships and the explanations for them have been shaped by racism. As Elizabeth Higginbotham remarks, in a deeply racist society "gender identity is inextricably linked to and even determined by racial identity. We are talking about the racialization of gender and class."[31] In 1955, Emmett Till, a fourteen-year-old black boy from the North, was murdered in Mississippi for allegedly whistling at a white woman. When his body was found, the testicles had been cut off. In the context of such assaults, the fact that black men held offices or were the formal leaders was not perceived as the critical issue for African American women. The struggle for the freedom of all black people remained at the center of their consciousness, and sustained their leadership efforts in the free spaces provided by the ideology of a participatory democracy and a decentralized nonhierarchical structure. It was within these free spaces that black women were able to act as leaders in SNCC.

Nevertheless, gender was a defining construct of power relations and shaped the structure of the movement.[32] Men and women clearly had differential access to structural and institutional power. Dr. King, for example, had access to the primary institutional hierarchy, or formal leadership track of the black church. For women, such a path to a position of formal leadership and power, even within a movement organization, did not exist. Instead, women held positions of power based upon their community work or extraordinary activism, but not from their position in a church hierarchy. Within this context, it is important to deconstruct leadership activities from their embeddedness in institutional hierarchies and structures.

In SNCC, many so-called "followers" or grassroots "organizers" operated as, what I term, "bridge leaders." They foster ties between the social movement and the community. They are the key links between what social scientists term pre-figurative strategies (aimed at individual change, identity and consciousness) and political strategies (designed to challenge existing relationships with the state and other societal institutions).[33] Indeed, the activities of bridge leaders in the civil rights movement provided the stepping stones necessary for potential adherents to cross formidable barriers between their personal lives and the political life of civil rights movement organizations. Bridge leaders were able to cross the boundaries between the public life of a movement organization and the private spheres of adherents and potential constituents.

Only by studying women was I able to discover this important area of leadership within social movements. Women comprised a large portion of those in this category of leadership, and were underrepresented in the formal leadership sector, even though their rates of movement participation exceeded those of men.[34] Bridge leaders were not always women, but it was the most accessible and acceptable form of leadership available to them. In general, women were excluded as formal leaders because of their sex, but this did not deter their leadership efforts in the movement. Women were not simply organizers within the civil rights movement, but as bridge leaders, were critical mobilizers of civil rights activities. Gender, which operated as a construct of exclusion, produced a particular context in which women participated. This gendered power structure served to strengthen the informal tier of leadership, thus providing a strong mobilizing force within the grassroots sector.

As discussed in my earlier work, women, as bridge leaders, may be characterized as follows. They become bridge leaders not because they lack leadership experience; but, rather because of a social construct of exclusion. They sometimes initiate organizations, do the ground work, and, when this is so, are more visible before an organization is formalized.[35] They operate in the movement's or organization's free spaces, thus making connections which cannot be made by formal leaders. They employ a one-on-one, interactive style of leadership for mobilization and recruitment. They have greater leadership mobility in nonhierarchical structures and institutions. They can act as a movement organization's formal leadership during moments of crisis, often catapulted to the fore by spontaneous and emotional events. They are more closely bound to the wishes and desires of the core constituency because, unlike formal leaders, they do not need legitimacy with the state. For the same reason, they tend to advocate more radical or non-traditional tactics and strategies. They can hold a formal leadership position in a specific social movement organization but tend to be considered outside the circle of formal leaders within the social movement sector (or among all of the movement organizations). Similarly, they may be formal leaders at the local level, but within movement organizations or within the movement sector, they are excluded from the primary formal leadership tier. In all cases, women's power was largely derived from autonomous pioneering activities rather than through their titled or hierarchical position within the organization.[36] Bridge leaders in the civil rights movement operated in "free spaces," providing a bridge which facilitated recruitment and mobilization. However, the position of women in the movement was to shift significantly with the rise of the black power movement.

The Rise of the Black Power Movement

On April 26, 1964, SNCC, whose philosophy was to build indigenous leadership within local communities throughout the Deep South, organized the Mississippi Freedom Democratic Party (MFDP). The MFDP was established to counter the continuing efforts of racist southerners to prevent blacks from voting. For example, in the Second District of Mississippi, 52.4 percent of the population was black, but only 2.97 percent had been allowed to register to vote.[37] The material conditions for rural black Mississippians were abysmal. A report compiled by the Council of Federated Organizations, (COFO), which included several active movement organizations in the state, described the desperate poverty. The 1960 census had found that more than half of Mississippi's rural homes had no piped water and three-quarters had no flush toilets, bathtubs or showers. For African Americans in the state, the situation was even worse with fewer than one in ten of their rural homes having flush toilets or bathing facilities. Poor sanitation was one reason why the infant mortality rate for the Mississippi Negro was more than twice as high as that of the white Mississippian. But poor diet among a population increasingly under-and unemployed was another. A COFO report explained: lack of work meant "surviving off of one meal a day, adults going without so that children may eat—in short it simply means slow starvation. Even when food is adequate it is composed largely of starches and fats."[38]

Many of the local people who assisted movement organizations had experienced such poverty. Fannie Lou Hamer who has been described as a charismatic leader, as one who, "when she sings can make a church tremble," knew hardship since childhood. Describing how her father's dreams of economic independence were destroyed by white sabotage, that forced him back to sharecropping and Mrs Hamer herself to drop out of school, she recalled especially her mother's struggles to feed a family:

> So many times for dinner we would have greens with no seasonin' ... and flour gravy. My mother would mix flour with a little grease and try to make gravy out of it. Sometimes she'd cook a little meal and we'd have bread.

> No one can easily say Negroes are satisfied. We've only been patient, but how much more patience can we have?[39]

In addition, black Mississippians were routinely murdered, harassed, beaten and intimidated even before the era of the civil rights worker. These acts, however, steadily increased as more and more local people attempted to register to vote.

At the first MFDP meeting representing four districts, a temporary State Executive Committee was elected of nine men and three women. All three women, Mrs Fannie Lou Hamer, Mrs Annie Devine and Mrs Victoria Gray, were active bridge leaders within their respective communities. Throughout the history of the MFDP, women were often elected to be delegates, but they were generally not elected as chairpersons. Women who served on the Executive Committee most often acted as secretaries. At the local level, men held most of the offices and were the committee chairs, even though half the membership in the MFDP was women. Most of the officers in the MFDP were young men.[40] But five of the three MFDP candidates running for office in 1964 were women. Although they did not hold offices within the organization, they were highly visible. The reasons for this visibility are not altogether clear. Describing her involvement in the MFDP, Victoria Gray remarked:

> I began simply by agreeing to go to the courthouse and become registered to vote and that was my initiation into the movement proper ... Just about everything I did, I was always a community oriented person.[41]

She, like many other leaders in the MFDP, had been active in community affairs prior to her civil rights activism. Gray describes the early activities of the MFDP and how she was elected as a delegate. This experience introduced MFDP members to each step of the electoral process as a process in which could actively participate. Her own nomination was, in part, a sign of how the high-risk nature of black activism in Mississippi encouraged the breaking of customary expectation. As she explains:

> ... women in government were somewhat of a rarity, period. So certainly it was different, and the other thing was finding people who were willing to be nominated into that situation. There really was just a handful of us. We did not have a lot of competition I assure you.[42]

So, because of these dangerous circumstances the custom that only men should be visible leaders was temporarily displaced. Indeed, many believed that men were at greater risk than women. Constance Curry, a former SNCC worker who has written a book about Mrs Mae Bertha Carter and her sharecropping family in Mississippi, explains:

> Mrs Carter said she was always more protective of her sons. She knew that if she were in a dangerous position, there were a lot of ways that she could use her wiles to protect herself. She knew that, traditionally, she was in a safer place than Matthew, her husband, or her sons. They were the ones who needed the most protection.[43]

The MFDP organization and philosophy of decision making came to parallel those of SNCC, creating an organizational climate more conducive for women's leadership. Women such as Mrs Hamer, Mrs Gray and Mrs Annie Devine were very vocal and involved in the planning and strategy meetings.[44] Mrs Gray often initiated discussions and suggested strategies and tactics. In fact, in several meetings, she spoke more than the men did. These women also took center stage in the MFDP newsletters, and often wrote press releases.[45] Even at the local level, men and women seemed to have equal input.[46] Mrs Gray describes the consensual nature of the decision making process: "No one person made the decision in the MFDP. Not ever. We insisted that whatever decisions were made, they were made by the body."[47] This reflected SNCC's influence upon the MFDP organizational philosophy. Many of those who worked closely with the MFDP espoused egalitarian values, such as Miss Ella Baker who ran its Washington, D.C. office, and SNCC workers Bob Moses, Charlie Cobb and Cynthia Washington.

During the campaign, many local women became involved in the necessarily clandestine task of mobilizing support for black candidates.

Mrs Mary Belk of West Point, Mississippi, for example, "had gone from house to house almost every night for a month, getting people out of the bed who had spent the entire day picking cotton, talking about the elections, urging people to run, urging people to vote." She captured the covert nature of her role, saying: "I work for the white folks in the daytime, and against them at night."[48] Similarly, MFDP member, Mrs Ada Holliday of Clay County, captured the courage and dedication of this local activism in a November 26, 1965 letter to the Department of Agriculture:

> We do not intend to let this work and effort go in vain. But more important than the work is the fact that all the candidates have put their bodies in the line of fire, and we will support them with our bodies if necessary ... we will go to jail again if needed, to make our participation in the control of our livelihood a reality. We have risked the burnings of our homes and churches and the loss of our lives. We have been harassed and intimidated by our white neighbors.[49]

The MFDP continued its courageous effort to combat the entrenched Jim Crow laws that kept blacks from voting. Despite increasingly violent reprisals, it succeeded in challenging the southern order through its alternative elections. With sixty-eight delegates and elected representatives, the challenge to the national Democratic Party Convention was well under way.

Upon arrival in Atlantic City, the delegation met other black civil rights leaders, including Reverend Martin Luther King Jr., Bayard Rustin, and Roy Wilkins, as well as long-time, white activist attorney Joseph Rauh. It was the latter who worked out the likeliest strategies for the MFDP's challenge to the seating of the white delegates elected under Jim Crow laws. At the same time, political tension over the challenge reached the White House. President Johnson, who had been in office less than a year, was determined to win the nomination. He was well aware that his commitment to civil rights had alienated many southern Democrats, and that he could ill afford to have his name linked to the MFDP or its actions at the convention. He was determined to stop the MFDP challenge endangering his nomination and party unity.

In addition to this concern, Johnson planned to select Senator Hubert Humphrey as his running mate. Humphrey had alienated many white southerners by standing up to segregationists at the 1948 convention and his presidential aspirations were further weakened by his defeat in the 1960 nomination contest. Under intense pressure to reshape his image so that he might be more palatable to southern whites and become Johnson's heir, Humphrey pressed the MFDP delegation to accept a compromise in committee rather than allow the seating decision to go to the floor. The latter raised the prospect of the nation witnessing the removal of southern white representatives and their replacement by blacks. Humphrey and Johnson understood that this powerful imagery could lose them the election.

To circumvent this possibility, a subcommittee to the convention's Credentials Committee was appointed. After this subcommittee brainstormed for an entire weekend, Humphrey emerged to urge movement figures to back compromise. At a meeting called by Representative Charles Diggs of Michigan, Humphrey met with Dr. King, Mrs Hamer, Aaron Henry, Joseph Rauh, white MFDP activist Rev. Ed King and Credentials Committee members, Representatives Robert Kastenmeier of Wisconsin and Edith Green of Oregon. Ed King recalls Mrs Hamer saying to Humphrey:

> "Senator Humphrey, I been praying about you; and I been thinking about you, and you're a good man, and you know what's right. The trouble is, you're afraid to do what you know is right.' She says, 'You just want this job [as vice president], and I know a lot of people have lost their jobs, and God will take care of you, even if you lose this job. But Mr Humphrey, if you take this job, you won't be worth anything. Mr Humphrey, I'm going to pray for you again."[50]

The only tenable offer to come out of that meeting was presented by Congresswoman Green, who suggested that any of the regular delegates willing to take a loyalty oath ought to be seated with the remaining seats open to the MFDP. Hamer consulted the MFDP delegation, which decided that this compromise was unacceptable. Mrs Hamer's steadfast position during these negotiations—that the delegation should not accept any compromise unworthy of their cause and their constituency back home—resulted in her deliberate exclusion from future meetings.

Meanwhile, attorney Rauh increasingly faced the weight of presidential power as he continued to lobby delegates. While many delegates supported the MFDP challenge, they were unwilling to do so publicly. Any support for the challenge would be construed as a vote against the Johnson/Humphrey ticket since they had succeeded in distancing themselves from the MFDP cause. Frustrated, and with waning support, Rauh agreed to a meeting with Walter Reuther, a powerful labor leader with financial ties to the movement, whom Johnson had persuaded to hammer out a deal. At yet another meeting with Dr. King, Bayard Rustin, Aaron Henry, Bob Moses and Rev. Ed King, a final compromise was offered. The MFDP would be given two seats as at-large delegates. Aaron Henry, as MFDP chair, and Rev. Ed King, as its most prominent white member, were appointed as these delegates, while the rest of the delegation would be "honored guests." The Credentials Committee would also make a public declaration that future state delegations would not be accepted if they were not legally elected or racially representative of their constituency. Rauh was horrified that the two seats were arbitrarily assigned to a white minister and a black middle-class druggist while the majority of MFDP delegates, the sharecroppers, were unrepresented. But even before he had time to report back to the delegation, pressure to accept the deal mounted. Walter Mondale, an aspiring politician and legal assistant to Senator Humphrey, presented the compromise to the Credentials Committee and rushed the measure through. Rauh likened the frenzy to that of a lynch mob, recalling: "They started hollering vote, even while I was still talking."[51]

Bowing to the atmosphere of near panic, Rauh and Mondale told reporters that a compromise had been reached. Bob Moses, meanwhile, had returned to the MFDP delegation's room where the compromise was debated. Some members worried that their representatives in the negotiation were too eager to surrender, that Moses was pressing the delegation to accept the compromise, and that Aaron Henry agreed because he felt beholden to Dr. King and Roy Wilkins for their support. But Henry recalls that the stumbling block was the assignment of the at-large seats to Ed King and himself rather than to the MFDP delegation as a whole to divide among themselves. He also remembered Bob Moses as someone who inclined the delegation to rejection rather than acceptance:

> I think we could have worked this thing out. I think
> that Bob [Moses] forced us into a hasty decision. I don't
> like to be critical of Bob, but I wonder really if he really
> wanted to win the situation. Now you know sometimes
> many of us feel more liberal every time we lose a battle.
> And because of the pressure that Bob was putting on so
> many of the delegates ... move now, not later, now, now,
> now, now, now, I wonder, you know, really if he felt that
> we might be able to work something out that would be
> amenable to the total delegation rather than to be

> panicked into an immediate decision. Certainly the two
> votes were completely unacceptable to me and to
> everybody else ... I don't want nobody handpicking me.[52]

Despite the pressure exerted on the delegation by Bob Moses, he and
Ella Baker were the only formal leaders to encourage the delegation to
make its own decision. In private, Dr. King was dissatisfied with the
compromise and confided to Ed King that if he were a sharecropper, he
would not have accepted it. But King was swayed by Humphrey's
private promise to wage war against racism in Mississippi. Other formal
leaders such as Roy Wilkins and Bayard Rustin urged the compromise.
During a heated argument, primarily with the women in the delegation,
Wilkins told them that they were ignorant of the political process,
should listen to their leaders and just return home. [53]

In an interview, MFDP delegate Mrs Unita Blackwell, recalled how
Mrs Hamer said to her:

> Girl, I'm going to tell you the folks didn't send us up
> here for no two seats. When we left Mississippi, we said
> that we wanted all of the seats or half because we wanted
> to be represented in our state.

In the debate over the compromise, it was Mrs Hamer's rejection that
caught the mood of the delegation when she declared: "We been
compromisin' all our life." But Blackwell also recalls that the incident
also captured the gulf between bridge leaders like her and formal leaders
like Roy Wilkins. As she puts it:

> And, honey, they looked at us and told us we were
> ignorant ... The rumor went around that we was sixty-
> eight ignorant folks from Mississippi and didn't
> understand politics ... and we looked at them and said,
> 'We do understand more than you understand. We
> understand what we come out of.'[54]

The delegation felt betrayed. Originally, they had come to combat
the Mississippi system of disenfranchisement, now they found
themselves battling their own. The compromise debate had highlighted
deep fissures inside the black community. As Mrs Blackwell recalled:

> Them people had not been talking to us poor folks.
> They had a certain clique that they'd talk to. The big
> niggers talk to the big niggers, and the little folks, they

couldn't talk to nobody except themselves, you know. They just goin' to push the thing on through and have us there for showcase. But we tore that showcase down. That's for sure. We told them what we think.[55]

Since the delegation had retained its principles, some leaders claimed a moral victory, but Mrs Hamer was more conscious of the sense of defeat and aware of the risks that still faced the MFDP. Later, she remembered herself saying:

What do you mean moral victory? We ain't getting nothing. What kind of moral victory was that, that we'd done sit up there, and they'd seen us on the television. We come on back home and go right on up the first tree that we get to because, you know, that's what they were going to do to us. What had we gained?[56]

Despite their sense of relative impotence at the convention, the women aired their anger to other MFDP members. Hamer, in tears, made a plea to the delegates not to go along with the black formal leaders who urged acceptance. She and Mrs Devine convinced Henry Sias, a sixty-nine-year-old farmer and chairman of the Issaquena County FDP in western Mississippi, to withdraw his support for the compromise. He recalls:

Those two women just shamed me right there. When they got through talking and whoopin' and hollerin' and tellin' me what a shame it was for me to do that, I hushed right then. See, I backed off and drew way back in that corner.[57]

Through emotional and impassioned pleas, the women were able to persuade many of the delegates that they had a responsibility to their constituents at home. When the vote was taken, the delegation decided to reject the offer. However, Rauh and Mondale had already announced the unanimous acceptance of the compromise by the delegation. Hamer and others were furious. In response, she and the other women leaders, holding "guest" tickets to the convention, forced their way onto the convention floor. They all stood in a circle for two hours, in silence.

The split between the formal male leaders of the movement organizations and the formal women leaders and most of the delegates, further illustrates the degree to which women and men without the status of a minister's title, were not considered formal leaders. Regardless of

Hamer's, Devine's, and Blackwell's preeminent positions within a civil rights movement organization, they were not acknowledged as formal leaders within the social movement sector. Their locations within the movement did not require a conciliatory relationship with white political leadership at any level, allowing them to maintain their affinity to the poor Mississippians back home.

The events at the Democratic National Convention were to have profound consequences for the future of the movement and for the black struggle, in general. It signaled the beginning of a deterioration in movement solidarity. Always strained, the disillusionment of grassroots movement members as well as many SNCC and CORE activists, particularly those working in Mississippi, led to a fractured movement and, structurally, the loss of the bridging tiers of the movement. In his autobiography, Cleveland Sellers, a black SNCC activist, sees the MFDP's rejection at the convention as a watershed, the point at which the movement lost faith in the so-called "good" people of America's willingness to change:

> We left Atlantic City with the knowledge that the movement had turned into something else. After Atlantic City, our struggle was not for civil rights, but for liberation.[58]

Dottie Zellner, a white SNCC activist, shares this view of the convention as the key turning point at which SNCC became more nationally visible yet simultaneously lost faith in the nation's willingness to reform. She says:

> … it actually was the beginning of the end. It was when people began to realize that society was not going to adapt. In other words, the doors looked like they were opened and they weren't.[59]

Fatefully, Zellner believes that SNCC proved unable to meet the challenge of developing new strategies at this stage when its members felt betrayed by liberal America:

> People felt they had been close and that the doors had been slammed on them again. They felt that the people that they had traditionally relied on, the white liberals, had betrayed them, which they had.

Most immediately, the convention questioned the value of the voter registration work in which SNCC and the MFDP had invested so much, particularly when the votes would be cast for the very white liberals who had betrayed them. As Zellner puts it: "How could they just keep on registering people to vote for ... who? Lyndon Johnson."

The sense of disillusionment strengthened the logic of a separatist position. SNCC had always been a black-led, African American freedom-seeking organization but now the appeal of separatism was far greater and more conspicuous. Throughout 1965, these sentiments grew stronger in the organization until the demand for an all-black organization was officially declared in the winter of that year. In Zellner's view, its articulation greatly strengthened the separatist camp: "Once they said it," she recalls, "of course, it became much more a possibility."

After their disappointment at the convention, SNCC activists and MFDP leaders, Fannie Lou Hamer, Bob Moses, Donna Moses, Julian Bond, James Forman, John Lewis, Ruby Doris Smith Robinson, Prathia Hall and others traveled to Guinea. The trip was arranged by Harry Belafonte, who was a staunch SNCC supporter and who had traveled to Mississippi to personally witness the conditions. The group was astounded to see a country run by blacks and to meet its president Sekou Toure.[60] The trip caused the group to ponder the fact that they could have been a descendent of some of the people in Guinea, but because of slavery, they had been ripped from their roots. They experienced a country of black people who were proud of their culture and heritage. Guinea had just gained its independence from France, and was deeply committed to the preservation of its culture. For the first time, Ruby Doris Smith Robinson, and the others, saw women wearing cornrows in their hair. Robinson let a Guinea woman braid her hair in this fashion.[61] The group experienced a growing sense of identity that was rooted in one's blackness, one's dark skin, one's kinky hair and one's culture.

When they returned from their trip, they found SNCC in crisis over its strategy, and Malcolm X's harsher view of white American society began to ring as true for these southern veterans as it had for northern ghetto dwellers. Mrs Hamer and the SNCC Freedom Singers appeared in rallies with Malcolm X on December 20, 1964. He insisted that theirs was the same struggle, declaring: "America is Mississippi. There's no such thing as a Mason-Dixon line—it's America."[62] He told the southern veterans that they had been wrong to believe national white politicians who put the blame for racial injustice on their southern counterparts. Interpreting their convention experience, he declared:

> The head of the Democratic Party is sitting in the
> White House. He could have gotten Mrs Hamer into
> Atlantic City. He could have opened up his mouth and
> had her seated. Hubert Humphrey could have opened his
> mouth and had her seated ... Don't be talking about some
> crackers down in Mississippi and Alabama and Georgia-
> all of them are playing the same game. Lyndon B.
> Johnson is the head of the Cracker Party.[63]

When he and Mrs Hamer shared a platform, she told of her brutal
beating in Winona jail. Following her moving account, Malcolm re-cast
her story of oppression in gendered terms:

> No, we don't deserve to be recognized and respected
> as men as long as our women can be brutalized in the
> manner that this woman described, and nothing being
> done about it, but we sit around singing "We Shall
> Overcome." We *need* a Mau Mau. (Emphasis in the
> original)[64]

Yet Malcolm X did not believe that women shouldn't be as fully
engaged in the struggle as men. He referred to Mrs Hamer as "the
country's number one freedom-fighting woman" and believed that "you
don't have to be a man to fight for freedom. All you have to do is be an
intelligent human being."[65]

Malcolm X's pronouncements, which were at variance with
SNCC's nonviolent origins, appealed to its disillusioned members. But,
although SNCC was shifting to a more radical politics and philosophy,
its immediate focus in late 1964 was the Mississippi Challenge,
organized through the MFDP. This involved challenging the seating of
Mississippi's congressmen in view of the violation of voting rights in
that state. As with the Atlantic City challenge, the federal law seemed to
support the MFDP's case. But, when Congress reconvened in January
1965, it rejected the challenge. This strengthened the view of those in
SNCC who believed that, even when black people played by the rules,
they couldn't succeed. Victoria Gray, one of the MFDP congressional
candidates contesting the seating, recalled that the deepening
disillusionment among the young activists was what hurt her the most;
since "many of them thought that when faced with the truth ... our
officials will do the right thing."[66] As Lawrence Guyot told MFDP
followers, when the challenge was rejected, a tearful Mrs Hamer
declared:

> I'm not crying for myself today, but I'm crying for
> America. I cry that the Constitution of the United States,
> written down on paper, applies only to white people. But
> we will come back year after year until we are allowed
> our rights as citizens.[67]

With a deepening pessimism over what working through the established political system could achieve, the tensions between SNCC workers and the SCLC reached its peak in Selma. In mid-January 1965, Dr. King and the SCLC announced a Selma-to-Montgomery march to draw national attention to voter registration violations in several Alabama counties. While SCLC prepared to march, it began small demonstrations, which SNCC felt detracted from its own ongoing efforts to mobilize and organize at the grass roots level.[68] SCLC was determined to publicize nationally the repression of African Americans in Alabama. SNCC felt this national orientation was apt to sacrifice local people's interests, but recognizing that the march would occur, it agreed not to denounce it, while still voting against SNCC's formal participation. Not all of its members were against the march, however, notably SNCC chairman John Lewis who was also a member of SCLC's board of directors. At the same time, President Johnson had exerted pressure against the march and King's aides grew concerned over the escalating death threats against him. Eventually, King capitulated to various demands and fears, and SCLC's Hosea Williams alongside John Lewis (on his own rather than SNCC's behalf) led the march.[69]

It was one of the bloodiest and most violent encounters in the movement's history, with the notoriously racist Sheriff Jim Clark deputizing hundreds of men and gaining the support of state troopers led by Major John Cloud. As the marchers crossed the Edmund Pettus Bridge, they were surrounded on both sides, tear-gassed and beaten. In chaos and panic, men, women and children fled for their lives, pursued by men on horseback brandishing nightsticks, cattle prods and chains. Seventy to eighty people were injured; among them, John Lewis—hospitalized with severe injuries to the head, and local leader Mrs Amelia Boynton, left unconscious from blows to the head and tear-gas inhalation. TV cameras captured the events and broadcasts prompted a public outcry against the brutality. Senators supporting voting rights legislation called for its passage as the least that could be done to honor the victims.[70]

Hearing the news, King immediately flew to Selma and conferred with local as well as national leaders. Many local people, as well as the bridge leaders in SNCC, supported a continuation of the march. But federal district court judge Frank Johnson, with a previous history of support for civil rights, blocked a second march with an injunction. King was torn. He had never defied a federal judge, but his commitment to the masses and the pressure exerted by indigenous and SNCC bridge leaders required a march. On the morning of the scheduled second march, former Governor LeRoy Collins of Florida, as director of the federal Community Relations Service established under the 1964 Civil Rights Act, came to mediate the situation. He proposed that Sheriff Clark and Colonel Al Lingo, head of the Alabama state troopers, agree not to attack the marchers if they would turn around once they reached the troopers. King could lead a symbolic march up to where the state troopers were waiting, and then turn around. This would avert bloodshed and allow King to support the masses and activists in favor of the march. King agreed to the plan. However, when King led the marchers, the troopers cleared a path, tauntingly giving the impression that they could have continued. King still turned the marchers around. They followed him, but once in Selma demanded to know why he had not continued on to Montgomery.[71]

King was forced to tell of his agreement with Collins. SNCC bridge leaders and participants were outraged. His deceit served to widen the gap between the primary formal organization and the bridge organization. SNCC had now been betrayed twice: in Atlantic City and in Selma. Once again, within the national movement sector, they possessed little or no power. While King's lack of candor incensed SNCC, he did gain the support of the federal government, and elicited the support of mainstream Americans. President Johnson demanded that Alabama's Governor Wallace insure the safe passage of marchers to Montgomery and supplied federal troops when Wallace refused protection. Moreover, in a televised joint session of Congress, he called for comprehensive voting rights legislation and signaled his allegiance by using the movement's slogan "We Shall Overcome."[72]

King had finally gained unprecedented presidential support, but SNCC workers were still being beaten in Alabama.[73] In the days that followed, the marchers, led by King and other movement leaders, continued the march from Selma, and this time they reached Montgomery. Joyous and hopeful, King delivered one of his most famous speeches warning of "a season of suffering" that still lay ahead, but holding out the promise that eventually "a society at peace with itself, a society that can live with its conscience," would be achieved. To the rhetorical question, "How long will it take?" he offered the reassurance: "However difficult the moment, however frustrating the hour, it will not be long." Repeating the call "How Long?" and response, "Not long" King built up to a rousing climax that drew a thundering ovation from the thousands of listeners."[74] That evening, a white mother of five, Mrs Viola Liuzzo, who had come to Selma from Detroit to assist the protest, was shot dead by Klansmen. She was on her way to take marchers back from Montgomery to Selma. Her murder, as well as the earlier killings of Reverend James Reeb and Marion County youth, Jimmie Lee Jackson, made it apparent that even federal support for civil rights could not eradicate the hate and racism so endemic to southern life. With passage of the 1965 Voting Rights Act, came the realization that African Americans in the South were now in the same position as Northern blacks, and that all the laws and legislation in the world would not bring equality and justice. A new approach was needed, one that did not try to appeal to moral imperatives for justice, but one which took one's rights by force.

SNCC bridge leader and social scientist, Joyce Ladner, studied black power advocates, dividing them into "locals" or those who only look at local problems, and "cosmopolitans" or those who connect local problems to the world. Describing the circumstances that led many SNCC activists to change their philosophy and approach to civil rights, she sees the perceived failure of the Freedom Summer of 1964 as the cause of the disillusionment among the "cosmopolitans." She writes that: "by the end of 1964, after the historic Mississippi Summer Project, the cosmopolitans began to feel that their organizational methods were just not effective."[75] Frequently frustrated and sometimes in despair over identifying more effective strategies, a number of cosmopolitans left Mississippi for well paid jobs or graduate training, while the more alienated among them became more interested in Africa and considered emigration. Still others left SNCC but joined other radical groups.[76]

Ladner saw the expulsion of whites from SNCC as the outcome of a debate initiated by the "cosmopolitans." The move was tied to the development of "black consciousness" which dispelled negative images of blackness derived from a white supremacist society and affirmed "the beauty of blackness." Committed patriotically to the development of African American institutions, such nationalists were not racists, Ladner explained, but were committed to "a move toward independence from the dominant groups, the whites." The SNCC experience had persuaded them that cutting themselves off from white people was an essential first step to true liberation. As advocates of such separatism put it:

> Indigenous leadership cannot be built with whites in
> the positions they now hold. They [whites] can participate

on a voluntary basis ... but in no way can they participate
on a policy-making level.

Equally, the acquisition of a new "black consciousness" was
fundamental because white supremacist assumptions were deeply
ingrained in the language and symbols of American culture.
Consequently, according to Ladner, the cosmopolitans argued that black
consciousness was needed before black "people can successfully
develop the tools and techniques for acquiring black power."

Embracing this new philosophy of black power was to have far-
reaching consequences. It was to become a positive base for black
identity, race pride and self-respect. As Ladner notes, Dr. King
appreciated the positive aspects of black power. He saw it as "calling the
Negro to a new sense of manhood, to a deep feeling of racial pride and
to an audacious appreciation of his heritage."[77] Although King
supported the central message of black pride, (and like the nationalists
viewed it in terms of a new black male identity) he did not agree with
the means by which many black nationalists wished to seize power.
Rather he felt that a nonviolent stance was more productive. Between
1963 and 1965, King and the SCLC had gained the unprecedented
support of the federal government. Yet, at the same time, the base upon
which the movement rested, the bridging tier, had begun to erode.

During 1965, COFO began to disband and scores of activists left
the Deep South. In the summer of that year, rioting broke out in Los
Angeles and other major cities outside of the South. Accordingly, King
urged the SCLC to shift its focus to the North. At the same time, both
SNCC and its main national movement collaborator in COFO, the
Congress Of Racial Equality (CORE), ejected whites from their
organizations, and elected new and more radical chairs, Stokely
Carmichael and Floyd McKissick respectively. Both men developed a
black power philosophy, explicitly rejecting nonviolence and interracial
membership. They proclaimed a black nationalist philosophy and
embraced the teachings of Malcolm X, with some spokesmen calling for
separatism, and the use of whatever means necessary to gain power. The
movement had begun to erode, but although these leadership changes
caught the headlines, the erosion came not from the top but rather from
its roots.

SNCC's transformation into a black power movement organization
was to have powerful consequences for women, and for the movement
as a whole. It brought a corresponding shift in organizational structure
and a collapse of the bridging nature of the organization. The change to

a black power philosophy brought the development of hierarchy and fewer "free spaces" for women's leadership. Prathia Hall, a bridge leader in SNCC, recalls "a collegiality and kinship between black men and women" before 1965. These solid friendships allowed people to share ideas and wrestle with issues in an atmosphere of mutual respect. Moreover, she agreed with Joyce Ladner that at that stage "if men had really gotten out of line or been demeaning or whatever, that women would have told them where to go! And in short order." Hall distinguished between the gender relations that characterized SNCC pre-1965 and those that existed later. Her reaction to the 1965 Waveland paper on the role of women had been ambivalent. She saw herself as "among the black women of the generations before [her] who wanted to see black men in leadership." But her reaction to the black power era with "all of the Black macho rhetoric and 'the best thing women can do for the movement is have babies?' and all the women walking—I've forgotten how many steps behind" was far from ambivalent.[78]

Hall left SNCC in 1965 to work for the National Council of Negro Women, and so viewed these changes from the outside. However, Jean Wheeler Smith Young, a community bridge leader, who remained in SNCC until 1968, offers a similarly negative response to the changes in the organization after 1965:

> I wasn't interested in the leadership that had evolved at that time. I thought there were a lot of strangers that I knew nothing about, and I wasn't about to follow them anywhere. Because so much of why it worked in the beginning was the people all knew each other and we knew that we could depend on each other. After there became so many new people that you couldn't know or depend on because of the way they came in or you'd never worked with them, it wasn't the kind of thing where you'd want to put you life on the line with somebody you never even met before, or you met ten minutes before.[79]

These comments suggest that not only did the new leadership style become more patriarchal and authoritarian but that the turnover of staff—including the expulsion of whites—damaged the distinctive *esprit de corps* that southern war zones had inculcated at SNCC.

Other members felt that the new regime was unfair and were saddened by the expulsions since many of the veteran white workers had sacrificed a great deal for the movement. However, SNCC had always found membership fluctuations traumatic. Muriel Tillinghast suggests that the large influx of new white volunteers during the Freedom Summer Project pushed many black participants into fighting for control of the organization, which eventually resulted in the expulsion of all white activists. Tillinghast also felt that many of the new black SNCC workers after 1965 were agents who infiltrated the organization in order to destroy it. Her own departure from SNCC in 1966 was impelled because, in her words "I couldn't tell the agents from my friends. I was getting to be ... extremely paranoid about some people ... I felt that the organization was going to explode and I didn't want to be there."[80] The leader of the Nonviolent Action Group in Cambridge, Maryland, Gloria Richardson, also has her doubts about the origins of the radical personnel changes at SNCC. Her organizational ties to SNCC ended in 1965 before the expulsion of white volunteers, but she shares the suspicion that infiltration accelerated SNCC's decline. Not only were experienced white activists expelled, but newcomers unknown to SNCC veterans like Cleveland Sellers, formed a dominant nationalist faction that, in Richardson's view, pursued a misguided, ideological organizing strategy. As she explains, they

> thought they could organize around Black nationalism alone when people were concerned about bread and butter issues—you have to talk about voting, you have to talk about housing, you have to talk about education, you have to talk about jobs—and I think that that killed it. And I think that was by design.[81]

Whether through outside infiltration or an internal shift of power, SNCC was no longer recognizable as the organization that had been so loved by black and white activists alike.

1966 was a difficult time in SNCC's history. With the expulsion of whites and the establishment of a leadership hierarchy, SNCC was irrevocably changed. However, Ruby Doris Smith Robinson, who died in her twenties, fought to keep the organization together. Bernice Reagon regards Robinson as the "glue" that kept SNCC together and believes that her efforts to sustain it in this difficult time "took her life."[82] Well-known black historian Paula Giddings believes that part of the crisis in SNCC was due to the fact that, whereas the early civil rights movement "had served to confirm masculine as well as racial assertiveness," when the movement "began to break down, that old nightmare of impotence resurfaced."[83] Though Ruby Doris Smith Robinson's track record of leadership and toughness made her the best hope of saving SNCC after her election as executive secretary in 1966:

Even so, she was plagued by chauvinistic attitudes. As James Foreman asserted, "She endured vicious attacks from the SNCC leadership. They also embodied male chauvinism in fighting her attempts as executive secretary to impose a sense of organizational responsibility and self-discipline, trying to justify themselves by the fact that their critic was a woman."

According to Giddings, the re-focusing of the freedom struggle on the North exacerbated the "exhibitionism of manhood" because outside of the South, black institutions "whose most vital resource was women" were weaker. The image of armed black young men became fashionable and reduced black power to "a metaphor for the male consciousness of the era." To illustrate this reductionism, Giddings cites CORE leader Floyd McKissick's declaration that: "The year 1966 shall be remembered as the year we left our imposed status as Negroes and became Black men."

With this shift, the position of black women in the struggle for equality and justice took an unprecedented turn. Never before had black women been "required" to "step back." While, previously, women may have voluntarily done so, always knowing that the step was really to the side, they were now explicitly receiving messages that dictated their positions as behind their men. Angela Davis, one of the few women leaders in the black power movement, said:

I ran headlong into a situation, which was to become a constant problem in my political life. Women should not play leadership roles, they insisted. A woman was to "inspire" her man and educate his children.[84]

She complained of the "brothers" who only attended occasional staff meetings rather than working for the organization on a daily basis, yet still denounced "women taking over the organization." They spouted the myth of black women being too domineering which implied, Davis reports, that "we wanted to rob them of their manhood." Some even went so far as to insist that by taking leading organizational roles, "we were aiding and abetting the enemy, who wanted to see Black men weak and unable to hold their own." Kathleen Cleaver, and Elaine Brown, both leaders in the black power movement, would echo this view.[85] Even longtime leaders such as Gloria Richardson, experienced the wrath of the new macho activists, who at one rally shouted her down as a "castrator."[86] While Malcolm X may have been supportive of women's activism, it is clear that the rhetoric of black nationalism centered on the development of a new black masculinity whereby black men could assert patriarchal power and seize their "rightful place" as men.

In a 1970s interview, Ella Baker had some harsh words for the way the rhetoric of black emasculation had put an extra burden on the black female inclining her to take "much more of a retiring role within the movement than she did in 1960."[87] The backlash against women's leadership was further fed by the body of literature that proliferated in the mid-1960s to the early 1970s which served to support the myth of the black matriarch in low income households.[88] Such a myth has been soundly refuted by scholars, many of whom argue that these findings are erroneous and based upon the false assumption that poor black women's earning power has given them more power in their relationships.[89] Sociologist, Robert Staples, notes that "in reality wives in poor black families contribute less to the total family income than do wives in non-poor black families because they are much less likely to be employed among the low income group ..."[90] Bonnie Thornton Dill similarly observes that black women have historically worked as household domestics, one of the lowest paid work in America, because they were black, poor and women.[91]

The new hierarchical form of power so vividly described by Elaine Brown in *A Taste of Power*, led to the erosion of the very qualities that had propelled the movement forward. By 1966, SNCC was no longer mobilizing to bridge the masses to the movement. As we have seen, Joyce Ladner explains the black power transition in terms of a division between locals and cosmopolitans with the latter's dominance ensuring that their disillusionment with the system led to a newfound identity and political orientation.[92] The MFDP's failed convention and Congressional challenges and the subsequent eviction of displaced sharecroppers from an inactive Air Force Base in Greenville, Mississippi, caused Ladner's "locals," also, "to pause and question the effectiveness of their traditional organizational tactics and goals." Like the cosmopolitans, they began to doubt the sincerity of federal promises to help African Americans, and among them, there were likewise locals who left the movement or "began to express strong anti-white sentiments."[93]

A common frustration, Ladner concludes, drew both cosmopolitans and locals behind black power.[94] For many of the locals, black power meant voter registration, political power held by blacks, black solidarity, and power over the black community.[95] Clayborne Carson has meticulously documented the fall of SNCC and he argues that the same critical rhetoric that paved the way for the black power platform simultaneously weakened SNCC itself.[96] Powerful women bridge leaders, Ella Baker, Muriel Tillinghast, Ruby Doris Smith Robinson and Faye Bellamy were openly critical of SNCC's failure to focus on programs, to develop indigenous leadership, and to build political power under Stokely Carmichael's chairmanship. All believed that individual aggrandizement had supplanted SNCC's course. When asked: "In what way has SNCC fallen short of its goal?" Ella Baker replied:

> It has not been successful in developing basic leadership in Mississippi, Alabama, Southwest Georgia. Its greatest difficulty has been in reconciling its genius for individual expression with the political necessity for organizational discipline. I myself approve of group discipline in general. The trend is more toward discipline, because the members of SNCC are a smaller and smaller band. This is because SNCC is no longer "the thing" and the civil rights movement is no longer "the thing."[97]

Exactly what Ella Baker meant by "the thing" is unclear, but what is clear is that SNCC had begun to fall apart and its change in organization, and philosophy were at the core of its collapse. SNCC's new chairman, Stokely Carmichael was becoming increasingly uncontrollable, making statements as *the* representative of SNCC without regard for the executive committee or SNCC members. Even Ruby Doris Smith Robinson, who supported the black power philosophy, criticized Carmichael on this score. As Carson shows, Robinson asked her fellow staff members how the impression had been created that "SNCC is only the organization that Carmichael has at his disposal to what (sic) he wants to get done?" In her view this was due to a combination of others failing to speak and the press seeking Carmichael "out for whatever ammunition could be found—FOR OUR DESTRUCTION." While conceding that Carmichael had, at his best, said what black people wanted to hear, Robinson was still dismayed by the lack of substance. Muriel Tillinghast echoed this complaint to Carson that after Carmichael became chair, "the chairman began to determine policy autonomously and the rest of us had to make a decision as to whether we were going with the chair or not." In a later meeting, Robinson, Faye Bellamy and Ralph Featherstone, as well as others, talked to Carmichael and convinced him to stop making speeches which included declarations and positions not approved by the rest of SNCC. He agreed to the request and decided to focus more on "developing programs and working on internal structure."[98]

As Ella Baker's comments indicate, SNCC failed to build on its Deep South achievements. By October 1966, two-thirds of SNCC's shrinking staff were in its Atlanta headquarters or in non-southern cities. Moreover, only a few veterans of the 1960-64 period remained with the organization. The departure of SNCC's most experienced organizers and the declining morale of those who remained further weakened its effectiveness. Perhaps most damning in the light of its earlier principles was the fact that SNCC workers increasingly tried to preach to and speak for local communities, rather than listening to them. As Carson sums up the situation:

> Instead of immersing themselves in protest activity and deriving their insights from an ongoing mass struggle, SNCC workers in 1966 stressed the need to inculcate among urban blacks a new racial consciousness as a foundation for future struggles.[99]

SNCC's philosophy and organizational shift away from the teachings of Ella Baker, and the methods developed by Septima Clark, destroyed the foundation of the movement. SNCC itself, which had been the major grass roots mobilizing force in the movement, collapsed in the early 1970s.

What this essay has sought to make clear, is that movement participants cannot be conceptualized in a dichotomous fashion as simply leaders and followers. Neither can it be suggested that women's civil rights movement participation was primarily of an organizing nature, as has been suggested by previous scholars. Charles Payne in his earlier work on black women's activism in the Mississippi Delta, has suggested that "men led, but women organized."[100] In a later analysis, which clearly enriches our knowledge of movement organizing in Mississippi, he labels them leaders, but describes their work as that of organizers.[101] Bernice McNair Barnett, who also studies black women in the civil rights movement, agrees with Payne that women organized and that their organizing was an important aspect of leadership.[102]

The present essay, and the larger study on which it draws, illustrates that African American women's activism included much more than organizing.[103] While formal networks, leaders, institutions and movement centers were significant factors in the recruitment process, they do not adequately address who, on a daily basis, provides the local leadership necessary to bridge the movement's message to potential recruits. Central to the success of a social movement is an intermediate layer of leadership, whose tasks include bridging potential constituents, and adherents as well as potential formal leaders to the movement. Women, as bridge leaders performed these tasks. In the case of the civil rights movement, the exclusion of most women from formal leadership positions created an exceptionally qualified leadership tier engaged in the task of micro-mobilization.

The social location of African American women, as defined by a gendered hierarchy, served the movement's need for a bridge between the pre-figurative politics of small towns and rural communities, and the strategic politics of movement organizations. Within this context, bridge leaders, who had no direct access to the power politics of the formal organization, could solicit potential constituents. This resolved the problems faced by many movement organizations that lacked such an intermediate layer of capable leadership. Ironically, gender exclusion was particularly useful because the movement could draw upon the resources of well educated and/or articulate women to act as carriers, as cultivators of solidarity, without the same set of leaders experiencing conflict between movement constituents and mainstream political compromise. In the case of the civil rights movement, these tasks were divided, though not exclusively, along gendered lines, thus providing the movement with a strong base of leadership.

In SNCC's early years, women bridge leaders succeeded because of SNCC's organizational form, which did not conform to the dominant, societal gender models. Through an ideology of inclusion, cooperation and individualism, as opposed to self-interest, SNCC broke down barriers to participation seeking not to indoctrinate, but to engage. Consequently, its organizational form, as created by its ideology, was able to incorporate women leaders into its leadership structure. It defied normative beliefs about the gender constructs and reorganized hierarchical lines into all-inclusive circles. While not completely successful, SNCC redefined the meanings of these constructs, because everyone in it was encouraged to question all cultural norms governing life in the 1960s. Subsequently, SNCC gave rise to the women's movement as well as the black power movement, as progressive extensions of SNCC's open, dialectical mobilizing frame.

However, with the rise of black nationalism, and a corresponding shift in ideology, came the imposition of hierarchy and the re-institutionalization of gender norms. Of course, the black power movement was not negative in its entirety. On the contrary, it created a positive base for a dramatic shift in racial identity and pride. However, the shift in movement ideology created a narrow action frame and mobilizing structure that undermined the bridging nature of SNCC. Power became centralized and followers became no more than acolytes for the leadership's ideological beliefs. Status was gained by a commitment to dogma rather than to community action and empowerment, and this undermined SNCC's effectiveness.

Movement leaders cannot simply preach a new creed or impose a new repertoire when creating a collective mobilizing action frame. Rather, such frames must evolve out of individual and subjective experiences of oppression. Bridge leaders Ella Baker and Septima Clark understood this fact. Moreover, they understood that resources, charismatic leaders, hierarchical structures, imposed action frames, and that political opportunities were not sufficient to sustain or even start a movement. Bridge leaders brought to the movement, a specific ideology of contention and, therefore alternative templates for organization that shaped corresponding action frames, mobilizing structures, political opportunities and outcomes. The bridging tier of women leaders was critical to the success of the civil rights movement.

The growing conflict between women bridge leaders and formal leaders after the Atlantic City convention marked the beginning of the movement's decline from below. The compromise so necessary to the relationship between the state and the movement's formal leaders created disillusionment in the bridging tier of the movement itself. The interplay of race, class, gender and culture all served to define that moment in terms of power, with white male elites having the most power, educated black male formal leaders having some power, and poor, uneducated black women having the least power to decide the fate of Mississippi and black representation in the political arena. As previously explored, women, because they could never possess the power of formal leaders within the movement sector, took a position much more in line with that of the masses they represented. On the face of it, the MFDP challengers had achieved an unprecedented victory, but to those at the movement's base, who suffered daily, and who were to return to impoverished conditions and oppression, the convention compromise marked a monumental defeat.

Rather than retaining the open organizational style, which sought to empower all members, SNCC's new ideological position resulted in a narrowing of its organizational power. While it shared many of the views of its local associates in the rural South, the new leadership abandoned this population, seeking instead to mobilize in northern cities. Its new dogmatism and attempts to deposit new cultural beliefs through rhetoric rather than dialogue, served to destroy its ability to mobilize the masses. At the same time, it embraced patriarchy, thus shrinking the "free spaces" once occupied by women leaders whose bridging work was critical to movement recruitment, mobilization and sustenance. The subsequent loss of many long-time activists, coupled with SNCC's failure to develop educational programs aimed at community empowerment, signaled the beginning of the end of the civil rights movement.

Notes

1. Joyce Rothschild-Whitt, "Collectivist Organization: An Alternative to Rational Bureaucratic Models," *American Sociological Review* 44 (1979): 509-527.

2. Myra Marx Ferree, "The Political Context of Rationality: Rational Choice Theory and Resource Mobilization" in A. Morris and C. Mueller, eds., *Frontiers of Social Movement Theory* (New Haven: Yale University Press, 1992), 45.

3. To give two examples: for the anti-nuclear power movement, see Gary L. Downey, "Ideology and the Clamshell Identity: Organizational Dilemmas in the Anti-Nuclear Power Movement," *Social Problems* 33 (1986): 357-373; and for the Pro-Choice Movement, see Suzanne Staggenborg, "Consequences of Professionalization and Formalization in the Pro-Choice Movement," *American Sociological Review* 53 (1988): 585-606.

4. Staggenborg, "Consequences"; for other feminist analyses, see, for example: Steven Buechler, *Women's Movements in the United States* (New Brunswick, NJ: Rutgers University Press 1990); Myra Marx Ferree and Beth H. Hess, *"Controversy and Coalition: The New Feminist Movement* (Boston: Twayne, 1985); Patricia Yancey Martin, "Rethinking Feminist Organization," *Gender and Society* 4 (1990): 182-206; Barbara Ryan, "Ideological Purity and Feminism: The U.S. Women's movement from 1966 to 1975," *Gender and Society* 3 (1989): 239-257; and Verta Taylor and Nancy Whittier, "Collective Identity in Social Movement Communities: Lesbian Feminist Mobilization" in Morris and Mueller, *Frontiers*, 104-129.

5. As exemplified by some Latin American guerila movements, see Linda Lobao, "Women in Revolutionary Movements: Changing Patterns of Latin American Guerila Struggle," and also the case of the German Green Party, Carol Schmid, "Women in the West German Green Party: The Uneasy Alliance of Ecology and Feminism," both in Guida West and Rhoda Blumberg, eds., *Women and Social Protest* (New York: Oxford University Press, 1990): 180-204, and 225-242 respectively.

6. Shrylee Dallard, *Ella Baker: A Leader Behind the Scenes* (NJ: Silver Burdett Press, 1990), 32.

7. Carol Mueller, "Ella Baker and the Origins of Participatory Democracy" on V. Crawford et al, eds., *Women in the Civil Rights Movement* (Brooklyn, NY: Carlson Publishing, 1990), 51-52.

8. Fay Bellamy, Interview, February 7, 1990.

9. Sara Evans and Harry Boyte, *Free Spaces* (New York: Harper and Row, 1986).

10. Anonymous Interviewee, March 16, 1989.

11. Anonymous SNCC member, Interview, March 16, 1989.

12. Persons Working out of the Atlanta Office, SNCC Papers, A:VI Box 28 #21.

13. Muriel Tillinghast, Interview, July 19, 1992.

14. Prathia Wynn Hall, Interview, November 9, 1992.

15. Bernice Johnson Reagon, Interview, November 30, 1992.

16. Reagon, Interview.

17. For a discussion of African American women and the church, see Evelyn Brooks, "The Feminist Theology of the Black Baptist Church, 1880-1900," in Amy Swerdlow and Hanna Lessinger, eds., *Class, Race and Sex: The Dynamics of Control* (Boston: G.K. Hall, 1983): 31-59; and Cheryl Townsend Gilkes, "Together and In Harness: Women's Traditions in the Sanctified Church," *Signs*, 10 (1985), 679.

18. Cynthia Neverdon-Morton, *Afro-American Women of the South and the Advancement of the Race: 1895-1925* (Knoxville: University of Tennessee Press, 1985), 6, 8.

19. E. Franklin Frazier, *The Negro Church in America* (New York: Schocken Books, 1963), 33.

20. Jacquelyn Grant, "Black Women and the Church" in Gloria T. Hull et al., eds., *All the Women are White, All the Blacks Are Men, But Some of Us Are Brave—Black Women Studies* (Old Westbury, NY: The Feminist Press, 1982), 145.

21. Hans A. Baer, *The Black Spiritual Movement—A Religious Response to Racism* (Knoxville: University of Tennessee Press, 1984), 154.

22. See Hortense Powdermaker, *After Freedom* (New York: Athenaeum, 1939), 272-276; St. Clair Drake and Horace Clayton, *Black Metropolis* (Chicago: University of Chicago Press, 1945), 632; and Milton Sernett, *Afro-American Religious History: A Documentary Witness* (Durham, NC: Duke University Press, 1985), 160.

23. For a more detailed discussion of this phenomenon, see Gilkes, "Together and in Harness," 678.

24. Reagon, Interview.

25. Fay Bellamy, Interview, February 7,1990.

26. Judy Richardson, Interview, August 7, 1990.

27. Anonymous Interviewee, March 16, 1989.

28. Bellamy, Interview.

29. Reagon, Interview.

30. Dorie Ladner, Interview, July 27, 1992.

31. Higginbotham, "African American Women's History and the Metalanguage of Race," *Signs* 17 (1992), 253-54.

32. On gender and power relations, see, for example, Rosabeth Moss Kanter, *Men and Women of the Corporation* (New York: Basic Books, 1977); Cynthia Cockburn, *Brothers: Male Dominance and Technological Change* (London: Pluto Press, 1983) and her later *Machinery and Dominance* (London: Pluto Press, 1985); R.W. Connell, *Gender and Power* (Palo Alto: Stanford University Press, 1987); and Catherine MacKinnon, "Feminism, Marxism, Method and the State: An Agenda for Theory," *Signs,* 7 (1982): 515-544. Also, see Joan Acker, "Hierarchies, Jobs, Bodies: A Theory of Gendered Organizations," *Gender and Society* 4 (1990): 139-158, for a discussion of the need for the analysis of gender as an organizational construct in organizational theory.

33. See Wini Breines, *Community and Organization in the New Left* (New York: Praeger, 1982); William Gamson, "The Social Psychology of Collective Action" and Sidney Tarrow, "Mentalities, Political Cultures and Collective Action Frames: Constructing Meaning Through Action," in Morris and Mueller, *New Frontiers,* 53-76 and 174-202 respectively.

34. See Charles Payne, *I've Got the Light of Freedom: The Organizing Tradition and the Mississippi Freedom Struggle* (Berkeley: University of California Press, 1994), 266. Also, Payne notes that Drake and Cayton's study of Chicago in the 1930s and 1940s suggests that activist women were trusted more than men because "they could not easily capitalize off of their activism." (275) This conclusion certainly reflects my findings. I disagree with Payne, however, when, in citing Arlene Daniel's work, he suggests that women's work in the movement was devalued. (276) Rather, my findings suggest that while their work was not in the formal sector, it was appreciated, acknowledged and viewed as important by men and women activists alike.

35. This phenomenon has been well documented by scholars. Women are often more visible and initiate movement activity and only tend to recede into the background later. See for example West and Blumberg, eds., *Women and Social Protest.*

36. Robnett, *How Long? How Long? African American Women in the Struggle for Civil Rights* (New York: Oxford University Press, 1997).

37. Howard Zinn, *SNCC: The New Abolitionists* (Boston: Beacon Press, 1964), 258.

38. COFO Proposed Community Centers, Mississippi Freedom Democratic Party Papers, Box 5:19, in the Martin Luther King Center for Non-violent Social Change, Atlanta, GA. [Hereafter MFDP Papers]

39. *The Nation,* (June 1, 1964).

40. Data compiled from the Minutes of Eighteenth Precinct Meetings and the list of six County Delegates and Alternatives, MFDP Papers, Box 4:15.

41. Victoria Gray, Interview, February 6, 1990.

42. Gray, Interview.

43. Constance Curry, Interview, August 22-23, 1992.

44. Report on November 10th. MFDP Meeting in Washington, D.C., MFDP Papers, Box 3: files 4-6 of 6.

45. Newspaper Clippings and Press Releases, MFDP Papers, Box 3:4 4 of 6; Minutes of Executive Committee Meeting, September 13, 1964, MFDP Papers, Box 20:20.

46. Minutes of FDP Statewide Convention, MFDP Papers, Box 20:21; Pinola Meeting, January 8, 1965, MFDP Papers, Box 20:19; Sunflower County Meeting, August 1, 1964, MFDP Papers, Box 20:19; Baker County Meeting, September 24, 1965, Charles Sherrod Papers, Box 3, File 2 in the Martin Luther King Center for Non-violent Social Change, Atlanta, GA.

47. Virginia Gray, Interview.

48. Clay County Report, November, 29, 1965, MFDP Microfilm, Reel 65 Frame #305 in the Congress of Racial Equality Papers 1944-1968. (Hereafter MFDP Microfilm).

49. Letter to the Department of Agriculture, November 26, 1965, by Mrs Ada Holliday, MFDP Microfilm, Reel 65, Frame #324.

50. Ed King, as quoted in Kay Mills, *This Little Light of Mine: The Life of Fannie Lou Hamer* (New York: Dutton, 1993), 125.

51. As quoted in Mills, *This Little Light,* 127.

52. Mills, *This Little Light,* 128.

53. Mills, *This Little Light,* 128-129.

54. Unita Blackwell, Interview, January 30, 1990.

55. Unita Blackwell, Interview.

56. Mills, *This Little Light,* 139.

57. As quoted in Mills, *This Little Light,* 130.

58. Cleveland Sellers [and Robert Terrell], *The River of No Return: The Autobiography of a Black Militant and the Life and Death of SNCC* (New York: Morrow, 1990), 111.

59. Dottie Zellner, Interview, July 27, 1992. All subsequent quotations from same interview, unless otherwise indicated.

60. Mills, *This Little Light,* 135.

61. Mills, *This Little Light,* 137.

62. As quoted in Mills, *This Little Light,* 142.

63. As quoted in Mills, *This Little Light,* 143.

64. Mills, *This Little Light,* 141. Malcolm was alluding to the Kenyan terrorist Mau Mau society led by Oginga Odinga whom the Freedom Singers had celebrated in one of their songs that day.

65. Mills, *This Little Light,* 144.

66. Mills, *This Little Light,* 170.

67. Mills, *This Little Light,* 171.

68. Sellers, *The River of No Return,* 117-118.

69. This account of the Selma campaign draws heavily on David Garrow, *Bearing the Cross* (New York: Vintage Books, 1986), 395-413.

70. Garrow, *Bearing the Cross,* 397-400.

71. Garrow, *Bearing the Cross,* 401-405.

72. Garrow, *Bearing the Cross,* 405-409.

73. Garrow, *Bearing the Cross,* 409.

74. As quoted in Garrow, *Bearing the Cross,* 413.

75. Joyce Ladner, "What Black Power Means to Negroes in Mississippi" in August Meier, ed., *The Transformation of Activism* (Chicago: Aldine, 1970), 131-154. All subsequent references to this source unless otherwise indicated.

76. Ladner, "What Black Power Means," 139.

77. As quoted in "What Black Power Means," 151. For the debate on black power, see also Harvard Sitkoff, *The Struggle for Racial Equality, 1954-1981* (New York: Hill and Wang, 1981), chapters 6 and 7.

78. Prathia Wynn Hall, Interview.

79. Jean Wheeler Smith Young, Interview, August 9, 1992.

80. Muriel Tillinghast, Interview, July 19, 1992.

81. Gloria Richardson, Interview, August 8, 1992.

82. Bernice Johnson Reagon, Interview, November 30, 1992.

83. Paula Giddings, *When and Where I Enter* (New York: Bantam Books, 1984), 314-315. Unless otherwise indicated, all subsequent references are to this.

84. Giddings, *When and Where I Enter*, 316-317.

85. For Cleaver, see *When and Where I Enter*, 315, and for Brown, see her *A Taste of Power* (New York: Doubleday, 1992), 357.

86. Giddings, *When and Where I Enter*, 317.

87. Ella Baker Oral History Transcript, 78, in the Civil Rights Documentation Project, Moorland Spingarn Center, Howard University, Washington, DC.

88. See, for example, Arthur Hippler, *Hunter's Point* (New York: Basic Books, 1974), 217; Daniel P. Moynihan, *The Negro Family: The Case for National Action* (Washington DC: US Government Printing Office, 1965); and more generally, Daryl Scott, *Contempt and Pity: Social Policy and the Image of the Damaged Black Psyche, 1880 - 1996* (Chapel Hill: University of North Carolina Press, 1997).

89. Rose Brewer, "Black Women in Poverty: Some Comments on Female Headed Families," *Signs* 13 (1988): 331-339; Vicky Cromwell and Ronald Cromwell, "Perceived Dominance in Decision-Making and Conflict Resolution among Anglo, Black and Chicano Couples," *Journal of Marriage and the Family* 40 (1978): 754-756; Robert Staples, *The Black Woman in America: Sex, Marriage, and the Family* (Chicago: Nelson-Hall Publishers, 1973),174-183; Annie Barnes, *Black Women: Interpersonal Relationships in Profile* (Bristol, IN: Wyndham Hall Press, 1986); Angela Davis, "Reflections on Black Women's Role in the Community of Slaves," *Black Scholar*, 3 (1971): 2-15; and Jacqueline Jackson, "But Where Are the Men," *Black Scholar* 3 (1972): 30-41

90. Staples, *The Black Woman*, 109.

91. Thornton Dill, "Race, Class, and Gender: Prospects for an All-Inclusive Sisterhood," *Feminist Studies* 9 (1983), 143.

92. Ladner, "What Black Power Means," 135.

93. Ladner, "What Black Power Means," 144-145.

94. Ladner, "What Black Power Means," 148.

95. Ladner, "What Black Power Means," 145-146.

96. Clayborne Carson, *In Struggle: SNCC and the Black Awakening of the 1960s* (Cambridge: Harvard University Press, 1981), 229.

97. As quoted in Emily Stoper, *The Student Nonviolent Coordinating Committee: The Growth of Radicalism in a Civil Rights Organization* (Brooklyn, NY: Carlson Publishing, 1989), 272.

98. Carson, *In Struggle*, 229-231.

99. Carson, *In Struggle*, 231, 232, quotation from 234-235.

100. Payne, "Men Led, But Women Organized: Movement Participation of Women in the Mississippi Delta" in Crawford et al, *Women in the Civil Rights Movement*, 158.

101. Payne, *I've Got the Light of Freedom*.

102. Bernice McNair Barnett, "Invisible Southern Black Women Leaders in the Civil Rights Movement," *Signs* 7 (1993), 176.

103. Robnett, *How Long? How Long?*

CHAPTER 6

The "Gun-Toting" Gloria Richardson: Black Violence in Cambridge, Maryland

Jenny Walker

Between 1962 and 1964, the spiritually and psychologically southern town of Cambridge, on the Eastern shore of Maryland, witnessed some of the most violent racial clashes of the supposedly "nonviolent" civil rights era. These confrontations were violent not only in terms of white mob terrorism, which was common enough, but also in terms of a black community in which some members were primed and prepared to defend themselves, with arms if necessary, against such oppression.[1]

In the midst of this racial tension and violence stood Gloria Richardson, the undisputed leader of the Cambridge Nonviolent Action Committee (CNAC)—a civil rights organization formed to challenge racial segregation in that city. Remarkably, this campaign and Richardson's leadership have received relatively little consideration from historians of the civil rights era. Serious work on Cambridge amounts to little more than a handful of articles and brief discussions in larger works on the civil rights movement. Yet even when historians have turned their attention to the Cambridge struggle, they have often misrepresented both its nature and the role of Richardson herself. On occasion, she has been portrayed as a young and militant, "gun-toting" woman, and the campaign has been interpreted as one in which, "blacks had stopped extolling the virtues of passive resistance" and "guns were carried as a matter of course."[2]

This essay seeks to demonstrate that such accounts are flawed. In reality, Mrs Richardson was a middle-aged, middle-class black woman who had never fired a gun. Contrary to the claims of some historians, she was an unfaltering advocate of nonviolent direct action. While black violence clearly occurred on a large scale in Cambridge, there is little evidence to show that any CNAC protester was ever involved in a violent act. In the process, this essay will also consider the way in which Richardson—as one of the few women to reach a position of prominence in a civil rights campaign—has subsequently been appropriated as a feminist icon. As we shall see, this has unfortunately resulted in historical accounts, which have distorted, rather than illuminated, what she did and what she represented.

Gloria Richardson: Violent Campaigner?

Cambridge was certainly not of the Deep South. Its economic base was in manufacturing, not agriculture. Railroad lines linked it to the major northern ports of New York and Philadelphia. Politically, its black residents had continued to vote since Reconstruction and their votes secured the election of two black councilmen: Nehemiah Henry in 1906 and, more significantly for this essay—Gloria Richardson's grandfather, Herbert Maynaidier St. Clair in 1912. St. Clair continued to hold this office until 1946. Furthermore, black policemen patrolled the city's streets. However, while geographically and in economic orientation Cambridge was northern, and there were other aspects of Cambridge life that far more strongly resembled northern habits than southern customs, white Cambridge still claimed a sort of honorary southern status, and spiritually and psychologically it was far more southern than northern in outlook.

In 1963, a *New York Times* article declared that "the city is more Deep South in its thinking than it is Maryland. Its citizens, in fact, feel more kinship with Virginia than with their own state."[3] In one of the few studies of Gloria Richardson, Annette K. Brock noted that Cambridge had an "established pattern of discrimination and segregation, like all Southern towns" and fellow historian Peter Levy also recognized that, "Cambridge had a southern look and feel."[4] Only five of the eighteen main restaurants in the downtown district were integrated and the remaining thirteen were legally segregated according to municipal law. While the employment of black policemen was progressive in southern terms, as in many towns of the Deep South, they had no legal power to arrest whites whom they suspected of breaking the law. Instead, they had to summon a white officer to the scene or, as a last resort, they had to obtain special permission to arrest the suspect themselves. Racial etiquette superceded effective law enforcement.[5] While desegregation plans for the city's public schools were drawn up after the *Brown* decisions of 1954 and 1955, there were still no integrated schools as late as 1962. Unemployment, though by no means a quintessentially southern phenomenon, ran some three times higher in the black population than it did in the white community. Most conspicuously, the white mobs that defended segregated public accommodations against civil rights demonstrators in Cambridge and the terrorist violence that ensued, far more closely resembled events captured on camera in Birmingham or St. Augustine in the Deep South than the generally more covert and systemic (some contemporaries termed it, subtle), though equally determined, opposition to black advancement in the north at this stage.

Formal civil rights activity in Cambridge began in late 1961 when two Student Non-violent Coordinating Committee (SNCC) workers, William Hansen and Reginald Robinson, began to investigate racial conditions in the city and its surrounding areas. They found a city with a deeply entrenched system of segregation, where most African Americans were poor, unemployment was disproportionately high, and educational provisions were inadequate. By January 1962, a campaign was under way which aimed to desegregate Cambridge's public accommodations. On January 13, a hundred-strong civil rights force staged sit-ins and other protests around the downtown area. About fifty of these participants were drawn from the local community, while the other half were either members of civil rights organizations, including the Congress of Racial Equality (CORE), SNCC and the Civic Interest Group (CIG)—a Baltimore civil rights organization—or students from Maryland State College—an historically black school in the area. As Reginald Robinson remembered: "The streets of Cambridge were lined with a great many jeering whites. Negroes also crowded the streets ... a number of incidents happened all over the downtown area. Picketers were shoved and jostled quite frequently." Describing a scene all too reminiscent of many of the more celebrated Deep South confrontations, Robinson continued:

> The most serious incident happened at the Choptank Inn. Bill [Hansen] and another demonstrator were the only two who got inside the restaurant. On the outside ... a crowd of about 150 very hostile whites gathered. Approximately fifty near-hysterical people were on the inside ... The mob on the inside converged on Bill and started beating him. He was thrown bodily out of the door. He got up again and entered the restaurant again. This time he was knocked down again, and kicked out of the door. When he tried to enter a third time he was again knocked down. At this juncture he was arrested for disorderly conduct, by a state policemen (sic) who had been standing nearby watching the entire proceeding.[6]

Following this dramatic example of nonviolent direct action protest in Cambridge, many more local black citizens joined the campaign,

especially when it became apparent that the authorities would not yield
to their demands for integration without a fight. In March 1962, CNAC
was formed as an affiliate of SNCC. Its first chairman was Frederick St.
Clair, Gloria Richardson's cousin. However, by June of 1962,
Richardson had taken his place and had assumed leadership of the
movement.

Protests continued throughout 1962 and tensions mounted, reaching
a climax in the spring of 1963. The Dorsett Theater, which had already
been a target of protests because its management confined black
customers to the segregated gallery at the top of the building, added
insult to injury by reducing the designated "Negro" area within the
gallery to only a few seats at the back. While African American
resentment smoldered at this affront, two black high school students,
Dwight Cromwell and Dinez White, were arrested while praying in
protest outside a segregated bowling alley. A local court sentenced them
to indefinite periods of incarceration at a Cambridge juvenile detention
center. Gloria Richardson, her mother, and her daughter, Donna, were
also arrested for demonstrating at segregated accommodations in the
area.

On June 12, in response to these and other incidents, racial violence
flared again. The trouble erupted when a white mob followed a group of
black demonstrators back to the black section of town where angry
residents were armed and waiting for them. Two white men were struck
in the chest by shotgun blasts and three white business establishments
were burnt to the ground. Tensions continued to mount and inter-
communal resentments reached such a fever pitch that the National
Guard was mobilized. With the deployment of these troops, violence
ceased temporarily. The city government, eager to avoid more violent
unrest, offered to pass a charter amendment that would end segregation
in the downtown restaurants and bars. But CNAC rejected this offer
arguing that any amendment would be subject to referendum and so,
given that the majority of voters were white, it would be likely to be
overturned. Robert Kennedy, in his capacity as Attorney General, also
attempted to intervene in a bid to avert further protests. He met with
Maryland's Democratic Governor, J. Millard Tawes, and negotiated an
agreement to desegregate the state's public schools completely by the
fall term of 1963. The charter amendment was unanimously passed by
the city council on July 2 and the National Guard left town. Thus,
government at all levels hoped that, thanks to these steps, the racial
situation in Cambridge would calm down. This proved to be a vain
hope.

Nonviolent marches and sit-ins at segregated facilities continued and, as previously, the protesters were met by angry, violent mobs. On the night of July 12, the violence far exceeded that of a month earlier, and the National Guard returned. This time it was to remain in the city for over a year. That night a group of whites drove through the black neighborhood shooting randomly at people and houses. Black residents returned fire, and white businesses again fell victim to arson attacks. By the end of the evening, more than twelve people had been shot, including two National Guardsmen and a twelve-year-old boy. Miraculously, no one was killed.

Violent incidents such as these have undoubtedly contributed to a widespread misunderstanding concerning Richardson's and CNAC's commitment to nonviolence. Certainly, some of the contemporary press accounts blamed CNAC and Richardson for, and sometimes implicated them in, these violent racial disturbances. Three weeks after the July 12 rioting, the white liberal magazine *Newsweek*, having informed its readers that Richardson was known as "the tough one, the most militant and mercurial of the stormy Negro revolt in Cambridge, Md." went on to discuss "her revolution." "Twice," the reporter commented, the Cambridge situation "had passed the flash point, and erupted into rioting It was now drawing dangerously close to the brink again—because of her [Richardson's] toughness, some people thought."[7] The *New York Times*, on the day after the riot, similarly labeled Richardson an "intransigent militant" who had ignored advice from the Justice Department to cease demonstrations. As a result, the report continued, "six whites were shot."[8]

Towards the end of 1963, such press reports became even more hostile towards Richardson. Their antagonistic tone was closely linked to events surrounding the city's passing of a charter amendment requiring the desegregation of public accommodations. Immediately after the council passed the amendment, segregationists in the city began to gather signatures to force a referendum on the issue. This petition drive was successful and a referendum was set for October 2. Cambridge's white moderate leadership, including businessmen and politicians, appealed to their fellow citizens to support the amendment, arguing that to reject it would threaten the "economic welfare of the city."[9] Mayor Calvin Mowbray worked especially hard towards these ends. The local National Association for the Advancement of Colored People (NAACP) chapter and several black ministers worked equally hard in an attempt to ensure that the African American vote turned out in force. Some commentators believed that if a majority of blacks voted in favor of the amendment, a 35 percent share of the white vote would be sufficient to secure the amendment.[10]

In the main, Richardson remained silent about the proposed solution to the segregated public accommodations issue. But she did remark that CNAC would not be actively encouraging the city's black voters to support the charter amendment. When pushed to explain why she simply stated that:

> Constitutional rights cannot be given or taken away at the polls. A first-class citizen does not plead to the white power structure to give him something that the whites have no power to give or take away. Human rights are human rights, not white rights.[11]

On October 2, the charter amendment was voted down by 1,994 votes to 1,720 and the segregationists were triumphant. The poll results showed that a little over the 35 percent of favorable white votes thought necessary to pass the amendment was secured, but only one out of every two registered black voters cast their ballot.[12]

Richardson's stand against the referendum seems to have helped to create the media myth that she had rejected nonviolent direct action. In opposing the referendum vote, she showed herself to be somewhat removed from the mainstream civil rights leaders and their liberal white allies, who broadly supported the freedom struggle's goal of equality before the law and the nonviolent tactics that it employed. The inference seemed to be that by disagreeing with the mainstream movement on one issue—namely that of the fairness of popular referenda—she had moved away from it on all issues including a commitment to nonviolent protest. Local NAACP leaders criticized her for "sending the wrong message to moderates who had stuck their necks out for blacks."[13] Martin Luther King criticized her for opposing the referendum at a time when others in the South were fighting for the right to vote. White leaders in Cambridge argued that she had opposed the referendum for personal motives rather than principled action.[14]

The mainstream media stepped up their direct criticism of Richardson. *Time* magazine labeled her a "zealot." By encouraging Cambridge's blacks to boycott the referendum, *Time* complained as had King, that Richardson offered "a strange brand of leadership, particularly at a time when in some parts of the U.S., her fellow Negroes were shedding blood in their struggle for the right to vote." Referring to the defeat in the referendum, the caption underneath her photograph

read, "Instead of a Win, a Whim." Of course, for Richardson, her
opposition was not capricious but highly principled, going to the very
heart of the human rights issues that underpinned the whole civil rights
movement.[15]

Murray Kempton, writing for the *New Republic*, also wrote
unfavorably about Richardson. Characterizing the charter amendment as
"a package it [the white Cambridge power structure] still thinks of as
total surrender," he castigated Richardson, claiming that she stood
"almost alone among Negroes with a voice" in her opposition. Kempton
also implied that motives of personal fame might have encouraged her
defiant stance. Though the argument had not been put as forcefully at
the time of that summer's violent confrontations, Kempton now put the
onus for the city's troubles on Richardson, suggesting that the state and
city leaders could be, "excused, as reasonable men, for blaming all this
on Gloria Richardson and everything she has done since she turned the
Negro school children out to demonstrate last Spring."[16]

By opposing the referendum, Gloria Richardson had opposed
democracy itself; at least so it seemed to white liberals. She therefore
stood outside the liberal coalition and was fair target for criticism. A
tortuous logic made her the villain of the piece. She had gone against
what "reasonable" people felt was acceptable in the struggle for equal
rights. Thus, having been proved to be an irresponsible leader, more
interested in maintaining her own leadership position than advancing the
cause she purported to espouse, it was quite possible that all the violence
that had taken place in Cambridge was in some way orchestrated by her.

For all their hostility towards Richardson, the white liberal print
media rarely claimed that Richardson had taken part, or had a leading
role in, the violence. Ironically, in the summer of 1963, such reporting
was far more prevalent in the black media, who celebrated the defiant
stance of Cambridge blacks. *Ebony* magazine, for instance, claimed that
over the course of the demonstrations "Negro *demonstrators* shot nearly
a dozen guardsmen in separate incidents, beat scores more with rocks
and stones and broke one Negro guardsman's arm when he tried to
throw a gas grenade". The article also went on to suggest that Gloria
Richardson and "her followers" had been "preparing for war with local
police, the National Guard and federal troops, if necessary, in an all-out
battle for their rights." "No-one," the magazine claimed, "really talks
seriously about practicing nonviolence in Cambridge."[17] The Nation of
Islam's *Muhammad Speaks* similarly linked the black violence in
Cambridge with Richardson. The article announced that, "Since the
Negro here first erupted for freedom in 1961, behind the unimpeachable,

not-for-sale leadership of Gloria Richardson, there have been boycotts, demands, demonstrations, tear gas, bullets, rocks." It also quoted a SNCC field worker who claimed that, because their demands for integration had been ignored: "The situation in Cambridge is hopeless. People are ready to kill or be killed."[18]

The print media, both white, but especially black, wrote story upon story, throughout the violent summer and fall of 1963, about Gloria Richardson and her violent campaign. However, they did so without offering any real evidence that she was in any way involved in these violent incidents. Justice Department attorney Burke Marshall, for his part, was quite sure that Richardson and CNAC had no part in that summer's violence. He reported in a July 1963 memorandum that, "the Negro community does not follow the leadership in terms of nonviolence or in demonstrations."[19] Nevertheless, even if such violent incidents were beyond the remit of Richardson and CNAC, there was still a considerable amount of black violence in Cambridge—far more than elsewhere in the "nonviolent" movement. In this climate, perhaps it is not surprising that the press would link the violence there to the groups who were stirring up racial tensions by encouraging black protest. But, given that there is so little other evidence to sustain such claims, why have Richardson and the CNAC been linked to the violence in subsequent historical accounts?

Historian Charles Payne, in an important bibliographic essay in his *I've Got the Light of Freedom*, recognizes that, "scholarly and popular histories of the movement have traditionally reflected the same underlying analytical frames as did contemporaneous media." As a result, there has been "a chorus of complaints from movement participants that they could not recognize their own movement in most histories." Payne goes on to suggest that, "The issues that are invisible to the media and to the current generation of Black activists are still almost as invisible to scholars."[20] The accounts of the Cambridge movement that appear in the contemporary press have certainly been replicated in the subsequent histories of the era. It would appear, as Payne points out, that this is due to the failure to develop an adequate, alternative framework to the one offered by the media, one which would interpret events more accurately. Both the media accounts and later histories fail to address important analytical issues such as what exactly constitutes an adherence to nonviolent direct action? Whether such an adherence can be seen in any other campaigns? Who exactly was perpetrating the violence? The shootings to which the *Ebony* article referred, were not carried out by "demonstrators," certainly not in the traditional sense of the term, but rather by black citizens not officially connected with the CNAC. This is a crucial difference, yet, unfortunately, one that subsequent historians also seem to have ignored.

Gloria Richardson: Feminist Icon?

The crudely militant view of Richardson can be partly attributed to the way in which she has been appropriated as a feminist icon. One example of this depiction is Paula Giddings's *When and Where I Enter*. While groundbreaking in its effort to restore black women to the center of black life and culture, the book impelled Giddings to embark on a seemingly relentless quest to find a more militant Richardson than ever existed. As a result, it gave an exaggerated, and often simply false, description of the Cambridge leader. This is especially disappointing when there is much in Richardson's story to impress without resort to hagiography.

It is worth pausing to consider precisely how Giddings frames her portrait of Richardson. Outlining her approach to African American history, Giddings comments that "in a group that depended on individual initiative and doers it was natural that women would play a major part." She goes on to explain that:

> whatever the political orientation of their families, most of the young women in SNCC had female doers as role models ... Many of the black women coming of age in the sixties not only had such women as role models but were encouraged to be independent, to do what had to be done, regardless of the prescribed gender roles.[21]

She then proceeds to talk about Jean Wiley, Angela Davis and Gloria Richardson as examples of this breed of young women activists. Later, Giddings acknowledges that Richardson was actually born in 1922. By conventional standards then, this means that Richardson actually came of age not "in the sixties," but in the 1940s. By the time she led the Cambridge movement in 1962 she was 40 years old—certainly not a young woman compared to the youthful SNCC activists. Richardson may well have had a superb role model in her mother, but she first became involved in the movement not because of her mother's example, nor because of her own youthful willfulness and independence, but because her teenage daughter Donna was deeply involved and she wanted to support her. Furthermore, what Giddings did not mention was that Richardson felt able to get involved because she belonged to the richest, and arguably the most powerful, black family in Maryland and was therefore, at least financially, relatively immune from attack by the white community. Richardson herself recognized that "they asked me if I would take that position [as head of CNAC] 'cos they thought I was least likely to be retaliated against," and if white Cambridge did try to attack her, she was at least the most able "to withstand retaliation in terms of economic reprisals."[22]

This, of course, does not detract at all from Richardson's bravery during the Cambridge struggle. But it does crucially revise our understanding of how and why she came to lead a civil rights campaign. However, by omitting the details of Richardson's background, Giddings seems to imply that a forty-year-old, divorced, middle-class and financially independent, mother of two is not an impressive enough image, or at least not her preferred image, for a successful and militant female civil rights leader. In doing so, she is actually in danger of belittling, rather than championing, Richardson's contribution. Similarly misleading is Giddings' statement that, "it is difficult to reconcile the soft-spoken, small-framed Richardson ... with the gun-toting militant of the Cambridge movement."[23] Frankly, it is even more difficult to guess exactly where this description originated. Standing five feet seven inches, and weighing 138 pounds in 1963, Gloria Richardson has recalled that "everybody—except me, my mother, my daughter—knew how to shoot. I did not know. Probably would have killed myself instead of, you know, somebody else."[24] Certainly, there seems to be little evidence to suggest that Richardson ever carried a gun. Not even the print media—even in the most hostile conservative or sensational black accounts—ever reported that she had, and none of the first-hand accounts from participants in the Cambridge movement have ever claimed that either. The only explanation for Giddings's use of the "gun-toting" tag seems to be a literary or stylistic aggrandizing of Richardson's actions in a bid to carve out a special place for her, as a woman, in civil rights mythology. But Richardson can rightfully claim such a place in an African American pantheon as an extremely brave and capable leader. Giddings's mythologization of Richardson actually threatens to demean Richardson's role. For the implication is that, in Giddings's eyes at least, the more historically accurate image of a rather tall and robust Gloria Richardson facing down a hostile mob unarmed, is not as worthy of praise and fame. Paradoxically, this undervalues a type of stoic heroism which many black women civil rights activists exhibited every day of their lives. Apparently, however, Giddings preferred a more martial style of black feminism and tried to force Richardson into this mould.

To be fair, Giddings is not alone in misrepresenting the nonviolent credentials of Richardson and the Cambridge movement. In a similar vein, Annette Brock states that Cambridge was one of the first campaigns where "nonviolence was questioned as a tactic."[25] Peter Levy also argues that Richardson and CNAC became "soured" on nonviolent direct action.[26] These statements, in part, testify both to an over-reliance on media accounts of the Cambridge campaign and to the limits of more recent, historical research. In addition, both claims are due to a disingenuous use of existing literature, especially with regard to issues of violence and nonviolence. Brock's source for her observations on the rejection of nonviolent direct action in Cambridge is none other than Giddings who provides no real evidence to sustain her thesis. After such a bold, yet isolated, statement, Brock provides no further evidence of her own, and does not return to the issue again in her twenty-three-page article on Richardson and CNAC. Steven Kasher in his book, *The Civil Rights Movement: A Photographic History, 1954-1968*, uses Brock's borrowed quotation from Giddings to describe the racial situation and the questioning of nonviolence in Cambridge but again provides no other independent research to warrant such a claim.[27] This is then, somewhat incestuous—compounding and extending error by repetition and in the absence of thorough research. Peter Levy is possibly the only scholar carrying out such research on the Cambridge movement at the present time. However, he is largely concerned with exploring the political and economic conditions in Cambridge and in revising our opinion of the supposed liberal coalition of the early 1960s. He therefore gives only a cursory mention of the dissatisfaction with nonviolent tactics in the Cambridge movement.

Gloria Richardson: Nonviolent Activist?

Richardson was actually no less an advocate of nonviolent direct action tactics than other leaders of civil rights campaigns in the South, such as Fred Shuttlesworth in Birmingham. There were many different levels of adherence to nonviolent discipline among activists in the civil rights movement. Some firmly believed that nonviolence was a way of life to be adopted at all times, while others viewed it as nothing more than a very effective tactic. Most activists sat somewhere in the middle, selecting nonviolence when it seemed practical but remaining prepared to defend themselves and their community. Even such a key nonviolent figure as Martin Luther King did not object to people defending their families and their own lives outside the protest arena. Writing in his 1967 book *Where Do We Go From Here?*, King declared, "the first public expression of disenchantment with nonviolence arose around the question of 'self-defense'. In a sense this is a false issue, for the right to defend one's home and one's person when attacked has been guaranteed through the ages by common law." It was only in the context of a nonviolent demonstration, however, that, "self-defense must be approached from another perspective."[28] It is in this context that we should view Gloria Richardson and her position on nonviolent direct action.

From the outset, when SNCC workers first arrived in Cambridge, Richardson had been impressed by the effectiveness of nonviolent protest. She remarked at the time that, "There was something direct, something real about the way the kids waged nonviolent war. This was the first time I saw a vehicle I could work with."[29] Once the CNAC had been established, it became their avowed goal to "show, through the medium of direct nonviolent action the desperate need to eliminate discrimination and segregation from all walks of Negro life."[30] This became Richardson's mission and, as far as it is possible to tell, she adhered to it. But it was a tactical rather than a moral adherence. In a 1996 interview she recalled that, nonviolence "was always a tactic for me ... I believed that you did a technical march ... you did that nonviolently ... I did not think that you were not supposed to respond if somebody attacked you outside of that framework."[31] This is very close to the position that Hosea Williams, later a prominent staff member in King's Southern Christian Leadership Conference, adopted in Savannah, Georgia in 1963 and also to that of Fred Shuttlesworth, founder of the Alabama Christian Movement for Human Rights in Birmingham. Although never involved in instigation or initiation of violence, both men typified the clearly flexible and pragmatic approach of most nonviolent activists to the tactics of nonviolent direct action—because they carried or tolerated the presence of weapons and accepted a stance of armed self-defense when whites attacked.

In 1961, when the Freedom Riders were attacked by a white mob in Anniston, Alabama, Shuttlesworth led a caravan of cars from Birmingham to rescue them. As Shuttlesworth recalled it, "every one of those cars had a shotgun in it." Shuttlesworth certainly had no problem with this, proclaiming at the time, "I'm a nonviolent man, but I'm going to get my people."[32] Hosea Williams recalled how, "I heard about Dr. King, and I was fascinated by him, and I started teaching nonviolence and training students in nonviolence, even though I didn't believe it. I started using it as a tactic, and I led the first sit-ins in Savannah." Much like Richardson, Williams never actually sanctioned violence, but later when violence erupted in Savannah while he was in jail, he recalled proudly, "they [black students] burnt Sears and Roebuck down. They burnt Firestone. Savannah was really in trouble."[33] As with Shuttlesworth, his brand of nonviolence made it possible for him to accept violence if it seemed an appropriate response in a given situation.

Given that these men, like Richardson, held a flexible position on nonviolence it is all the more surprising that their nonviolent credentials have survived their rendering as heroic figures in the movement's historical literature while Richardson's have not.

With little or no evidence to suggest that Richardson actively encouraged violence, the issue of whether she actively discouraged it remains complex. In order to explore Richardson's position more fully here, it is vitally important to determine exactly who was carrying out the violence. Richardson certainly would not tolerate black violence breaking out on her organized nonviolent protests and therefore did actively discourage it. "People pretty much understood" she recalled, "we told them, you know, if you can't do it don't go [on a nonviolent march]."[34] Stanley Wise, a SNCC field worker and campus organizer, similarly remembered that, "basically what she did is, she told them what our plan was and if you were not part of our plan ... then you had to go out and develop your own. But you don't come to the back end of ours and do these disruptive things which could injure all kinds of other people and pretend that you were being revolutionary."[35]

But what of those people who did develop their own plan? There was a considerable section of black Cambridge that did not subscribe to nonviolent direct action. Many of these citizens were army veterans who had "returned to Cambridge resolved to demand full citizenship." Richardson recalled that although she never attended their meetings, people in Cambridge knew that they were indeed organized and provided an alternative organization of sorts to the nonviolent CNAC. According to Richardson they had "amassed medical supplies and guns and stuff in case at the final analysis ... they had to use those things." And at night, "the ones that could not submit to nonviolence were the ones that were out ... protecting the perimeters of the community, armed."[36]

The extent of this organization is evident from the events of May 11, 1964. George Wallace was in town canvassing for support in the Maryland presidential primary election. That night, a furious CNAC held a mass meeting followed by a nonviolent demonstration downtown. Before long, the National Guard confronted the demonstrators informing them that their march was illegal and that they would have to turn back. When Richardson refused, the Guard attacked the marchers with a noxious gas and fired rifles at them. According to Cleveland Sellers, "a lot of people would have been seriously injured if a small group of black men had not started shooting at the guardsmen in order to slow them down." According to Sellers, this was a well-practiced maneuver on the part of the black defenders: "The men would run a few steps, crouch on one knee and fire; run a few steps, crouch on one knee and fire."[37] As Richardson stated, "it was an immediate response ... they had to be pretty well organized for it to have happened that quickly."[38]

Stanley Wise recalled this "non-nonviolent" side of black Cambridge with equal amounts of mirth and horror:

> It was terrifying ... Somebody broke into the armory ... a group of whites ... and took a case of rifles ... and so word spread in the black community that this had been done, and the blacks went over there and took three cases of hand grenades and brought one of them and set it on my back step ... Oh I was so terrified I didn't know what to do.[39]

Wise similarly remembered that one way the National Guard attempted to monitor the night marches was to bring searchlights into the streets:

> Somehow the word spread in the black community that if you got in the way of this light for more than three minutes, it made you sterile. And so they told him [General Gelston of the National Guard], "we'll blow the thing up" if he didn't get it out of town and he didn't believe it. So they blew up something in the town to show him that they were serious.[40]

Speaking of these black Cambridge residents who did behave violently but outside of her campaign (in as much as they were ready and able to defend themselves against attack), Richardson recalled that "they saw that [violence] as part of the protest ... we certainly didn't condemn that." Far from discouraging this element of black violence, she regarded the tension between the nonviolent and violent black elements of Cambridge as a creative force. She even believed with hindsight that, "if it had not been for that tension, the things that were accomplished may not [have been], because that is what attracted Washington. It was embarrassing for them to have that within a hand's throw."[41]

Like the tactical commitment to nonviolence, this pragmatic view was common among civil rights leaders by the end of 1963. Certainly, many were aware of the usefulness of black violence in highlighting the need for the white establishment to yield to the more "responsible" demands of the more "responsible" leaders. Even in the most celebrated of all the speeches of the nonviolent era, King's "I Have a Dream" speech of August 1963, the movement's archetypal "man of peace" used the threat of black violence to try to persuade federal government to pass civil rights legislation. Recalling the racial turmoil of 1963—not least the trouble in Cambridge, but equally the black violence that occurred during his own campaign in Birmingham, Alabama—King threatened that:

> This sweltering summer of the Negro's legitimate discontent will not pass until there is an invigorating autumn of freedom and equality.
>
> Nineteen sixty-three is not an end, but a beginning. And those who hope that the Negro needed to blow off steam and will now be content, will have a rude awakening if the nation returns to business as usual.[42]

Richardson then, like King, recognized that there were occasions when black violence could be useful in coercing the government to act. Unlike King, but far more like Hosea Williams, she was less inclined to take positive steps to discourage this violence from breaking out. This may indicate that she was not as committed to nonviolence as a way of life as King was. However, it does not mean that she had rejected or even questioned nonviolent direct action as a tactic any more than the riots that took place in Birmingham after the Gaston Motel bombing illustrated that King and Shuttlesworth had abandoned their commitment to it. Certainly, Richardson's reluctance to criticize other black citizens outside of her organization, for adopting armed self-defense in the face of vicious white provocation or for being primed and prepared to resort to violence, is critically different from the image of a "gun-toting" leader.

In conclusion, we can see that the nature and sources of the black violence in Cambridge have been misunderstood and misinterpreted by movement historians. Richardson and CNAC, though perhaps not believing in nonviolence as a way of life, were certainly as dedicated to it as a repertoire of tactics as most nonviolent activists of this era. Despite accounts to the contrary, Richardson and CNAC were consistent and unfaltering in their adoption of and adherence to nonviolent direct action.

This account of the Cambridge movement in the historical literature—of the misunderstandings and misinterpretations that have distorted our understanding of that movement—can serve to remind us of the pitfalls that can be encountered when writing history. Many of the errors in the interpretation of the nature of the relationship between nonviolence and violence in the Cambridge campaign can be attributed to an over reliance on media accounts rather than those of movement participants. This problem is compounded when historians cite each other's work too readily without the corroboration of primary sources.

As for the work of historians like Paula Giddings, it can be seen that history with an explicitly political agenda can be a double-edged sword. While it can ask questions which may otherwise remain unasked and under-explored, it can also lead to a distortion of the truth. Without the kind of feminist history that Giddings pioneered, the story of Richardson and countless other women would probably remain untold. This would be a tragedy and a grave distortion of history that would seriously undermine our understanding of the civil rights movement. However, the ideological motives that prompted feminist historians to re-write women into history may also inspire them to represent them inaccurately. In Richardson's case, that impulse distorted the portrayal of Richardson and her role in the Cambridge campaign. In the quest for images of militancy that would have a resonance for a later audience, groomed to associate political radicalism with a para-military posture, the figure of the "gun-toting woman" served to strengthen the misperception of Richardson as violent.

Notes

1. This account of the Cambridge, Maryland, movement has been drawn largely from Peter B. Levy, "Civil War on Race Street: The Black Freedom Struggle and White Resistance in Cambridge, Maryland, 1960-1964," *Maryland Historical Magazine*, 89, (Fall 1994): 291-318 and Annette K. Brock, "Gloria Richardson and the Cambridge Movement," in V.L. Crawford et al., eds., *Women in the Civil Rights Movement: Trailblazers and Torchbearers* (New York: Carlson, 1990), 121-143. Unless specified, references are to these two studies.

2. Paula Giddings, *When and Where I Enter: The Impact of Black Women on Race and Sex in America* (New York: Bantam 1985), 292; Cleveland Sellers, *The River of No Return: The Autobiography of a Black Militant and the Life and Death of SNCC* (Jackson: University of Mississippi Press, 1990), 68.

3. *New York Times* June 12, 1963, 23.

4. Brock, "Gloria Richardson," 123; Levy, "Civil War on Race Street", 291.

5. The experiences of black policemen in Cambridge were very similar to those of black policemen in the Deep South. Former black Atlanta policeman and later State Representative, Billy McKinney, recalled that, as a policeman in the late 1940s and early 1950s, he "couldn't arrest white people ... I would go back to the black leadership saying that we were working under terrible conditions." Just as in Cambridge, McKinney remembered that if a black policeman found a white person committing a crime, "white policemen had to come." Billy McKinney, interview with Brian Ward and Jenny Walker, October 19, 1995, University of Newcastle upon Tyne Oral History Collection. (Hereafter UNOHC).

6. Levy, "Civil War," 296.

7. *Newsweek*, August 5, 1963, 26.

8. *New York Times*, July 13, 1963, Clippings Folder-1963, Reel 10, Bayard Rustin Papers, Microfilm Collection, Alderman Library, University of Virginia, Charlottesville.

9. Levy, "Civil War," 306.

10. Murray Kempton, "Gloria, Gloria," *New Republic*, November 16, 1963, 15.

11. Levy, "Civil War," 306.

12. Kempton, "Gloria," 15.

13. Levy, "Civil War," 306.

14. Brock, "Gloria Richardson," 138.

15. *Time*, October 11, 1963, 30.

16. Kempton, "Gloria," 15.

17. *Ebony*, July 1964, 23-24. Emphasis added.

18. *Muhammad Speaks*, June 19, 1964, 10.

19. Burke Marshall, "Memorandum re: Cambridge, Maryland, Situation," (July 1963), Reel 2, Civil Rights During The Kennedy Administration, Part II, Microfilm Collection, Alderman Library, University of Virginia, Charlottesville.

20. Charles Payne, *I've Got The Light of Freedom: The Organizing Tradition and the Mississippi Freedom Struggle* (Berkeley: University of California Press, 1995), 413.

21. Giddings, *When and Where*, 277-78.

22. Gloria Richardson, interview with Jenny Walker, (March 11, 1996), UNOHC.

23. Giddings, *When and Where*, 292.

24. *Ebony*, July 1964, 23. Richardson interview, UNOHC.

25. Brock, "Gloria Richardson," 124.

26. Levy, "Civil War on Race Street," 306.

27. Steven Kasher, *The Civil Rights Movement: A Photographic History: 1954-1968* (New York: Abbeville, 1996), 130.

28. James Washington, ed., *A Testament of Hope: The Essential Writings and Speeches of Martin Luther King, Jr.* (New York: Harper, 1986), 589-590.

29. *Newsweek*, August 5, 1963, 26.

30. 'Report - Cambridge Nonviolent Coordinating Committee', n.d., Student Nonviolent Coordinating Committee Papers, A-IV-65, Manuscripts Division, Library of Congress, Washington, D.C.

31. Richardson Interview, UNOHC.

32. Howell Raines, *My Soul Is Rested: Movement Days in the Deep South Remembered* (Harmondsworth, England: Penguin, 1983), 115.

33. Raines, *My Soul*, 439, 441.

34. Richardson interview, UNOHC.

35. Stanley Wise, interview with Brian Ward and Jenny Walker, (October 19, 1995), UNOHC.

36. Richardson interview, UNOHC.

37. Sellers, *River of No Return*, 74.

38. Richardson, interview.

39. Wise, interview, UNOHC.

40. Wise, interview.

41. Richardson, interview.

42. Washington, *Testament of Hope*, 218.

CHAPTER 7

"It's a Doggy-Dogg World": Black Cultural Politics, Gangsta Rap and the "Post-Soul Man"

Eithne Quinn

"Post-soul man" is an amalgamation of two terms: *post-soul* and *soul man*. I have appropriated the term *post-soul* from cultural critic Nelson George, who writes, in the introduction to his 1992 book (subtitled *Notes on Post-Soul Black Culture*):

> Over the last 20 or so years, the tenor of African American culture has changed. I came up on the we-shall-overcome tradition of noble struggle, soul and gospel music, positive images, and the conventional wisdom that civil rights would translate into racial salvation. Today I live in a time of goin'-for-mine materialism, secular beat consciousness, and a more diverse, fragmented, even postmodern black community.[1]

Clearly this is a notional, probably overstated, and rather nostalgic appraisal of changing black structures of feeling, pointing to shifts—since the early 1970s—in the social, political and cultural realms. Still, it is a suggestive and useful statement, not least because its sentiments seem to be so widely shared in contemporary black America. In relation to the music industry, the post-soul shift may be broken down into changing aesthetic, industrial and ideological imperatives. Briefly summarized, the aesthetic shift is from a sense of live performance and emphasis on *authentic* songwriting and vocalization to new technologies of sound production and the ascendant role of producers.[2] Industrially, the shift is towards increasing mass mediation (corporate conglomerates, the rise of MTV, the evolution of black radio), a presumed commodification of product at the expense of the independent producer, and an assimilationist opening up of the "core black audience" to crossover markets.[3] Ideologically, the move, principally conveyed through the lyrics, seems to be from the sacred to the secular, from the activist to the lumpen-proletariat, from spiritualist to materialist, and from a sense of congregation to one of individualism. Post-soul becomes a metonym for the fragmented, "feel-bad" politics and poetics of recent neo-conservative times, just as soul serves as a symbol for the perceived ethical certainties and positivist politics of the civil rights era. The popular and highly contentious prefixing of *post* indicates a sense of both sequentiality and backlash: a relinquishing of soul-searching spiritualism and sacrifice, at once born out of and as a reaction against these previous cultural traditions.[4] If my epochal generalizations strike the reader as crudely stereotypical, my concern is with *popular imaginaries* in the 1990s concerning changes in black cultural politics between 1960s and 1990s black America, so my "potted" account of shifts suffices. A central shifting co-ordinate is the perceived changes in dominant cultural modes of black masculinity: from the often idealized, middle-class-identified men of the civil rights era, to the predominance of post-soul street masculinity.

Thus, I appropriate the term *soul man* from the title of Sam and Dave's 1967 gospel-influenced black anthem, that serves to index the archetypal masculine mode circulating in the previous era of black popular music. Rooted in the gospel and blues tradition, soul music reached its peak in the expansive mid-1960s and remained ascendant through the later 1960s and into the early 1970s as its sound and political complexion evolved: soul exemplified the mood of both civil rights and black power periods. A range of artists developed highly distinctive versions of the soul sound, united by a pervasive sense of black authentic voicing, of racial pride and salvation, and of "a better tomorrow" (in black idiomatic terms, the preoccupation with "gettin' over"); and usually these imperatives were played out through narratives of romantic love.[5] As one music critic puts it, the dialectical soul sensibility is concerned with "sexual connection as salvation and rebirth, lovers as guiding lights, the profane as sacred, as wholly holy love."[6] The emotionally expressive soul man serves as an umbrella term for a kind of paternalist, faithful, and sexually dynamic black masculinity so firmly associated with the prevailing sensibilities of the 1960s, as Brian Ward outlines in his essay. And this black masculine type was deeply embedded in a committed political and religious enterprise. To be sure, the soul man was a patriarchal figure, upholding the dominant discourses of hard-working, bread-winning, paternalist masculinity circulating in both black and white America. Considered retrospectively, there seems to be an unproblematic celebration of the "positive images" of the soul man, which reflects both the wider, unquestioned patriarchal frame within which these debates are operating, and an idealized, highly contingent account of the gender politics of the civil rights era. Still, in light of the post-soul masculinity I discuss in this essay, the soul man does present a more sensitive archetype.

The dogg persona of gangsta rap provides a powerful, perhaps even exemplary, articulation of the *post-soul man*.[7] The great notoriety and commercial success of macho and misogynist gangsta rap, which came into ascendance at the beginning of the 1990s, renders it especially instructive to a discussion of the politics of black masculine representation. I want to examine how gangsta's masculinist figures—and particularly the dogg figure of the G-Funk Era—constructed themselves and in turn were constructed by critics as a product of the time, and often in opposition to the assumed soul man of an erstwhile era. The emotional expressiveness and patriarchal responsibility of the soul man is seen to have been replaced by the retributive, loveless and regressive masculinity of gangsta. Stuart Hall suggests that "identities are the names we give to the different ways we are positioned by and position ourselves in the narratives of the past."[8] I want to pursue this idea by exploring the ways in which music serves as a key narrative tradition through which contemporary black masculinity is constituted and contested by artists and by critics. And the politics and poetics of the civil rights era present a particularly potent narrative of the past. Thus, although the framework of this essay stems from diachronic shifts, my central concerns are synchronic: how this mythologized past is invoked and re-articulated in contemporary cultural discourses about black men.

All music is, of course, political, but highly successful and influential African American music has long been the site of particularly overt political contestation. Music can forge a sense of collective identity and community and therefore it has been a powerful medium for mobilizing and shaping political constituencies. The well-established and important links between music and racial resistance have fostered, within the black community, a pronounced discourse of responsibility circulating in and around the musical field. As Nelson George registers, black music is furnished with the role of disseminating positive and progressive political messages. Cornel West shares the widely-held view (particularly of middle-class, older, and religious sectors of the African American community) that artists should produce responsible black music:

> Since black musicians play such an important role in
> African American life, they have a special mission and
> responsibility: to present beautiful music which both

sustains and motivates black people and provides visions
of what black people should aspire to.[9]

That many black and leftist critics have lauded the uplifting and racially
galvanizing music of the 1960s, then, is as unsurprising as their reproval
of gangsta rap. Some critics argue for an incontrovertible breach
between soul man and what I am calling the post-soul man. The
rhetorical force of this critique often works to obscure continuities and
complexities. In what follows, I will trace the formal vocabularies of
gangsta's masculine mode, and through an examination of the genre's
black critical reception, analyze some of the cultural contestations over
representations of black masculinity in the post-soul era. Thus, I will
loosely construct a framework of shifting conversations between the
residual "soul man" and the post-soul men of gangsta; and between
soul-identified critics and an emergent generation of what Manning
Marable has described as "post-civil-rights critics." Along the way, I
suggest ways in which these two conversations—in the musical and
critical field—intersect.

Soulless: The Dogg Figure in Gangsta Rap

Gangsta rap emerged in the late 1980s and is still around today. The
genre is populated by a series of intersecting black male folk and street
heroic types, the products of a complex interplay of socio-cultural
antecedents that have been transposed into a mass-mediated and
commercial form. They include the pimp, the hustler, the gangster, and
the *baadman* and these subcultural types are united in part by their
lyrical preoccupation with macho street toughness and "cool poses."
Gangsta rap's stars have adopted different versions of post-soul
masculinity: from N.W.A.'s murderous and misogynist nihilism, Ice
Cube's versatile gangsterism, Too Short's abusive and comic pimp
persona, to Ice-T's politico-player image. The dogg figure incorporates
many of the strands of these personae, offering in some ways the
crystalization of gangsta's regressive masculine modes. During the self-
proclaimed "G-Funk era"—from 1992 to 1996—a stable of artists
adopting dog iconography emerged out of the Death Row record label.
Snoop Doggy Dogg (Calvin Broadus: *Doggystyle*, 1993; *The
Doggfather*, 1996), his group Tha Dogg Pound (*Dogg Food*, 1995), and
Nate Dogg (Nathaniel Hale), all came together under the innovative G-
Funk sound of producer Dr Dre (Andre Young), on his ground-breaking
album *The Chronic* (Interscope, 1992). The popular-cultural reach and
importance of the G-Funk era, both in terms of sales and controversy,
was phenomenal.[10] The music found a mass audience among urban
black and MTV-viewing white adolescent males.[11] From the contexts of

production to those of consumption, this was a profoundly masculine project, constituting spatially dispersed audiences of young men across class and race lines, united by a pronounced patriarchal imagination. The pleasures, fantasies and desires mobilized by the music fostered affinities between black and white young men, at the same time as registering a sense of heightened racial difference. The G-Funk era was predicated on a lyrical and visual proliferation of dogg figuration: the notorious *Doggystyle* album cover presents a semi-pornographic cartoon image of an anthropomorphized dogg (presumably Snoop) in the center of the frame chasing a "bitch," with a white adult male "dogg catcha" voyeuristically looking on. Snoop, one of the first gangsta rap artists to be heavily rotated on MTV, famously morphed into a dog in the video "What's My Name?" Tha Dogg Pound play with dogg metaphors on the track titles "Dogg Day Afternoon" and "Dogg Pound Gangstaz." The lyrics of these tracks are often punctuated by smutty canine rhymes, such as the following sample from Snoop's "G-Funk Intro": "Foaming at the mouth"; "of keen sense of smell"; "in heat"; "we travel in packs"; "we do it doggystyle"; and "he buries his mutherfuckin' bone." These lyrics offer a characteristic G-Funk tale: the lewd narrative centers on hypersexual male doggs, who boast about their pursuit and exploitation of an objectified female (referred to as "bitch" and "ho," a black idiomatic variation of "whore"). Clearly, there is no sense of the redemptive vigor or sacred/profane dialectic associated with the soul tradition. Instead, the lyrics present fables which have been stripped of their moral message. Masculinist pleasure and desire is generated from the rather cartoonish debasement of sexuality and from the hyper-sexual assertions of the domination of females.

Usage of the multivalent word *dog* as a designation for street-wise black males dates back at least to the beginning of this century, and continues to sustain common currency in black vernacular discourse.[12] Emerging out of this repertoire, the gangsta dogg can be distilled into three main meanings. First, the noun *dog* (rather like the player or hustler) denotes a supersexual and street-identified black male, thus constituting a heroic type in gangsta. The dog-as-player is highly derivative of George Clinton's P-Funk hit "Atomic Dog" (1982), from which the captions on the cover of *Doggystyle* are taken ("Why must I feel like dat?," "Why must I chase da cat?," "Nuttin' but da dogg in me!!!"), and which is heavily sampled on this album.[13] The dog mantle has recently been taken up by DMX, one of the most successful rappers of 1998 (with tracks like "Get At Me Dog," "For My Dogs," and his trademark phrase "Where My Dogz At?"). The G-Funk drug of choice, marijuana, captures the "lumpen," "don't-give-a-fuck" (perhaps even ethically anaesthetized) posture of the dogg. The laid-back player image is evoked through the slower rapping delivery and bass-driven, "low metabolism" sound that became so firmly associated with the Death Row label. The sense of dogs travelling in packs, betokened by the group title Tha Dogg Pound, reflects a romanticized investment in male bonding and group loyalty in gangsta rap. Masculinist bonding is privileged over more conventional and institutional ties such as familial or romantic affiliation. The dogg is chiefly a baadman of the sexual arena. The macho dog and the term "bitch" are in many ways concomitant in black vernacular discourse, although dog contains none of the latter's pejorative resonances. In the familiar process of semantic revision, one of the few commercially successful female gangsta rap groups called themselves B.W.P (Bytches With Problems), reinflecting the term "bitch," with dozens-playing tracks like "Two-Minute Brother" (deriding male sexual inadequacy), and "We Want the Money" (celebrating materialism, and constructing sexual and romantic liaison in terms of economic exchange). The term "bitch" then is multivalent and should not be reduced to its predominantly pejorative meanings. Still, the "dog" moniker, when deployed by black men in vernacular culture, is always a term of respect. And even in the famous reproving refrains sung by black women—in Bessie Smith's "you low down dirty dog" and Big Mama Thornton's "hound dog"—there seems to be a sneaking admiration for their abusive partners.

A posture of adolescent irreverence characterizes the masculine subjectivity presented in these explicit dogg narratives. The sexual mores expressed in the repetitive and rather axiomatic doggerel of "If We all F---," by Tha Dogg Pound, offer a representative G-Funk statement. A typical verse goes:

> Kurupt: Now if I fuck
>
> Daz: And if I fuck
>
> Snoop: Yo, and if I fuck
>
> Kurupt: Then we all gone fuck (beeeyaaatch!)

The three doggs are served by a "flock of hoes" and, typically, references to *fellatio* abound. The boastful, rather childlike sing-song chants of Snoop's verse ("Drip drop drop drip / Look at these hoes all over my dick / Tic toc toc tic") draw attention to a lack of emotional investment in the sexual encounter. The humor and the irreverence stem partially from a pronounced sense of arrested development intimated through the unsophisticated syntactic and semantic priorities. For Robin

Kelley, Snoop's lyrics sound "more like little kids discovering nasty words for the first time than some male pathos."[14] Both the lyrical and tonal semantics of these group-sex scenarios, in all their paltry, adolescent display, seem precisely to eschew a sense of patriarchal responsibility. Snoop's enormous sexual appetite is repeatedly alluded to in throw-away boasts like, "How many hoes in ninety-four will I be bangin'? / Every single one, to get the job done," from "Gz and Hustlas." Here, his "job" seems to be, rather than a traditional occupation, simply the maintenance of his sexual reputation. Unlike most of gangsta's pantheon of heroes, the dogg is in no way defined by occupational role, thus to qualify for this designation one simply needs an abundance of masculine mystique. Importantly, this flies in the face of the hard work ethic and the bourgeois discourse of the black male as familial breadwinner.

In some ways coterminously, the verb *to dog* means to mistreat or demean someone (usually one's sexual partner), and this hierarchical meaning of dog (to exploit, "to treat like a dog") holds particular historical resonances of political and economic oppression for African Americans.[15] The preoccupation in dogg narratives is with sexual—and not racial—domination: the verb is mobilized in tales of exploitative and loveless sexual conquest. At the center of gangsta narratives is always a power negotiation, and sexual practices tend to be reducible to such an economy. Snoop's oft-repeated refrain, "I really don't love hoes," points to an insistence on the rejection of love and romance which are construed as signs of a vulnerable masculinity. Thus, the dogg is closely linked to the street-heroic pimp figure. The influence of pimp-identified gangsta rapper Too Short, whose cartoon-graphic cover of *Short Dog's in the House* (1990) clearly informed G-Funk's dogg iconography, is notable. Too Short and G-Funk artists are united by the insistence on their reputation with and power to control women. Exploitative sexual encounters are often indexed in gangsta by references to oral sex: *fellatio* is celebrated and frequently invoked (for example, on the tracks "She Swallowed It" and "Findum, Fuckum & Flee" by NWA, "If We All Fuck" and "Some Bomb Azz (Pussy)" by Tha Dogg Pound, "Deeez Nuuuts" by Dr Dre, "Ain't No Fun" by Snoop, and "Freaky Tales" by Too Short); but *cunnilingus* (to "brown nose") is rarely mentioned and almost always reviled. The descriptions of *fellatio* in gangsta are strikingly repetitive and often rather unimaginative, indicating more a fascination with the subordination of the female than with eroticism. The term "doggystyle" corroborates the bawdy bestialization of sexual practices. Thus, *to dog*— an assertion of the exploitative ways in which these sexual liaisons are conducted—is often the narrative's very *telos*. In this way, gangsta is acting out and re-articulating the long-standing black-as-bestial racial stereotype: a stereotype that the black middle class have long been trying to demobilize through the promulgation of "positive images" of an assimilated black masculinity, which downplays symbols of racialized difference.[16]

Gangsta is grounded in the *dog-eat-dog* ethos of ghetto survivalism, opportunism and extreme individualism. This meaning of dog extends beyond the "battle of the sexes" to male ghettocentric codes more generally. The phrase suggests mutually destructive competition and intra-male power negotiations (which are often settled violently), indexing the nihilism for which this music has been so heavily criticized. From a track on Dr Dre's *The Chronic*, Snoop half-sings the onomatopoeic hook: "Rat-tat-tat-tat and a tat like that / Never hesitate to put a nigga on his back," which captures the genre's postulated devaluation of human life. As gangsta rapper Bushwick Bill of Geto Boys quipped in interview for *The Chicago Tribune*: "It's dog eat dog, and some of them have rabies."[17] Critic bell hooks corroborates this rappers' summation: "gangsta rap celebrates the world of the material, the dog-eat-dog world where you do what you gotta do to make it even if it means fucking over folks and taking them out. In this world view killing is necessary for survival."[18] And it is from the extremely individualist phrase *dog-eat-dog* that the G-Funk mantra "Doggy-Dogg World" is derived. It is a male-dominated soundscape of dangerous yet exciting survivalism. The doggy-dogg world-view can certainly be situated in diametric opposition to the sensitive, nonviolent male consciousness evident in the "beloved community" ideal of Martin Luther King. This summary of the dogg figure, which pervaded the G-Funk Era of gangsta, evokes a profound sense of moral and spiritual bankruptcy: from the "profane as sacred" (Mark) to profanity for profanity's sake; from "positive images" (George) of black masculinity to "negative" ones; and from an investment in the future of "racial salvation" (George), to the gratuitous and short-term pleasures of the moment.

The "reasons" why black men have historically adopted the "cool pose," exemplified by the dogg, have been the subject of close critical scrutiny.[19] Sociologists tend to agree that it partially stems from black men's historic exclusion from the normative properties and symbols of manhood, principally as patriarchal breadwinner. The recent deindustrialization of America's urban centers and the de-skilling and insecurity of labor markets have produced a situation of chronic unemployment and occupational immobility among lower-class males across racial lines. The Californian post-industrial geographies of urban Los Angeles, Long Beach and Oakland, the towns from which these artists emerged, have been particularly hard hit.[20] The effects of institutional racism, of course, exacerbate the diminished opportunities for blue-collar black males. The employment insecurities facing working-class men, and black working-class men in particular, are inscribed in the production of this music and may also partly explain why gangsta found such a widespread cross-racial male youth audience. The recent resurgence of retributive and regressive modes of masculinity in popular culture, such as gangsta's extremist dogg figure, may be considered as the retrenching products of their time. The vicious demeaning of the female and the assertion of masculine dominance can also be understood in part as a defensive, "compensatory" move. Kobena Mercer posits—if rather one-dimensionally—that "the incessant dissing of "bitches" ... in rap betrays a vulnerable ego whose existence can only be confirmed by the degradation of others."[21] This "vulnerable ego" may have particular contemporary resonances associated with a sense of black matriarchal authority and the disruption of traditional gender roles and relationships in American culture more generally. Political scientist Michael C. Dawson, among many others, has thoroughly detailed the steady decline in black/white income parity in all regions except the South since the mid-1970s, and shows that the income disparity between black and white men is much greater than that between women.[22] Henry Louis Gates, in the introduction to *Thirteen Ways of Looking at a Black Man*, describes certain socio-economic ways in which black women are faring comparatively better than black men, including the fact that there are roughly eighty percent more black women than black men in graduate programs in America (the compound effect of educational differentials at each stage of schooling). He draws the conclusion that "black men are dramatically less likely to achieve middle-class status" than their female counterparts.[23] It would be interesting to pursue the idea that this class-based gender disparity is resulting in the preponderance of a more aspirational imagination among working-class black females compared to a greater investment in ghettocentric belonging among black men. Consequentially, there may be reason for a perceived sense among black men of a feminization of the black bourgeoisie.

The street macho of gangsta rap can be contextualized in these sociological ways (as a product of real conditions of existence for young black men), but it is, of course, essential to avoid equating lived experience and popular-cultural representation. As Robin Kelley argues, it is particularly important not to resort uncritically to the clichés about African Americans promulgated by the "ethnographic imagination" (and in particular the ethnographer's fascination with black masculinity) as expounded by the rather sensationalist "underclass" discourses of pathology, nihilism and dysfunction.[24] To counter the critical move of explaining gangsta in terms of black male pathology, bell hooks asserts that gangsta rappers are, instead, the subjects of "white supremacist capitalist patriarchy." In her article, "Gangsta Culture—Sexism, Misogyny: Who Will Take the Rap?," hooks usefully reminds us that gangsta rap is not the authentic product of a lived black urban experience, but a highly commodified, pop-cultural form. She argues that the "patriarchal ways of thinking and behaving that are glorified in gangsta rap are a reflection of the prevailing values in our society," rightly framing gangsta within a wider Western matrix of oppressive masculine modes. Gangsta's largest audience group is young white men, thus the influence of this market sector—of which G-Funk artists are explicitly aware—has been considerable. The oft-repeated argument that gangsta artists to some extent compromise themselves by trading in the stereotypes of black masculinity for record sales is certainly valid. Along these lines, hooks argues that the masculinism of gangsta artists (and in particular Snoop) is not "an expression of their 'manhood', it is an expression of their own subjugation and humiliation by more powerful, less visible forces of patriarchal gangsterism." This argument may have its merits, but it is also overstated, simplistic and, I want to argue, politically unhelpful. hooks sets up a colonial topography of center and margin, placing gangsta as a wholly co-opted product of the center, in contrast to her own oppositional stance. When she argues that gangsta rappers are "duped" by "white supremacist capitalist patriarchy," her monolithic account does not seem to engage with the complex articulations of difference mobilized by gangsta's "expressions of manhood." Reducing highly self-conscious and dialogic gangsta rappers to cultural "dupes" who "labor in the plantations of misogyny and sexism," neglects the core cultural conversations taking place and altogether precludes self-determination.[25] This critical position overlooks the crucial intra-black cultural dialogues and contestations circulating in and around gangsta. Such explanations, which activate the discourses of "internalized oppression" and "false consciousness"—mobilizing complex discursive dynamics of race and class—position black male subjectivity in terms of its otherness or its negative relationship to white masculinity and white patriarchy. This kind of approach is in danger of altogether denying agency to the subject of study.[26] In light of this concern, the focus on black cultural dialogue and contestation in my discussion below is not intended to deny the important influence of wider patriarchal and commercial contexts, but instead reflects a tactical move away from the pitfalls of prevailing critical positions.

What is sometimes neglected in critical discourses surrounding gangsta (which tend to substitute rhetorical force for systematic explication), is that the genre's ethics and aesthetics have as much to do with formal pleasures as with functional strategies. As I have explored elsewhere, the masculinist bluster and braggadocio of gangsta are informed by the highly developed and performative language use of black vernacular discourses.[27] These diasporic black men are conspicuously and knowingly tapping into the narrative and formal conventions of baadman and pimp narratives (the tall tales of Dolemite, Stackolee, Iceberg Slim), at the same time as they draw from male-dominated movie genres (chiefly Italian Gangster, blaxploitation, and action-adventure). Gangsta's sexual practices and politics are highly derivative of toasts—extended and improvised narrative poems, traditionally performed in the male-coded spaces of the street, the barbershop and, archetypally, the prison. When Bruce Jackson describes the sexual economy in pimp toasts, he could equally well be describing Snoop's "doggystyle" tales: "sexual relations in toasts are invariably affectionless and usually affectless. There is an apparent inconsistency too important to ignore: sexual conquest of the female is usually presented as being important, yet the object of the conquest is consistently denigrated."[28] Thus, as Brian Ward's essay on gender politics in black music demonstrates, gangsta rap is only one rather extremist point in a long and varied trajectory of masculine modes and of misogynist enunciations in black male expressive culture. What is particularly distinctive about G-Funk is the combination of this continuity within black cultural repertoires (say, with the blues man) at the same time as it registers a deep structural opposition to soulful masculinity. The hyper-masculinist, emotionally inarticulate dogg is constituted relationally, in diametric and often self-conscious opposition to the responsible and emotionally expressive black masculinity of the soul man. I want to pursue this oppositional relationship as it has been constructed by gangsta's "soul-identified" critics.

The Soul Ethic: Black Critical Responses to Gangsta Rap

The dogg era of gangsta rap became embroiled in a series of national debates and public discourses, constructed as a powerful emblem for much that was "wrong" with young black men in particular and American society in general. According to Kobena Mercer, "black masculinity ... is a key site of ideological representation, a site upon which the nation's crisis comes to be dramatized, demonized, and dealt with," an assertion which is powerfully substantiated by this case study.[29] In the same year as *Doggystyle*'s release, Snoop was involved in an incident for which he would be tried for accessory to murder (he was eventually acquitted). Although this paradoxically helped sales, his name became a byword for "pathological black male."[30] He entered the national consciousness, serving as a totem of its fears and anxieties, but also of some of its pleasures and fantasies. In February 1994, Congressional hearings were held which centered on gangsta rap (Snoop in particular) and declining family values. One of those curious coalitions was formed (which the fraught issue of censorship seems to spawn) when the National Political Congress of Black Women, led by C. Delores Tucker, joined forces with prominent conservatives, notably Bob Dole (a Senate Majority leader) and William Bennett (Secretary of Education), to attack gangsta and call for censorship. The "corporate responsibility" pressure imposed by this coalition led to the jettisoning of Interscope Records (Death Row's distributor) by its parent company, Time Warner, on the release of the notorious, number-one album *Dogg Food* by Tha Dogg Pound in 1995. Across the board, this music has been vilified: by feminists (for its sexism and misogyny); by the moral right (for "polluting" the minds of America's youth); by radical intellectuals (for it's a-politicism); and, as I want to pursue here, by black community leaders and intellectuals (chiefly, for its nihilism and for reinforcing negative stereotypes about black people).

The 1990s marks a transitional period, when the generation of black leaders and critics who had lived through the great advancements and sense of optimism of the civil rights movement began to give way to a new post-civil rights generation who had come to know the 1960s at second-hand only: through childhood memories, the testimony of elders, history books, and cultural forms like music. Gangsta rap in some ways became a measure of how far removed were the new times, an emblem of the waning of the civil rights legacy. At the same time, the passing of soul men and women into post-soul offered new opportunities for mythologizing the past. Now that it seemed so irrevocably past, so anachronistic, the mythic era of civil rights activism was furnished with new evocative and emblematic force. These residual and emergent strains in black public discourse fuelled new charged intergenerational conversations, and in what follows I will be focusing on dialogues between soul "fathers" and their post-soul "sons."[31]

Much of gangsta's black critical reception has read the form as a symptom of a current "crisis" of black masculinity. The genre is conceived as an extreme and troubling articulation of a secular consciousness, and as such, it is often positioned as antithetical to the critics' own soul-based sense of racial responsibility. In his 1990 press article, "Why Does Rap 'Dis' Romance?," historian Mark Naison offers an early example of the perceived breach between soul and post-soul man, which would become a characteristic structural device in gangsta criticism:

> one of the most precious themes in African-American popular music seems to have been lost—romance and tenderness. When black Rhythm and Blues took America by storm in the 1950s and 1960s, it did so not only with the power of its beat, but with beautiful harmonies and lyrics propagating images of love and longing ... partisans of rap need to ponder why an earlier generation of black artists dealt with male-female relationships as the repository of hopes and dreams rather than an arena for violence, competition and naked aggression.[32]

Naison assumes a lamenting note, invoking the discourses of declension and responsibility, as he charts the passing of "reverent" and "caring" masculine modes. And the article's graphics suggestively present the same story through the changing face of black masculinity: a photo of "soulful" Otis Redding is set beside a grimacing gangsta rapper, with the caption, "[f]rom a fever to a chill: Otis Redding's romanticism supplanted by the cruelty of Ice Cube."[33] Roger D. Abrahams paraphrases the soul man posture towards love and romance as the "'see how much you have hurt me baby' feeling," where "most of them seem to say, 'I'll come to you, baby, and on your own terms, too'."[34] By setting up this frame of reference through the picture of Redding, Naison powerfully highlights the emotional inarticulateness and retributive masculinity of gangsta.

Bakari Kitwana, in his lambasting book, *The Rap on Gangsta Rap*, also castigates gangsta masculinity:

> In this world-view, Black, male youth are savage, devoid of vision, non-thinking, incapable of love, violence-prone, and ultimately, schizophrenic ... It is important to stress that the problem is not with artists exploring notions of erotica and/or sensuousness, but with graphic and often crude, violent, self-hating, women-hating, and anti-Black, abusive sexual representations.

He goes on to ask rhetorically, "Where is the Black cultural tradition's moral center articulated in sex-violence rap?"[35] Both critics position gangsta as the furthest outreach of a recent secularization in black cultural traditions and do so by invoking its opposition to an emotionally expressive, faithful and authentic masculinity exemplified by soul music. Similarly, critic Armond White asserts: "There's nothing on *Doggystyle* that isn't a disgrace to hiphop as a politicized pop form made by alert, thinking young artists," positioning Snoop in opposition to a "moral center" in rap music.[36]

Naison, Kitwana and White are representative of a dominant mode of criticism which constructs gangsta as a charged symbol and symptom of the age. There is an implicit—and often explicit—value judgement attendant on many of these soul/post-soul distinctions. The lamenting and often condemnatory tone these critics adopt gestures towards gangsta's low stock of cultural capital among the black middle class, and also points to concerns about the socio-historical context of this musical form. Gangsta rap is seen both to reflect and be constitutive of the worsening problems facing African American communities and especially black males. To take one example, Naison states:

> The journey from Otis Redding's "Try a Little Tenderness" to Slick Rick's "Treat Her Like a Prostitute" is not progress; it is a sad commentary on the decline of humanistic values in African-American communities and in American society as a whole.[37]

Traced through changing black male singers and their postures towards courting rituals, the "doggy-dogg" world-view is seen to reflect a deteriorated lived experience (the antithesis of progress), in opposition to "humanistic values." These critics tend to move rather uncritically between gangsta's portrayals of black masculinity and "real" black men, both of which are deeply troubled (self-hating, woman-hating, non-humanist, abusive). Popular-cultural forms often become sites around which the social discourses of the day are played out, and so it was with gangsta rap. The genre and its critics need to be situated within the growing concern, since the 1980s, with single-parenthood and "poor fathering" in the African American community, culminating in the men-only Million Man March in 1995.

The oppositional stance and soul-centered tone of gangsta's critical reception mirrors the civil rights-inflected rhetoric often mobilized by black intellectuals more generally. In his influential and oft-cited article published in the year of G-Funk's emergence, "Nihilism in Black America" (1992), Cornel West rightly blamed the despondency which "increasingly pervades black communities" on worsening socio-economic conditions, and went on to describe the "lived experience of coping with a life of horrifying meaninglessness, hopelessness, and (most important) lovelessness." And, in preacherly fashion, he called forth the soul sensibility of African American exceptionalism:

> Black people have always been in America's wilderness in search of a promised land. Yet many black folk now reside in a jungle with a cut-throat morality devoid of any faith in deliverance or hope for freedom.[38]

West's description of the mindsets of besieged black urban communities presents one frame through which gangsta rap can be read. Still, the disparity between West's civil-rights rhetoric (wilderness, promised land, faith in deliverance, hope for freedom) and the purported mindsets of the constituency he is presumably trying to mobilize is striking. The gulf between the (lost) politics of hope and the (current) descriptions of despair seems absolute. The point I want to stress is that certain black critical voices are rhetorically and substantively immersed in a value system (the soul ethic of progress) which they configure in diametric opposition to gangsta's symbolic constituency: young, black, working class men. Ostensibly deployed to mobilize a sense of collective activism, the moral charge of the language may in fact inhibit inter-generational and cross-class cultural dialogue (rather like a parent lecturing a delinquent adolescent who stopped listening some time ago). Straight soul rhetoric may be outmoded, for it implies a faith in the system, in American liberalism, which fits most uneasily with the disaffected, disenfranchised and disappointed post-civil rights era.[39] The rhetorical burden some critics place on gangsta and the determinist ways in which they read it (which are certainly informed by a heartfelt concern for the declining socio-economic position of the black working class) are born out of a civil rights rhetoric of responsibility and uplift which exemplifies the residual ethical certainties of the soul sensibility.

Some cultural critics, however, have relinquished moral certainties and political positivism in their readings of gangsta rap and black working-class masculinity. The two critics I discuss below—Michael Eric Dyson and, particularly, Robin Kelley—have been instructively described by Manning Marable as on the "vanguard of the post-civil-rights generation of new scholarship on black identity, cultural and social history," whose "commitment is to theoretical and cultural engagement, analyzing the meaning of race, gender and class issues in the context of a post-civil-rights reality."[40] Dyson's book title, *Between God and Gangsta Rap*, succinctly positions the genre as the furthest outpost of secularization, tapping into the term's great symbolic purchase. In the introduction, he asserts: "black culture is constantly being redefined between the force of religious identities and secular

passions. Somewhere between God and gangsta rap."[41] Dyson describes
the fraught negotiations in contemporary black culture "in-between" the
secular and sacred, presenting the emblematic "preacher" and "gangsta"
as the two polar points on a whole spectrum of black male types.
Interestingly, though his prose is embedded in religious metaphors and
the sacred/profane dialectic of soul (indicated by the essay titles
"Between Apocalypse and Redemption" and "Minstrelsy or Ministry?"),
he emerges as an alternative kind of soul-identified voice. From a soul
dialectic he seems to move into a project of soul dialogics. Both through
his engagement with the gangsta rap genre and through his knowing
mobilization of evangelical rhetoric without assuming the moral high
ground, he playfully exposes the continuities and contradictions in black
cultural politics.[42] In the *New York Times* article, "When Gangstas
Grapple With Evil," Dyson sets up the usual contrast between past and
present, this time between the views of Martin Luther King and of
gangsta rappers. But then, in a second move, gesturing towards my
argument below, he concludes—in opposition to Kitwana—that rappers
are in fact "connected to a moral tradition they have seemingly
rejected."[43] The accessible and at times trite style (with phrases like
"horniness or holiness"), in marked opposition to the overbearing
earnestness of soul critics, encourages an inclusive, non-determinist (and
some might say compromised) politics.

The scholarship of neo-Marxist cultural historian Robin
Kelley—stylistically and politically of a very different complexion to
Dyson (an ordained Baptist preacher, deeply embedded in a religious
humanism)—displays a serious commitment to the popular-cultural
forms of America's black youth. In the most rigorous and even-handed
work on gangsta to date, the 1994 article "Kickin' Reality, Kickin'
Ballistics," Kelley presents a range of social, political and cultural
frameworks through which gangsta rap needs to be understood. He
offers a positional appraisal of the form, identifying a new black,
"ghettocentric" masculinity in the section entitled "Niggas in Post-Civil
Rights America."[44] This periodized account of gangsta explores the
form's post-soul contexts, suspending determinist value judgements.
The charged discourses surrounding gangsta not only influence the
genre but extend to its black critics, who may feel pressure to take up
the "authorized" polemical line. The argument seems to be that the
modes of black masculinity in gangsta are so morally reprehensible and
their political meanings so transparently negative that discussion should
not exceed condemnation. In conversation, Kelley explained how he felt
"under siege" by the weight of critical attacks he received after the
publication of his article. He was cast as a gangsta apologist who was
"too soft on gender" and for "not taking seriously the issues of urban

America," criticisms which seem to have far more to do with the climate of critical opinion than with a lack of political commitment in his work.[45] Towards the end of Kelley's article, the even-handed tone shifts to a more dismissive note (in "afterWORD: A Genre Spent?"), followed by a further shift (in the epilogue, marked by italics) in which he insists on the formal pleasures of gangsta rap, and which in conversation he described as "another set of confessionals." These structural tensions demonstrate Kelley's open acknowledgement of his own ambivalence and the dialogic approach he takes. Thus, there may be certain affinities between the burden placed on the "post-soul sons" of gangsta and its critics. I want to go on to argue that the non-determinism and contingency inscribed in the structure of this post-civil rights scholarship in some ways complements the structural tensions at work in the post-soul masculinity of G-Funk.

Post-soul Masculinity and the Aesthetics of G-Funk

The G-Funk sub-genre has worked as a self-conscious reaction against the soul sensibility and particularly soul masculinity, at the same time as being a product of this very (musical and ethical) tradition. Unlike the critical tendency to concentrate on a few (particularly offensive) lyrics or images in gangsta rap, I want to argue that much of G-Funk's power and importance stems from a conjunction of lyrics, vocal delivery and instrumentation. A great deal of G-Funk's offensiveness and appeal was derived from the intersection of the southern, soulful vocalization and seductive, accessible music—resonant of and often sampling highly evocative tracks from black music repertoires—with the a-moralist and secular lyrics and iconography. George characterizes the shift from "a distinctly country-accented optimism" of the civil rights era to an "assimilated-yet-segregated citified consciousness flavored with nihilism ... and consumerism."[46] G-Funk seems precisely to force an irreverent sonic conjuncture between these two sensibilities. This innovative synthesis of symbolically contradictory styles served as a point of articulation around which new generational resonances of black masculinity coalesced.

It is the surprising tension between the hyper-masculine lyrics and the feminized, Southern-tinged tonal semantics which renders the most infamous G-Funk voices of Snoop, Nate Dogg and to a lesser extent Warren G so provocative and suggestive. Snoop's tonal inflection—soft-spoken, languid, smooth, half-sung—belies the profane and nihilist lyrical content.[47] Critics have remarked on the power of this most distinctive and inherently contradictory voice. Despite his disapproval, Kelley admits: Snoop has "the coolest, slickest 'Calabama' [California meets Alabama] voice I've ever heard";[48] and Adario Strange from *The Source* magazine describes his "famous syrupy drawl of biting twangs and soft whispers."[49] Both commentators point to the kind of country-inflected optimism or *faux*-naivety, an inflection which asserts a rejection of assimilationist, bourgeois blackness. According to another critic, "the complex (or hypocritical) Snoop sings like a gangland thug, but talks like a choirboy," pointing to the unlikely conflation of church and street in the same vocal space.[50] Music critic Steven Daly speaks of his "sleepy almost feminine delivery," which stands in striking opposition to the macho lyrical priorities. In all cases, the effect is not to set up the heightened sacred/profane dialectic of the soul sensibility; instead the soul-identified vocal serves to emphasize, as the critics intimate, a post-soul sense of insouciance, apathy and street toughness. The female-coded vocal delivery actually enhances Snoop's masculine mystique. For Daly, Snoop's implacable persona communicates "a hard man with nothing to prove, someone who could drown out the thuggish braying with a mere whisper."[51] He does not have to avow his "hardness" because he has, so to speak, masculinity to spare. When Snoop *half-sings,* in his laconic drawl, the mantra "I don't love them hoes," the tonal semantics do not overtly suggest a testy disavowal or fear of female sexuality. Instead, they imply the implacable masculinity of a super-cool player: in short, a dogg. The *frisson*, then, is created by the softest, smoothest rapping and the hard, profane and secular lyrics.

The vocal ambiguities and innuendoes of Nate Dogg produce similar evocative tensions. Raised in the gospel tradition (like Snoop), as a member of the Hale Family Singers, Nate Dogg's vocal timbre is sensuously spiritual. But, as *Source* critic Donnell Alexander asserts, "his soul-stirring voice is his only obvious legacy from the gospel indoctrination." Alexander's article is entitled "Teflon Blues" which succinctly captures the oxymoronic conflation of the G-Funk era.[52] Drawing on musical traditions (blues) whilst re-articulating them in the postmodern present (Teflon) signposts the post-soul shift. Musicologist Gino Stefani explains that a pitched (sung) voice requires relaxation of the muscles involved in phonation, and this implies a state of quiet, peace and *tenderness* in the person.[53] Certainly, this characterizes the "meaning" conveyed by the sound of Nate's voice. However, in that characteristic G-Funk reversal, this renders the lyrical content of murder and lust even more shocking. Part of the power comes from the way in which his "foreboding voice of mean R&B" and "chilly singsong" nostalgically invoke the soul sensibility, whilst jettisoning its meanings.[54] Thus, Nate Dogg registers some of the same longings as the soul men of the past, at the same time as communicating their untenability in the present. The heightened macho posturing in gangsta rap points at once to the fantasies *and* the anxieties of male identity. The points of *suture* in masculine subjectivity are often self-consciously exposed in gangsta, in part reflecting the diasporic and socio-psychological tensions of African American men. However, in G-Funk and in the voices of Snoop and Nate, these tensions and anxieties seem to be resolved. The points of tension become barely perceptible, replaced by what Andrew Ross has called an "affectless masculinity."[55]

The 1994 G-Funk anthem "Regulate" by Nate Dogg and Warren G, from the sound-track to the gangsta movie *Above the Rim*, draws together many of the aesthetic and discursive imperatives of this post-soul genre.[56] The highly popular and influential track cross cuts the hesitant and again country-inflected rapping of Warren G with the soulful singing of Nate Dogg as they recount the cinematic tales of an evening's adventures in sex, robbery and murder. In "Regulate," Warren G heavily samples the whistled chorus hook from (white soul man) Michael McDonald's love song, "I Keep Forgetting" (the title implies the rest of the memorable phrase: "we're not in love anymore").[57] The listener recalls the sentiments of the forlorn, yearning love song depicting a soft and vulnerable masculinity as s/he confronts the overlaid, emotionally antithetical G-Funk lyrics. After sonic scenes of violent and sexual conquest, "Regulate" ends with a reflexive G-Funk statement that takes on manifesto resonances:

> I'm tweaking into a whole new era,
>
> G-Funk, step to this, I dare ya,
>
> Funk, on a whole new level ...

This song, which exemplifies the G-Funk aesthetic, actually constructs itself as inaugurating a new era. Thus, G-Funk presents a matrix of pathos (it does powerfully tap into pervasive generational resonances) and bathos (its overblown, self-referencing grandeur). Usually the hailing of a new era is accompanied by the grand discourses of moral achievement and progress. Instead, G-Funk's new era is marked by a rejection of any ethical basis or of any commitment to the future, compellingly offering its own "post" periodization. The G-Funk manifesto is precisely apathy. Tracks like "Regulate" assert a signal denial of traditional notions of black committed politics and its attendant correct forms of masculinity, as these have long been promulgated in black music.

The familial upbringing of G-Funk artists sheds light on the continuing influence of the soul era in black memory. These artists attest to the strong influence of their (southern-born) parents' record collections. An article in the *Los Angeles Times* describes Warren G "searching through his father's stacks of dusty vinyl and soaking up the sounds of Al Green, Bobby Womack, Les McCann," a tableau which incorporates the young artist's real and sonic soul fathers.[58] In interview, Snoop speaks of his mother playing soul music when he was growing up: "Al Green's lyrics were real deep, they were reality at the time. My lyrics are about what's goin' down on the streets nowadays."[59] Tellingly, Snoop's mother was a single-parent, thus the soulful masculinity Snoop recalls (Al Green is "still in love with you") may have more to do with musical memory and the domestic soundscape of his upbringing than with its lived experience. Of course, we shouldn't simply take Snoop's comment at face value for the artist is also making a rhetorical move by activating the discourse of authenticity—he offers an "address to truth"—to defend his much-maligned music. What is interesting though is the post-soul imagination his comment enunciates. In his negotiation of the legacy of the civil rights era, Snoop sounds rather like his critics! Both artist and critics invoke a golden age of soulful masculinity and responsible fathers that was far more iconic than actual. Snoop nostalgically invokes a sense, and acknowledges the influence, of the black musical past, registering a kind of musical historicity. Snoop's interviewer confirms the notion of the "changing same" of his post-soul music: "on 'Doggystyle', you'll hear the influences of soul singers from his youth, like Curtis Mayfield, Marvin Gaye, LJ Reynolds of the Dramatics, and Al Green. Wide-collar love men, none of whom would ever call their lady a bitch or ho."[60] The soul men of the past, then, bear heavily on the post-soul sons of the present. The important point here is that the soul/post-soul contrast is actually, sometimes even knowingly, built into the formal vocabularies of G-Funk with the particular intention to mark socio-cultural change. Furthermore, just as these repertoires are encoded in the songs so they are being understood and decoded by the audience I am chiefly concerned with here: young black men. This social group, who grew up in the 1970s and after, acquire a sense of the 1960s—its politics and its culture—to a great extent through the highly partial and idealizing medium of music. This complicates the accusation of nihilism implicit in Kitwana's rhetorical question ("where is the black cultural tradition's moral center articulated in sex-violence rap?") quoted earlier.

Interesting connections can be drawn between the "wide-collar love men" and their G-Funk sons, and the patriarchal family of black cultural politics. G-Funk's articulations of irresponsible and adolescent black masculinity, in self-conscious opposition to the paternalist soul man, can be understood in part as a rejection of what Paul Gilroy has identified as "the familialization of [black] politics." He takes issue with this constricting black discursive regime, which is preoccupied by a sense of "generational responsibility" and in which the "invocation of 'race' as family is everywhere":

> The family is not just a site of cultural reproduction; it is also identified as the mechanism for reproducing the cultural dysfunction that disables the race as a whole. And since the race is nothing more than an accumulation of families, the crisis of black masculinity can be fixed. It is to be repaired by instituting appropriate forms of masculinity and male authority, intervening in the family to rebuild the race.[61]

Gilroy instructively ties the proliferation of familial metaphors in black cultural politics to the peculiarly overburdened politics of black masculinity. The trope of the family informs the rhetoric of gangsta's black critics who advocate responsibility and, as Gilroy argues, quite often (overtly or implicitly) propose the resumption of traditional patriarchal family structures. The 1990s dogg figure can, in part, be positioned within the black discursive field as an irreverent rejoinder to the "appropriate forms of masculinity and male authority" deemed necessary to "rebuild the race." Gangsta can be read as a calculated attack on a seemingly complacent black bourgeoisie.[62] It is interesting here to think about the ways in which both the pleasures and the offensiveness of G-Funk masculinity stem from a self-conscious rejection of this burden of responsibility. And within the popular-cultural field, this becomes a rejection of the black male "burden of representation" (a term that has been generatively theorized recently by Kobena Mercer and Henry Louis Gates among others).[63] G-Funk, in its adolescent amorality, can be seen as a reaction against the fraught politics of "the black man's burden" and the longstanding middle-class-identified notion of the "race" artist who must present positive and ennobling images of the race. As a backlash, it takes seriously the "burden of *ir*responsibility," as it were. Clearly, both the reverent "black patriarch" and the irreverent "hypermasculinist dogg" are highly charged cultural-political symbols and as such are engaging in (class-based and generational) negotiations about representative forms of black masculinity. Thus, in some ways G-Funk is engaging in black cultural-political dialogues, assuming one particularly extremist position. Consequently, it is important not simply to view the form as reflecting (as Stuart Hall puts it) "how life really is out there," nor to read it as a totally commodified, co-opted product (as bell hooks does).

The pleasures of G-Funk are derived in part from subverting the "positive" role model of the soul man. Thus, this music institutes a different patriarchal structure (with an alternative set of—all be they more troubling—masculinist and sexist co-ordinates to those of dominant black discourses). What emerges is a complex interface between the post-soul ethics of gangsta and much of its reception among the black public intellectuals of its parent culture, still firmly rooted in the "old" vocabularies which I code here as the soul sensibility. This is a cultural conversation clearly informed by class, religious and geographic as well as generational differentials (not to mention the fraught feminist and sexual contestations which are not my subject here), so to say "old" is not to impose some simple chronology.

Discussing contemporary black masculinity, Henry Louis Gates asserts:

> I distrust the rhetoric of crisis. It's at once too gloomy
> and too hopeful: the Hippocratic trope of "crisis" invokes
> a turning point, beyond which lies recovery or death, and
> neither one seems on the cards for us.[64]

In his problematization of the "soulified" dialectical tension between gloom and hope for the future, Gates seems to be registering his own "post-soul" discursive move. The rhetoric of crisis—and its often attendant discourse of racial uplift through "self-help"—seems inappropriate, perhaps even irresponsible, in the face of the deep and endemic structural conditions of urban America, which are resultant of both neo-conservative policies and increasingly globalized market forces. The often galvanizing and sensational rhetoric of crisis (with its in-built sense of possible recovery) is almost entirely denied in G-Funk. Instead, G-Funk luxuriates in a knowing a-politicism and a performed nihilism which in some ways offer a timely rejoinder to, what Robin Kelley calls, the "negrocon" (black neo-conservative) over-emphasis on black men taking "personal responsibility."[65] The sense of optimism and aspiration of the civil rights era, enunciated by the soul man, seems to have dissipated, and this is understandably registered in some of the modes of black masculinity in contemporary pop culture. The posture of the gangsta dogg in some ways concords with Gates's perspective (though obviously approaching the problematic from widely divergent positions), insofar as they both throw into question the usefulness of deploying soul-inflected rhetoric to describe the socio-cultural products and predicaments of the present.

Underlying the flagrant and oft-noted nihilism in gangsta is a pronounced note of nostalgia. Because these dogg artists have grown up at the tail end of the soul era—at the dawning of George's post-soul historical moment—the "golden age of soul" is not so much a remembered as an imagined past. They access this era of responsible masculinity and political engagement via popular culture, which in no way renders it less powerful. The soul man is a kind of patriarchal father to the dogg figure, and, as I have shown, this crucial and complex relationship is actually mobilized in the formal features of gangsta rap. Thus, when black critics berate the nihilism and irresponsibility of gangsta and set it up in direct opposition to their own politically engaged, "soulful" posture, the opposition is in many ways a false one. The cultural exchange is knowing, and the polemical positions assumed are strategic: both rappers and critics have certain audiences in mind. Moreover, both rappers and critics are registering some of the same longings and anxieties. In the post-soul world there circulates a much wider range of black masculine types, and the conditions and contexts of production and consumption of cultural artifacts are far more complex. Perhaps the most important shift between soul and post-soul cultural periods is the decline of authorized representations of black identity. In the post-soul arena, the soul man becomes a kind of moral and political bedrock or point of reference for artists and critics alike, from which articulations of black masculinity are constituted and adjudged.

Where does this leave the question of resistance? I certainly don't want to try to overturn the reservations of G-Funk's detractors by recuperating or defending the models of masculinity the genre presents. My concern is not to find a means of decoding "against the grain" in order to uncover a resistive politics in what seem to me, on the whole, highly regressive articulations of masculinity as such. However, what may be politically enabling is the critical move of untying this popular cultural form from the strictures of overworked and perhaps politically disabling critical positions. Negative, unauthorized or "bad" black-produced popular-cultural depictions of black masculinity—of which the gangsta dogg is an exemplar—are usually understood in two ways. Either they are positioned as the "dupes" of the regulatory regimes of dominant culture and so are co-opted (a one-way dialogue between white and black culture, a position promulgated by bell hooks which precludes black agency); or they are positioned as reflections of a lamentable reality (the discourse of black authenticity is mobilized).

Both these explanations of black popular culture, I would argue, have lost some of their political efficacy and explanatory power. Instead, to position gangsta rap inside a *black* cultural dialogue over competing versions of masculinity, a dialogue that is often self-conscious, seems to be a timely and instructive exercise. The type of circumspect pop-cultural investigations of Marable's "post-civil-rights critics" offer fresh ways of thinking about representations of black men: ways which jettison some of the encumbering discursive baggage which discussions of black masculinity tend to come up against. Prescriptive pronouncements about the moral and political role of pop music and calls for uplifting gender representations are remnants of tactics deployed in a previous era of cultural politics. Instead, scholarship that is concerned with what Kelley calls the "hidden transcripts" of popular culture, its "infra-red" politics (or "infrapolitics"), is creating new ways of thinking and posing new kinds of questions about the black political terrain.[66] In order to understand the political outlook and the complex identificatory make-up of young black men (the ways in which they imagine themselves—as individuals and as a group—and the ways in which they understand the present through the lens of the black cultural and political past), it is incumbent on critics to engage carefully and systematically with the different forms of popular culture which reach and influence this social group, however distasteful or regressive one might find them.

Notes

1. *Buppies, B-Boys, Baps & Bohos* (New York: Harper Perennial, 1992), 1. The titles and content of two of George's other books capture the same sense of passing and regret: *Where Did Our Love Go?: The Rise and Fall of the Motown Sound* (New York: St Martin's Press, 1985); and *The Death of Rhythm and Blues* (London and New York: Omnibus Press, 1988). I want to thank Steven Daly, Mary Ellison, Michael Langnas, Eugene Quinn, and especially Peter Krämer.

2. For an overview of aesthetic changes, see, for instance, Portia K. Maultsby, "Music in African American Culture," in Venise T. Berry and Carmen L. Manning-Miller, *Mediated Messages and African American Culture: Contemporary Issues* (California, London and Delhi: Sage Press, 1996), 241–262; for aesthetic changes focusing on the development of rap, see Tricia Rose, *Black Noise: Rap Music and Black Culture in Contemporary America* (Hanover and London: Wesleyan University Press, 1994).

3. For industrial changes, see, for instance, George, *The Death of Rhythm & Blues*; Ellis Cashmore, *The Black Culture Industry* (London and New York: Routledge, 1997).

4. To gesture briefly towards the problems of positing a "post-soul" black culture, it is obvious that many continuities exist between the black music of the 1960s and of today. For instance, Motown Records—the center of soul production—was, of course, a highly commercial, "cross-over" enterprise, successfully marketing a sense of black authenticity; secondly, with contemporary artists like R Kelly, Boyz II Men and Blackstreet, it could be argued that soulful masculinity is alive and well in black music today.

5. Following George, my main concern is with the "soul" of the civil rights rather than the black power era, thus the soul men I have in mind include Otis Redding, (early)

Marvin Gaye, Smokey Robinson, Wilson Pickett, up until "the last of the great soul singers," Al Green in the early 1970s.

6. M. Mark, "It's Too Late to Stop Now," in Greil Marcus ed., *Stranded: Rock and Roll for a Desert Island* (New York, Da Capo Press, 1996), 12–13. The term "soul," as both a sociopolitical and cultural concept, extends far beyond the designation of a musical genre, as Portia Maultsby succinctly outlines in, "Ain't We Still Got Soul?," in Monique Guillory and Richard C. Green, eds., *Soul: Black Power, Politics, and Pleasure,* (New York and London: New York University Press, 1998), 270–3. For a classic discussion (where "soul" is understood as "the lower-class urban Negro's own 'national character'"), see Lee Rainwater, ed., *Soul* (Transaction Books, 1970), especially, "The Significance of Soul," Ulf Hannerz, 15–30.

7. I use the alternative spelling of "dogg" in this essay to signify the term's gangsta rap usage.

8. Cited in Henry Louis Gates, "The Black Man's Burden," in Gina Dent, ed., *Black Popular Culture* (Seattle: Bay Press, 1992), 77. Gates's invocation of Hall here betokens the influence of the latter's work on recent African American scholarship. Many of the intellectual positions in this paper are informed by recent black British cultural studies and in particular Hall's work on the "politics of representation." The fullest exposition of these approaches can be found in the collected volume D. Morley and K. Chen, eds., *Stuart Hall: Critical Dialogues in Cultural Studies* (London and New York: Routledge, 1996).

9. Cornel West, *Keeping Faith: Philosophy and Race in America* (New York: Routledge, 1993), 289.

10. Snoop Dogg's album *Doggystyle* (Death Row, 1993) sold 803,000 copies in its first week, making it the first debut album in pop music history to go instantly to number one on the American charts, and it went on to sell more than four million copies, *The* (London) *Times* , March 19, 1994, 20); Dr Dre had sold 15 million records by 1996, *Vibe*, February, 1996, 47.

11. I am centrally concerned with the black male audience of gangsta in this essay, which I call its "core" audience—not because it's the biggest (white adolescent males are gangsta rap's largest audience sector)—but because it is the primary audience; that is, the community from which and for which these artists usually claim to speak.

12. To give only a sample of the cultural circulation of the word "dog," there are standard numbers such as "Salty Dogg Blues," "Doggie House Boogie," "Hound Dog," "How Come My Dog Don't Bark," "Walking the Dog," and artists like Swamp Dogg and Tim Dog. I've found scant scholarly treatment of the dog figure, so my discussion is informed by a number of invaluable conversations conducted in 1997—I especially want to thank Todd C. Roberts, Editor of *URB* magazine.

13. The sound and imagery of G-Funk (short for 'Gangsta Funk') are heavily influenced by George Clinton's 1970s P-Funk ('Parliament-Funkadelic'), which was itself an early post-soul form.

14. Robin Kelley, *Race Rebels: Culture, Politics, and the Black Working Class* (New York: Free Press, 1994), 224.

15. As the most exploited and, as it were, "dogged" social group in the antebellum period, slaves were not allowed by law to own dogs.

16 This section can be usefully compared to Paul Gilroy's discussion of "Snoop's affirmation of blackness in dog-face," in "'After the Love Has Gone': Bio-politics and Etho-poetics in the Black Public Sphere" in The Black Public Sphere Collective, ed., *The Black Public Sphere*, (Chicago and London: University of Chicago Press, 1995), 53–80.

17. Quoted in Greg Kot, "Rock Turns Mean and Ugly," *The Chicago Tribune,* November 18, 1990, Arts 4.

18. bell hooks, *Outlaw Culture: Resisting Representations* (London and New York: Routledge, 1994), 117.

19. For a seminal sociological account, see Robert Staples, *Black Masculinity* (San Francisco: Black Scholar Press, 1982); for a cultural studies survey account, see Kobena

Mercer "Black Masculinity and the Sexual Politics of Race," in *Welcome to the Jungle: New Positions in Black Cultural Studies* (London and New York: Routledge, 1994), 131–170; and Thelma Golden, ed., *Black Male: Representations of Masculinity in Contemporary American Art* (New York: Whitney Museum of Modern Art, 1995).

20. On the profound social and economic restructuring of the Los Angeles area, see, for instance, the critical urban studies collection, Allen J Scott and Edward W Soja, eds., *The City: Los Angeles and Urban Theory at the End of the Twentieth Century* (Berkeley and Los Angeles: University of California Press, 1996).

21. Kobena Mercer, *Welcome To the Jungle*, 167.

22. Michael C. Dawson, *Behind the Mule: Race and Class in African American Politics* (New Jersey: Princeton UP, 1994), 15–44

23. Henry Louis Gates, *Thirteen Ways of Looking at a Black Man* (New York: Vintage Books, 1998, xv.

24. Robin Kelley offers a powerful critique of these over-worked "explanations" of popular culture in *Yo Mama's Disfunktional!*, 15–42.

25. hooks, *Outlaw Culture*, 116, 122–123.

26. In his wide-ranging and insightful account of "Black Masculinity and the Sexual Politics of Race," Mercer seems to come to some similar conclusions to hooks, when he claims that gangsta rap seems "to be based on an unconscious *identification* with the hegemonic white master model," and that a gangsta rap movie "unwittingly discloses that black masculinities are actually rather similar to white ones," in *Welcome to the Jungle*, 167. Mercer and hooks are right to point up the connections between the patriarchal expressions of black and white masculinity, but why is black male identification "unconscious," and the disclosure "unwitting"? In power-driven America, why are black men cast as "dupes" if they are as patriarchal as their white counterparts? Underpinning the "false consciousness" logic of these critiques is a binary sense of center and margin that may have outlived its political usefulness.

27. Eithne Quinn, "'Who's The Mack?': The Performativity, Politics and Play of the Pimp Figure in Gangsta Rap," *Journal of American Studies* (Cambridge: Cambridge University Press, forthcoming).

28. Bruce Jackson, *'Get Your Ass in the Water and Swim Like Me': Narrative Poetry from Black Oral Tradition* (Cambridge, Mass.: Harvard University Press, 1974), 17.

29. Mercer, "Endangered Species: Danny Tisdale and Keith Piper," *Artforum, 30* (Summer 1992), 75.

30. See, for example, the rather sensational cover photo and story of Snoop in *Newsweek*, November 29, 1993.

31. My general focus in this discussion is on male critics, so I use the term "post-soul *sons*" advisedly. For interventions by female critics on gender issues see (aside from hooks), above all, Tricia Rose, *Black Noise*.

32. Mark Naison, "Why Does Rap Dis Romance?," *Newsday*, 29 October, 1990, 48.

33. Of course, this clear-cut opposition would work less well if Otis Redding were replaced by the more sexual soul man, James Brown.

34. Roger D. Abrahams, *Deep Down in the Jungle*, revised ed. (Chicago: Aldine, 1970), 84–85.

35. Bakari Kitwana, *The Rap on Gangsta Rap: Gangsta Rap and Visions of Black Violence* (Chicago: Third World Press, 1994), 52-54.

36. Armond White, *Rebel For the Hell of It: The Life of Tupac Shakur* (New York: Thunder's Mouth Press, 1997), 135.

37. Naison, *Newsday*, 48.

38. Cornel West, "Nihilism in Black America," *Black Popular Culture*, 41.

39. In "Gangster Rap and Nihilism in Black America: Some Questions of Life and Death," *Social Text*, No. 43, Fall 1995, 89–132, Nick De Genova dismissively refers to West's "facile sermonizing on the subject of 'nihilism'" which he counterposes with the "radical politics" of gangsta rappers. This romanticizing, underhistoricized critique does

not take into account the widely differing agendas of black cultural workers nor the divergent cultural terrain (in time and space) they are contesting, and I certainly want to distance my own reservations about West's article from those of De Genova.

40. Manning Marable, "Black Intellectuals in Conflict," *Beyond Black and White: Transforming African American Politics* (London and New York: Verso, 1995), 171-172.

41. Michael Eric Dyson, *Between God and Gangsta Rap: Bearing Witness to Black Culture* (New York and Oxford: Oxford University Press, 1996), xviii.

42. See Dyson, "Gangsta Rap and American Culture," and "Ice Cube: Gangsta Rap's Visionary," *Between God and Gangsta Rap*, 176–86, 172–5; "Between Apocalypse and Redemption: John Singleton's *Boyz N The Hood*," in Jim Collins, Hilary Radner and Ava Preacher Collins, eds., *Film Theory Goes To the Movies*, (London and New York: Routledge), 209–227; and "Performance, Protest, and Prophecy in the Culture of Hip-Hop," in *Black Sacred Music*, 5:1, Spring 1991, 12–24.

43. Dyson, *The New York Times*, March 30, 1997, 2:34.

44. Kelley, *Race Rebels*, 209–214.

45. Conversation with Robin Kelley in New York, April, 1997.

46. George, *Buppies, B-Boys, Baps & Bohos*, 7.

47. Curtis Mayfield shocked audiences in a commensurate way with his deceptively sweet falsetto voice, singing blaxploitation tales of *Superfly* Priest the drug dealer in 1972.

48. Kelley, *Race Rebels*, 223.

49. Adario Strange, "Angel of Death," *The Source*, December, 1996, 104.

50. MacIntyre, "Shooting From the Hip," *The London Times*, March 19, 1997, 20.

51. Steven Daly, "A Dogg's Tale," *The Face*, February, 1994, 47, 48.

52. Donnell Alexander, "Teflon Blues," *The Source*, February, 1997, 55.

53. Richard Middleton, *Studying Popular Music* (Milton Keynes and Philadelphia: Open University Press, 1990), 262.

54. Strange, "Angel of Death," 106; Robert Christgau, "Gangstas and Niggaroes," *The Village Voice*, July 12, 1994, 55. The success of Nate Dogg's gospel-gangsterism inaugurated a new wave of R&B singing on gangsta tracks (notably leading to Coolio's 1995 smash hit single "Gangsta's Paradise," featuring singer L.V.).

55. Andrew Ross, "The Gangsta and the Diva," in *Black Male: Representations of Masculinity*, 171.

56. *Above the Rim* (Death Row / Interscope, 1994) sold one million copies in three weeks and produced three top twenty singles.

57. This track was originally written by Jerry Leiber and Mark Stoller who were largely responsible for the soul music of the Stax record label, again pointing to the influence of the soul era on G-Funk instrumentation.

58. Cheo H. Coker, "G Marks the Spot," *Los Angeles Times*, May 21, 1995, Calendar, 3.

59. Daly, "A Dogg's Tale," 50.

60. Daly, "A Dogg's Tale," 50.

61. Paul Gilroy, "It's a Family Affair," *Black Popular Culture*, 305-315.

62. This point is developed by Davarian Baldwin, "Black Empires, White Desires: The Spatial Politics of Identity in the Age of Hip Hop" (unpublished paper).

63. See Mercer, *Welcome to the Jungle*, 233–258; Gates, "The Black Man's Burden," *Black Popular Culture*, 75–83.

64. Gates, *Thirteen Ways of Looking at a Black Man*, xvi.

65. Kelley, *Yo' Mama's Disfunktional!*, 89.

66. Robin Kelley, "'We Are Not What We Seem': Rethinking Black Working-Class Opposition in the Jim Crow South," in *The Journal of American History*, Vol. 80 (1), June, 1993, 77.

CHAPTER 8

Revisiting the 1960s in Contemporary Fiction: "Where do we go from here?"

Sharon Monteith

This essay examines the tension between representations of the private man and the public figure, and between the individual event and its locus within the concatenation of episodes that is civil rights history in fiction. Novels published by two African American men in the 1990s refocus the struggles and the legacies of Martin Luther King Jr. and the civil rights movement for our times. Julius Lester's *And All Our Wounds Forgiven* (1994) and Charles Johnson's *Dreamer* (1998) each considers the inevitable alienation of civil rights leaders from the status quo they sought to change. They draw out the tensions between the different styles of male leadership and the contradictory images of black manhood that preoccupy politicians and historians today. They interrogate the visceral feelings that shape contemporary crises of polity and progressive action since, as James R. Ralph, Jr. has summarized, the story of the civil rights movement is "one that speaks directly to our own time," most specifically because of the movement's failure to overcome racial and gender divisions.[1] The failure to pass on an effective program for social transformation impinges on post-civil rights fictions and, as a result, they remain discursively locked. The feeling of declension that characterizes contemporary African American political struggles is ultimately more confining than the history of the civil rights movement that grounds the novels. I will consider this historical-literary impasse whilst examining the ways in which *Dreamer* and *And All Our Wounds Forgiven* are innovative fictions of moral complexity and philosophical enquiry, which begin to unpick the network of images that creates romantic heroes out of civil rights leaders like Martin Luther King.

Angela Davis in the 1988 introduction to her *Autobiography* (1973) reflects that the "frantic pace of events" in the 1960s and early 1970s precluded "the kind of contemplative attitude necessary to chronicle and interpret those struggles from the standpoint of history."[2] This is indeed a feature of civil right histories and of memoirs; Myrlie Evers's *For Us The Living* (1967), re-issued with new introductions in 1996, is also a reminder that she waited thirty-three years before Byron De La Beckwith was finally convicted for the murder of her husband, civil rights leader Medgar; poetry like Sonia Sanchez's "A Letter to Dr. Martin Luther King" (1984) deliberates reflexively on what would have been the leader's fifty-fourth birthday. In the 1990s a painful reconnection with the past is also keenly asserted via post-civil rights fictions and memoirs since, as King himself opined, "no society can repress an ugly past when the ravages persist into the present."[3]

The danger of reading contemporary fictions like Lester's and Johnson's astigmatically—in this context solely in terms of an African American literary tradition of protest writing—is that what may be innovative about these fictions tends to be undervalued or even repressed. The risk is still greater when one seeks only "authentic" documentation and a verifiable historical record in a fiction and fails to see what is also prospective in the work. There is a danger in trying to explain the workings of the imagination too literally as the restorative or recuperative fusion of politics and history, instead of recognizing that the emblems of the 1990s are the simulacra of the 1960s. Contemporary writers look through the prism of the civil rights movement in order to assess current crises of political and national progress; they create composite characters in order to aggregate events; they enter into debates on issues like leadership, but they also seek to tell stories. As James Baldwin once observed, "The resolution of a story must occur within us, with what we make of the questions with which the story leaves us. A plot, on the other hand, must come to a resolution, prove a point: a plot must answer all the questions which it pretends to pose."[4] Lester eschews plot preferring to compose a medley of voices and Johnson brushes history against the grain, decanting mysteries like the FBI involvement in King's death into an anxious exhortatory text since: "the way of agapic love, with its bottomless damands" has proved "too hard for this nation."[5]

King: The Dream and the Nightmare

Ralph Abernathy's eulogy at King's funeral is memorable for the analogy he made between King and the Biblical Joseph: "Let us slay the dreamer, and see what shall become of his dream." Charles Johnson's philosophical and historical concerns are the foundation of *Dreamer*, a novel that is a creative intervention into the last two years of King's life via the Chicago campaign. Johnson is best known as winner of the National Book Award for *Middle Passage* (1990) and his literary criticism in books like *Being and Race* (1988) locates him securely in an African American intellectual tradition. Historiographical fiction provides a forum through which readers become cognizant of struggles and events in which they themselves may have played no part and Lester and Johnson have each written narratives in which slavery is reconfigured as a site of African American history and memory. *Middle Passage* is a neo-slave narrative and Lester's *Black Folktales* (1969) for children and his Uncle Remus stories are highly creative forays into African American history that rework the seam of slavery. In their most recent novels, however, Lester and Johnson have turned their attention to glossing events of their own lifetimes.

King wrote in 1968, "Every revolutionary movement has its peaks of united activity and its valleys of debate and internal confusion."[6] Johnson descends into a valley of despair as well as into intra-Southern Christian Leadership Conference (SCLC) debate when he focuses on what King had determined would be the "action phase" of the Chicago campaign. The novel opens with King in bed in his Lawndale flat after two days without sleep. He is disturbed by his devoted aide, Matthew Bishop, who wishes him to see a face so like his own that Chaym (Cain) Smith leaves King speechless. He is the mirror image of the civil rights leader but also his antithesis, having risen from the recesses of African American culture. *Dreamer* speaks through two motifs intimately entwined—the dreamer and the underground man. King described the Northern slum dweller as inhabiting a "schizophrenic social milieu,"[7] and himself as two separate people.[8] Consequently, the Cain and Abel story of two brothers differently judged by God becomes the fulcrum of Johnson's novel. *Dreamer* is born in the interstices of previous texts, including the Bible, philosophical tracts, histories and biographies of King, and the palimpsestic fictional world Johnson creates across his own fictions. It is a world populated by men who struggle for power and visibility, a world in which women inhabit the private sphere as grieving widows, or provide maternal or sisterly strength as the keepers of family history.

Houston Baker fixes on 1966 as the point by which "both blacks and whites knew that America was destined for extremes."[9] In other words, the reformist phase was over and black power politics was pushing the civil rights movement to the brink of destruction. It is the year in which King began his Chicago campaign and the year in which the Black Power slogan, first coined during the Meredith March Against Fear in June of 1966, began to have particular resonance for younger movement workers. The slogan, described by King as "a psychological call to manhood,"[10] epitomized a shift in attitude and agenda for those who remained disaffected after legislation failed to translate into concrete social gains. In 1966 the interracial Student Non-violent Coordinating Committee (SNCC) expelled white colleagues, entrusting them to continue the struggle in alternative forms outside of the new all-black organization. Similarly, "black consciousness" marked the demise of the term "Negro" and signaled a shift in movement ideology to align the racial struggle in the United States with anti-colonial struggles around the world. Continuing struggles for integration jarred with calls for separatism. The times signify a splintering of the movement and a divergence of its goals.[11] King's faith in Platonic justice and the sacred principle of equality was shaken but his public persona remained crucial in centering the movement, and maintaining dialogue with CORE, SNCC and the NAACP until his death. For this reason, he remains a potent symbol for writers who choose to explore the nexus of race and rights in their fiction.

The tensions between allegiances and alliances were highly visible by 1966, and the impatience that would split radicals and liberals by 1968 undermined coalition politics. The SCLC had moved to Chicago to work with its native sons, most notably Al Raby, to coordinate the fight against institutional injustices and *de facto* segregation in January of 1966. Johnson's novel opens into the zenith of community disorder on July 17, by which time SCLC was scapegoated by Mayor Daley's office and by the press for the rioting and looting taking place on the city's streets, and King was already writing *Where Do We Go From Here: Chaos or Community?* On July 10, the Freedom Day rally at Soldier Field had culminated with King, in a symbolic reiteration of Martin Luther at Wittenberg, nailing his own measures for improvement to the door of Chicago's City Hall. Two days later, on an intensely hot day, police pulled over a group of black children who had opened a fire hydrant on the South Side to refresh themselves. The children retaliated and soon riots were underway. Three died before the National Guard returned the streets to simmering order and the faltering nonviolent alternative to black power was condemned on all sides.

It was in Chicago that King began to be most consistently criticized as he openly denounced the government's involvement in the war in Vietnam and the administration's failure to allot sufficient funds to combat poverty at home, as promised by Lyndon B. Johnson in his national program for "The Great Society": "The bombs in Vietnam," King declared, "explode at home; they destroy the hopes and possibilities for a decent America."[12] The press denied his right as a civil rights leader to speak against the war and unmitigated criticism from younger activists on a number of fronts affected King deeply, leaving his closest aides worried that "Martin is not only waging a war on the war, he's waging a war on sleep."[13] Johnson keeps his novel close to these historical events—even the description of the slum apartment echoes Coretta Scott King's almost word for word.[14] But having set the parameters, he breaks them open. At the midnight hour in riot-torn Chicago, Johnson has Chaym Smith appear to King, the living symbol of his belief that northern cities were the products of Cain.

In *Strength to Love* (1963), in the sermon "A Knock at Midnight," King had employed the metaphor of "the darkness of midnight" to stress the dual focus on hope and despair that drove him on:

> This would be an unbearable world were God to have only a single light, but we may be consoled that God has two lights; a light to guide us in the brightness of the day when hopes are fulfilled ... and a light to guide us in the darkness of midnight when we are thwarted and the slumbering giants of gloom and hopelessness rise in our souls.[15]

In Lester's novel Chaym Smith becomes the slumbering giant, King's doppelgänger, another of Chicago's native sons but this time a veteran, a drug user from the projects, and the distillation of all the problems King was to fail to solve in Chicago. Chaym is reminiscent of Rutherford Calhoun in Johnson's *Middle Passage*. Both belong in the tradition of the trickster-survivor and Chaym, as the FBI inform him in *Dreamer*, is also descended from Balaka, a free woman of the African tribe, the Allumuseri, introduced by Johnson in the earlier novel. For Johnson, as for King and Malcolm X, slavery is the crucible in which the weapons of the civil rights movement were forged and differences over anti-slavery ideology transmogrify into splits in the civil rights coalition symbolized by Cain and Abel. Chaym is Cain, the angry revolutionary to King's Abel; the rejected angry brother endures and the historical continuum that he represents survives beyond him.

The dominant metaphor in the novel is of doubling the point; in *Dreamer,* as in *And All Our Wounds Forgiven*, King becomes a two-dimensional character. Chaym performs a specific symbolic function here and in Lester's novel the character is split; John Calvin Marshall performs in public and "Cal" lives out a private, secret life. As will become clear, neither novel succeeds in creating a multi-faceted King. His anxiety over performing a series of roles is voiced but only on one occasion, in *Dreamer*, is he represented as a father, for instance, playing with his son. Imagining a double life serves to raise certain anomalies and conflicts; Johnson asks why the philosopher "Citizen King" has not invested more time in those like Smith: "He was the kind of Negro the Movement had for years kept away from the world's cameras: sullen, ill-kept, the very embodiment of the blues ... Neglected like the very building we were in. Everything about him was in disrepair."[16] The economic and psychological problems Chaym's lifestyle bespeaks are the perennial problems King sought to put an end to in Chicago. His inevitable failure is bound up with a loss of the ethical imperative that was King's legacy. Imagining a complex amalgam of conflicting, overlapping roles perhaps risks blurring the distinction that can be made between self and other.

Chaym Smith is an inauspicious repository for King's values. He is coached to act and speak like King but his own dreams are heroin-induced and his world-view jars with King's own; he speaks of "brotherhood malarkey" (55) and places his individuality over all else, "Shit, as long as he's alive, I guess I'll always be nothing." (130) *Dreamer* imagines what happens when King's double becomes known to the FBI; whisked away by agents in the days preceding King's assassination, Chaym's final allegiances remain unclear. The agents who, independently of King, concur that his schedule is "suicide on the installment plan" (187) and who describe him as a "liability," extort "help" from Chaym by threatening to re-open the cases on his past crimes. The final section of the novel presages Chaym's demise, King's murder and Matthew Bishop's broken future after Memphis. But, "King" has already been "killed." Chaym, taken for the pastor, is shot by an old man and left so close to death that Bishop sees in his agonized face the death of his hero and mentor. Similarly, as the nation mourns King's death, Johnson projects forward and reels back to encompass other assassinations. His juxtaposition of cross-eyed detectives, "clearing" the area to "look for evidence," with Bishop's belief that Cainites killed King, is searing.

Chaym Smith is a version of a recurring figure in African American fiction: more streetwise and cynical than Richard Wright's Bigger Thomas, he is recognizable from Leon Forrest's cycle of Chicago novels which includes characters who can be read as forerunners of Smith, as in the epic *Divine Days* (1993) set in 1966 on Chicago's Southside. Forrest's novels explore the hybrid of conflict and dream, history and biblical allusion which also animates Johnson's *Dreamer*. Analogies are frequent and thought-provoking: brother to brother and self to other, King and Chaym are likened to Jesus and Judas, Gandhi and Godse, Romulus and Remus and Jacob and Esau. But, the most powerful intertext is Genesis 4:1-8. Johnson writes in the Byronic tradition, in that his Cain is revised up into a tragic, alienated individual and Abel often seems flawed and lacking in selfhood: "the Movement left no room for subjectivity." (138) Whilst Chaym is made over, King remains a remote figure, perhaps in order to signal the kinds of worrying disconnections that C. Vann Woodward began to describe in *The Burden of Southern History* when he wrote that: the stirring events of the civil rights movement were such that "nothing comparable had ever happened before in our history ... these are unforgettable moments ... and yet they seemed at the same time so remote, so improbable."[17] The odd gesture belies King's tiredness, lack of confidence or, on one occasion, guilty sexual desires, but only in short italicized interchapters does the narrative ever enter King's confidence, and then expressly in third person narrative form.

Johnson has said that King is "someone we think we know ... but despite the overwhelming presence of this man in our lives, he is strangely absent." He began *Dreamer* in an effort to combat his ignorance of King the man: "I wondered if there was any way I could claim to understand him, or his position at the time of his death, or what he means to us today," by capturing what he calls the "eidos," or essence, of King's life.[18] The narrative structuring reflects the difficulties Johnson faced in extricating the private man from the iconic figure. Outside of the short interchapters, the story of King in Chicago is only ever told from the point of view of Matthew Bishop, the aide who first introduces Chaym to "Doc," the witness-participant figure who believes himself to be inconsequential (a "callow prop in the background of someone else's story" but whose job it is to record events, "preserving ... secrets for posterity." (102) In *Dreamer*, the main woman character, who contends for attention, is Amy, but she is an "Abelite, lost to ambiguity," as described by Bishop who, in his admiration, hoped she would be the "pious woman [who] might lead a man to the Lord. "(109) Bishop, like Simon the Cyrene, the African designated to carry Christ's cross to Golgotha, "on stage for only one sentence" in Matthew 27:32 (212), carries the story only in this metaphorical sense and Amy and her grandmother, Mama Pearl, provide an almost stereotypically resilient backdrop, even if its context is the movement. It is through such figures that Johnson creates the quotidian but it is Chaym Smith he proclaims as the novel's protagonist and who remains intractably the more forceful in the primary literary pairing.

Hayden White has suggested: "As distinct from the present the past is alien, exotic, or strange; as continuous with it this past is familiar, recognizable, and potentially fully knowable. The historical past is, in a word, 'uncanny,' both known and unknown, present and absent, familiar and alien, at one and the same time." He concludes that, "Thus construed, the historical past has all the attributes that we might ascribe to the psychological sphere of 'the imaginary'."[19] Johnson slips between the prevailing ideologies of civil rights history and historically skewed representations of black manhood to disentangle King and re-present him in interrogative and imaginative ways for a contemporary readership, yet when he imagines an alter ego for Martin Luther King in *Dreamer*, he does not imagine a woman. The "sphere of the imaginary" of which White speaks remains bound historically into ideas of leadership as a masculine preserve. Finally, Johnson cannot fathom the essence of his stated subject, King; the ideas are larger than the space in which they may be realized. Johnson can only approach King through his avatar Chaym or his apprentice—the Crito to his Socrates—Bishop. He veers towards the bewitching Chaym who charms Bishop as easily as he fascinates the reader. Bishop is very much a child of his time, the 1950s, but cursed with "a shy Victorian personality" (164), whereas the dark, brooding Chaym, who King might have described as one of the "ill-starred and deeply wounded veterans of ... 'slum shock',"[20] is the most disturbingly postmodern figure in the text. He is the symbol of present anxieties and future failures and, consequently, he eclipses the charismatic hero he is employed to impersonate.

Love and Death in the Civil Rights Movement

The civil rights messiah is a recurring figure in fiction and film that seeks to mine the territory of the 1960s. Like Ralph Ellison in *Invisible Man* (1952) and John A. Williams in *The Man Who Cried I Am* (1967) who also turned away from naturalism (Williams even to consider King's adultery), Julius Lester disguises historical figures as fictional characters to exert a speculative and allusive investigation of a civil rights collective. In many ways, this allows him to be bolder than Johnson. He reconstitutes civil rights mythology and fragments it through multiple narrators—male and female—purposefully situating John Calvin Marshall's messianic presence alongside the workers on the ground (Robert Card), the wife waiting at home (Andrea Calvin Marshall) and the white lover (Lisa Phelps). Andrea and John Calvin meet in Boston like King and Coretta Scott and, like them, marry before he devotes his life to the movement. But, Lester's Marshall is an ex-centric, centrifugal King rather than a remote figure. He leads the Southern Committee for Racial Justice, which recalls the SCLC but incorporates allusions to the work of CORE with the Freedom Rides and SNCC's field-work in Mississippi.

The northern white woman activist and lover—problematized in Alice Walker's "Advancing Luna and Ida B. Wells" (1971) and *Meridian* (1976) and in Rosellen Brown's *Civil Wars* (1984)—is a device through which much of the hidden sexual history of the civil rights movement may begin to be written. Coleman Dowell created the ubiquitously sad Ivy in *White on Black on White* (1983) but his work has received scant critical attention. Julius Lester, however, creates Lisa as a key voice in his chorus; it is in her arms that John Calvin Marshall dies and her confession to his dying wife ("tell andrea i never stopped loving her"), postponed for thirty years, signals the beginning of the deferred atonement and forgiveness that is the fragile center of Lester's project. The interest in women characters for post-civil rights writers reflects the impact those like Sara Evans, Casey Hayden and Mary King have had on our broader understanding of interracial movement politics. In Lisa, Lester creates another composite figure and draws on the life stories and memoirs of white women activists to do so. Lisa's memories of joining the movement—what drew her to the cause and why she stayed—are very close to those of Candie Carawan (formerly Anderson) who, like Lisa, moved from California to join the Fisk Exchange Program in 1960. Her feelings as described in *Sing For Freedom* are echoed in Lisa; Carawan remembers the endless self-questioning, "What could a white student do? What would my presence at a lunch counter mean?"[21]

Lester was involved in different ways in representing aspects of the cultural climate of the 1960s. Renowned for writing the angry polemic *Look Out Whitey! Black Power's Gon' Get Your Mama!* (1968), more recently, the ex-field-marshal for SNCC has been labeled a neo-conservative. What Lester brings to the field of literary enquiry is a historiography of the civil rights movement in which he was involved but which he explores very differently thirty years on. In *Look Out Whitey!* Lester ridiculed King as Booker T. Washington's successor and castigated him for his ideas of agapic love, "What is love supposed to do? Wrap the bullet in a warm embrace? Caress the cattle prod?"[22] In *And All Our Wounds Forgiven,* it is precisely to love and personal relationships that he turns in an effort to distil the essence of the civil rights era, but to *eros* rather than *agape* and to sex rather than civic virtue. His most recent work has been acclaimed by mainstream critics, in a way that his earlier radical essays resisted, and this may reflect a new willingness to engage with gender issues.[23]

Lisa, eleven years younger than Marshall, sustains a relationship with him over seven years but their connection is not highly politicized. The pair treat each other as exotic prizes; she exalts his skin color and the size of his penis whilst he "needs" her to be blonde and blue-eyed.

(142) But, as Marshall says, "in the sixties a lot of black men and white women tried to heal history with their bodies ... i also know that some of history's wounds could not have been tended any other way." (73) Theirs is a communion with death and desire. For Lisa:

> I turned off the shower, took the bar of soap and began covering him with lather as thick as desire, but this was not the desire for sexual union as the desperate desire that he should live and not die, that this body whose every pore I had touched with my hands, my tongue, my breasts ... not begin its journey toward dust so soon ... (206)

Even though the politics of interracial relationships in the 1960s South have begun to be explored by Alice Walker, it is only more recently that issues of black male sexuality have received similarly interrogative treatment. Walker's representation of Truman Held in *Meridian* prompted specifically masculinist criticism, from Stanley Crouch most notably, who feared Walker's and Morrison's representations of "black brutes" undermined black men who remain vulnerably susceptible to criticism in American society.[24] Lester, in many ways, writes in the equally controversial tradition of James Baldwin who, of all writers in the African American tradition, has been the most consistently courageous in articulating the significance of sexuality and cross-racial sexual relationships. Lester could be said to respond to Gloria Naylor's call, post-Baldwin, for black men to write novels about that largely "unexplored territory in our literature" that is "waiting for some man who is courageous enough to enter it." Naylor is concerned that to confront love, desire and death takes courage because, "given this society's definition of what it is to be a 'man', for a male and especially a black male" to represent the frailty and vulnerability of black men remains difficult and rare.[25]

In the case of King, the context is further complicated by the impossibility of public figures living private lives, an immensely topical issue in the late 1990s, as President Clinton's affair with Monica Lewinsky demonstrates. Writers and journalists have been preoccupied with this feature of public office since James Callender accused Thomas Jefferson of having an affair with one of his own slaves.[26] In the modern context, James Baldwin's prescient commentary on the issue of privacy occurs in *Tell Me How Long The Train's Been Gone* (1968) when Leo Proudhammer, leaving hospital after a serious operation, provides a telling indictment of the loss of privacy that public service or celebrity status entails: "It makes me feel a tremendous obligation to stay well. It makes me know that I did not make myself—I do not belong to me."[27]

Lester echoes this idea: "Cal lived in terror that one day ... he—Cal—would not awaken because John Calvin Marshall would have swallowed him ..." (48) Baldwin's actor-activist, based, one imagines, on Harry Belafonte and Sidney Poitier, highly visible civil rights activists who shared platforms with King and marched by his side, feels he is constantly under surveillance, by the people, by the police and, one is tempted to add, by the FBI.[28] Similarly, in *And All Our Wounds Forgiven*, a public discussion of citizenship and social enfranchisement, law and legislation is decanted into a literary exploration of King's *imagined* private life and relationships in a broad dissection of the American social fabric. Fiction becomes a forum for intimate exposé. Do a man's deeds outweigh his human failings? One might imagine that the narrative options available to a writer who knows his civil rights history diminish unless the object is to fuel the debates as to King's sexist posturing or the controversy surrounding the FBI's COINTELPRO campaign. Lester skates very close to this assumption with regard to his King figure but reasserts an alternative historical line that reacts to the problems of remaining charismatic and heroic in tight personal and political corners.

Marshall's affair remains secret, except from Hoover and the FBI who are unable to frighten him into ending the relationship: "i thought about opening the paper one morning to see stories about my relationship ... and a giddiness swirled inside me ... my god! i thought. i would be free! i wouldn't have to be john calvin marshall anymore ..." (60) But, its impact on Andrea, his wife, is given significant time and space in the novel. Through eight days in 1993 she lies in a Nashville hospital awaiting death. Silenced by a stroke, she becomes the repository of Lisa's and Card's confessions and the source of forgiveness. The relationship between Andrea and Lisa, silent with each other for so many years, is one of the sites in which Lester grapples with the contestations of race and gender. Lisa is drawn to Andrea but in a certain safety that she can open her heart to a woman who may never be able to respond. I have written elsewhere about fictions in which black women are made to remain silent whilst white women's voices dominate in the text.[29] But, Lester makes it clear that Andrea should not respond in any case, she has no need, "in the hearing was the atonement." (219) It is she who continues to hold the primary connection with the past and her death signifies her own release from her pain, as it signifies a new phase for those who remain behind. In his efforts at reconciliation, Lester foregrounds the healing of his black characters whilst allowing his white characters to begin to heal themselves, once they understand that their limitations were as important as their strengths in the struggles of the 1960s. Andrea is so much a part of Marshall that for Lisa, "I would be free only when all of his truth meant as much to me as my own truth. Part of his truth was that he loved her." (227)

Reading Lester's novel, the reader is immediately disoriented by Marshall's first person narration and by the truths that torque and twist within it. Presented in lower case and largely unmarked by punctuation, it generates an anxious circling narrative. Ascribing an interior monologue to a civil rights leader renowned for public speaking begins the relocation of the public figure in the realm of the personal. It also begins the project that Cornel West has described as imperative when examining iconic figures. West cites the importance of "questioning King's sexism and homophobia and the relatively undemocratic character of his organization," not to sabotage his legacy but to reactivate its meaning in a changed context.[30] *And All Our Wounds Forgiven* widens the focus on King whilst jamming a foot in the door it appears to open; that John Calvin Marshall is a fictionalized permutation of King allows for an elastic portrayal but it also allows space to dwell on what is biographically different (Cal is born in Alabama, he participates in the Freedom Rides, he dies in a white woman's arms) rather than what sustains the comparison. Marshall haunts the text; his presence equivocates between the biographical narrative which recreates King as a unitary historical figure for others, and the imaginary which allows Lester to step outside what is biographically "known" about King. The relation between story and history is made ambivalent from the very first page when Marshall, the absent leader, speaks. His is the voice of a dead man and the novel begins long after his death but circles around that "fact," pushing back and forth; back to the 1950s and 1960s and up to 1993 since, as he says "neither my life nor my death constitutes the story."(1) Lester explores the wider ramifications for the movement as a whole, as Johnson does when he describes the week of King's funeral as "the longest week in modern history" (227), in the belief that those ramifications will persist into the next century.

Lester's King becomes a marshal, marshalling the troops on the ground like his young lieutenant, Robert Card. In a complicated exploration of post-civil rights anxieties, the hermeneutic code of the novel is pitted against the teleological, and the chain of recorded events which culminated in King's assassination. Lester pushes his protagonists so far as to create an analogy between love of race as a passion for death; in his last years Marshall feels defeated that a "subterranean stream of racial chauvinism" has broken like lava over the civil rights movement. (161) Since Marshall exists in a liminal space in the text, his voice echoes down the years to absorb the hatred and *ressentiment* those around him continue to feel. In a multi-voiced exploration of an era, the liminal zones or interstitial spaces between lives are the real sites of what King himself referred to more than once as the "bruised history" of blacks and whites.

As in *Dreamer*, the King figure is not indisputably the novel's central character. The text is polyvocal and Marshall is only one of four major interpreters of the constellation of events which leave the characters dead and alive, forgiven and forgiving. The most memorable of these characters is Robert Card. At the 1963 March on Washington, John Lewis of SNCC alleged "We shall crack the South into a thousand pieces and put it back together again in the image of democracy."[31] In order to remake the South, black male southerners burdened by pernicious stereotypes shot through with desire, hatred and fear, had to become citizens. Lester's fractured modernist enquiry pursues how those who live after Marshall might make that transition. Robert Card's character is a composite of fieldworkers like Bob Moses, posted to McComb, Mississippi, in 1961 under SCLC and SNCC sponsorship, and others like Charles Sherrod and Cordell Reagon, primarily associated with the Albany campaign. Bobby Card is the most troubling presence in the novel; he drags his wounded body and tormented mind in and out of a series of mental institutions and into every bar and bed he can find down the years after Shiloh. Lester's Shiloh is moved out of Tennessee to the state of Mississippi, "where colored people looked at trees and saw gallows." (100) It forms the epicenter of Robert Card's tragedy and of his forbearance; in Biblical terms, a sanctuary which was destroyed, Shiloh becomes a place where he develops meaningful relationships within the black community but where white hatred ultimately forces him to annul Robert and to rename himself Card. After Card's father figure is shot in the back for daring to work for voter registration, Card stays in Shiloh and "did everything he knew to force somebody to use one of those bullets—talked back to highway patrolmen, cursed the sheriff, dared plantation owners to shoot him, and he almost succeeded the night a shotgun blast covered him with glass as he lay sleeping, or the first time he took someone to the courthouse to register to vote and a mob beat him into unconsciousness."(111) This aspect of the novel may be based on Robert Moses's grief over the death of Herbert Lee. (37)

Death would make Robert Card a civil rights martyr and the sheriff knows how to shake his faith in selfhood and survival without risking such distinction. Violence, sexuality and power pivot on a white sheriff's nod and gruff: "Don't you worry none. I ain't going to kill you. In fact, I'm not going to leave a mark on you. But I guarantee you when I get done, you'll never forget me." (117) The sequence in which Sheriff

Zebediah Simpson tortures the young man falls at the center of the novel. Unlike most descriptions of torture, there is no interrogation. What Simpson's victim knows is of no consequence; it is his resilience in the face of implacable white power that the Sheriff must conquer. The Sheriff opens Card's fly and carefully brushes his knife along his penis until he is fully aroused against his will. His *piéce de resistance* is the two black men he has commandeered to perform oral sex, leaving Card "limp, exhausted, sexually satisfied and intent on his own death." (119) Unable to stem the serial murdering of black men who dare to speak out against segregation and powerless to defend his own body against abuse, Card's masculine foundations are rocked. It is only when Wylie, who the Sheriff forced to abuse him, offers his hand in friendship that Card begins the slow fight back with the knowledge that for his friend life is wretched in a way he had never imagined: "If you think being a nigger is hard, it ain't half as hard as being a faggot in a small town in Mississippi where everybody knows you a faggot and they treat you like shit but late at night, them's the one that come scratching at your back door." (121)

Lester tries to peel back each stereotype and assumption about black masculinity to reveal the ordinary and the fragile; to show that it was precisely those qualities against which King's success and the success of other male civil rights workers should be measured. When Marshall, meets with "X" two months after his split from the Nation of Islam to form the Organization of Afro-American Unity, they talk but "X" talks more and faster, making awkward apologies for doing so. Lester provides a critique of the failure to commend what was ordinary about those like King who have been sanctified:

> he did most of the talking. i doubt that had been his intent, but i sensed he was nervous. people often were when they met me. perhaps it was the disparity between what i looked like physically and what i had done. our culture has its images of courage as it does of beauty and courage dresses in biceps. i had none. yet in their minds were the pictures of me being beaten at the bus station in birmingham, me standing before the quarter of a million that august day in washington, me leading a march along mississippi highways. (213)

Only in death do John Calvin Marshall the public hero and Cal the fragile, flawed individual become one. But Card, left behind to hemorrhage from his wounds, is rendered almost mad with rage and regret. As with Chaym in *Dreamer*, it is really his character that plumbs the depths of civil rights pain and power, more terribly even than John Calvin Marshall: "I cannot think of anyone in this century who lived in constant relationship to death like those of us who sought to make America whole and broke ourselves into pieces instead." (190)

In this novel, interracial sexual contact between Marshall and Lisa is graphically described; the more intimate the representation of sexual relations, the more the racial binary is dissolved but the binary gender divide is affirmed; Cal and Lisa's voices and thoughts merge more than once in the acting of making love. Card's experience of rape as homosexual oral sex would also seem to subvert gender categories but the racial divide is reinscribed; this episode operates within a context racialized as black. Had the rape been *committed* by white men, the violation would have carried different connotations. As it stands, Card's black manhood is an important integer for Lester's belief that "our racial suspicions and hatreds have made us one nation"(68) but that we need to work through them. Finally, Card is left re-establishing his relationship with the black woman who is the mother of his child, working to re-constitute a post-civil rights black family in the 1990s, in spite of his fears and regrets.

Re-Evaluating the Civil Rights Movement in Contemporary Fiction

As reconsiderations of past decades dominate contemporary cultural production, critics are invited to engage with narratives written not just to "account for" the past but to imagine new kinds of connections with it. History is inevitably a site of aporia and anxiety as both Johnson and Lester demonstrate. Walter Benjamin, Hayden White and, more recently, Alun Munslow's work at the seam of "new cultural history," probes historical discourse and its relation to literary representation. Critical and dramatic distance, particularly in the 1990s when there are fewer visible social movements through which to channel one's political allegiances, ensures that a fiction's intersection with the historical record becomes an interaction. The historical novel has given way to the historiographical metafiction and protest fiction has mediated into manifestly alternative scripts for the future.[32]

Post-civil rights fictions like *Dreamer* and *And All Our Wounds Forgiven* might be best described as parapolitical texts, they are novels which ponder and probe the trajectory from self to the civil rights movement in politicized discourse. They follow roads not previously taken in earlier literature and pastiche and parody figure significantly in fictions which revisit and re-assert civil rights history. The narrative strategies and their effects are quite different from those deployed in novels of the 1960s and 1970s; the politically charged realism of a novel like Gil Scott-Heron's *The Nigger Factory* (1972) or William Melvin Kelley's *A Different Drummer* (1962) and John O. Killens's '*Sippi* (1967) contrasts markedly with the modernist and postmodernist texts Lester and Johnson write. The conviction with which we read realist novels has come under attack from structuralists and poststructuralists alike. Opening out the relationship between fiction and the illusions of "realism" has succeeded in multiplying the modes in which writers represent "the historical" in fiction. Lester and Johnson create referential narratives that tell stories previously told by historians and biographers; they write, as Daniel W. Lehman has described "from the outside in," peering over "the edge of history," but they manipulate the historical record in an effort to overcome its aporia or to graft their memories on to the next generation.[33]

Beginning to take the long fictional view means working within and against the traditional boundaries of history and fiction, being able to "slip into the breaks and look around," to borrow Ralph Ellison's phrase for his Invisible Man's disquisition on historical time and its elasticity. Contemporary novels may be less insurgent than those written in the 1960s and 1970s but they are potentially much more open and dialogic; writers are necessarily in dialogue with historians' interpretations. Johnson feels that in his fiction, for example, a "concern with boundaries" has replaced a "concern with roots" and that boundaries do not "merely separate, divide, or protect but instead function as signifiers of the biological, physical, cultural exchanges going on across them as well."[34] In fiction, the historical record is only one tool in the imaginative reconstruction of a cultural and historical context and a vestigial thesis emerges in which historically verifiable facts undergo a sea change; facts are malleable and unstable and fictions phenomenological, so that in Johnson's *Dreamer* the 1960s is described as "the first truly *theatrical* decade," when "role-playing and how things appeared took primacy over reality (and who, after all, knew what *that* was anymore?)." (164) The slippage between imagination and the facts that historical commentators work so assiduously to retrieve, becomes the creative wellspring for writers of fiction for whom strict allegiance to the facts may limit what they can do with them.[35]

In recent years, writers like Lester and Johnson, Alice Walker and Leon Forrest, have succeeded in offering disturbing and sometimes visionary heterotopic spaces in which post-civil rights anxieties may be addressed. The impact of this fiction has not yet been sufficiently examined within the historiography of the civil rights movement and post-nationalist African American ideologies. Richard H. King, amidst one of the few sustained discussions of civil rights fictions, considers novelist E.L. Doctorow's idea that "truths of the imagination" can be much more hostile to the status quo than historical facts.[36] This idea is prevalent in American literature from William Wells Brown's *Clotel* (1853) in which the slave daughter of a founding father is sold on the auction block to Faulkner's *Absalom, Absalom!* (1933) in which it is posited, "There is a might-have-been which is more true than truth." However, the impact of fiction on the American public is necessarily limited by its audience. Films like Spike Lee's *Malcolm X* (1994) and Melvin and Mario Van Peebles's *Panther* (1995) are mass marketed and, consequently, fire the public's imagination as they fortify the bridge between contemporary experiences of America and those of past decades; the opening sequence of Lee's *X* combines newsreel footage of civil rights rallies with the eighty-second long videotape George Halliday made of the beating of Rodney King in 1991. But the danger of fetishizing "Brother" Malcolm or "Saint" Martin or of creating a delimiting taxonomy of black leadership or black manhood, is most imaginatively interrogated in literary works. Even fictional representations, however, cannot blithely surmount the feeling of declension that characterizes the post-civil rights era.

Literary and historical reconsiderations of masculinity and sexuality have begun to energize new readings of the civil rights movement and, most particularly, to unsettle stereotypes of black men. George P. Cunningham, for example, reads the movement as a "narrative of African American male bodily agency." He draws on Michael Dyson's idea that images of black men's public deaths and murders underpin a story of the civil rights and black power movements that is recursive.[37] Lester's Robert Card exemplifies this idea. However, as Cunningham acknowledges parenthetically, Rosa Parks was the first person to use her body symbolically in this way. Women's contributions to the civil rights movement remain underexplored in fictional representations of the period. One begins to wonder why the boundaries between black men and women, and between white and black women activists that Alice Walker determined as salient, have not yet received more developed examination. Novels may chronicle events and personalize civil rights history; as in *Meridian* and Meredith Sue Willis's *Only Great Changes* (1985). But, as decade supersedes decade, novelists are clearly more free to intervene creatively as well as critically, so that, as Fred D'Aguiar has said, "The act of looking back not only acknowledges the present in the past, it admits, too, the future in the past ... Each generation demands something different from those stories, some shift in emphasis or focus, some alteration in tone or nuance, that has a direct bearing on the ease of their own inherited hurt."[38]

Johnson and Lester's novels demand that we consider inherited hurts in terms of what Adrienne Rich has designated "episodes of collective civil loss, shame, betrayal" which "dwell in the national psyche unacknowledged, embedded like shrapnel, leaving a deep recurrent ache in the body politic."[39] Inter-movement disputes, homophobia and sexism, violence and conspiratorial assassinations characterized the 1960s; betrayal and loss are as palpable in historical memory as the March on Washington or the passing of the Civil Rights Act in 1964. In *And All Our Wounds Forgiven* and *Dreamer*, psychological and physical wounds cluster as motifs to characterize a past that has survived into the present, the effects of which are yet to be fully played out. If the public discourse on race still believes that the personal can subvert the misconstruction that constitutes racialized identity, the public discourse on gender in the civil rights movement does not offer a way in which the personal might transcend the misconstruction that constitutes manhood or womanhood. If writers of the 1960s and early 1970s sought to correct and control images of black men vitiated by racism, by the 1990s the tendency is to disarm the arbitrariness of gender constructions and to broaden the context in which black men are represented. However, contemporary novelists continue to codify black leadership as male and masculinist in the way that Belinda Robnett has exposed in her examination of distinctively male and female modes of bridge and formal leadership models.[40] The masculine model of non-elected leadership remains charismatic and this is a primary reason why King remains central in literary as in other investigations of the topic.

Contemporary fictions are often more effective when readers are precipitated into an anxiety of interpretation rather than hurtled through a series of incendiary episodes; to write beyond the historical "ending" may be the salient difficulty, as with Van Peebles's *Panther*.[41] The assassination of King and the disbanding of the Panthers may be *ideés fixés*, unequivocal factors in a novel's composition, but they need not scotch the imaginative leaps one might take. Like Don DeLillo's *Libra* which delves into the conspiracy around J.F. Kennedy's assassination and former CIA agent Robert Andrews's novel of conspiracy *Death in A Promised Land* which does the same, less successfully, for King, each of these novels asks the same question in different ways: where do we go from here?

Where Do We Go From Here?

King's own question, raised by Lester's John Calvin Marshall and by Johnson's King, is also advanced by those who search for a new and dynamic black leadership for the twenty-first century. It features significantly in discussions in the press and political arena and characterizes essays by historians and philosophers like Manning Marable and Cornel West: "We need leaders—neither saints nor sparkling television personalities—who can situate themselves within a larger historical narrative of this country ... who can grasp the complex dynamics of our peoplehood and imagine a future grounded in the best of our past, yet who are attuned to the frightening obstacles that now perplex us."[42] Michele Wallace is more acerbic: "When you look at so-called black leadership as reflected by the mainstream media, what you see is a motley crew of the narcissistic, the vaguely ridiculous, and the inept."[43]

The contemporary crisis of African American leadership has precipitated fictions which take place on a discursive terrain in which the historical narrative of the civil rights and black power movements is examined in relation to millennial concerns surrounding models of leadership. Writers endeavor to unlock what was one of the decade's most notable features, its debates and struggles around race and rights as codified by civil rights leaders and black power revolutionaries. Novelists, like historians, contest the meaning of the decade; what persists in each of their works is the need to investigate a turbulent period which has been variously described as the "most dynamic and icon-shattering decade of the twentieth century" when "everything seemed possible for a brief shining moment"[44] and a decade in which "murder became an accepted form of political discourse."[45]

"In the ruins of ideology, bereft of messianic leadership, the African-American community reaches a moment of painful introspection," reports Manning Marable: "Black America still sees itself as the litmus test of the viability and reality of American democracy."[46] Such preoccupations are reflected and interrogated in contemporary fictions which revisit earlier struggles for black freedom with an eye to the impasse of the last two decades in African American politics. They are especially effective when the focus is constructions of black male community leaders, as in Lester and Johnson's novels. In 1990 Marable asked, "Will black leaders exist in the twenty-first century?" His concern was the absence of a dynamic black leadership that could speak across class divisions and community borders to identify common ground and common goals. Fictional interrogations of leadership models which incorporate women are yet to be imagined in post-civil rights fictions. Revisiting what was participatory about grassroots politics for both genders, and bridge leadership for women activists in the civil right movement, would develop what is already an interrogative genre. It was King who said, "Ultimately a genuine leader is not a searcher for consensus but a molder of consensus," a nonconformist.[47] Lester and Johnson are beginning to allow the nonconformist a place; fiction is often the forum in which controversial subjects are first explored, and representing icons as flawed hero-humans begins the process of reinvesting in today without a debilitating nostalgia for what might have been. As Diane Nash says, "instead of saying they wish Martin Luther King were here to lead, they should think of the movement as a whole and ask 'What can I do?'"[48]

The 1990s is a decade in which commemorations of the deaths of civil rights leaders and anniversaries of civil rights legislation proliferate. Summarizing the views of many, Martin Carnoy alleges that, "a generation after the Civil Rights Act and the Great Society, the American landscape is still marked by most of the problems these efforts were meant to solve."[49] In Jasper, Texas in 1998, James Byrd's murder by white men who dragged him behind a pick-up truck long enough to break his body into pieces, brought the Klan and the New Black Panthers out in force and shook the ambivalent calm of small town America. Byrd's final journey ironically began on Martin Luther King Drive where he was offered a ride by his murderers. Images of racial violence were raked through every news bulletin and President Clinton called, as he had in 1997, for a new dialogue about the "old, unfinished business between black and white Americans."[50] John Hope Franklin, head of Clinton's commission on race, recently asserted, "The color line is alive and well, and flourishing in the final decade of the twentieth century ... public efforts must be combined with private efforts to promote mutual respect":

> If we can somehow teach ourselves these lessons in human relations, perhaps we can take the first feeble steps toward creating the kind of community about which some of our forebears spoke and wrote, and the kind of nation about which many of us have dreamed but never realized.[51]

One of Johnson's characters wonders, "Would the wounds uncovered ever heal?" (61) and later, after King is dead, he is more certain, "I believed in each of us there was a wound, an emptiness that would not be filled in our lifetime." (236) A continuing history of racial murders and violence provokes in each of the writers a nostalgia for a discourse of mutuality. But, it is muted by fears that millennial hopes will be cut through with new lacerations as well as old wounds. Whereas religion and rebellion often combined in the 1960s, the moral and political in the 1990s diverge in ever more complicated permutations of mistrust; and so it is that the charismatic moral leaders constructed as symbols of protest and progress in the 1950s and 1960s persist in the memories and imaginations of writers.

Johnson and Lester do go some considerable way towards interrogating the cult of personality that grew up around civil rights leaders and what Marable has called "the messiah complex": a hierarchical organisation structured on the model of a pyramid ensures that eventually the death or demise of the charismatic leader will "freeze his organizational lieutenants and disorient most loyal rank-and-file members."[52] Thus, the overriding reaction becomes one of fear that the leader is irreplaceable. This fear has characterized recent decades and Lester produces a post-civil rights novel in the post-reform era which bespeaks the isolation and fragmentation of ex-activists, male and female. He re-creates a leader with feet of clay, whose humanity finally overbalances the superhuman credibility of his legacy. Each character is emotionally disabled by their experiences in the 1960s. Johnson ensures that we remember that fiction is "a meditation on remembrance" (74); and Lester that history is "taloned and beaked and lusts for blood," as much as for forgiveness. (55) For Lester, history "hums like the drone of a bagpipe, insistent, monstrous and present." (123) It is this description that best summarizes the legacy of the civil rights movement for the 1990s.

Notes

1. James R. Ralph Jr., *Northern Protest: Martin Luther King Jr., Chicago and the Civil Rights Movement* (Cambridge, Mass.: Harvard University Press, 1993), 6. See also Pat Watters, *Down to Now: Reflections on the Southern Civil Rights* Movement (Athens: University of Georgia Press, 1993). Watters, a white activist, reissued his 1971 memoir describing the 1960s as a decade which "produced a shimmering vision of what life between the races might be, and more than that, what life in America for all people might be," 20. In 1993 he seeks to understand how events and people coalesced in the movement but why that "movement mentality" has not lasted.

2. Angela Davis, *An Autobiography* (London: The Women's Press, 1988), x.

3. Martin Luther King, Jr., *Where Do We Go From Here: Chaos or Community?* (Boston: Beacon Books, 1968), 109.

4. James Baldwin, *The Devil Finds Work* (New York: Bantam Doubleday Dell, 1990), 53.

5. Julius Lester, *And All Our Wounds Forgiven* (New York: Harcourt Brace (Harvest), 1996), 142. Subsequent references will be included in parenthesis.

6. King, *Where Do We Go*, 32.

7. King, *Where Do We Go*, 19.

8. David J. Garrow, *Bearing the Cross: Martin Luther King Jr. and the Southern Christian Leadership Conference* (London: Jonathan Cape, 1988), 289.

9. Houston A. Baker, *The Journey Back: Issues in Black Literature and Criticism* (Chicago: University of Chicago Press, 1980), 80.

10. King, *Where Do We Go*, 38.

11. The Meredith March also indicated how leaders prioritizing different agendas might still unite, although the march failed to make permanent that organizational unity. Cleveland Sellers describes King marching with Stokely Carmichael and others, "shoulder to shoulder with the troops." See Cleveland Sellers with Robert Terrell, *The River of No Return: The Autobiography of a Black Militant and the Life and Death of SNCC* (New York: William Morrow and Co. Ltd., 1973), 157.

12. King, *Where Do We Go*, 86.

13. Andrew Young, *An Easy Burden: The Civil Rights Movement and the Transformation of America* (New York: Harper Collins, 1996), 434.

14. Coretta Scott King, *My Life with Martin Luther King, Jr.* (London: Hodder and Stoughton, 1970), 289, 291-294.

15. Martin Luther King, *Strength To Love* (New York: Harper and Row, 1963), 66.

16. Charles Johnson, *Dreamer* (New York: Scribner, 1998), 33. Subsequent references will be included in parenthesis. I would like to thank Trudier Harris who introduced me to this novel through her paper, "The Power of Martyrdom: Martin Luther King and his Philosophy in African American Literature," Martin Luther King Memorial Conference, University of Newcastle, May 1998.

17. C. Vann Woodward, *The Burden of Southern History* (Baton Rouge and London: Louisiana State University Press, 1968), 171-2.

18. See Charles Johnson, "Fictionalizing King" the *Seattle Times*, 1998, www.SeattleTimes.com

19. Hayden White, *The Content of Form: Narrative Discourse and Historical Representation* (Baltimore and London: The Johns Hopkins Press, 1987), 89. Andrew Young describes watching footage of the SCLC's 1968 march in Chicago's Gage Park, when bottles and bricks were thrown at King and others, almost thirty years later, and still feeling frightened, "It seems bizarre and unreal." (Young, *An Easy Burden*, 413) Young's feeling of emotional continuity is ruptured by his recognition of the past's "unreality" when regarded in the light of the present.

20. Ralph, *Northern Protest*, 89.

21. There are clearly no correlations between the Lisa, who sustains a long and meaningful affair with the composite King figure, and Candie Carawan. However, Lester, a folk singer who has recorded a number of albums, knows the Carawans well and may have drawn on passages in *Sing For Freedom* for Lisa's early memories. See Guy and Candy Carawan, *Sing For Freedom: The Story of the Civil Rights Movement Through Its Songs* (Bethlehem, PA.: Sing Out Corporation, 1992), 20-21.

22. Julius Lester, *Look Out Whitey! Black Power's Gon' Get Your Mama!* (New York: The Dial Press, 1968), 106.

23. *And All Our Wounds Forgiven* was one of only twenty-five books nominated for the National Book Critics Circle Award in its year of publication. David Nicholson in the *Washington Post* went so far as to compare Lester to Faulkner and Ellison.

24. See, for example, Stanley Crouch, *The All-American Skin Game, or, The Decoy of Race* (New York: Vintage, 1995), 79.

25. Gloria Naylor, "Love and Sex in the Afro-American Novel," *The Yale Review*, 78:1 (1989), 30-31.

26. See Michael Dury, *With the Hammer of Truth: The Autobiography of James Callender* (Charlottesville: University of Virginia Press, 1990) and Sharon Monteith, "America's Domestic Aliens: African Americans and the Issue of Citizenship in the Jefferson/Hemings Story" in Deborah Cartmell et al. eds., *Alien Identities: Exploring Difference in Film and Fiction* (London: Pluto Press, 1999), 31-48. During the mid-term

elections of November 1998, the *New York Times* reported that new evidence from DNA testing had concluded that Jefferson fathered at least one black son. The commentary which follows the claim states that a "truth that should be self-evident" is that: "Our heroes—and especially presidents—are not gods or saints but flesh and blood humans." see Peter Beaumont, "Jefferson fathered his slave's child" the (London) *Observer*, November 1, 1998.

27. James Baldwin, *Tell Me How Long The Train's Been Gone* (London: Michael Joseph, 1971), 277.

28. Baldwin's representative public figure can be located within the discourse of race and rights that permeates his essays, and especially his descriptions of finding himself under government surveillance in *The Devil Finds Work.*, 107-111.

29. See, for example, Sharon Monteith "Between Girls: Kaye Gibbons' *Ellen Foster* and Friendship as a Monologic Formulation," *Journal of American Studies*, 33: 2 (1999), 1-20.

30. Cornel West, *Race Matters* (Boston: Beacon Press, 1993), 45-46.

31. Garrow, *Bearing the Cross*, 282.

32. For example, the murder of fourteen-year old Emmett Till in Mississippi in 1955, the subject of Gwendolyn Brooks's bleak and barbed poems in the 1960s, continues to preoccupy black and white writers alike; in *Reckless Eyeballing* (1986), Ishmael Reed reworks the Till case via his character Ham Hill in metafictional fashion and, more recently, Lewis Nordan's award-winning *Wolf Whistle* (1993) extrapolates on the same events in a surreal and acidly sardonic postmodernist parody.

33. Daniel W. Lehman, *Matters of Fact: Reading Nonfiction Over the Edge* (Columbus: Ohio State University Press, 1998).

34. Charles Johnson, *Being and Race: Black Writing Since 1970* (London: Serpent's Tail, 1988), 291.

35. Charles Johnson praises John McCluskey's short story, "Chicago Jubilee Rag" (1983) in which Frederick Douglass, Paul Laurence Dunbar and Scott Joplin meet, for its ability to "breathe life into historically accurate fiction that *opens* the past in such a way that we feel the emotions of the individual actors beneath dry facts." See *Being and Race*, 72. His words might stand as a writing plan for his novel *Dreamer* completed ten years later.

36. Richard H. King, "Politics and Fictional Representation: the Case of the Civil Rights Movement" in Brian Ward and Tony Badger, eds., *The Making of Martin Luther King and the Civil Rights Movement* (London: Macmillan, 1996), 164.

37. George P. Cunningham, "Body Politics: Race, Gender and the Captive Body" in Marcellus Blount and George P. Cunningham, *Representing Black Men* (New York: Routledge, 1996), 132.

38. Fred D'Aguiar, "The Last Essay About Slavery" in Sarah Dunant and Roy Porter eds., *The Age of Anxiety* (London: Virago, 1996), 142.

39. Adrienne Rich, *What Is Found There: Notebooks on Poetry and Politics* (New York: W.W. Norton, 1993), 106.

40. Belinda Robnett, *How Long? How Long? Women in the Civil Rights Movement* (New York: Oxford University Press, 1997. Although there have been a number of African American women who play significant political roles (Ella Baker, Fannie Lou Hamer, Septima Clark, Shirley Chisolm, Carol Mosely Braun, Maxine Waters), the main public aspirants to leadership are still male and it is this trajectory which continues to underpin even the most innovative representations of black leadership in fiction.

41. Eldridge Cleaver, characterized as "El Rage" after his breakaway from the Panther organization, and Bobby Seale, presented as less inspiring than Huey Newton, have charged Van Peebles with mealy-mouthing the "facts." *Panther* (Edinburgh: Payback Press, 1995) thrives on conspiracies and is prefaced by an extract from the Senate Select Committee's investigation of domestic intelligence operations in 1976.

42. West, *Race Matters*, 7.

43. Michele Wallace, "Masculinity in Black Popular Culture: Could it be that Political Correctness is the Problem?" in Maurice Berger et al, eds., *Constructing Masculinity* (New York: Routledge, 1995), 303.

44. Manning Marable, *Beyond Black and White: Transforming African-American Politics* (London: Verso, 1995), 207.

45, Garrow, *Bearing the Cross*, 310.

46. Marable, *Beyond Black and White*, 24.

47. King, *Where Do We Go*, 63.

48. Garrow, *Bearing the Cross*, 625.

49. Martin Carnoy, *Faded Dreams: The Politics and Economics of Race in America* (Cambridge: Cambridge University Press, 1995), 6.

50. See, for example, Steve Berg, "Riots of 1960s changed the race discussion ... President Clinton calls for new conversation, the nation recalls events that changed the terms," *Star Tribune*, July 20, 1997, 1A.

51. John Hope Franklin, *The Color Line: Legacy for the Twenty-First Century* (Columbia: University of Missouri Press, 1993), 72-74.

52. Manning Marable, *Race, Reform and Rebellion: The Second Reconstruction in Black America 1945-1990* (Jackson: University Press of Mississippi, 1991), 223-224.

CHAPTER 9

"The Struggle Continues": Black Women in Congress in the 1990s

Britta Waldschmidt-Nelson

Since the late 1960s and early 1970s, African American women have continued the fight for equal rights and social justice. By this stage, many of them realized that the time had come to gain political office themselves in order to change the system from within. This development can be illustrated by looking at the black women who have been elected to the United States Congress since the 1960s, particularly in the 1990s. The first to be elected to the House of Representatives was Shirley Chisholm in 1968. Yvonne Burke, Cardiss Collins and Barbara Jordan joined her in 1973. Until 1993, there were never more than four black women serving in Congress at the same time, and from 1985 to 1992 Cardiss Collins was the only one. Between 1993 and the 1998 elections, however, there were twelve African American women in the House of Representatives and one, Carol Moseley-Braun, in the Senate.[1] A significant change had occurred. Drawing on interviews with these remarkable women, this essay seeks to answer the following questions: why was there such a remarkable increase in the number of black female representatives in the 1992 election? In what ways have gender, race and class influenced the political agenda of these women? What have been their major legislative successes? And does the presence of African American women in Congress actually make a difference?[2]

The Election of 1992

It is not very difficult to explain why there were so few black women in Congress until the 1990s. Minority status generally makes it more difficult for African Americans and for female candidates to be elected to national office. A contributory factor is that they usually have significantly less campaign funding than the average white male candidate.[3] The simple majority rule of the American electoral system also presents a general disadvantage for minority candidates, and until very recently, the major parties didn't give them enough support. Party skepticism reflected the fact that a significant number of white voters retain prejudices against black and/or female candidates.[4]

The more challenging question is why was this previous pattern overturned in 1992? The 1992 elections produced a dramatic increase in the number of female members of Congress (from 31 to 55), of black members (from 26 to 40) and, especially, of black female members (from 4 to 10). A number of journalists and scholars dubbed 1992 "The Year of the Woman" or "The Year of the Black Woman."[5] There are a number of explanations for this outcome. First, the creation of a number of black majority districts in 1991 was a major factor that opened the way for new black representation on Capitol Hill. Redistricting occurred after the 1990 Census, under the terms of the 1982 Extension of the Voting Rights Act. Despite the Voting Rights Act of 1965, a number of southern states had still systematically prevented their African American and Hispanic populations from electing a representative of their ethnic group to Congress. North Carolina, for example, with a 22 percent African American population, had elected no African American to Congress since Reconstruction.[6] Such states were now forced to create new voting districts that would favor the election of minority candidates. As a result of the redistricting, eleven new, black representatives (including two from North Carolina) and six new Hispanic representatives were elected to Congress. Five African American women were among them: Corrine Brown, Carrie Meek, Cynthia McKinney, Eva Clayton and Eddie Bernice Johnson.[7]

While redistricting was probably the major reason for the increase in minority representation, the work of political support groups explicitly for women aided the increase in female representation in 1992. To counteract timid party support and relatively low campaign finances, female activists had organized Political Action Committees (PACs) for women since the mid-1970s. Their objectives had been to build up networks, raise funds and conduct skill-training programs to increase female candidates' chances. Besides the cumulative advantages of long-established PACs, there were other factors that significantly increased membership of and donations to Women PACs in 1991 and 1992.[8] One was the encouraging presence of an unusually high number of "open seats." The so-called power of incumbency has always withheld resources from new political candidates. Between 1892 and 1992, incumbent members of Congress were normally re-elected, and since most of them were—and still are—white males, this trend blocked the arrival of female and minority candidates.[9] The best chance for a new candidate to win a congressional race occurs when he or she can run for an open seat; either in a newly created district or in one where the incumbent is not seeking re-election. Redistricting had created several new congressional seats for the 1992 election. In addition, many incumbents decided not to run again because of their involvement in one of several big scandals affecting the 102nd Congress. The total of 91 open seats in the election for the 103rd Congress was an important precondition for the election of a record number of female and minority representatives.[10]

Given the scandals, there was widespread voter discontent with the existing members of Congress. This growing anti-incumbent mood also reflected public anger at the huge federal deficit, a discontent with politics in general and a growing mistrust of "Washington insiders." "Voting for Change" became an oft-cited motto in 1992 and since white men had dominated Congress for so long, women and minority candidates were automatically seen as symbolizing change.[11] The collapse of the Soviet Union and the end of the Cold War also presented a further advantage to female candidates. These global changes ensured that the campaign of 1992 was dominated by domestic rather than foreign policy issues. Traditional gender stereotyping credits women with more competence on so-called *compassion issues* (education, welfare, and health care) rather than *force issues* (such as crime, military build-up and war). Consequently, the prevalence of domestic over foreign policy issues may have prompted some voters to favor female candidates.[12]

There was one highly gender specific incident which had a major impact on both voters and potential female candidates: the Anita Hill-Clarence Thomas Affair.[13] In June 1991, the only black member of the U.S. Supreme Court, Justice Thurgood Marshall, announced his resignation. Since Marshall had been a strong supporter of women and minority rights, African Americans and feminists followed the process of nominating his successor very closely. President Bush nominated conservative black judge, Clarence Thomas, and asked the Senate to confirm his appointment. Although some Senators doubted whether Thomas possessed all the qualities expected of a Supreme Court justice, a majority seemed satisfied with the nominee after the first round of hearings.[14] But, in October 1991, Thomas's nomination was suddenly jeopardized by the testimony of black law professor, Anita Hill, who accused him of sexual harassment during the 1980s when she had been on his staff. Hill had decided to bring her case forward because she felt that a man of such grave character defects should not sit on the US Supreme Court. The three days of hearings were broadcast on television and generated national debate. Public opinion regarding the trustworthiness of Hill and Thomas (who denied Hill's allegations) and, consequently, the latter's suitability for high office was sharply divided. While many Senators equivocated, the final vote on October 15, 1991 saw a 52 to 48 majority in favor of confirmation.[15] But this did not end the public debate which continued into the campaign season. The spectacle of fourteen, old, white men questioning one, young, black woman sometimes in an aggressive and chauvinist fashion had infuriated feminists all over the country. The Senators' general failure to recognize sexual harassment as a serious public concern angered many other Americans. Some concluded that the only remedy was to elect more women—and more minority representatives—to a Congress so blatantly dominated by white men.[16]

The Hill-Thomas hearings served as a catalyst for change on three levels. It contributed to the willingness of voters to elect more women in 1992. It also motivated a number of female politicians, who had been previously hesitant, to run for national office. Carol Moseley-Braun, has stressed that the hearings, especially the manner in which Illinois Senator Alan Dixon interrogated Anita Hill, compelled her to run against him.[17] More importantly, there was a sharp increase in membership and financial contributions enjoyed by PACs for women. *EMILY's List*, for example, saw its membership rise from 3,000 to over 24,000 between October 1991 and November 1992. Whereas the organization had had less than a million dollars to spend in 1990, it was able to contribute over four million dollars for political training of female candidates and for individual campaign support in 1992. All the black women who ran for Congress that year were supported by *EMILY's List*.[18]

In a cumulatively reinforcing way, these effects of the Hill-Thomas affair ensured that the election chances for women, especially black women, in 1992 were higher than ever before. Thus, it was an exceptional combination of factors—redistricting, the high number of open congressional seats, the support of Women's PACs, the general anti-incumbent mood among voters, and the Anita Hill-Clarence Thomas hearings—that produced the remarkable increase in black female representation on Capitol Hill. The "Year of the Black Woman" was no ordinary year.[19]

A Gendered Agenda?

The analytical categories of class, race and gender do not exist in isolation or independently of one another. Consequently, the legislative agendas pursued by these women were shaped simultaneously by class, race and gender concerns. Nevertheless, by examining their legislative conduct, it is evident that their priorities reflected a special sensitivity to the poor and the disadvantaged, among whom African Americans figure disproportionately. It is also clear that their legislative remedies were informed by a recognition of the interplay between race and gender in structuring the plight of unemployed young black males and African American female heads of household or single mothers. In the mid-1990s black unemployment was twice as high as white unemployment. While unemployment has generally declined during the decade (from 6.3 percent in 1992 to 4.9 percent in 1997), the jobless rate of African Americans has stayed high (8.5 percent in 1997, compared to 3.6 percent of whites). Particularly worryingly is the rate of black youth unemployment which in 1997 was over 30 percent nationwide, and exceeded 50 percent in some inner cities. Almost a third of the black community still lived below the poverty line. Average black family income was 63 percent of the average white family income. Over half of all black children (54 percent) lived in female-headed households compared to 17 percent of white children, and the poverty rate of these households was 68 percent compared to 47 percent for white female-headed households.[20]

These facts made progressive social welfare legislation one of the most important priorities of black women on Capitol Hill. Among their attempts to fight unemployment and crime was the *Economic Stimulus Package* (H.R. 1335) of March 1993. This provided $16.2 billion for public works projects, creating over 150,000 new jobs in public housing, and canal, road and railway construction, as well as a summer jobs program for teenagers and a scholarship program for poor students. It included the *Job and Life Skills Improvement Act* (H.R. 1020), offering special stipends, including counseling and financial aid, for unemployed Americans, aged 17 to 30, who were willing to participate in an intensive job-training program. Representing the district of South Central Los Angeles, the center of the LA "race riots" or rebellion in 1992, Maxine Waters urged her congressional colleagues to address the deepening urban crisis and the alienation of young black males by passing H.R. 1020:

> After twelve years of retrenchment, abandonment and neglect of our cities ... the children and young adults of our inner cities need more than economic growth. They cry out for hope. These young people—mostly minority males—don't count as unemployed. Many of them have never had jobs ... [they] don't show up in the statistics. They have literally dropped off the agenda. Our purpose

> today is to end the hopelessness, anger, and despair that
> engulfs our inner cities ... Without a substantial
> commitment to empower our young people, we stand to
> lose an entire generation. The urgency cannot be
> overstated. The price of inaction is unthinkable.[21]

All the black Congresswomen also strongly supported the *School-To-Work Opportunity Act* (H.R. 2884) of May 1994, which allocated $300 million to promote practice-oriented job-training programs for high schools. Since the program targeted pupils unlikely to go on to college, it was of particular benefit to black high school students.[22]

To help families affected by long-term unemployment, like those in her home district in Detroit, Congresswoman Collins initiated the *Emergency Unemployment Compensation Act* (H.R. 920), passed in March 1993. It enabled unemployed Americans who no longer received state welfare benefits to apply for federal aid for up to six months.[23] After long and heated debates in August 1993, the black women on Capitol Hill, especially Representatives Waters, Collins, Johnson, and McKinney, and Senator Carol Moseley-Braun, secured the *Earned Income Tax Credit* (EITC) as part of the *Omnibus Budget Reconciliation Act* (H.R. 2264). All persons, supporting at least one child under the age of 18, who had worked for a full year and earned under $23,050 a year became eligible for a government "tax credit." For instance, after filing her tax return, a parent of two children, whose minimum wage job brought in less than $9,000 a year, would receive an EITC of almost $3,000, that would raise the family income to the federally established poverty line for a family of three.[24] Most liberals inside and outside of the Beltway lauded the *Earned Income Tax Credit* as one of the most important congressional steps to promote social justice since the 1970s. Black female politicians helped to secure this measure of practical family support, aware of its importance to the disproportionate number of single headed low-income households in their community.[25]

Other initiatives pursued by these politicians seem to confirm their continuance of a well-established female social welfarist tradition. The *Comprehensive Childhood Immunization Act* appropriated $1.2 billion for a new federal child immunization program to vaccinate all small children in the United States. This included $500,000 for the US Center for Disease Control and Prevention to develop new vaccines. In 1993 only 55 percent of American children had been properly vaccinated against diseases such as polio, measles, smallpox or meningitis. Many children—mostly from poor families without health insurance and that disproportionately meant minority children—contracted these diseases needlessly each year. Eddie Bernice Johnson, a former nurse, who had seen too many of such cases, championed the measure, but all her black female colleagues supported it.[26] Similarly, Eleanor Holmes Norton proposed what became the *Mickey-Leland Childhood Hunger Relief Act* in the 102nd Congress. After almost three years of lobbying, she and other Congressional Black Caucus (CBC) members finally obtained its passage, appropriating $7.1 billion for a federal program to provide nutritious meals and food supplements to poor children.[27]

Children benefited from two other bills ardently supported by the black Congresswomen. The *Head Start Reauthorization Act* (H.R. 4250) of May 1994 nearly tripled the annual appropriation for the federal Head Start program. Created in the 1960s as part of the War on Poverty, Head Start supports education programs for preschool children from underprivileged families. Funding for the program had been drastically cut during the 1980s. Only 20 percent of those children who were eligible for Head Start were able to attend its courses in the early 1990s. But after passage of H.R. 4250, the number of participating children almost doubled within one year. Corrine Brown called the fuller funding of Head Start one of the most important accomplishments of the 103rd Congress.[28] One of the most comprehensive American education reform bills since the 1960s, the *Goals 2000: Educate America Act* (H.R. 4250) of March 1994, contained initiatives particularly beneficial to minority youth. One example, the Midnight Basketball League Training and Partnership program, proposed by Senator Carol Moseley-Braun, sought to decrease high school drop-out rates using evening and nightly basketball training and games at school. It combined three strategies: first, the physical activity made coming to school more attractive to teenagers, especially to black males; second, each member of such a basketball-league was obliged to participate in an academic and job-training workshop after each game; and third, the program kept at-risk youth away from the streets at night (i.e. away from gang violence, drug dealing and other criminal activities.)[29] Midnight Basketball Programs had already enjoyed considerable success in Moseley-Braun's hometown, Chicago, and after long debate she secured five million dollars for such programs nationwide.[30]

The black Congresswomen cooperated closely with the Congressional Caucus on Women's Issues (CCWI) on bills promoting women's rights and gender equality. The CCWI's job, according to Congresswoman McKinney, was:

> to look after those issues that don't necessarily beep
> very high on the male radar screen. Children, of course, is

one of them, women's rights is another one. It never
ceases to amaze me how men can dictate to women what
women are going to do with themselves, with their
bodies, with their lives—and they act as if they are all
knowing.[31]

McKinney's comments highlighted the strength of feeling in the 103rd
Congress over the question of the federal protection of a woman's right
to have an abortion. Even though the Supreme Court's *Roe v. Wade*
decision of 1973 granted women the right to abortion during the first
three months of pregnancy, some states had subsequently passed laws
limiting this right by prohibiting the use of public funds for abortions,
by installing mandatory anti-abortion counseling sessions or 24-hour-
waiting periods, and by demanding written parental consent from minors
seeking a termination, or even by allowing abortions only in cases of
rape, incest or danger to the mother's life.[32] Many of the black female
members of Congress are very religious and have strong moral
reservations about abortion. As a Catholic, Senator Moseley-Braun said
she would personally always oppose an abortion. The others similarly
stressed that they viewed abortion as a terrible, last resort for an
emergency situation. They would rather concentrate on improving sex
education and access to contraceptives to prevent unwanted pregnancies.
Nevertheless, they all described themselves as "pro-choice," believing
that this decision should be left to each woman's own conscience. As
Carrie Meek explained:

> My [personal] views are not the issue. Whatever I
> feel or believe, I have no right as a politician or as a
> legislator to impose my view on an issue that must remain
> private, confidential and be in the best interest of the
> individual woman and all the circumstances she is faced
> with.[33]

Consequently, all black female members of the 103rd Congress
supported the so-called FACE bill, *Freedom of Access to Clinic
Entrances Act* (H.R. 796), which made it a federal crime to intimidate or
attack women seeking to enter clinics where abortions were performed,
or to harass the staff of these clinics. Given the sharp increase in violent
attacks on abortion clinics by "pro-life" radicals, the passage of FACE
in May 1994 was an important defensive measure.[34]

The black Congresswomen also fought against actions to restrict
access to abortion to those who could afford private medicine. One
attempt in particular resulted in a notable conflict between the white and

the black Congresswomen. Congressman Henry Hyde, a white Republican from Illinois, now famous for his role in President Clinton's impeachment, had successfully attached an anti-abortion amendment to the *Labor-HSS-Education Appropriation Bill* every year since 1977. His amendment strictly prohibited the use of any federal funds (including Medicaid) for abortion on whatever grounds. Hyde insisted that the 1.5 million abortions in the United States each year constituted "cruel and terrible mass murder" and must never be financed by the taxpayer. His opponents argued that the taxpayer already indirectly subsidized abortions for middle-class and upper-class women whose private health insurance was tax-deductible. The black Congresswomen were particularly eager to defeat the Hyde amendment, since fewer black women had such insurance and the black abortion rate was almost twice that of whites in 1993.[35] Cynthia McKinney declared that the Hyde Amendment amounted to discrimination "against poor women, who happen to be disproportionately black." By funding childbirth but not abortion, McKinney argued, "the federal government is practicing discriminatory politics." She demanded that the government act "in a non-discriminatory manner in the childbearing choices of women."[36]

Despite her arguments, the Hyde Amendment secured a majority in June 1993. Its opponents did manage to have cases of rape and incest excluded from the general prohibition of federal funding, but the bill's passage was a major disappointment. Black Congresswomen were particularly upset that some white female colleagues, who were generally "pro-choice", had still voted for this amendment to expedite the appropriations bill. Angered that "freedom of choice" should be limited to those who could afford private health, black women withdrew their support for the *Freedom of Choice Act* in July 1993 to the dismay of white CCWI members.[37] This revealed how in cases of conflict, the factor "race"—especially when combined with "class" concerns—was more important than "gender" alone to the decision-making process of the black female politicians.

However, in most cases, white and black female members of Congress worked closely together and co-sponsored legislation, enabling them to pass important bills. *The Family and Medical Leave Bill* first introduced in 1985 by Patricia Schroeder, a white Democrat Congresswoman from Colorado, was fully supported by her female colleagues. It required companies with more than 50 employees to grant them an unpaid leave of up to twelve weeks in cases of childbirth, adoption or a severe family illness. Personal experience of the difficulties of juggling home and career commitments made black Congresswomen, like Barbara-Rose Collins, ardent supporters of the bill. By 1985 60 percent of all American women (70 percent of black women) with children under the age of six, and 80 percent of all American women (90 percent of black women) with school-age children, worked outside of the home. They could lose their jobs if they took time off for the reasons mentioned above. Thus, most American families—black and white—viewed the passage of the *Family and Medical Leave Act* in February 1993 positively.[38] Directly following this success, Schroeder introduced the so-called *Violence Against Women Act* (H.R. 1133) appropriating $1.6 billion for a federal program to prevent such violence, especially rape, and to the support of battered women shelters and the creation of a national domestic violence telephone hotline. The act contained a mandatory arrest provision in cases of domestic violence and declared interstate stalking (crossing state lines in order to harass or harm a former spouse or partner) a federal crime. Many male members—especially older Republicans—felt the bill interfered too much in what they regarded as people's private lives. But CCWI members countered that "protecting the private sphere of marriage" had allowed violent husbands to escape punishment for their abuse for too long. Eventually the measure, which had been supported by all of the African American congresswomen and their black colleagues (except Republican Gary Franks) was passed in September 1994 as part of the *Violent Crime Control and Law Enforcement Act* (H.R. 3355).[39] In this case, concern for the safety of women, and the fact that the measure contained over $10 billion for so-called "preventive measures" which included social welfare provisions, overcame the justifiable misgivings of most African American members about the racism of US law enforcement agencies that made the CBC resist hard-line "law-and-order" proposals. Two black congresswomen (Waters and Norton) and fourteen of their male CBC colleagues did not vote for the bill because it failed to include a racial justice act.

Supported by their white female colleagues, the African American congresswomen also pushed for another bill protecting women from physical harm: the *Federal Prohibition of Female Genital Mutilation Act* (H.R. 3247). The practice of female genital mutilation—referred to as "female circumcision" by its supporters—is a female initiation rite. Common among African Muslims, it consists of cutting out the clitoris and labia and then sewing up most of the vagina. Practiced by some Afrocentric factions of the black community in the United States since the 1970s, the rite is supposed to guarantee the women's virginity at marriage and fidelity thereafter. Supporters see it as an important, ancient tradition, but opponents, including all the black congresswomen, regard it as cruel mutilation and a violation of human rights.[40] While the black female representatives failed to pass H.R. 3247, Senator Moseley-

Braun did obtain passage of a Senate-Resolution, strongly condemning the "Cruel and Torturous Practice of Female Genital Mutilation" in the United States and worldwide.[41] In this matter, humanitarian concerns superceded cultural nationalism.

The black and white women in the 103rd Congress worked intensely for legislation against gender discrimination in education, work, health care and retirement. Among important successes in education was the *Gender Equity in Education and Equity in Athletics Disclosure Act* (H.R. 1793), prohibiting the unequal funding of sport and physical education programs for females and males in high schools and universities. The black congresswomen also amended the *Elementary and Secondary Education Act* (H.R. 1794) to require the establishment of an "Office of Women's Equity" in the Department of Education and secured a federal appropriation to promote gender equity in schools and teacher training programs. Similarly, as two of only three female members of the Committee on Veterans' Affairs, Corrine Brown and Maxine Waters had fought for the passage of the *Veterans' Benefits Improvement Act* (H.R. 5244), which became law in November 1994. It created a new "Office for Women's Issues" within the Department of Veterans' Affairs and made additional women's health services available to female veterans. Since almost half (48.7 percent in 1992) of all female army veterans are black, the improvement of their condition was particularly important to Brown and Waters.[42]

Among other legislative initiatives supported by black female representatives to promote women's health were major amendments to the *Labor-HHS-Education Appropriation Act* (H.R. 2518), which secured over $500 million for the early detection and treatment of breast cancer as well as additional funding for other new women's health care programs.[43] The black congresswomen also contributed significantly to the passage of the *Social Security Domestic Employment Reform Act* (H.R. 4278) which rectified a longstanding racial and gender injustice. The Act created new regulations and stricter enforcement provisions for the payment of unemployment and retirement benefits to domestic workers. A majority of these workers were minority females who had previously worked for very low wages without any social benefits. In cases of unemployment, incapacity or old age, these workers had no source of public financial support. Opponents warned of the burden of additional costs that the measure would place on the—mostly white, middle- or upper-class—employers of domestic help. However, lawmakers were deeply impressed by Representative Carrie Meek's moving recollection of the difficulties and anxieties of her time as a domestic servant, and ultimately, H.R. 4278 was passed.[44]

All in all, the 103rd Congress passed more laws favorable to women (65 in total), and appropriated over twice as much federal money as any previous Congress for programs promoting women's health and safety. This reflected the increased female representation on Capitol Hill and, in most instances, female cooperation across racial and class lines. Many bills promoting social welfare and women's rights were particularly beneficial to African Americans and other minorities. However, the Hyde Amendment debate and the failure of the Freedom of Choice bill was one instance when white blindness to the race and class concerns of black female members was re-paid by a reciprocal reluctance to give feminism exclusive priority. For the black congresswomen, the fight against racism and discrimination remained the legislative priority.[45]

A Racial Agenda?

African American women have been among the most outspoken advocates of affirmative action on Capitol Hill. As former Congresswoman Shirley Chisholm stated once:

> If it were not for affirmative action in this country we wouldn't have the number of women and African American people being able to move up the ladder, being able to have an opportunity to enter into those realms which heretofore were closed to them because of their race or sex. The men who have been in power never used the authority and never had the morality of their consciences to treat everyone in the same fashion so long as they had the prerequisites for holding certain jobs. Therefore affirmative action has definitely been needed and continues to be needed.[46]

Sharing this conviction, the black female members of the 103rd Congress supported the *Equal Employment Opportunity Commission Amendment of 1993* (H.R. 126). Sponsored by Cardiss Collins and Eleanor Holmes Norton, it would have strengthened the power of the Equal Employment Opportunity Commission (EEOC) to enforce nondiscrimination policies in federal employment. Despite support from Democratic CBC-members and most CCWI-members, it failed. [47] Collins did, however, obtain passage of two important amendments to the comprehensive Telecommunications Act of 1994. The first prohibited discrimination against minority or female contractors or workers in the construction of a new telecommunication infrastructure. The second established set-aside-programs, requiring a certain percentage of all federal contracts for creating this "Communications Super Highway" to go to either minority or female owned businesses.[48]

Another important piece of anti-discrimination legislation was sponsored by Congresswoman Waters in order to end so-called "redlining" in the inner cities. This is the practice by banks and credit-agencies of labeling certain "special risk areas" as unsafe for investment. Since these were predominantly inhabited by African Americans, many CBC members regarded redlining as a major obstacle to their community's economic renewal. Access to capital, Waters pointed out to her congressional colleagues, was "critical to a community's ability to empower itself, to revitalize itself ... In this regard, our financial services industry has let down low-income and minority communities in a profound way."[49] As a result of Waters's effective lobbying and strong support from all CBC members, Congress finally passed the *Community Development Banking Act* and the *Loan Guarantees for Cities Act* in 1994. These included provisions against redlining and a new "Community Reinvestment Program," giving economic incentives for infrastructural improvements in the inner cities, and raising the federal credit loan guarantees for such projects to two billions dollars a year.[50]

If one legacy of the civil rights struggle was visible in the congresswomen's quest for economic empowerment, another was even more conspicuous in their fervent defense of black enfranchisement. One of the key pieces of legislation supported by the black women—and men—in the 103rd Congress was the *National Voter Registration Act of 1993* (H.R. 2), often referred to as the *Motor Voter Bill*. Unlike most European countries, the United States does not have a centralized citizen registration procedure. Every citizen has to register him or herself at a special registration office to qualify to vote before an election. In 1965 the *Voting Rights Act* prohibited discriminatory voter-registration practices (such as literacy tests or "good conduct clauses") which had been a common means of black disenfranchisement in the southern states. As a result, black voter registration in these states more than doubled and the number of African Americans elected to political office in the South increased from 72 in 1965 to 2,000 in 1976 and nearly 5,000 in 1993. Despite this progress, only 64 percent of African Americans (compared to 70 percent of white Americans) were registered to vote in 1993. Black participation in congressional and presidential election between 1970 and 1992 had been about 10 percent lower than that of white Americans and the Hispanic voter participation rate (28 percent) was even lower still.[51]

African American members of Congress felt that one reason for these sizeable differences in voter registration and turnout was the fact that voter registration offices were located in big cities and open during business hours (i.e. Monday through Friday, 9am-5pm). Blue-collar workers, especially from small villages or rural areas, found it hard to register since they had to take time off work to reach the nearest registration office. Since black and other minority Americans were disproportionately blue-collar workers, current practice constituted indirect discrimination. Moreover, studies showed that the process of voter-registration itself—going to the office and dealing with public officials—was intimidating to many poor, less-educated Americans, especially minorities.[52] To remove obstacles to voter registration that disproportionately affected their constituents, the black members of Congress and other supporters of reform, introduced the *Motor Voter Bill*, so called because one of its provisions made it possible to register to vote at any of the many local offices of the Department of Motor Vehicles (DMV). To encourage voter registration among those groups who traditionally had very low voter participation rates (people on welfare, single parents, unemployed and handicapped people), the bill also listed the offices of public assistance agencies as places of voting registration.[53]

Republican opponents argued that this was a partisan Democratic measure because the people that the agency-based provision would encourage to register were likely to vote Democrat. In rebuttal, Senator Moseley-Braun stated that her Republican colleagues were opposed to removing barriers to voter registration because they feared true democracy. Congresswoman McKinney accused the bill's opponents of wanting to exclude certain groups. What kind of voters will be registered by this legislation, she asked her House colleagues rhetorically, "'What kind of voters?', I ask, 'American voters!'"[54] Of course, McKinney's implication that the opponents of the *Motor Voter Bill* had racist motives led to an outcry of indignation and protest among her Republican opponents.[55] But in the end, McKinney, Moseley-Braun and the other supporters of the bill managed to convince a majority of both houses to vote in its favor, and the *National Voter Registration Act of 1993* was signed into law in May of 1993.[56]

"Those who believe in freedom cannot rest" was one of the axioms of the generations of African Americans who forged the civil rights movement. It has become equally self-evident to their successors. As a result of the 1994 election, leadership in both houses passed from the Democrats to an ideologically conservative Republican Party. All of the black congresswomen were re-elected and Sheela Jackson-Lee joined them from Texas. But, even though the number of black members actually increased from 40 to 41, the legislative impact of the overwhelmingly Democratic CBC was inevitably smaller than before. During the next two years, the 104th Congress passed a flood of conservative legislation and Democratic President Clinton tacked towards the right-of-center. In many cases, this reversed the progressive legislative trend of the 103rd Congress. For example, the Republican majority was able to pass a very restrictive, welfare reform package, abolishing one of the nation's oldest family-aid programs (Aid for Families with Dependent Children) and cutting funding for many of the social programs initiated in 1993 and 1994. However, had it not been for the steadfast opposition of representatives like the African American Congresswomen, the cutbacks would have been even worse.

Recognizing the significance of majority minority districts within a progressive coalition, conservatives challenged their legitimacy through the courts. Five white citizens of North Carolina filed suit against the creation of black majority districts in their state. In *Shaw v. Reno* of June 1993, the US Supreme Court finally ruled that by making race the overarching determinant of its re-districting, North Carolina had violated the equal protection guarantees of the Fourteenth Amendment. This decision represented a major setback for African American politics, and was harshly criticized by black and white civil rights activists and politicians as a violation of the spirit of the Voting Rights Act.[57] *Shaw v Reno* established a precedent for similar rulings rendered between 1993 and 1996, in which the Supreme Court declared the basis for the creation of six of the eleven black majority districts to be unconstitutional. As a result, four of the black congresswomen from the South—Corrine Brown, Cynthia McKinney, Eddie Bernice Johnson, and Sheila Jackson Lee—faced tough re-election battles in 1996, since they now had to run in white-majority districts. To the surprise of many, they were all returned to Congress. Benefiting to some extent from the incumbency advantage that had previously worked against them, these black women had also obviously managed to overcome racial prejudice by the quality of their legislative work.[58] With the exception of Barbara-Rose Collins (who lost her seat to another black woman, Carolyn Kilpatrick) and Cardiss Collins (who retired from politics after twenty-three years in office), the other black female members of the 104th Congress—Eva Clayton, Carrie Meek, Eleanor Holmes Norton, Maxine Waters, and Juanita Millender-McDonald (who had been appointed to fill out the term of a resigning representative from California)—were safely re-elected in 1996. In addition, two more black women were elected: Julia Carson from Indiana and Donna Christian Green, the new delegate from the Virgin Islands.

The most recent election in November 1998 continued this positive trend. Only Senator Carol Moseley-Braun, whose political fortunes had been blighted by financial scandals, did not manage to retain her Senate seat. All the other black congresswomen returned to 106th Congress. Moreover, Barbara Lee from California and Stephanie Tubbs Jones from Ohio (who won the seats of retiring CBC veterans Ron Dellums and Louis Stokes respectively) joined the ranks of African American women in the House of Representatives, increasing their number to an all-time high of fourteen.[59]

Despite this steady, encouraging increase in the number of black female members of Congress since 1992, the total number of black representatives has stagnated at around forty. It dropped to thirty-nine after the 1998 election, and it may decrease further as a result of future re-districting decisions. Thus, while the success of black women in Congress has been impressive, the issues of further increasing black political representation, of protecting minority rights and the interests of the under-privileged remain as vital as ever in a nation still ravaged by race hate crimes and institutionalized discrimination. As representatives with a special sensitivity to the cumulative burden of gender, class, and race, African American Congresswomen remain committed to the ideals of the civil rights movement. They now face a new century, in which the struggle must continue.

Notes

1. These are the black female representatives in chronological order: Shirley Chisholm (NY, 1969-1983), Yvonne Burke (CA, 1973-1979), Barbara Jordan (TX, 1973-1979), Cardiss Collins (IL, 1973-1997), Katie Hall (1983-85), Barbara-Rose Collins (MI, 1991-1997), Eleanor Holmes Norton (1991-), Maxine Waters (CA, 1991-), Corrine Brown (FL, 1993), Eva Clayton (NC, 1993–), Eddie Bernice Johnson (TX, 1993–), Cynthia McKinney (GA, 1993–), Carrie Meek (FL, 1993–), Sheela Jackson Lee (TX, 1995-), Julia Carson (IN, 1997–), Donna Christian Green (VI, 1997–), Carolyn Kilpatrick (MI, 1997–), Juanita Millender-McDonald (CA, 1997–), Barbara Lee (CA, 1999) and Stephanie Tubb Jones (OH, 1999–). Carol Moseley-Braun served as Senator for Illinois from 1993 to 1999.

2. This paper summarizes the results of a larger study on the political work of black women: Waldschmidt-Nelson, *From Protest to Politics: Schwarze Frauen in der Bürgerrechtsbewegung und im Kongreß der Vereinigten Staaten* (Frankfurt: Campus, 1998). Besides other sources, I interviewed more than eighty civil rights and community activists, black politicians, leaders of national black organizations and their staff to obtain information on the personal experiences of black female civil rights activists and politicians as well as on the everyday life and power dynamics on Capitol Hill.

3. Regarding the question of financial resources, see Interview with Cynthia McKinney, May 12, 1994. According to data of the Federal Election Commission (FEC) black members of the US House of Representatives spent on the average $370,000 for their election campaign, average House member spent $543,000. v. J. Nelson, "Carol Moseley-Braun," *Essence*, (October 1992), 56-63.; "Campaign Finance: Spending 'Off

and Running'," *CQ*, October 31 (1992), 56ff. and Susan Caroll and Wendy Strimling, *Women's Routes to Elective Office*. (Cambridge: Harvard University Press, 1983).

4. Caroll and Strimling, *Women's Routes*, 61-82, Elizabeth Cook, Sue Thomas and Clyde Wilcox , eds., *The Year of the Woman* (Boulder, CO: Westview Press, 1994), 88-89, 161-180; R. Darcey and C. Hadley, "Black Women in Politics: The Puzzle of Success," *Social Science Quarterly*, 69 (1988): 629-645.

5. See, the title of Kitty Dumas article "The Year of the Black Woman?," *Black Enterprise*, August (1992): 35; also see title of Cook, Thomas and Wilcox's 1994 study.

6. For further comments on racial gerrymandering and the general disadvantage of multi-members at-large elections for minority candidates v. C. Davison and G. Korbel, "At-Large Elections and Minority Group Representation," *Journal of Politics*, 43 (1981): 982-1005; F. McCoy, "Tools For Empowerment?," *Black Enterprise*, 8 (March, 1991), 19; and F. Flake, "How To Undo a Century of Racism in Politics," *New York Times*, [*NYT*] July 11, (1993), 18.

7. As members of their state legislatures' redistricting committees of Florida, Georgia and Texas, Meek, McKinney and Johnson had helped to create new black majority districts in their respective states. v. B. Beneson, "Arduous Ritual of Redistricting Ensures More Racial Diversity", *CQ*, October 24 (1992): 3353-3363 and Flake, "How To Undo," 18.

8. Caroll and Strimling, *Women's Routes*, 61-82; Cook, Thomas and Wilcox, *The Year of the Woman*, 161-196.

9. For the adverse effect of incumbency on increasing the number of women in Congress, *The Year of the Woman*, 9, 125.

10. Two of the major scandals of the 102nd Congress were the so-called "post-office scandal" and the "house banking scandal." For their effect on the election of 1992, v. B. Wolf, "Voter Anger Is Loud and Clear," *USA Today*, March 18 (1992), 8A and *The Year of the Woman*, 133-135, 164.

11. For women as political "outsiders," v. L. Phillips and P. Edmonds, "Special Report: Women in Congress," *USA Today*, April 1 (1992): 1-5A; R. Berke, "With Outsiders In, Female Candidates Are the Rage," *NYT* April 29 (1992); C. Trueheart, "Politics' New Wave of Women: With Voters Ready for a Change, Candidates Make their Move," *Washington Post*, [*WP*] April 7 (1992); M. Schwartz, "Female Candidates Break Record," *WP*, May 25 (1992), A1+A18 and K. Dumas, 35.

12. v. Cook, Thomas and Wilcox, *The Year of the Woman*, 12-13, 123-137; R. Wolf, "Incumbents Face 'Triple Whammy' in November," *USA Today*, March 19 (1992), 5A and D. Howlett, "For Some, a Great Notion: Parity," *USA Today*, April 1 (1992), 4A.

13. For more information, v. Toni Morrison, ed., *Race-ing, Justice, En-gendering Power: Essays on Anita Hill, Clarence Thomas, and the Construction of Social Reality* (New York: Pantheon, 1992); M. Schwartz, "Female Candidates," *WP*, May 25 (1992), A1+A18, and M. Feinsilber, "Anita Hill Apparently a Powerful Symbol," *The Philadelphia Inquirer*, April 28 (1992), A 12. For Hill's own account and sympathetic commentaries by Patricia Williams, Barbara Smith and Eleanor Holmes Norton v. "Capitol Hill's Worst Kept Secret: Sexual Harassment" in *Ms.* Jan./Feb. (1992): 32-45; for opposing views v. G. Will, "Anita Hill's Tangled Web" *Newsweek*, April 19 (1993), 74.

14. Thomas had been director of the EEOC under Reagan who then nominated him to the Circuit Court of Appeals in 1990. A conservative Republican and strict Catholic, he was generally assumed to oppose abortion. However, since he had never practiced as a public lawyer, he had not published commentaries on this and other constitutional issues. Opponents of his nomination stressed his undistinguished qualifications. His rapid rise under Republican Presidents was partly due to the dearth of highly qualified African American lawyers in the Republican camp. Pleased that Bush had at least nominated a black candidate, many white liberal Senators limited their criticism of Thomas.

15. While most African Americans in opinion polls supported Thomas, civil rights organizations such as the NAACP or the Rainbow Coalition opposed his nomination. The

Hill-Thomas affair also led to a new debate over gender relations within the black community, v. bell hooks, Michelle Wallace, Andrew Hacker, Derrick Bell et al., "The Crisis of African American Gender Relations," *Transition* 5, No. 66 (Summer 1995): 91-175.

16. Barbara Ehrenreich's comment in "What Do Women Have to Celebrate?" *Time*, November 16 (1992), 55 and "The Thomas Vote: What the Senators Said," *USA Today*, October 17 (1991), 9A.

17. Moseley-Braun's statement in J. Nelson (October 1992), 57; A. Moore, "The Thomas-Hill confrontation is Showing up in Primary Voting," *Philadelphia Inquirer*, April 30 (1992), A1; M. Schwartz, "Senate Upset Reflects Powerful Legacy of Thomas Hearings," *WP*, March 19 (1992), A15; I. Wilkerson, "Cracking The Club" in *NYT*, March 19 (1992), A 20; and Interviews with Senator Moseley-Braun, May 19, 1994, and her Chief of Staff, Mike Frazier, June 3, 1993.

18. Candice Nelson's comment in Cook, Thomas and Wilcox, *The Year of the Woman*, 181. EMILY is an acronym for "Early Money Is Like Yeast (it makes the dough rise)" and expresses the PAC's intention, to help in the early financing of female candidates. *EMILY's List*, founded in 1985, is currently the largest American women's PAC and supports only Democratic candidates. The oldest one, the *Women's Campaign Fund* (WCF), established 1974, is bi-partisan, while the *WISH-List*, founded March, 1992 supports only Republican, "pro choice" candidates.

19. In 1992 the percentage of women in Congress rose from 5.8 to 10.2 percent, but within this group black women enjoyed the largest percentage increase. In the 103rd Congress, 25 percent of all black members were women, compared to 15.8 percent of Hispanic members, 14.3 percent of Asian and no Native American members were women. Although African Americans (12.1 percent of the American population according to the 1990 census) held only 7.5 percent of all Congressional seats in the 103rd Congress (1993/94), their political representation was higher than that for other American minority groups or for women for that matter.

20. Children's Defense Fund [CDF], *The State of America's Children: Yearbook, 1994* (Washington, DC: CDF, 1994); C. Rexroat, *The Declining Economic Status of Black Children* (Washington, DC: Joint Center for Political and Economic Studies, 1994); E. Montgomery "Income Inequality within the Black Community" in *FOCUS: The Monthly Magazine of the Joint Center for Political and Economic Studies*, November (1996), T3-4 and M. Simms, "Whose Robust Economy," *FOCUS*, April (1997), T3-4.

21. "Floor Statement of Congresswoman Maxine Waters: Introduction of the 'Youth and Young Adult Empowerment Initiative'," February 18, 1993.

22. The rate of African Americans who attend college is less than half that of whites; e.g. in 1992 24 percent of white high school graduates, but only 12 percent of blacks obtained a college degree. v. W.R. Allen and J.O. Jewell, "African American Education since *An American Dilemma*," *Daedalus* 124, No. 1 (1995): 77-100. Also v. "President Clinton Signs School-To-Work Act," *FOCUS*, June (1994), 3 and Robert Reich, "Two Million Jobs Are Not Enough," *FOCUS*, July (1994), 3.

23. The other black women strongly supported Collins's initiative and even voted against their own pay raise in 1993 in order to help finance this measure.

24. The official US poverty line for the annual income of a household of three was $11,890 in 1993. The annual wage of a full-time, year-round minimum wage worker at that time was $8,840.

25. Maxine Waters, for example, said, "This initiative the EITC will make the most important difference in the lives of low-income Americans of anything contained in the package H.R. 2264!" v. "Statement of Maxine Waters in Favor of Clinton Budget," *Press Release*, August 1993 and CDF, *Yearbook*, 1994, 3.

26. CDF, "A Healthy Start for Children" *CDF Reports*, November (1993), 1-2, 5-10; CDF, *Yearbook, 1994*, 15-16 and E.B. Johnson, "Newsletter: Dear Constituents" (Spring/Summer 1993).

27. Michael "Mickey" Leland, the African American chairman of the *House Select Committee on World Hunger*, died in a plane crash after visiting a refugee camp in Ethiopia in 1989. v. CDF, *Yearbook, 1994*, 45 and "Legislative Initiatives Supported by Congresswoman Eleanor Holmes Norton" (1991).

28. Interview with Brown, June 29, 1994; also v. CDF, *Yearbook, 1994*, 33 and M. Jordan, "Head Start's Big Test," *WP*, March 29 (1993).

29. The national average of teenagers who left school without graduating was 26 percent for white and almost 40 percent for black teenagers in the early 1990s, and in the predominantly black inner-city ghettos drop-out rates were even higher. Moreover, the number of black teenage criminals in the inner cities had increased 30 percent since the 1985; in 1993 black teenagers were arrested for violent crimes five times as often as white teenagers and in 1994 25 percent of young black men between 17 and 27 were either in jail, in prison or on probation. v. CDF, *Progress and Peril: Black Children in America* (Washington; DC: CDF, 1993), 83-99; N. Taifa, "Drug Laws 100 Times Harder on Blacks," *FOCUS*, April (1995), 5-6; C. Spohn, "Courts, Sentences, and Prisons," *Daedalus*, 124: 1, Winter (1995), 119-143; also see "Statement of Senator Carol Moseley-Braun on Goals 2000: Educate America Act," *Press Release*, March 25, 1994.

30. Moseley-Braun commented on the success of her initiative: "If midnight basketball helps keep even one of the participating young people out of our criminal justice system, this program will have served the taxpayers very well. v." Senate Approves Moseley-Braun Amendment to the Goals 2000 Bill," *News Release* from the office of the senator, February 3, 1994.

31. Interview with McKinney, May 26, 1994. All of the black women were members of the CCWI, but they also stressed that their first loyalty always belonged to the Congressional Black Caucus. Most of the time the CCWI and the CBC supported the same legislative issues. However, as will be pointed out later, in the few cases where there was a conflict of interest between both groups, the black women always supported their CBC colleagues.

32. For more detailed information on the abortion debate in the United States, v. F. Davis, *Moving the Mountain: The Women's Movement in America Since 1960* (New York: Simon and Schuster, 1995), as well as C. Costello and A. Stone, *The American Woman, 1994-1995* (New York: W.W. Norton, 1994).

33. Interview with Meek, July 14, 1994, and "Blueprint 2000: Carrie Meek's Congressional Platform for the Future," *News Release*, Fall 1992. Also see, interviews with the other Congresswomen and their staff and "Statement of Senator Carol Moseley-Braun on Reproductive Health Care," *News Release*, July 21, 1993. Being "pro-choice" as opposed to being "pro-life" are terms expressing that one either supports or opposes the right to have an abortion.

34. The fact that a doctor of an abortion clinic in Florida was actually killed by a fundamentalist Christian member of the militant anti-abortion group "Rescue America" in 1993 added to the determination of the Congresswomen to get H.R. 796 passed. See, Costello and Stone *The American Woman*, 215; "Women on the Hill: Can They Make a Difference?," *Ms.*, January/February (1995): 85-90. Corrine Brown, who represented the district in which this murder had occurred, was furious about this violence. v. "Brown Outraged at Senseless Murder" *News Release*, March 11, 1993 and Interview with Brown June 29, 1994.

35. F. Attaguile, "We'll All Pay for Denying Abortion to the Poor: A Medical Nightmare," *NYT*, July 12 (1993), A16, "There is no Choice for Poor Women," *NYT*, July 2 (1993); F. Wilkinson, "Guess Who's Coming to Legislate," *Rolling Stone*, May 19 1994: 46-47 and M. Margolies-Mezvinsky, *A Woman's Place: The Freshmen Women Who Changed the Face of Congress* (New York: Crown Publishers, 1994), 111-134.

36. "Hyde Amendment," *CR*, June 30, 1993, Vol. 139; No. 94 and "Statement of Cynthia McKinney: Repeal of the Hyde Amendment," *Press Release*, June 30, 1993. The fact that the abortion rate among women who live below the poverty line is almost three

times as high as those of middle- or upper-class women also supports the argument that it is not lack of money that stops women from having an abortion but probably better sex-education, and more information as well as access to contraception. v. F.D. Brown, "More Fuel for the Abortion Debate," *Black Enterprise*, October (1990): 31-33 and Attaguile (1993).

37. Even Moseley-Braun, who was one of the initial sponsors of the bill in the Senate, withdrew her support. v. "Senator Moseley-Braun Withdraws Name From Freedom of Choice Act," *News Release*, July 8, 1993, and R. Toner, "Middle Ground on Abortion Shifting into Terra Incognita" in *NYT*, July 15, 1993, A1.

38. CDF, *Yearbook, 1994*, 76 and CDF, *Progress and Peril*, 37-38; Collins, Speech on House Floor on February 3, 1993. The black female members I interviewed would have also supported a form of *paid* family and medical leave (such as exists in most European countries), but they knew that they would not be able to get a majority for this in Congress. v. Interviews with Congresswomen, and Waters, "Statement on the Family and Medical Leave Act," *Press Release*, February 3, 1993.

39. C. Collins, McKinney and Clayton had been direct co-sponsors of the bill. v. *Legislative Profiles* of and interviews with the Congresswomen and their staff. Also see, CCWI, "Record of Accomplishments for women in Congress: Summary of Legislative Action in the 103rd Congress," *News Release*, October 13, 1994 and K. Golden and G. Kirshenbaum, "1994 in Review: The Good News," in *Ms.*, January/February (1995): 46-53.

40. Barbara-Rose Collins, who introduced H.R. 3247 in October 1993, said her tolerance for traditional heritage and religious freedom ended at the point where essential human rights were being violated. In her view, "female genital mutilation" was just another traditional tool of male oppression of women and male control over female sexuality. She also pointed out that a number of girls had suffered from lasting shock and some had died as a result of uncontrolled bleedings or infections after this "operation." See, "Congresswoman Barbara-Rose Collins' Initiative" (press release, May 1994) and interview with Collins. For more details on the continuing debate about this practice, which is also found among Africans living in Europe, see, A.M. Rosenthal, "On My Mind: Female Genital Torture," *NYT*, November 12 (1993), A33, M. Merwine, "How Africa Understands Female Circumcision," *NYT*, November 24 (1993), A24; D. Hecht, "Fighting for Their Rites," *Newsweek*, October 14 (1996), 57 and M. Haas, "Mit dem Messer in die Hochzeitsnacht: Frauen-Beschneidung: Eine Folter mitten in Europa," *Süddeutsche Zeitung*, December 10 (1997), 3.

41. See, text of Senate Resolution 263 as well as Golden and Kirshenbaum, "1994 in Review," 48.

42. Costello and Stone, *The American Woman*, 301; Hine, *Black Women in America*, 791-797; "Can They Make a Difference?," *Ms.*, January/February (1995): 85-90; Interviews with Brown, June 29, 1994, and with Waters' legislative director, Bill Zavarello, April 25, 1994.

43. H.R. 2518 was passed in October 1993. On the whole the 103rd Congress appropriated more federal means for women's health care than any other Congress before (e.g. 70 percent more money than the 102nd Congress). v. CCWI, "Record of Accomplishments For Women in Congress (1994).

44. H.R. 4278 was passed in October 1994. Meek and most of the female members of her family had worked as domestics for white families in Florida. v. M. Dowd, "Growing Sorority in Congress Edges into the Ol'Boys Club," *NYT*, March 5 (1993):A1; "Women on the Hill," and Margolies-Mezvinsky, *A Woman's Place*, 140.

45. See, Maxine Waters' statement: "In this country, we have institutionalized racism. Because of that, public-policy decisions have not been made to help people who are considered invisible or less than human beings. These powerless people happen to be people of color. And it is usually people of power and wealth—white people—who make

the decisions." v." Straight Talk from South Central," *Ladies Home Journal*, August 1992): 112. Also see, interviews with the other Congresswomen.

46. Interview with Chisholm, June 23, 1993.

47. Norton had been director of the EEOC during the Carter Administration. v. P. Lamson, "Eleanor Holmes Norton Reforms the EEOC," in J. Barber and B. Kellerman, eds., *Women Leaders In American Politics* (Englewood Cliffs, NJ: Prentice Hall, 1986), 340-345. For more information about the EEOC's role and the affirmative action debate, see, H. Walton, *When the Marching Stopped: The Politics of Civil Rights Regulatory Agencies* (Albany: State University of New York Press, 1988); G. Horne, *Reverse Discrimination: The Case for Affirmative Action* (New York: International Publishers, 1992), and D. Ruffin, "Affirmative Action Myth and Realities," *FOCUS*, August (1996), 7-8.

48. "Collins Gets Amendments to Telecommunications Bill," *Jet*, April 11 (1994), 36.

49. "Maxine Waters' Agenda for the 103rd Congress," *News Release*, April 1993; Waters was a member of the House Banking Committee and had fought against redlining since 1991.

50. "Maxine Waters' Agenda for the 103rd Congress," *News Release*, April 1993 and Interview with her legislative director, Bill Zavarello, April 25, 1994.

51. S. Lawson, *Running for Freedom: Civil Rights and Black Politics in America Since 1941* (Philadelphia: Temple UP, 1991); US Bureau of the Census, 20-466, "Voting-Age Population; Percent Reporting Registered, and Voted: 1978-1992; Joint Center for Political and Economic Studies, *Black Elected Officials. A National Roster*, 1971-1994, 23 vols., Washington, DC, 1971-1994 and D. Bositis, "Blacks and Democrats," *FOCUS*, September (1996): 3-4.

52. K. Arrington and W. Taylor, *Voting Rights in America: Continuing the Quest for Full Participation* (Washington, DC, JCES, 1992), 143-204 and League of Women Voters (LWV), "Patterns of Participation: Survey of Voters and Nonvoters," *LWV-Report*, May 30 (1996).

53. See, text of *National Voter Registration Act of 1993* and D. Ruffin, "Motor Voter Bill: Extending the Franchise," *FOCUS*, May, 1993, T1. McKinney's speech in support of the *Motor Voter Bill* expressed why she as a black woman had a particular interest in this issue: "While individuals must take responsibility for exercising their right to vote, elected officials must take responsibility for reducing the red tape associated with registering to vote. Not too long ago, Congress permitted laws and practices that prevented black Americans from exercising their constitutional right to vote. Many citizens of the 11th District of Georgia were victims of those laws and practices ... I am in Congress today because of efforts to expand voting rights and voter participation. On behalf of [the civil rights activists] who have dedicated their lives to voting rights for all Americans I urge my colleagues to support this effort to make voting just a little easier for our people," v. "Floor Statement of Congresswoman Cynthia McKinney on the Motor Voter Act," February 4, 1993.

54. "Floor Statement of Congresswoman Cynthia McKinney on the Motor Voter Act," April 1, 1993; also see, Senator Moseley-Braun, "Statement on the Motor Voter Legislation," in *CR-Senate*, May 7 (1993): S.5679-5680: "I am beginning to reach the conclusion that perhaps there really is a fear of participation ... there really is a fear that if we remove the barriers the gauntlet will come down and we will really have a democracy ... Our hopes are that people will participate. Our hopes are that we will expand the franchise - that is why we want to have motor-voter."

55. Newt Gingrich (R-GA) was particularly angry about McKinney's assertion and stressed his reasons for opposing H.R. 2: "This bill would create a nationwide Chicago, where the dead can vote, illegal aliens can vote, and the political machine can pressure people to vote for their candidate" v. J. Cummings, "Georgia Lawmaker Provokes GOP Anger," *The Atlanta Constitution*, April 2, 1993, 1.

56. The law made it mandatory for all states to offer voter registration services in all DMV and social welfare offices as well as to allow for registration by mail (which had only been legal in certain states before). As a concession to conservatives, the law also included a provision declaring all military recruitment offices as mandatory registration sites. See, text of H.R.2/S. 460 and Ruffin, "Motor Voter Bill."

57. Clarence Thomas cast the decisive vote against the black majority district in this 5–4 ruling; v. J. Biskupic, "N.C. Case to Pose Test of Racial Redistricting," *WP* April 20 (1993), A4, and F. Parker, "The Supreme Court's Blind Eye on Voting Rights," *The National Voter*, January (1994): 14-17.

58. The African American voting population in McKinney's district was reduced from 64 percent to 38 percent, in Brown's district from 55 percent to 45 percent; v. D. Ruffin, "Congressional Elections: New Faces and Tough Races" *FOCUS*, September (1996): T1-3, and "1996 Election Results," *FOCUS*, November (1996), T1-2.

59. D. Ruffin, "Black Voters Assert Their Power" and "1998 Election Results for Black Candidates to Congressional and Statewide Offices," *FOCUS*, December (1998), 3-4, 8, and T1-3; Center for the American Woman and Politics (CAWP) "Women Who Will Serve in the 106th Congress," at http:www.rci.rutgers.edu/~cawp/106thcongress.html [a fact sheet produced by CAWP, National Information Bank on Women in Public Office, Eagleton Institute of Politics, Rutgers University].

Contributors

Marisa Chappell received her doctorate in U.S. history from Northwestern University. She is currently a Franklin Postdoctoral Fellow at the University of Georgia and is revising her manuscript, *From Welfare Rights to Welfare Reform: The Politics of AFDC, 1964–1984*, for publication.

Jenny Hutchinson completed an M.A. in African American history and race relations at the University of Newcastle upon Tyne where she focused on the role of the black popular press in helping to raise black consciousness during the 1950s.

John A. Kirk is lecturer in U.S. history at Royal Holloway, University of London. He is the author of *Redefining the Color Line: Black Activism in Little Rock, Arkansas, 1940–1970* (2002), which won the Arkansas Historical Association's 2003 J. G. Ragsdale Book Award. He is currently working on a volume on Martin Luther King for Longman's Profiles in Power series.

Peter Ling is Reader in American Studies at the University of Nottingham, England. He is the author of *Martin Luther King, Jr.* (2002) and *The Democratic Party* (2003). His articles on the civil rights movement have appeared in *Journal of American Studies*, *History Workshop Journal*, *Prospects*, and *Comparative American Studies*. He is currently working on a series of articles on political education in the movement.

Sharon Monteith is Reader in American Studies at the University of Nottingham. Her books include *Advancing Sisterhood?: Interracial Friendships in Contemporary Southern Fiction* (2000), *Pat Barker* (2002), and *South to a New Place: Region, Literature, Culture* (2002). She is completing a book on representations of the civil rights movement in popular cinema.

Eithne Quinn teaches American studies at the University of Manchester, UK. Her book *Nuthin' but a "G" Thang: The Culture and Commerce of Gangsta Rap* will be published in 2004.

Belinda Robnett is a professor of sociology and former director of African-American studies at the University of California, Irvine. She is the author of *How Long? How Long? African-American Women and the Struggle for Civil Rights* and the coauthor of *Social Movements: Identity, Culture, and the State.* She is currently working on a book titled *Our Struggle for Unity: African Americans in the Age of Identity Politics* and has published numerous articles on race, gender, and social movements.

Britta Waldschmidt-Nelson is an assistant professor of American history, politics, and culture at the America Institute of the University of Munich. Her publications include *From Protest to Politics: Schwarze Frauen in der Burgerrechtsbewegung und im Kongreb der Vereinigten Staaten* (1998) and *Gegenspieler: Martin Luther King, Jr., and Malcolm X* (2000) which is now in its third edition.

Jenny Walker is a former graduate student of the University of Newcastle upon Tyne where she completed a Ph.D. on black violence and nonviolence in the civil rights and black power eras. She is the author of "A Media-Made Movement: Black Violence and Nonviolence in the Historiography of the Civil Rights Movement" in *Media, Culture, and the Modern African American Freedom Struggle*, edited by Brian Ward (2001).

Brian Ward currently teaches and is chair of the department of history at the University of Florida, Gainesville. He is the author of *Just My Soul Responding: Rhythm and Blues, Black Consciousness and Race Relations* (1998), which won a number of prizes, including an American Book Award from the Before Columbus Foundation, the James A. Rawley Prize from the Organization of American Historians, and the European Association for American Studies Network First Book Prize. It was also named a "Notable Book of 1998" by *The New York Times Book Review* and an Outstanding Academic Book of 1998 by *Choice* magazine. His other publications include *The Making of Martin Luther King and the Civil Rights Movement* (edited with Tony Badger; 1996), and another edited collection, *Media, Culture and the Modern African American Freedom Struggle* (2001). His latest book, *Radio and the Struggle for Civil Rights in the South* will be published in 2004.

Index

Abernathy, Ralph, 83, 102, 105, 216
Above the Rim, 205
Abrahams, Roger D., 44, 199
Absalom, Absalom! (Faulkner), 231
"Adam, Come And Get Your Rib," 47
"Advancing Luna and Ida B. Wells" (Walker), 223
Aid to Families with Dependent Children, 253
Alexander, Donnell, 204
Allen, Joseph, 94
"All She Wants to Do Is Rock," 46
Alston suit, 31
"Always," 51
And All Our Wounds Forgiven (Lester), 10, 215, 219, 223, 225, 226–229
Andrews, Robert, 232
Arkansas Council on Human Relations (ACHR), 36, 37
Arkansas Democrat, 35
Arkansas Democratic Voters' Association, 30
Arkansas State Conference of Branches (ASC), 17, 32, 33
Arkansas State Press, 28, 29–30, 32, 35, 75, 77, 96
"Atomic Dog," 191
Autobiography (Davis), 215

"Backstabbers," 57–58
Badger, Tony, 11
Baker, Ella, 9, 12, 102–108, 132, 134, 160, 161, 162, 164
Baker, Houston, 217
Baldwin, James, 2, 8, 224
Baptist Church, Sixteenth Street bombing, 117
Baraka, Amiri, 10
Barnett, Bernice McNair, 162
Barry, Marion, 53
Basie, Mrs. Count, 77
Bates, Daisy, 7–8, 12, 17–19, 75
 as ASC president, 33–34
 church/religion and, 23–24
 father (adopted) of, 20–23, 26
 father (biological), 26
 marriage, 28

mother (adopted) of, 22–23
mother (biological) of, 20,
  25–26
NAACP and, 31–35
racism, encounters with, 20,
  23, 25
relations with neighborhood
  women, 24–25
relations with whites, 27–28
State Press, 28, 29–30, 32, 35,
  75, 77, 96
Bates, L. C., 18, 28, 75
Bearcats, 46
Beasley, Edward, 78
Being and Race (Johnson), 217
Belafonte, Harry, 95, 151
Belk, Mary, 145
Bellamy, Faye, 133, 138, 139, 161
Belling, Sarah, 79
Benjamin, Walter, 229
Bennett, Constance Motley, 12
Bennett, Lerone, 91
Bennett, William, 198
Benton, Brook, 50, 80
Berry, Chuck, 51
Berry, William, 78–79
"Beside You," 48
Between God and Gangsta Rap
  (Dyson), 201
Bevel, Diane Nash, 134
Bevel, James, 12, 102, 117,
  118–119, 122
"Bewildered," 57
"Bicycle Tillie," 48
"Big Leg Woman…," 58
Big Mama Thornton, 192
Billy Ward and the Dominoes,
  45, 48, 58, 78
Black Folktales (Lester), 217

*Black Macho and the Myth of
  Superwoman* (Wallace), 7
Black Power movement, effects
  on women, 155–165
Blackwell, Randolph, 125
Blackwell, Unita, 148–149, 150
Blasingame, Odis von, 88
Bo Diddly, 51
Bogle, Donald, 5
Bond, Julian, 151
Booker, James, 94
Boyd, Eddie, 45
Boynton, Amelia, 153
Boyte, Harry, 133
Branch, Taylor, 90, 110
Brock, Annette K., 170, 179
Brooks, Sadie, 94
Brooks Higginbotham, Evelyn, 2
Brothers Johnson, 58
Brown, Corrine, 240, 245, 249,
  253
Brown, Elaine, 159, 160
Brown, James, 57
Brown, Rosellen, 223
Brown, Roy, 45–46
Brown, William Wells, 231
Brown v. Board of Education, 34,
  79
Bullock, H. A., 80
Burden of Southern History, The
  (Woodward), 221
Burke, Solomon, 56
Burke, Yvonne, 239
Bushwick, Bill, 194
Bussey, Charles, 29–30
Butler, Jerry, 51
Byrd, James, 234

Cadets, 49

Cadillacs, 49
Callender, James, 224
Cambridge, Maryland, 169–184
Cambridge Nonviolent Action
    Committee (CNAC),
    169–184
Campbell, Luther, 63
Caretners, Solar M., 31
Carmichael, Stokely, 3, 53, 156,
    161
Carnoy, Martin, 234
Carolina Times, 81
Carr, Mrs. Johnnie, 86, 91
Carson, Clayborne, 55, 160, 162
Carson, Julia, 253
Carter, Clarence, 58
Carter, Eugene, 92, 93
Carter, Mae Bertha, 144
Carter, Willie, 93–94
Castelles, 48
Caucus on Women's Issues, 11
Caute, David, 58
Chafe, William, 13
Chandler, Gene, 51
Chappell, Marisa, 8, 69–96
Chicago Defender, 75, 77, 79,
    87, 93
Chi-lites, 59, 60
Chisholm, Shirley, 239, 250
Chords, 49
Church, Eugene, 51
Civic Interest Group (CIG), 171
*Civil Rights Movement: A
    Photographic History,
    1954–1968* (Kasher), 179
Civil Wars (Brown), 223
Clark, Dee, 51
Clark, Jim, 153, 154
Clark, Kenneth, 4

Clark, Septima, 9, 12, 106–107,
    120, 123–125, 162, 164
Clayton, Eva, 240, 253
Cleaver, Eldridge, 55
Cleaver, Kathleen, 159
Cleveland Call & Post, 93
Clifford, Linda, 62
Clinton, Bill, 234, 253
Clinton, George, 191
Clotel (Brown), 231
Cloud, John, 153
Collins, Barbara-Rose, 247–248,
    253
Collins, Cardiss, 239, 244, 250,
    253
Collins, LeRoy, 154
Colvin, Claudette, 85
Committee on Negro
    Organizations, 32
Community Development
    Banking Act, 251
Comprehensive Childhood
    Immunization Act, 244–245
Congress, women in
    election of 1992, 239–242
    gendered agenda, 242–250
    racial agenda, 250–254
Congressional Black Caucus, 11
Congressional Caucus on
    Women's Issues (CCWI),
    245–246
Congress of Racial Equality
    (CORE), 13, 101, 156, 171
Cooke, Sam, 50, 80
Cothran, Tilman C., 34
Cotton, Dorothy, 120, 122
Council of Federated
    Organizations (COFO), 142,
    156

Council on Community Affairs
(CoCA), 37
"Court of Love," 58
Crawford, Vicki, 9, 17
Crenshaw, Jack, 84
Cromwell, Dwight, 172
Crook, General, 58
Crouch, Stanley, 224
Crows, 49
Cunningham, George P., 231
"Cupid," 50
Current, Gloster B., 33, 34
Curry, Constance, 144

D'Aguiar, Fred, 231–232
Daly, Steven, 204
Dance, Daryl Cumber, 44
Davis, Angela, 7, 55, 159, 177, 215
Davis, Tyrone, 59
Dawson, Michael C., 195
Death in a Promised Land
(Andrews), 232
De Knight, Freda, 75
De La Beckwith, Byron, 216
Delfonics, 59
DeLillo, Don, 232
D'Emilio, John, 13
Devine, Annie, 143, 149, 150
Different Drummer, A (Kelley),
230
Dill, Bonnie Thornton, 160
Dixon, Alan, 242
Doctorow, E. L., 231
"Doggin' Around," 51
Doggy-Dogg figure in gangsta
rap, 190–197
"Do It For Me," 58
Dole, Bob, 198
"Dollars for Daisy" campaigns, 36

Dolomite, 44
Dominoes, 45, 48, 58, 78
"Don't Give It Away," 60
"Don't Mind Dyin'," 49
Dowell, Coleman, 223
Dr Dre (Andre Young), 190, 194
Dreamer (Johnson), 10, 215,
216–222
DuBois, W. E. B., 70–71
Du-Droppers, 46
"Duke of Earl," 51
Dunaway, Edwin E., 31
Durr, Clifford, 86
Durr, Virginia, 86–87
Dykestra, Wilma, 87
Dyson, Michael Eric, 4, 201–202

Earned Income Tax Credit
(EITC), 244
"Earth Angel," 49
East End Civic League, 29–30
Easy Burden, An (Young), 12
Ebony, 75, 78–79, 88, 90, 95, 175
Eckford, Elizabeth, 70
Economic Stimulus Package Act
(H.R. 1335), 243
Elementary and Secondary
Education Act (H.R. 1794),
249
Elks, 82
Ellison, Mary, 11
Ellison, Ralph, 1, 2, 8, 222
Emergency Unemployment
Compensation Act (H.R.
920), 244
EMILY's List, 242
Equal Employment Opportunity
Commission Admendment
(1993) (H.R. 126), 250

Evans, Sara, 3, 18–19, 133, 223
Evers, Medgar, 112, 216
Evers, Myrlie, 216

Fairclough, Adam, 11–12, 115
Family and Medical Leave Act,
    247–248
Farrakhan, Louis, 7
*Fatheralong: A Meditation on
    Fathers and Sons, Race and
    Society* (Wideman), 7
Faulkner, William, 231
FBI, 102, 109–110
Featherstone, Ralph, 161
Federal Prohibition of Female
    Genital Mutilation Act (H.R.
    3247), 248–249
Ferree, Myra, 131
Five Royales, 47
Flamingos, 48
"Florence," 49
Flowers, William Harold, 32–33
Floyd, Gwendolyn, 77
Forman, James, 151
Forrest, Leon, 230
For Us the Living (Evers), 216
Fosdick, Franklin, 76
Foster, Thomas, 29
Frankie Lymon and the
    Teenagers, 49
Franklin, Clyde, 4, 6
Franklin, John Hope, 234
Frazier, E. Franklin, 42, 74–75,
    137–138
Freedom of Access to Clinic
    Entrances Act (FACE) (H.R.
    796), 246
Freedom of Choice Act, 247
Freedom Rides, 115, 180

Freedom Summer of 1964, 101,
    155
Freeman, Garman P., 37
French, Edgar, 88, 89
Funkadelic, 59
"Furry's Blues," 45

Gaines, Kevin, 72
Gandhi, Mohandas, 112
Gangsta rap, 10, 61, 62, 64, 189
    critical responses to, 197–203
    Doggy-Dogg figure in, 190–197
Garrow, David, 91, 110
Gates, Henry Louis, 195, 207,
    208
Gaye, Marvin, 56, 59, 206
Gaynor, Gloria, 62
"Gee," 49
Gellatly, Mary Sue, 135
Gender Equity in Education and
    Equity in Athletics
    Disclosure Act (H.R. 1793),
    249
Genovese, Eugene, 42, 71
George, Nelson, 187, 189, 203
G-Funk Era, 189
    post-soul masculinity and
        aesthetics of, 203–210
Giddings, Paula, 85, 158, 159,
    177, 178, 184
Gilmore, Glenda, 72
Gilroy, Paul, 54, 207
"Gimme Some," 58
Glass, Thelma, 93
Goals 2000: Educate America
    Act (H.R. 4250), 245
"Golden Teardrops," 48
Goodgame, Rev., 103–104
"Good Good Lovin'," 57

"Goodnite Sweetheart Goodnite," 49
Gordon, Jacob, 7
Gordon, Majors, 7
Grant, Jacquelyn, 138
Gray, Fred, 94
Gray, Victoria, 143–144, 152
Green, Al, 59, 206
Green, Donna Christian, 253
Gutman, Herbert, 42
Guyot, Lawrence, 152

Hale, Nathaniel, 190, 203,
    204–205
Hall, Grover, 91
Hall, Prathia, 135, 151, 157
Hall, Stuart, 189
Halliday, George, 231
Halpern, Rick, 11
Hamer, Fannie Lou, 9, 122,
    142–143, 148, 149–150,
    151, 152–153
Hansen, William, 171
Hare, Nick S., 84
Harptones, 48
Harris, Wynonie, 46–47
Hawkins, Jeffrey, 30
Hayden, Casey, 3
Head Start Reauthorization Act
    (H.R. 4250), 245
Henry, Aaron, 147–148
Henry, John, 44
Hesitations, 58
"He Will Break Your Heart," 51
Higginbotham, Elizabeth, 140
Hill, Anita, 241–242
Hine, Darlene, 9
Hoare, Ian, 56
Holliday, Ada, 145
Holmes, Eleanor, 250

Hooker, John Lee, 45
hooks, bell, 43
"Hopefully Yours," 48
"Hot Pants," 57
Houston Juvenile Delinquency
    and Crime Commission, 80
Howard, John, 13
Howlin' Wolf, 45
Humphrey, Hubert, 145–146
Hutchinson, Earl Ofari, 11
Hutchinson, Jenny, 8, 69–96
Hyde, Henry, 247

"I Can't Leave Your Love
    Alone," 58
Ice Cube, 190, 199
"I Like My Baby's Pudding," 46
"I'll Always Love My Mama," 59
"I'll Go Crazy," 57
"I'm A Man," 51
"I'm A Sentimental Fool," 48
"I'm In Love," 56
In Friendship, 103
Interscope Records, 190, 198
Intruders, 58, 59
Invisible Man (Ellison), 222
"It Ain't The Meat It's The
    Motion," 48
"It's A New Day," 57
I've Got the Light of Freedom
    (Payne), 176
Ives, Amelia B., 31
"I Wake Up Crying," 51

Jackson, Beatrice, 93, 94
Jackson, Bruce, 197
Jackson, Bullmoose, 46
Jackson, Chuck, 51
Jackson, George, 55

Jackson, Jesse, 102
Jackson, Jimmie Lee, 155
Jackson, M. A., 36–37
Jackson-Lee, Sheela, 252–253
James, Elmore, 45
Jayhawks, 49
Jefferson, Thomas, 224
Jenkins, Esau, 107
Jim Crow South, 19–28
Jobs and Life Skills Improvement
    Act (H.R., 1020), 243
Jody the Grinder, 44
Johns, Vernon, 90
Johnson, Charles, 10, 215,
    216–222, 230, 233–235
Johnson, Eddie Bernice, 240,
    244, 245, 253
Johnson, Frank, 154
Johnson, June, 53
Johnson, Lyndon, 145, 153, 154
Johnson, Robert, 45
Johnson, Syl, 60
Jones, Lafayette, 36
Jones, Stephanie Tubbs, 254
Jordan, Barbara, 239
Jordan, Louis, 91
Jordan, Richard, 94

Kasher, Steven, 179
Kelley, Robin, 2, 41, 195–196,
    201, 202–203, 210
Kelley, William Melvin, 230
Kempton, Murray, 175
Kennedy, Robert, 172
Kenyatta, Jomo, 112
Killens, John O., 230
Kilpatrick, Carolyn, 253
Kilpatrick, James Jackson, 69
King, Alberta Williams, 106, 111

King, Ben E., 51
King, Coretta Scott, 95–96, 105,
    108–109, 110–111, 116
King, Ed, 147
King, Martin Luther, Jr., 2, 10,
    12, 179
    And All Our Wounds Forgiven
        (Lester), 10, 215, 219, 223,
        225, 226–229
    black power and, 156
    Crusade for Citizenship,
        104–105
    Dreamer (Johnson), 10, 215,
        216–222
    extra-marital relations, 101, 110
    "I Have a Dream" speech,
        182–183
    nonviolence and, 108–119
    respectability and early civil
        rights movement, 80, 83, 88,
        89, 90–92, 95–96
    Richardson and, 174
    Selma/Montgomery marches,
        154–155
King, Martin Luther, Sr., 111
King, Mary, 3
King, Richard H., 11, 231
King, Rodney, 231
Kirk, John A., 7–8, 12, 17–38
Kitwana, Bakari, 199
"Knock Her Down," 49

Labor-HSS-Education
    Appropriation Act (H.R.
    2518), 247, 249
Ladner, Dorie, 139–140
Ladner, Joyce, 42, 155, 156, 160
Lampkin, Daisy, 103
"Land of Ladies," 58

Lane, Mary, 134
Larks, 48
"Laundromat Blues," 47
Lee, Barbara, 254
Lee, Bernard, 102
Lee, Herbert, 117
Lee, Spike, 4, 231
Lee Andrews and the Hearts, 49
Lehman, Daniel W., 230
Lerner, Gerda, 58–59
Lester, Julius, 10, 215, 216, 217,
    219, 223, 222–229, 230,
    231, 233–235
"Let Me Bang Your Box," 47
"Let Me Be The Man My Daddy
    Was," 60
Letter from Birmingham Jail
    (King), 126
"Letter to Dr. Martin Luther
    King, A" (Sanchez), 216
Levine, Lawrence, 42
Levinson, Stanley, 103
Levy, Peter, 170, 179
Lewinsky, Monica, 224
Lewis, Furry, 45
Lewis, John, 151, 153
Libra, 232
Ling, Peter J., 12, 101–126
Lingo, Al, 154
Little Anthony and the Imperials, 49
Little Richard, 51
Little Rock Classroom Teachers'
    Association (CTA), 31
Little Rock School crisis, 7, 34,
    70, 112
Little Rock Urban League, 31
Liuzzo, Viola, 155
Loan Guarantees for Cities Act,
    251

Loeb, Charles, 93
Long Shadow of Little Rock, The
    (Bates), 7, 18, 19
*Look Out Whitey! Black Power's
    Gon' Get Your Mama!*
    (Lester), 223
Louis, Joe, 78
"Love Bandit," 49
"Love Bones," 58
"Love Man," 56
"Lovin' Dan," 45, 58, 78
"Lovin' Machine," 47
Lynn, Susan, 77

MacPhatter, Clyde, 50
Malcolm X, 4, 115, 151–152,
    156
Malcolm X, 231
"Man's Temptation," 51
Man Who Cried I Am, The
    (Williams), 222
Marable, Manning, 4, 190, 201,
    210, 233, 235
Marshall, Burke, 176
Marshall, Thurgood, 31, 241
Marylanders, 48
"Mary Lee," 49
Masciana, Gerry, 75
Matriarchy and machoism, myths
    of, 41–45
McClinton, I. S., 30
McDonald, Michael, 205
McGee, Willie Ester, 134–135
McKinney, Cynthia, 240, 244,
    245–246, 247, 252, 253
McKissick, Floyd, 156, 159
Meek, Carrie, 240, 246, 249,
    253
Mercer, Kobena, 195, 197, 207

Meridian (Walker), 223, 224
"Me Tarzan, You Jane," 58
Meyerowitz, Joanne, 77
Mickey-Leland Childhood
   Hunger Relief Act, 245
Middle Passage (Johnson), 216,
   217
Mighty-Mighty Men, 45–48
Milburn, Amos, 46
Millender-McDonald, Juanita,
   253
Million Man March, 7
"Mirror Mirror," 57
Mississippi Freedom Democratic
   Party (MFDP), 9, 108,
   142–152
Mississippi Summer campaign of
   1964, 101, 155
"Mr. Soul Satisfaction," 58
Mixon, Gregory, 71
Mondale, Walter, 147
Monteith, Sharon, 10, 12,
   215–235
Montgomery bus boycott, 8,
   83–96
Montgomery Improvement
   Association (MIA), 8, 90,
   91
Moonglows, 49
Moore, Amzie, 107
Morris, Susie, 31–32
Morrison, Jessie, 135
Moseley-Braun, Carol, 239, 242,
   244, 245, 246, 248–249,
   252, 254
Moses, Donna, 151
Moses, Robert, 117, 147–148,
   151
Motor Voter Bill, 251–252

Mowbray, Calvin, 173
Moynihan, Daniel, 42
Muddy Waters, 45
Mueller, Carol, 132
Muhammad Speaks, 175–176
Munslow, Alun, 229
Murray, Pauli, 12
Music
   gangsta rap, 10, 61, 62, 64,
      189, 190–203
   G-Funk Era, 189, 203–210
   soul, 188–189
Music, gender depiction in
   black pop and the civil rights
      movement, 50–54
   Black Power and, 54–61
   matriarchy and macho in
   Rhythm and Blues, 41–45, 79–81
   in the post-revolutionary era,
      61–65
   the shouters and the Mighty-
      Mighty Men, 45–48
   vocal groups, 48–50
"Music For My Mother," 59

Naison, Mark, 198–199, 200
Nash, Diane, 234
Nate Dogg (Nathaniel Hale), 190,
   203, 204–205
National Association for the
   Advancement of Colored
   People (NAACP), 173
   Bates and the Little Rock,
      31–35
   sexism and, 101
National Council of African
   American Men (NCAAM), 7
National Council of Negro
   Women, 30, 35, 157

National Political Congress of Black Women, 198
National Urban League, 101
National Voter Registration Act (1993) (H.R. 2), 251, 252
Naylor, Gloria, 224
"Negro Leadership in a Crisis Situation" (Cothran and Phillips), 34
Nelson, Britta Waldschmidt, 10–11
Newsweek, 173
Newton, Huey, 4
New York Times, 173
Nigger Factory, The (Scott-Heron), 230
"Nihilism in Black America" (West), 200–201
Nixon, E. D., 83, 85–86, 91
"Nobody But You," 51
Norton, Eleanor Holmes, 245, 253
NWA, 62, 64, 190, 193

O'Jays, 57–58
100 Percent Proof Aged in Soul, 58
"One Less Bitch," 62
"One Man's Leftovers...," 58
Only Great Changes (Willis), 231
Orbits, 49
Osborne, Louise, 93
Ouachita County Training School, 82

Palmer, Phyllis, 2
Panther, 231, 232
"Papa Don't Take No Mess," 57
"Papa's Dream," 60
"Papa Was A Rolling Stone," 60

Paragons, 49
Parker, Sammy Dean, 70
Parks, Rosa, 12, 77, 83–90, 93, 231
Patton, Charley, 44
Payne, Charles, 17, 31, 38, 162, 176
Payne, Ethel, 79
Penguins, 49
Penn, Garland, 71–72
Philander Smith College, 35
Phillips, William, Jr., 34
Pickens, William, 104
Pickett, Wilson, 56
Pittsburgh Courier, 109
Platters, 80
Poitier, Sidney, 225
Political Action Committees (PACs), for women, 240, 242
Ponder, Annell, 122
"Pony Blues," 44
Popper, Karl, 5
"Pop the Pussy," 62
Porter, Mrs. H. L., 31
Post-soul man, 187–190
Pouissant, Alvin, 4
Powell, Adam Clayton, Jr., 77
"Pretty Girls Everywhere," 51
"Prisoner Of Love," 57
Project X, 117–118

Quinn, Eithne, 10, 187–210

Rainbows, 49
Ralph, James R., Jr., 215
Rap, Kool G., 62
Rap on Gangsta Rap, The (Kitwana), 199
Rauh, Joseph, 145, 146

Reagon, Bernice Johnson, 82, 136–137, 138, 139
"Real Woman," 60
Redding, Otis, 56, 199–200
Reeb, James, 155
Reese, Jeanetta, 94
Reid, Clarence, 60–61
Respectability, role of black media in the promotion of, 74–82
Rhythm and Blues, 10, 41–45, 79–81
Rich, Adrienne, 232
Richardson, Donna, 172
Richardson, Gloria, 5, 158, 159
   as a feminist icon, 177–179
   as a nonviolent activist, 179–184
   as a violent campaigner, 170–177
Robinson, Gwen, 135
Robinson, Jackie, 113
Robinson, Jo Ann, 52, 83, 86, 89
Robinson, Reginald, 171
Robinson, Ruby Doris Smith, 134, 151, 158–159, 161
Robinson, Smokey, 51
Robnett, Belinda, 3, 9, 11, 13, 17–18, 107, 131–165
Roediger, David, 2
Roe v. Wade, 246
Rogers, Lois, 135
Ross, Andrew, 205
Rothschild-Whitt, Joyce, 131
Rustin, Bayard, 102, 147–148

St. Clair, Frederick, 172
St. Clair, Herbert Maynaidier, 170
Saints, 57

Sampson, Frances, 32
Sanchez, Sonia, 216
School-to-Work Opportunity Act (H.R. 2884), 244
Schroeder, Patricia, 247, 248
Scott, Hazel, 77
Scott-Heron, Gil, 230
Sellers, Cleveland, 150, 158, 181–182
Sellers, Clyde, 84
Selma, Alabama, 153–155
"Sex Machine," 57
Shakur, Afeni, 62
Shakur, Tupac, 62
Shaw v. Reno, 253
"Sh-Boom," 49
Sheppherdson, Carrie, 31
"She's Got It," 51
"She Swallowed It," 62
Shirelles, 80
Shuttlesworth, Fred, 105, 179, 180, 183
Sias, Henry, 149
Simon, Joe, 59
"Sincerely," 49
Sing For Freedom, 223
Singleton, John, 4
Sippi (Killens), 230
"Sixty Minute Man," 45, 58, 78
Slick Rick, 62
"Slip Away," 58
Slyvester, 62
Smith, Al, 88
Smith, Bessie, 192
Smith, Ernest, 93, 94
Smith, Mary Louise, 85–86
Smith, O. C., 60
Smith v. Allwright, 29
Snead, James, 5

Snoop Doggy Dogg, 190,
197–198, 203–204, 206
Social Security Domestic
Employment Reform Act
(H.R. 4278), 249
"Somewhere Over The Rainbow,"
48
"Son of Hickory Holler's
Tramp," 60
"Soul Superman," 58
Southern Christian Leadership
Conference (SCLC), 11
conflict with SNCC, 153
gender relations in, 101
nonviolence and the return of
the repressed, 108–120
origins of, 102
rejection of Ella Baker, 102–108
Young, role of, 120–126
Southern Leadership Conference
on Transportation and Non-
Violent Integration, 102
Southern Mediator Journal, 35
Spaniels, 49
"Speedoo," 49
Staggenborg, Suzanne, 131
"Stand By Me," 51
Staples, Robert, 4, 6, 160
_State of Alabama v. Martin
Luther King, Jr._, 91
State Press, 28, 29–30, 32, 35,
75, 77, 96
Steele, C. K., 105
Stevenson, Brenda, 43
Stokely, James, 87
Strange, Adario, 204
Strength to Love (King), 219
Student Non-violent
Coordinating Committee

(SNCC), 9, 53, 101
Cambridge, Maryland and, 171
collapse of, 160–162
conflict with SCLC, 153
empowerment of women and
transformation of positions,
136–142
ideology and organizational
structure in early years,
132–133
rise of the Black Power movement and effects on women,
155–165
titled positions and role of
women, 133–136
Stylistics, 59
Sullivan, William C., 110
Summer, Donna, 62
"Sunday Kind of Love, A," 48
Sutton, Ozell, 35
Swallows, 48
"Sweet Little Sixteen," 51
"Sweet Honey in the Rock," 81

"Talk Like Sex," 62
Talmadge, Eugene, 95
Tan, 75, 76, 77, 78, 79, 81, 82
Taste of Power, A (Brown), 160
Tate, Greg, 63
Tawes, J. Millard, 172
Taylor, Johnnie, 58, 60
Taylor, Marcus, 32, 33
"Teardrops," 49
"Tears On My Pillow," 49
Telecommunications Act (1994),
250
_Tell Me How Long the Train's
Been Gone_ (Baldwin), 224
Temptations, 60

Tex, Joe, 56, 60
"These Foolish Things," 48
*Thirteen Ways of Looking a a
    Black Man* (Gates), 195
"32-20," 45
Thomas, Clarence, 241–242
Till, Emmett, 112, 140
Tillinghast, Muriel, 134, 135,
    157–158, 161
Time, 69, 174–175
Tolbert, Israel, 58
"Too Many Cooks...," 58
Too Short, 190, 193
Toppers, 47
Tourne, Sekou, 151
Townsend, W. H., 37
"Treat Her Like A Prostitute," 62
Tucker, C. Delores, 198
Turner, Joe, 46
Turner, Sammy, 50, 51
Tushnet, Mark, 32
2 Live Crew, 62, 63
Tyson, Tim, 112

Unifics, 58
Upshur, Evangeline, 37

Van Peebles, Mario, 231, 232
Van Peebles, Melvin, 4, 231, 232
Vaughan, Sarah, 51
Veterans' Benefits Improvement
    Act (H.R. 5244), 249
Veterans' Good Government
    Association, 29
Violence Against Women Act
    (H.R. 1133), 248
Violent Crime Control and Law
    Enforcement Act (H.R.
    3355), 248

Voting Rights Act, 251

Waldschmidt-Nelson, Britta,
    239–254
Walker, Alice, 223, 224, 230,
    231
Walker, Jenny, 169–184
Walker, John, 36
Walker, Wyatt Tee, 12, 102, 113,
    117–118, 124
Wallace, George, 154, 181
Wallace, Michele, 7, 233
Ward, Brian, 8, 10, 11, 12,
    41–65, 69–96, 188, 197
Warren G, 203, 205–206
Washington, Booker T., 71
Washington, Cynthia, 135
Washington Post, 92
Waters, Maxine, 243–244, 249,
    251, 253
Welke, Barbara, 71
West, Cornel, 4, 189–190,
    200–201, 226, 233
Wheatstraw, Peetie, 45
Wheeler, John, 37
When and Where I Enter
    (Giddings), 177
Where Do We Go From Here?
    (King), 179, 218
White, Armond, 200
White, Barry, 59
White, Deborah, 43
White, Dinez, 172
White, Hayden, 221–222, 229
White, J. A., 33
White, John, 11
White, Lulu B., 33
White, Matthew, 44
White, Walter, 33

White on Black on White
    (Dowell), 223
"Who's Making Love?," 60
"Why Do Fools Fall In Love,"
    49
Wideman, John Edgar, 7
Wiley, Jean, 177
Wilkins, Roy, 33, 104, 113, 148
Williams, Hosea, 102, 117,
    119–120, 123, 125, 126,
    153, 180
Williams, John A., 222
Williams, Odessa, 93
Williams, Patricia J., 6–7
Williams, Robert, 112–113
Willis, Meredith Sue, 231
Willis, Timmy, 58
"Will You Be Mine," 48
Wilson, Jackie, 51
Wise, Stanley, 181, 182

Withers, Ernest, 6
*Women in the Civil Rights
    Movement: Trailblazers and
    Torchbearers, 1941–1965*
    (Crawford), 9, 17
Woodward, C. Vann, 221
F.W. Woolworth, sit-ins at, 35

Yamato, Gloria, 2
Young, Andre, 190, 194
Young, Andrew, 12, 102,
    105–106, 108, 120–126
Young, Jean Wheeler Smith, 157
Young Negro Democrats, 30
Young Women Christian
    Association (YWCA), 30,
    107
"You Send Me," 50

Zellner, Dottie, 150–151